Eduard Wilhelm Eugen Reuss, David Hunter

History of the canon of the holy scriptures in the Christian Church

Eduard Wilhelm Eugen Reuss, David Hunter

History of the canon of the holy scriptures in the Christian Church

ISBN/EAN: 9783743367678

Manufactured in Europe, USA, Canada, Australia, Japa

Cover: Foto ©Lupo / pixelio.de

Manufactured and distributed by brebook publishing software (www.brebook.com)

Eduard Wilhelm Eugen Reuss, David Hunter

History of the canon of the holy scriptures in the Christian Church

HISTORY

OF THE

CANON OF THE HOLY SCRIPTURES

IN THE

CHRISTIAN CHURCH.

BY

EDWARD REUSS,

PROFESSOR IN THE UNIVERSITY OF STRASBURG.

TRANSLATED FROM THE SECOND FRENCH EDITION, WITH THE
AUTHOR'S OWN CORRECTIONS AND REVISION, BY

DAVID HUNTER, B.D.,

LATE SCHOLAR AND FELLOW IN THE UNIVERSITY OF GLASGOW.

EDINBURGH:
JAMES GEMMELL, GEORGE IV. BRIDGE,

1887.

TABLE OF CONTENTS.

	PAGE
CHAP. I.—Use of the Old Testament in the Apostolic Church	1
Reading of the O. T. in the Jewish Synagogues	1
This reading continued in the Christian churches	4
Was the canon of the O. T. closed then?	6
The bearing of the Septuagint on this question	7
The apostolic theory of inspiration	12
CHAP. II.—The Writings of the Apostles in the Primitive Church	15
How these writings were disseminated	15
How the custom arose of reading them in public	17
Their growing influence on Christian teaching	21
But no notion yet of any canon of Scripture	24
CHAP. III.—First Beginnings of a Collection of Apostolic Writings	28
The prejudice in favour of the early closing of the canon	28
Arguments advanced for the early closing,	29
The inspiration of the apostles was not at first held to apply to their writings	33
Facts against the early closing	35
Examination of Christian writers between 130 and 180	37
Papias	37
Epistle to Diognetus	38
Hegesippus	39
Melito of Sardis	39
Claudius Apollinaris	40
Dionysius of Corinth	41
Treatise against Montanism	42
Athenagoras (†117)	43
Letter from the Church of Lyons	44
Martyrdom of Polycarp	45
Martyrdom of Ignatius	45
The *Pastor* of Hermas	45
Justin Martyr	46
CHAP. IV.—Heresy	57
Attitude of heretical writers towards apostolic books	57
The Jewish Christians	58
The Gnostics	61
The attitude of both prove non-existence of a canon	64
Marcion's treatment of the gospels	66
Tatian's *Diatessaron*	69
The existence of pseudonymous books	71
Marcion and the Pauline epistles	72
CHAP. V.—Catholicism	77
Growing importance of tradition	77
And increasing value of the apostolic writings	79

	PAGE
Influence of Montanism and Gnosticism on the conception of Scripture	82
Opinion of certain Catholic writers—	
Theophilus of Antioch	84
Irenaeus and Tertullian	85

CHAP. VI.—THE COLLECTIONS IN USE TOWARDS THE END OF THE SECOND CENTURY ... 92
 The Muratorian Canon (180-190), ... 94
 Discussion of its statements ... 98
 Irenaeus (†202) ... 103
 Tertullian (190) ... 106
 Clement of Alexandria (190) ... 112

CHAP. VII.—BIBLIOGRAPHY ... 117
 Two distinct parts in the collection of the N.T. ... 117
 The order of the books in the collection ... 120
 The term *Catholic Epistles* ... 123

CHAP. VIII.—THE THIRD CENTURY ... 125
 Slow progress of the canon in the third century ... 125
 The Syriac version or *Peschito* ... 127
 Origen (184-253) ... 129
 The School of Alexandria and the Apocalypse ... 138
 The Apostolic Constitutions ... 141
 Cyprian of Carthage (†260) ... 144

CHAP. IX.—THE FOURTH CENTURY—STATISTICAL RETROSPECTIVE 146
 Eusebius of Caesarea (270-340) ... 148
 His difficulty about the Epistle to the Hebrews and the Apocalypse ... 154
 His position towards certain apocryphal books ... 156
 Testimony of Codex Sinaiticus and Codex Clermontanus 158
 The Bibles prepared for the Emperor Constantine ... 160

CHAP. X.—ATTEMPTS AT CODIFICATION—THE EASTERN CHURCH ... 163
 Athanasius (296-373) ... 164
 Gregory of Nazianzus (†390) ... 167
 Cyril of Jerusalem (†386) ... 169
 Didymus of Alexandria (†394 or 399) ... 171
 Epiphanius of Salamis (†403) ... 172
 The School of Antioch—Theodore of Mopsuestia (†428) 174
  Chrysostom (†407) ... 175
  Theodoret (†450) ... 177
 Council of Laodicea (363) ... 180
 Apostolic Canons ... 181

CHAP. XI.—ATTEMPTS AT CODIFICATION—THE WESTERN CHURCH 185
 Hilary of Poitiers (†368) ... 185
 Philastrius of Brescia (†about 387) ... 187
 Toranius Rufinus (410) ... 192
 Different estimates of certain books in East and West ... 192
 Jerome (329-420) ... 193
 Augustine (354-430) ... 200
 The Synod of Carthage (397) ... 205
 The Epistle of Pope Innocent I. (405) ... 207

	PAGE
CHAP. XII.—THEORY AND TERMINOLOGY	208
Uncertainty still prevails about the canon	208
Results established by the previous chapters	210
Meaning of the term *canon, canonical*, etc.	217
The books placed by the Fathers in a second canon	220
Meaning of the term *apocryphal*	223
General criticism of the testimony of the Fathers	226
CHAP. XIII.—THE MIDDLE AGES	232
Various catalogues of the biblical books	232
The decree of Pope Gelasius I. (492-496)	233
The Synopsis of Holy Scripture	236
Junilius, *De partibus legis divinæ*	238
Cosmas Indopleustes (535)	240
Euthalius (459)	241
Leontius of Byzantium (590)	242
Anastasius Sinaita (†599)	242
Cassiodorius (†562)	242
Pope Gregory the Great (†604)	243
Isidore of Seville (†636)	244
The Council of Trullum (691-2)	247
John of Damascus (†754)	248
Nicephorus of Constantinople (†828)	249
Raban Maur of Mayence (†856)	250
The evidence of Bibles and Manuscripts	252
Peter of Clugny (†1156)	257
Hugo of St. Victor (†1141)	257
John of Salisbury (†1182)	258
Thomas Aquinas	258
Nicephorus Callistus (fourteenth century)	260
Peter of Blois (†1200), and Hugo of St. Cher (†1263)	261
Nicolas de Lyra (†1340)	262
The Albigenses, Cathari, and Waldenses	263
CHAP. XIV.—THE RENAISSANCE	266
Position of the canon at the end of the fourteenth century	266
Bull of Pope Eugenius IV. (1439)	267
Thomas Cajetanus	270
Erasmus	271
CHAP. XV.—OFFICIAL AND MODERN CATHOLICISM	274
Decree of Council of Trent	275
Discussion of the decree	280
Sixtus of Sienna	282
Decisions of the Eastern Church	283
Metrophanes Kritopoulos (1625)	284
Cyrillus Lucaris (1629)	285
Present state of the canon in the Eastern Church	287
CHAP. XVI.—THE THEOLOGY OF THE REFORMERS	290
The principles of the Reformation, and their application to the canon	290
Opinions of Calvin, Zwingle, and Petrus Vermilius	294
Statements in the Helvetic Confessions of Faith	298
Statements in the Scotch Confession and the thirty-nine Articles	299
All these base canonicity on the witness of the Holy Spirit	304

	PAGE
Practical difficulties of this theory	306
As seen in the position assigned to the Apocrypha	307
Opinions of Luther	320
His principle of canonicity	332
Opinions of Melanchthon, Brentz, Flacius	333
Carlstadt (†1541)	336
Translator's note on the position of the Apocrypha in early English Bibles	339
CHAP. XVII.—THE CONFESSIONAL SCHOOLS	341
The common neglect of the theologians of 17th century	341
Apparent adherence to the principles of Calvin and Luther	343
Gradual return to the principle of tradition	345
The treatment of the O. T. Apocrypha	352
Relation of the terms *Scripture* and *Word of God*	354
The *Consensus Helveticus* (1675)	357
Attacks made by Protestants on the Apocrypha	359
The Synod of Dort (1620)	362
Treatment of the N. T. books	363
The polemic of Martin Chemnitz	366
CHAP. XVIII.—CRITICISM AND THE CHURCH	371
Some words of retrospect and prospect	371
Influence of Protestant theology on the notion of the canon	373
Similarity of results among Protestants and Catholics	374
Growth of traditionalism in the Reformed Churches	376
Recoil from excessive traditionalism	379
Influence of Pietism on the Lutheran Church	382
Influence of Rationalism	385
Rise of the historical method	388
Semler	388
Semler's use of internal evidence	390
His theory of inspiration	393
His theory of the canon	396
Concluding remarks—hopes for the future	400

AUTHOR'S PREFACE TO THE FRENCH EDITION.

The History of the Canon of the Holy Scriptures in the Christian Church recounts all the facts relating to the collection of the Apostolic writings, considered as a distinct whole and possessing a special dignity and value for the Church, for its creed and its theology. It traces the origin of this collection, its gradual formation, its vicissitudes down to the present day, and the dogmatic theories connected with it. And as the Christian Church has at all times recognised a similar or equal value in the sacred code of the Jews, this history will also include the facts relating to the Old Testament, in so far as these belong to the history of Christianity or of the Christian schools.

This is not the first time that I have publicly entered on a discussion of these matters. A discussion of them forms part of my book in German on the general history of the New Testament.[1] Several people have honoured me by expressing a desire to see that book translated into French, but I have refused on the ground that its method and form were unsuitable to French readers. This present book, therefore, is quite new. It deals with the same materials, but for different readers, and on a different plan. I hope thus to make response to a very flattering appeal, without incurring the reproach of repeating myself.

The French work first appeared in the form of detached articles in the *Revue de Théologie*, published at Strasburg. From these articles a selection was made, with some changes and additions to form this work, so that this second edition, which has been called for in a few months, is really a third edition. It has further been carefully revised, and enriched with some accessory details.

As to the matter and spirit of the book, I do not believe it to be necessary for me to make a profession of principles. I wish to be an historian, and nothing more. I shall leave the facts to speak for themselves; or, at least, the commen-

[1] *Geschichte der Heiligen Schriften N. T.*, by Ed. Reuss. A fifth improved edition of this work appeared in 1874.

taries which I may have to add when the real or apparent contradictions of the witnesses might arrest the reader, will never be confused with the materials furnished by the history, and, in this way, each one will be left to form his own opinion. When the points on which the historian must touch are still burning questions, it is his duty more than ever to make the facts tell their own tale. And he fails in this duty, not only when he interprets them wrongly, but also when he does not present them in their natural order, or when he is reticent regarding them.

My readers who are familiar with theological controversy, will be astonished, perhaps, to find no special chapter discussing several books recently published in our language on the canon; but I have simply to reply that, though these books have suggested the writing of my own, I have sought to avoid all polemical dispute. True science disdains forms which are not homogeneous with it. Where these books deal with the historical facts, I have implicitly expressed my opinion regarding them by the manner in which I have handled the same facts; the reader will form his own from the documents placed before him. But he will readily be convinced that these books are rather theoretical works, and as such, only reproduce a conception which is already old, and which has been sufficiently discussed, in the place belonging to it, in the general scheme of the evolution of ideas and institutions.

TRANSLATOR'S PREFACE.

M. REUSS'S *History of the Canon* has long been known to scholars; it is now translated in the hope of bringing it more prominently before the English-reading public. I share the opinion of many, in believing it to be the best history of the canon that has yet been written. Much has been published in Britain of recent years on the subject, but chiefly in support of a dogmatic prepossession against, or in favour of, the canon as it now stands in our English Bible. The treatment of the whole subject has been too often based on the quotation of proof passages from the early Fathers. Thus, on the one hand, a book like Charteris's "Canonicity," while valuable in its accumulation of facts, may mislead where it does not confuse, since it tacitly assumes the existence of a closed canon at a very early date. A weight is laid on the passages which they cannot bear, and the historical growth of the canon is altogether ignored. On the other hand, writings like "Supernatural Religion," when discussing the bearing of the same passages on the origin of the gospels, are equally deficient in historical imagination. On both sides, it seems to be believed that, if the Scriptures are to have any value, they must have come into existence, as did Minerva in the mythological fable, distinct, full-grown, complete. The defenders of the canon, as it now stands, labour to prove that it was so; its assailants find it very easy to demolish all such proof. But, on both sides, the main question is overlooked. For it is not enough to argue that this book was used by Justin Martyr, that other quoted by Irenaeus, when the real question is—"How came the canon of Scripture to be composed of these books, so many and not more?" Nor is it sufficient to demonstrate that Justin Martyr was not acquainted with our present gospels, when we remember that there must have been stages of transition, before the written book gained more authority than the spoken word, and the occasional and scattered writings of the apostles were collected to form a *New* Testament. The great value of M. Reuss's work lies in his clear conception of an historical growth in the canon. He bases his discussion, not on single passages, but on the general position which the Scriptures held in the Christian writings of succeeding generations. Perhaps the most striking feature is his discussion of the theologians of the Middle Ages and of the Reformation. His wide acquaintance with the facts, his impartial weighing of the evidence, his historical insight, and the clear logic of his exposition, make the study of his book an epoch in the reading of every candid student of Scripture.

A scientific conception of the history of the canon is still far from being general in Britain, and there are probably many who will be astonished to find that the closing of the canon, in the proper sense of the term, did not take place till the period of the Reformation and the Council of Trent, if even then; while there are others who may be agreeably disappointed to find that there has been so much practical consensus of opinion on the question. The claims of such minor books as Esther, Jude, 2 Peter, 2 and 3 John to canonicity may be considered very doubtful; but there is no reasonable doubt that the other books of Scripture have universally, and from an early date, commended themselves to the Christian consciousness as containing the revealed word of God. If it be asked on what grounds these books, and no others, commended themselves—*i.e.*, what principle of definition guided the formation of the canon—it must be answered that no such principle was ever formulated by the early Church. Even still, there is much division of opinion regarding the definition. The common principle, which may be stated in the words of Dr. Westcott, "It is to the Church that we must look, both for the formation and the proof of the canon,"[1] is simply an appeal to tradition. It is diametrically opposed to the principle laid down by the Reformers, especially by Calvin, which principle is clearly stated in the Westminster Confession: "The authority of the Holy Scripture dependeth not upon the testimony of any man or church, but wholly upon God," and this testimony of God is further explained to be "the inward work of the Holy Spirit, bearing witness by, and with, the word in our hearts." If M. Reuss himself gives no strict definition of the canon, he at least prepares the way for one; and on this point his last two chapters are very suggestive.

The translation has been made from the second French edition, with certain additions and corrections made by M. Reuss for a future third edition. The proof-sheets have been revised by him throughout, but I willingly hold myself responsible for any errors which may still be found in the text. DAVID HUNTER.

ST. MARY'S, PARTICK, GLASGOW, *Oct.*, 1883.

[1] Westcott, History of the Canon of the N. T., p. 12.

HISTORY

OF THE

CANON OF THE HOLY SCRIPTURES

IN THE CHRISTIAN CHURCH.

CHAPTER I.

USE OF THE OLD TESTAMENT IN THE APOSTOLIC CHURCH.

In the times of Jesus Christ and of the apostles, the sacred books of the Old Testament were used for the purposes of edification in the Jewish communities; and hence they were regularly read to the people in the synagogues, both on festival-days and at the ordinary meetings for prayer. The origin of this practice is unknown. The tradition of the Talmud traces it back to Moses, and founds it on the facts related in Deut. xxxi.;[1] but in the entire history of the Israelites previous to the exile, there is no trace of the existence of the synagogues, nor of readings of the kind

---

[1] Comp. also Josephus, *Contra Apionem*, ii., 17: ἑκάστης ἑβδομάδος ἐπὶ τὴν ἀκρόασιν τοῦ νόμου ἐκέλευσεν (ὁ νομοθέτης) συλλέγεσθαι.

indicated. The first allusions to such institutions are found only in the literature posterior to the exile,[1] and all this organisation appears to have been the fruit, and also one of the most powerful means, of the ecclesiastical and national restoration, by which Judaism at last entered on the path of its final consolidation.[2] In the time of the apostles, the custom was already ancient,[3] existing wherever there was a synagogue, and essentially bound up with the local or sabbatic worship.

It is natural to suppose that at first these readings were made solely from the Mosaic law. That is the opinion of some Jewish scholars, who trace the practice of reading passages from the prophets likewise, to the time of the persecution of King Antiochus, during which the Jews are said to have had all copies of the Pentateuch taken from them. This explanation, it is true, does not appear to me very probable. The high esteem in which the second volume of Holy Scripture was held, could not fail to obtain for it at an early period a place similar to that assigned to the first; but it appears to me to be true that the use of the prophetical books is more recent, because select portions only were read from the various books of the collection, while the law was read consecutively from beginning to end. In Palestine the text of the Pentateuch was formerly divided into 153 *Sedarîm* (paragraphs), corresponding to the sabbaths of three consecutive years; later, in the synagogues of Babylon, there was adopted a division into 54 *Parasches* (sections), calculated for a single year. This last division finally came into general use, and is now

---

[1] Nehem. viii.—The fact related in 2 Kings xxii. has quite another bearing.

[2] See Reuss, *History of Christian Theology in the Apostolic Age*, B. 1, chs. ii. and iii.

[3] Acts xv. 21: ἐκ γενεῶν ἀρχαίων—κατὰ πόλιν—ἐν ταῖς συναγωγαῖς κατὰ πᾶν σάββατον—

marked in all editions of the Hebrew Bible. As to the prophets, we must remember, in the first place, that the Jews included under that collective name, not only the fifteen prophetical books proper (Isaiah, Jeremiah, Ezekiel, and the twelve Minor Prophets), but also the books of Joshua, Judges, Samuel, and Kings. From a period before the apostolic age, religious exercises usually ended with the reading of a passage taken from one of these books. These passages, therefore, were disconnected fragments, isolated from one another, simply pericopes or lessons, as they were called afterwards in the Christian Church. Such a custom was subject to many variations; and indeed the scanty information we possess on these points, goes to show that successive changes were made in practice. In any case, the *Haftares* (final lessons) marked now in our printed Hebrew Bibles, do not appear to go back farther than the middle ages.

Apart from all this, the New Testament bears testimony to the fact that the custom of this double reading already existed. It is true that all the passages which may be cited on this point are not equally explicit. From what Luke relates of the preaching of Jesus at Nazareth (Luke iv. 16), it might be inferred that the reader was left perfectly free in his choice of a passage. The same author in a verse already quoted (Acts xv. 21), and Paul also (2. Cor. iii. 15), make express mention only of Moses as read in the synagogues. But in another place (Acts xiii. 27), the prophets are mentioned formally in the plural, and there is nothing to prevent the inclusion of Moses in the number. In the same chapter a few lines before,[1] mention is made of the reading of the law and the prophets, in terms which undoubtedly show that the author is speaking of a regular and official practice. But there is more than this. This same practice is attested still

---

[1] Ver. 15: ἀνάγνωσις τοῦ νόμου καὶ τῶν προφητῶν.

more strongly by the frequent use of the phrase, *the law and the prophets*,[1] on all occasions when the Scriptures of the Old Testament in general are spoken of. This means that at that time these two parts alone were used in ordinary reading, and therefore, in the minds of the hearers, represented the sacred code.

Such was the state of things at the death of Jesus, when His disciples began to associate more closely with one another, and to form communities more and more numerous and distinct. I do not need to remind my readers, that those of the believers who belonged to the Jewish nation did not cease to frequent the synagogue, and that to them the public reading of the sacred books continued therefore to be a familiar practice. They soon introduced into their own special meetings, even before their final separation from the Jews, the same means of edification as were used in the Jewish religious gatherings; and later, when the schism was complete, these means were preserved, and bequeathed to succeeding generations. I shall not stop here to collect the passages which speak of prayers, of singing and preaching; I shall confine myself to what concerns the public reading of the texts. There is, indeed, in the whole of the New Testament only one passage (1 Tim. iv. 13) where mention is made of this reading. The attempts made to find positive traces of it elsewhere[2] have been vain. But we may succeed in establishing the fact by very probable inductions. In the first place, it is indisputable that in the second century and later, the Church read the Old Testament, and it is hardly probable that a return would have been made to this practice if the apostles had

---

[1] Or, also, *Moses and the Prophets* (Matt. v. 17, vii. 12, xi. 13, xxii. 40; Luke xvi. 16, 29, 31, xxiv. 27, 44; John i. 46; Acts xxiv. 14, xxviii. 23; Rom. iii. 21). See Reuss, *Geschichte der Heiligen Schriften des A. T.*, § 413.

[2] Acts ii. 47; Eph. v. 19; Col. iii. 16.

let it drop. Then it is obvious, not only from the didactic books of the New Testament, but also from all that we are told of the preaching of the first missionaries, that the evangelic teaching was primarily and essentially based on Scripture prophecy, and that the texts of Scripture were continually quoted, either to give to the facts of the gospel history their religious and providential meaning, or to give sanction to the doctrines contained in them. Quotation was made most of all when the doctrines seemed to be in contradiction with the former revelation or opposed to the traditional beliefs. Hence there is hardly a page in the New Testament in which the Old is not cited with a dogmatic purpose, or indication given by the writers of great familiarity with its texts. But if this is a fact beyond dispute for writers and preachers, we must suppose something of the same familiarity to have existed among readers and hearers, in so far, at least, as we cannot imagine them to have been entirely passive in presence of the great questions put before them.[1] Now, when we think of the extreme rarity of copies among individuals, how impossible it was for most members of the Church to procure and possess all that vast and precious library, we naturally infer that their acquaintance with the Old Testament must have come from public readings. In most cases, these readings must have been the only possible means, and in all cases they were the most direct and simple means of such a familiarity. The Pagan or Jewish origin of the various members of the Church made no difference on this point. They all received the same instruction from the apostles. Besides, many of the Greek proselytes had frequented the synagogues before presenting themselves for baptism; and the apostles, who never for a moment thought of diminishing the dignity of the Old Testament, or of doubting its Divine origin, had

[1] See on the contrary, Acts xvii. 11, viii. 28; Gal. iv. 21, &c.

as little intention of founding the faith of their Pagan disciples on any basis other than that on which their own convictions rested.

But here arise some special questions, all the more interesting that they will recur all through the history of the Christian canon, and are not settled to this very day.

It has, for instance, been asked what was the form or the extent of the collection of sacred books in the apostolic age. Was the canon of the Old Testament closed, and was it the same as we have now in our Hebrew Bibles? or did it not, perhaps, include some other books? Every possible answer has been given to these questions without arriving at any certain result. There are, however, some facts which should not be neglected in the discussion.

In the first place, we must not lose sight of the fact that all Christians could not make use of the original Hebrew. The ancient language of the prophets was no longer spoken; it differed as much from the usual language of the Palestinian Jews, as the French of Sire de Joinville or the English of Wycliffe differs from that of the nineteenth century; and it could not be understood without some literary education. Hence the reading of the texts was accompanied with an interpretation in the vulgar idiom. This interpretation was still more indispensable for the Jewish communities, which, either in the maritime towns of their own land, or still more in foreign lands, had absolutely forgotten the language of their fathers, even in its latest forms, in order to adopt Greek, or what they believed to be Greek. It cannot be proved that so early as the first century of our era, readings were made in the synagogues of sacred texts in the Aramean dialect, but this was incontestably the case in later times; the interpretation may still have been oral. With greater reason we must admit that it was the same with Greek, although there already existed written translations. We know that long after, in the time of the Emperor Justinian, opposition was still made by the Jews to the official use of these Greek translations.[1] But what was the custom of the Christians? Did they submit to the demands of this linguistic orthodoxy, or did their pressing desire for edification prevail over the tenacity of forms? We do not know. We know absolutely nothing of the fortunes of the celebrated Greek version of Alexandria (the Septuagint) before the time when the Church and Christian theology made use of it almost exclusively.

This historical point would be less obscure if the numerous quotations from the Old Testament in the apostolic books were of a nature to guide our judgment. But on the one hand we have a series of texts, undoubtedly taken from the Septuagint, and faithfully reproducing the peculiarities, the unusual forms of expression, various readings, and exegetical mistakes of that version; while, on the other hand, we have as many texts in which the Christian writers seem to have translated the original themselves, whether agreeing with the Hebrew against the Alexandrine translators, or adopting a version equally remote from both texts. I shall not stop to prove these facts by analysing some passages of special significance; that would take me too far away from my main subject. I content myself with asserting the fact that the Septuagint was known among Christians, and was consulted by them from the first century, but that it did not enjoy an absolute or exclusive authority as was afterwards the case, and apparently was not used even where its use might have been of great advantage. In fine, we are unable to form any clear idea of the manner in which the readings from Scripture may have been organised within the primitive Church, especially in Greek-speaking countries. On the one hand, we cannot affirm

[1] *Codex*, Tit. 28, *Nov.* 146.

that in all the churches copies of the Septuagint already existed and were used. Still, on the other hand, as there must have been very few persons out of Palestine who could have understood the original well enough to give an oral interpretation to a Greek audience after a reading from the Hebrew, the use of a written Greek translation, among Christians at least, becomes very probable.

Now, it is important to remember that the Hebrew Bible and the Greek Bible were not in all respects alike, even apart from the value of the translation. It is well known that the latter includes several books not found in the former—viz., the books of Judith, Tobit, The Wisdom of Solomon, Ecclesiasticus, and Maccabees—which were afterwards known in the Church as the Apocrypha of the Old Testament. Were these books also in the hands of the Greek Christians of the first century, and were they put on the same level as the others, in so far at least as the Septuagint was used? This question has been answered sometimes in the affirmative, sometimes in the negative. Some have contended that these books had no authority even among the Greek Jews; others have found in the New Testament numerous allusions to one or other of them. Certainly, very striking parallels may sometimes be found between the Epistle of James and Ecclesiasticus, between the Epistle to the Hebrews and the Wisdom of Solomon—nay, between certain passages of St. Paul and the same works; but though the ideas already current in society, or common to thinkers of the same century, may appear in their writings, this does not prove that the last-comers borrowed directly from their predecessors, and above all, it does not prove that in borrowing they acknowledged them to have a dogmatic authority. This is the aspect of the question which is most essential. In all the New Testament, no one has been able to point out a single dogmatic passage taken from the Apocrypha and quoted as proceeding from a sacred authority. Hence, whatever may have been the practice followed in the various Christian communities, it must be said that the apostolic teaching, so far as we are acquainted with it, adhered to the Hebrew canon.

Still it would be a mistake to exaggerate the importance of this fact. There are some considerations which seem to me to prove that what we call in our day the question of the canon, was not for the apostles and their immediate disciples, as it has been for Protestant theologians, a matter of supreme moment or a matter depending on *à priori* criticism and a precise theory of inspiration.

In the first place, if the silence of the authors of the New Testament regarding the Greek books, called the Apocrypha, were of itself sufficient proof that these books were not in the hands of the first Christians, were neither read nor consulted by them, this same argument might be advanced against certain writings in the Hebrew collection, which also the New Testament does not mention, and to whose authority it makes no appeal. Among these writings there are not only historical books, whose contents were not suited to the apostles' teaching (Ezra, Nehemiah, Esther), but also writings in which the traditional orthodoxy professes to find very positive and very detailed revelations of the Gospel (Canticles), or, at least, texts to be used with a similar purpose (Ecclesiastes). It is evident that for the apostles these books had no canonical value in the Christian sense of the word—*i.e.*, they could not be used in constructing the dogma of the New Covenant. This observation is not new; it was made in the sixteenth century, by very orthodox Lutheran theologians, as we shall see further on. It acquires special importance from its connection with a still greater question. Is it quite true that the Hebrew canon, as we possess it, was closed before the time of the apostles? No one can prove it.¹ On the contrary, I have established elsewhere, that in the time of Josephus the books, called the Hagiographa,² were not yet gathered into a clearly defined collection, and that certain Hebrew documents, which now form part of them, seem even to have been unknown to that author. Commonly the attempt is made to prove the integrity of the Hebrew canon for the apostolic age, by the terms which Luke uses (xxiv. 44); but it is easy to see that in that passage he is simply enumerating the books in which Messianic prophecies were found. The name *Psalms* cannot possibly have included also such books as Ezra and Chronicles.

In the second place, though the apostles in their writings are silent regarding certain canonical books of the Old Testament, they make quotations which prove that the notion of the canon, as it was afterwards defined by theology, and above all by Protestant theology, was unknown to them. I do not wish to insist here on certain passages which cannot be found in the Hebrew text—*e.g.*, John vii. 38; Luke xi. 49; 1 Cor. ii. 9; James iv. 5; Matt. ii. 23, etc.— and which not only many modern interpreters, but also Origen and other fathers, have believed to be taken from apocryphal books now lost; for after all they may be considered as quotations made from memory, and for that very reason more or less inaccurate. I shall insist more on facts to which they allude for a didactic purpose, and which are indisputably drawn from extra-canonical sources. What Paul says of the magicians of Egypt (2. Tim. iii. 8) is not necessarily extracted from a book, but it is at any rate taken from a tradition which may appear open to suspicion. The examples of religious courage and constancy extolled

¹ See on this point, Reuss, *Geschichte der Schriften des A. T.*, § 411 ff, 544, 579 ff.

² Psalms, Proverbs, Job, Canticles, Ruth, Lamentations, Ecclesiastes, Esther, Daniel, Ezra, Nehemiah, and Chronicles.

by the author of the Epistle to the Hebrews (xi. 34, ff) are undoubtedly copied in part from the history of the Maccabees; and just as he presents these latter to the admiration of the faithful as having claims equal to those of the heroes of sacred antiquity, so the documents relating the life of both must have had an equal value in the eyes of the writer quoting them. The Epistle of Jude (vers. 9. 14.) not only reproduces some traditions which are somewhat peculiar and may very well have been taken from works of an apocryphal nature, but it makes an express appeal, as to an authority existing before the Flood, to a book which we have still in our hands, and which no one assuredly is willing to consider authentic or divinely inspired.[1]

From all this it follows, at least, that we should not be too hasty in attributing to the apostles the theories regarding the canon which were formulated by Protestant theology. We shall find, by-and-by, analogous facts in the writings of their disciples and immediate successors. But this is not all. I have still another very singular fact to put before my readers, a fact too often neglected though of considerable importance for the history of the canon. Among the books of the Old Testament, there are several in which the Greek text is very different from the Hebrew text, either because it is a new form of it, or because additions have been made by other hands. Thus in the book of Daniel, the Greek recension inserts the Song of the Three Children in the furnace, and the stories of Susanna, of Bel and the Dragon. Thus the book of Jeremiah has not only undergone a complete

---

[1] [This is the much-discussed book of Enoch. It had long disappeared; but in 1773 Bruce brought three MSS. from Abyssinia containing a translation in Ethiopic. It was edited, and translated into English by Archbishop Lawrence in 1838; but the standard edition is now that of Dillmann (Leipsic, 1851). The allusion in ver. 6 of Jude has also been traced to this book. According to Origen, allusion is here made to an apocryphal work, *The Ascension of Moses;* but the passage does not appear in the fragment that has survived in Latin.]—*Tr.*

transformation in the order of its contents and chapters, but there have been also added to it an epistle of the prophet and what is called the book of Baruch. The book of Esther has been enriched by a series of documents professing to be official. Finally, the book of Ezra[1] occurs twice in two very different forms. Now it is not merely probable, it is proved by testimonies which I shall present in their proper place, that the Christians who made use of the Greek Bible and were not, like Origen and Jerome, sufficiently learned to compare it with the original, knew and read the books just mentioned only in the form of the Greek version, or, we would now say, in the apocryphal form. To what date does this fact go back? We are no longer able to determine the exact time when these additions were made, but very possibly they were in existence before the Christian era. I have shown that the historian Josephus knew only the Greek recension of several of these books. We shall see later, that this was the case with almost all the fathers of the Church.

Having thus proved that the history of the canon of Scripture in the apostolic age is not so simple and clear, nor so consistent with the notions commonly received as some would like to make it, I shall further say a word or two regarding the theological aspect of the question. On this point there is not the least doubt that the apostles, and, as a rule, the Christians of their time held the law and the prophets to be divinely inspired,[2] and therefore held the words of Scripture to be, not the words of men, but the words of God. It is the Spirit of God who speaks by the mouth of the sacred authors;[3] and the prophets in writing

---

[1] [Ezra and Esdras are different forms of the same name. In our English Bibles, Ezra is applied to the canonical book and Esdras to the two books of the Apocrypha; in French, the one form Esdras is applied to both.]—*Tr.*

[2] For this whole question, I refer my readers to Reuss, *History of Christian Theology in the Apostolic Age*, i., p. 352.

[3] Acts i. 16, iii. 18, 21; Heb. iii. 7, iv. 7, ix. 8, &c.

hold a special position which excludes the idea of any common and human mistake (ἐν πνεύματι, Matt. xxii. 43). In this respect, king David, considered as the author of all the Psalms (Acts iv. 25; Heb. iv. 7), shared in the privilege of the prophets (Acts ii. 30, &c.); and in consequence of the liturgical use made of these sacred songs by the synagogue, the book of which he was supposed to be author shared the honours rendered to the two parts of Scripture which were used for the public reading (Luke xxiv. 44). But above all, by studying the exegetical methods of the Jewish doctors and the apostles, which were all but identical, we come to the conviction that the notion of inspiration then included all the elements of excellence and of absoluteness which have been given to it in later definitions. Indeed, it is only from this point of view that we can explain to ourselves how so many texts relating to a distant past—simple narratives, songs expressing the joys or regrets of an individual, or of the people at a particular crisis—could continually and confidently be translated into positive and special predictions, such as might occupy the spirit of speculation in the schools, or nourish and exalt the religious sentiment of the masses. When we see an essentially divinatory method of interpretation applied to members of phrases detached from the context, to words completely isolated,[1] this method which no one now would venture to apply to any work sacred or profane, is in exact harmony with the conception formed of inspiration. For inspiration was not supposed to be restricted to a general direction of the mind of the authors, but to imply also the dictation of the very words. In any other view we should have to charge the apostles with being purely arbitrary in their exegesis, as we know to be actually the case in numerous instances which put the science of our days to great difficulty.

[1] For instance, Matt. ii. 23; 2 Cor. iv. 13; Heb. ii. 13, &c.

Here, then, are two facts duly established at the outset of our discussion: on the one side, a theory of inspiration which permitted no confusion between sacred and profane literature; on the other side, a practice which betrays some hesitation, a certain vagueness in the demarcation of the two literatures, or, more exactly, the absence of any decision definitely and rigorously limiting the canonical code, and enumerating the books which it ought to include. In other words, in selecting the books which were to compose the Scriptures, we might either take a theological or dogmatic point of view, in which case we should be disposed to restrict the number; or we might take a practical or pedagogic point of view, in which case we should rather be inclined to extend the circle of books having a religious value. We shall find that the entire history of the canon in the Christian Church resolves itself finally into alternations between these two points of view.

CHAPTER II.

THE WRITINGS OF THE APOSTLES IN THE PRIMITIVE CHURCH.

ALL that I have said hitherto relates to the Old Testament only, and has a bearing on the usages introduced into the Church, owing to the natural connection of the latter with the synagogue. I have not yet spoken of the writings of the apostles, because I am in a position to assert that these writings, during the remainder of the first century and at least the first third of the second, were not yet read publicly in any regular and liturgical fashion, as I believe the books of the prophets to have been read. I shall devote this second chapter to proving this assertion, relating in general terms the varying fortunes during the period indicated, of the books which afterwards composed the New Testament.

The first point to be examined here, is the mode in which these books were disseminated; for when we remember the limited means of publicity in the apostolic age, it would be wrong to suppose that the apostles had nothing to do but send copies to all the existing churches. Nevertheless that is the unconscious supposition of those who hold that the *canon*—*i.e.*, the official collection—was formed simultaneously everywhere as each new text was issued.

The apostolic books may be divided into two categories according to their origin and the form of their publication. There are, in the first place, those which were originally addressed to particular communities. These had from the first a public character, and were in a very advantageous position for acquiring authority, and, consequently, for being disseminated. In this category we naturally place the Epistles of Paul, except where the authenticity of one or other of them may be disputed on sufficient grounds. If, as most critics think, the Epistle to the Hebrews was written for a particular church (certainly not the church at Jerusalem), it too must be mentioned here. Now we see clearly enough, from texts we can consult, what took place in regard to these epistles. Generally they reached their destination by means more or less accidental.¹ Sometimes the occasion of writing them was equally accidental. They were addressed or sent to the heads of the communities, who on that account were charged with general and individual salutations,² and who caused them to be read to the meeting of the faithful, a course so natural, that the apostle only speaks of it once (1. Thess. v. 27) in his earliest epistle. The same officials had to communicate these letters to other neighbouring communities when the apostle expressed a desire for it. In this way, of course, the Epistle to the Galatians must have been put in circulation after its arrival in the leading church of the province; for if there had been only one church there, we would not understand how it should be nowhere designated by the name of its locality. Thus, the Epistle to the Colossians must have been communicated to one other church at least, if not to several (Col. iv. 16; comp. ii. 1). Thus also the Epistles to the Corinthians, at anyrate the second (1 Cor. i. 2; 2 Cor. i. 1), are encyclical, and it is well-known that many exegetes have adopted a similar hypothesis regarding the Epistle to the Ephesians. The epistles may have been communicated in various ways, either by the transmission of the original, or by copies. Even in the former case, it is very probable that every church that received a missive of this kind, took care to have it copied before returning the loan. For all

---

¹ Rom. xvi. 1; 1 Cor. xvi. 17; 2 Cor. viii. 18 f; Eph. vi. 21 f; Col. iv. 7; Tit. iii. 13.

² These salutations are always introduced by the exhortation : ἀσπάσασθι.

the churches which had had personal and often very intimate relations with the author of the writing communicated, were alike interested in preserving it as a pledge of affection, as the precious title-deed of a relation whose ineffaceable remembrance was the happiness of the first generation, and the glory of those that came after. There is no trace, in the literature of that epoch, that these epistles were publicly read on fixed days from the very date of their arrival. As they were in part devoted to special circumstances, that does not seem probable. Some time elapsed before they were read regularly; and even long afterwards, when they had been diffused among Christians at a distance, we do not find that they were used for liturgical or periodical readings.

What I have just said is not founded on bare assertions, or on inductions more or less plausible. Some works or fragments, which have survived to us from the fifty years following that of the apostles, contain direct information on this point; but before collecting them, and to avoid repetition, let me further say a word regarding the second category of the apostolic writings. This contains the writings intended for a wider circle of readers—*e.g.*, the gospels and some of the epistles, commonly called Catholic. I include in it also the two books of Luke, though apparently they are addressed to a single individual; for at that time dedication rather favoured than limited the circulation of a book. So, too, the introductions to the First Epistle of Peter and to the Apocalypse have more of the nature of a dedication than of an epistolary address. These books, which, moreover, were almost all more lengthy than Paul's letters, must, like all writings of that age, have acquired a circulation among the public, in proportion to the interest attached to their authors when known, or still more to their contents. Thus we see that in this respect they were not all placed in the same position, and had not the same chances of success. Luke's work, certainly the latest of the historical writings, and also the most complete, made its way into notice much more slowly than the others;[1] while the Epistle of James had much difficulty in attracting attention beyond the locality of its publication. In general, the writings of this second category appear to have had more difficulties to overcome than the Epistles of Paul. The latter were pastoral letters, having a certain official character, and were therefore public property; while the others were, at first, only private property, in the hands of persons who had in some way or other procured them. So much was this the case that, during all the period of which we are now speaking, we find no mention of any public use of them, and almost no trace of their existence, though I do not mean to call it in question. In any case, the diffusion of all these writings was not regulated, organised, or directed by the care or action of any central power, which for that matter never existed after the destruction of Jerusalem. If indeed such a power did exist for a few years, it had completely lost control of the religious movement which was spreading in the heathen world, long before Paul wrote his first epistle. I do not on that account admit that the work of diffusing the rising literature of Christianity was done by commercial speculation, or, as we might now say, the book-trade. The immense majority of the Christians were common people, and the common people did not read. The gospel was still diffused, or, rather, had all along been diffused and put into shape, by oral instruction. The need for replacing this by other less simple means would not be felt, since the apostles and their successors continued to visit the

---

[1] Papias was acquainted only with the two first gospels, and quotations from texts peculiar to Luke are very rare in the authors of the second century, in comparison with those taken from Matthew.

churches,[1] and everywhere, even in the smallest community, the traditional teaching was abundant and careful.[2] The men chosen to direct the churches and to preserve untouched the sacred trust of the gospel are recommended to the faithful as guides to be relied on, worthy of their submission and esteem.[3] The numerous terms used in the New Testament to designate the teaching of the apostles express, without exception, the idea of oral instruction. Everywhere the question is of speaking and hearing, of discourses and auditors, of preaching, proclamation, and tradition,[4] and never once of writing and reading, except where there is express allusion to the books of the Old Testament. And later, when the writings of the first disciples and missionaries came within reach of persons who were literate, they might decidedly prefer the oral source for acquaintance with evangelic facts, because it was more abundant.[5] At any rate, while the great value of the apostolic documents was recognised, it was not forgotten that the publication of

---

[1] Acts viii. 14, ix. 32, xi. 22, xiv. 21, xv. 25, 36, 41, xviii. 23, xx. 1, 17; 1 Cor. iv. 17, xvi. 10, 12; 2 Cor. vii. 6f, viii. 6, xii. 18; Phil. ii. 19f, Col. iv. 10; 1 Thess. iii. 2; 2 Tim. iv. 10; Titus iii. 12.

[2] Acts xx. 17, 28; Titus i. 5, 7; Eph. iv. 11; 1 Pet. ii. 25; Phil. i. 1; 1 Cor. xii. 8, xiv., &c.

[3] 1 Cor. xvi. 15; Phil. ii. 29; Col. i. 7; 1 Thess. v. 12; Clement *Ep. ad Cor.* i. 42; Ignat. *ad Philad.* 7; *Magnes.* 8, 13.

[4] Εὐαγγέλιον, εὐαγγελιστής, εὐαγγελίζεσθαι, Rom. i. 1; 1 Cor. iv. 15, etc.; Luke ix. 6; Acts viii. 4, etc.; 2 Tim. iv. 5.—Κήρυγμα, κήρυξ, κηρύσσειν, Titus i. 3; 1 Cor. ii. 4; 2 Tim. i. 11; Matt. x. 7; Acts xx. 25.—Παράδοσις, παραδιδόναι, 2 Thess. ii. 15; Luke i. 2; Acts xvi. 4.—Μαρτυρία, μαρτυρεῖν, μάρτυς, Acts i. 8, xxii. 18, xxiii. 11; Rev. i. 9; 1 Cor. xv. 15, etc.—Ἄνοιξις τοῦ στόματος, Eph. vi. 19.—Λόγος, Acts iv. 31; James i. 22, etc.—Λόγος ἀκοῆς, 1 Thess. ii. 13; Heb. iv. 2.—Λαλεῖν, Acts xviii. 15; Titus ii. 15.—Ἀκούειν, Eph. i. 13; 1 John ii. 7, etc.—Ἀκροᾶσθαι, James i. 22, etc. Comp. especially Rom. x. 14-17; 2 Tim. ii. 1, 2; Gal. iii. 2, 5; Heb. ii. 1-4.

[5] Papias, apud *Eusebium*, iii. 39: Οὐ γὰρ τὰ ἐκ τῶν βιβλίων τοσοῦτόν με ὠφελεῖν ὑπελάμβανον ὅσα τὰ παρὰ ζώσης φωνῆς καὶ μενούσης. This testimony is all the more interesting that the author professes to be acquainted with *two* written accounts of the life of the Lord, the one by Matthew, written in Hebrew, and the other by Mark (about the year 120).

those few pages was but a very small part of the work of evangelising the world. "Guided by the Holy Spirit and endowed with a miraculous power, the apostles carried everywhere the proclamation of the kingdom of God, caring very little about committing it to writing, because they had to fulfil a ministry more elevated and exceeding human strength. Paul, the first among them by his power of speech and the excellence of his ideas, left but a small number of very brief epistles, though he might have said many things more which God had deigned to teach to him alone. The other companions of the Lord, the twelve apostles, the seventy disciples, were not less instructed, and yet only two of them composed memoirs, and that through force of circumstances."[1]

But if, fifty years after the destruction of Jerusalem and the death of most of the first disciples of Jesus Christ, their writings were not yet used regularly and periodically for the common edification of the faithful at the hours of meeting and prayer, it does not follow that these writings were forgotten or disregarded. On the contrary, the unbroken relations which the churches, especially those of Greece and Grecian Asia, maintained with one another, soon led to the interchange of the Christian writings which each possessed. I say *Christian writings* purposely, for I do not mean to confine this remark to the apostles only. Correspondence went on between the disciples of the apostles and their churches, as Paul had given example, and even if the writings attributed to what are called the Apostolic Fathers,[2]

---

[1] Eusebius, *Hist. Eccles.* iii. 24.

[2] This expression is generally taken to denote men who knew the apostles personally. This interpretation is erroneous if we look to the origin of the term, and could not be applied to all the *Apostolic Fathers*. The term ἀποστολικός is met for the first time in the *Martyrology* of St. Polycarp, ch. 16; but, as it is joined there to προφητικός, it clearly does not contain any chronological signification. He is speaking of the religious tie which united the bishop of Smyrna to the apostles, and of the gift of prophecy which he possessed (ἐν τοῖς καθ᾿ ἡμᾶς χρόνοις διδάσκαλος ἀπ. καὶ προφ. γινόμενος).

—*i.e.*, to the writers who must have flourished between the years 90 and 130—were not all authentic (which is very probable), they are at least of high antiquity, and, in any case, they may be of use to us as evidence. Clement of Rome then was said to have written to the Corinthians, Polycarp of Smyrna to the Philippians, Ignatius of Antioch to a certain number of churches, chiefly in proconsular Asia. These letters were not the only ones in their time; far from it. From them I shall draw considerable material for my History of the Canon.

In the first place, these letters establish the fact of the interchange mentioned above. Thus, Polycarp says to the Philippians, at the very end of his epistle:[1] "I have received letters from you and from Ignatius. You recommend me to send on yours to Syria; I shall do so, either personally or by some other means. In return, I send you the letter of Ignatius, as well as others which I have in my hands, and for which you made request. I add them to the present one: they will serve to edify your faith and perseverance." We do not know what the letters were, of which this author is here speaking. If they were apostolic writings, then the Philippians did not yet possess them all; if they were later works, then the churches at this time were using for their edification other writings than those of the apostles. Certain it is, that this epistolary exchange continued to a still later date.[2]

In the second place, these same epistles furnish us with direct proof that the writings of the apostles had not only extended beyond the narrow circle of their first origin or local destination, but that they were already exercising a

---

[1] Polycarp, *ad Phil.* ch. 13; comp. Euseb. iii. 36, 37. I quote this text and some others, without inquiring into its authenticity, which is sufficiently doubtful. The inferences to be drawn from them lose nothing of their value, even if these texts are of a later date.

[2] Euseb. iv. 23, v. 25.

marked influence on the teaching. There are, indeed, in these epistles no quotations by name, with some rare exceptions to which I shall return by-and-by, and the texts of the apostles are nowhere appealed to expressly and literally as authorities; but they are sometimes made use of tacitly, in a way not to be mistaken. In certain passages, the exhortations are couched in the formulas employed by those illustrious predecessors, and the conviction is readily formed that the writers of this second generation were already studying the works of the first. Thus, the Epistle of Clement presents accurate enough reminiscences of some passages in the Epistles to the Romans and to the Corinthians, and above all, in that to the Hebrews;[1] those of Ignatius, more numerous and certainly more recent, contain others, which take us back to the Epistles to the Corinthians and to the Galatians, as well as to the Gospel of John;[2] finally, the very brief Epistle of Polycarp has frequent allusions to apostolic passages, notably to Acts, the First Epistle of Peter, the First of John, the Epistles to the Romans, the Corinthians, the Galatians, the Ephesians, the First to Timothy.[3] One point more: this use is purely homiletical or rhetorical. Nowhere is the reader warned by an apostle's name, or by a formula of quotation, or by any notice whatever, that the words which we at once recognise as borrowed have a special value different from that of their context.[4]

I said that there exist some exceptions to this usage.

---

[1] Clement, *ad Cor.* i. 24, 32-36.

[2] Ignatius, *ad Magnes.* ch. 10; *ad Ephes.* ch. 18; *ad Rom.* ch. 3, 7; *ad Philad.* ch. 1; *ad Smyrn.* ch. 6, etc.

[3] These allusions are more precise in that part of the epistle of which the Greek text is lost. Like Daillé and other critics, I am suspicious of the authenticity of that part.

[4] This homiletic use goes back further still. See, in the Reuss, *History of Christian Theology in the Apostolic Age*, Vol. II., p. 264, what I have said on the use which the Epistle of Peter makes of James, Romans and Ephesians.

These are interesting in several respects. The three authors now before us do speak by name of certain Epistles of Paul, when they are writing to the churches which had received these epistles. They speak of them as documents belonging still to those churches, as being their special heritage. They speak of them by way of reminder, or of exhortation to read them and meditate on them. Such an exhortation therefore was still necessary. Thus Clement tells the Corinthians to take Paul's letter to convince themselves that the Apostle had written to them before of matters analogous to the subject of their dissensions.[1] Polycarp, in order to preach righteousness to the Philippians, avails himself of the example of the illustrious and blessed Paul, who preceded him among them, both in his preaching directly and in the letter written to them, which letter will still serve to edify them, if they are willing to study it.[2] Ignatius, finally, reminds the Ephesians[3] that they are the colleagues of Paul, that elect instrument of God, in whose footsteps he himself desires to walk, and who in his epistle professes always to pray for them.

Let me add, in order to omit nothing, that in these same authors occasional mention is made of the evangelic history and of certain words of Jesus.[4] In most of the cases, it is difficult to say whether the facts have been taken from a written source or from oral tradition. If the former be the case, we must at least admit that the quotations have been made from memory. They do not agree with our canonical texts. I shall cite some instances. Ignatius relates that

---

[1] Clement, *loc. cit.*, ch. 47 : ἀναλάβετε τὴν ἐπιστολὴν τοῦ μακαρίου Παύλου τοῦ ἀποστόλου. Τί ὑμῖν ἔγραψεν;

[2] Polyc., *loc. cit.*, ch. 3 : ὃ καὶ ἀπὼν ὑμῖν ἔγραψεν ἐπιστολὰς εἰς ἃς ἐὰν ἐγκύπτητε δυνηθήσεσθε οἰκοδομεῖσθαι κ. τ. λ.

[3] Ignatius, *ad Ephes.* ch. 12; comp. Paul, *Ephes.* i. 16.

[4] See, *e.g.*, Ignat. *ad Ephes.* ch. 14, ch. 19 ; *ad Smyrn.* ch. 1 ; *ad Polyc.* 2. Polycarp *ad Phil.* 2. Clement *ad Cor.* ch. 46, &c.

Jesus, when risen, said to the disciples, "Take hold, touch me, and see that I am not a spectre without body."[1] Clement quotes the following words: "Be merciful, that you may obtain mercy; pardon, that you may be pardoned; according as you do, so will be done to you: according as you give, so it will be given to you; according as you judge, so will you be judged; according as you will show kindness, so will kindness be shown to you—with the same measure with which you will mete, it will be measured to you again."[2] A still more curious fact of the same kind is found in the epistle which bears the name of Barnabas, and is earlier, in my opinion, than those of which I have been speaking. When it comes to treat of the Sabbath, it declares that the Christians spend the eighth day in rejoicing, because on that day Jesus rose again, appeared to His disciples, and ascended into heaven.[3] Whoever wrote this sentence was either unacquainted with the gospels of Matthew, of Mark, and of John, and with the Acts of the Apostles, or did not regard them as authoritative; for none of these documents permit us to suppose that the resurrection, the appearances, and the ascension of Jesus took place on one and the same day, as the text of the third gospel seems to represent.[4]

These extracts, which might be multiplied, will convince us that there is as yet no question of textual quotations of canonical gospels, consulted exclusively for the history of the Lord. But there is more. In place of the canonical texts which sometimes fail us, we find others to which the

---

[1] Λάβιτι, ψηλαφήσατί με καὶ ἴδετε ὅτι οὐκ εἰμὶ δαιμόνιον ἀσώματον (ad *Smyrn.*, ch. 3; comp. Luke xxiv. 39).

[2] Clem. *loc. cit.* i. 13; comp. Luke vi. 36 ff.

[3] *Ep. Barnab.* ch. 15: ἄγομεν τὴν ἡμέραν τὴν ὀγδόην εἰς εὐφροσύνην ἐν ᾗ καὶ ὁ Ἰησοῦς ἀνέστη ἐκ νεκρῶν καὶ φανερωθεὶς ἀνέβη εἰς τοὺς οὐρανούς.

[4] Comp. also the last phrase of ch. 7, appealed to as a word of Jesus Christ and not found in our gospels. Another of the same kind in ch. 4.

Church did not afterwards assign the same value. Thus I must direct attention to the fact that Clement does not hesitate to invoke, along with the "blessed" Paul, the "blessed" Judith,[1] thus placing on the same line and using the same term for writings which we are accustomed to consider very different from a theological point of view. But that was not this writer's point of view; his conception of the canon was different from ours, or, rather, there was at that time no precise conception of the canon. After this, we shall raise no dispute on finding in the same writer a quotation taken from the Book of Wisdom,[2] no doubt an indirect quotation—*i.e.*, not preceded by a formula distinguishing it from the context, but, in this respect, exactly like nearly all those taken from the epistles of the New Testament. Clement had read Wisdom as he had read certain epistles: he makes use of his readings for the advantage of those he wishes to instruct; that is all.

But even when these authors have express formulas of quotation, and of Scriptural quotation, we are not always sure of finding the formulas followed by canonical texts. Thus the same Clement uses "*It is written*" to introduce phrases for which we might vainly search the whole Bible, but which may have been taken from apocryphal books.[3] The author of the epistle which bears the name of Barnabas quotes, as taken from a *prophet*, the following words: "When shall these things be consumed? When the wood shall be cut down and lifted up, and there shall drop blood from it."[4] In another place, the *Scriptures*, according to him,

---
[1] Clement *loc. cit*, ch. 55. It is the first mention of the book of Judith among the ancients.

[2] Clement, *loc. cit.*: Τίς ἐρεῖ αὐτῷ· τί ἐποίησας; ἢ τίς ἀντιστήσεται τῷ κράτει τῆς ἰσχύος αὐτοῦ; comp. Wisdom xii. 12.

[3] Ch. 50 : γέγραπται μνησθήσομαι ἡμέρας ἀγαθῆς καὶ ἀναστήσω ὑμᾶς ἐκ τῶν θηκῶν ὑμῶν; comp. 4 Esdras ii. 16.—ch. 23 : ἡ γραφὴ λέγει ταλαίπωροί εἰσιν οἱ δίψυχοι οἱ διστάζοντες τὴν ψυχήν κ. τ. λ.

[4] *Epist. Barn.* ch. 12.

say: "At the end of the times, the Lord will deliver to destruction the sheep of the pasturage, their fold and their tower."[1] In Ignatius, too,[2] we find a quotation of this kind, in which he tells us the *Holy Spirit* said, "Do nothing without your bishop!" These are evidently not canonical texts; and the formula, "*It is written*," and others similar to which so much weight is now attached, ought to awaken suspicion, especially on the part of those who attach most importance to them. I fully admit that these formulas imply the recognition of a scriptural authority specially inspired, and therefore exalted above every purely human work of literature. It is all the more significant that they are scarcely ever employed in the Greek texts of the apostolic fathers, when they are quoting from the words of the apostles, whereas they often occur in connection with quotations of a suspicious origin.

All these facts might be supported further by considerations based on the nature and tendency of the evangelic teaching contained in the documents in question. It might very easily be shown that the allusions made in them to phrases of St. Paul do not prove that the authors intended to reproduce exactly the teaching of the apostle, to confirm or comment on it. I have elsewhere[3] given an exposition of the dogmatic substance of the epistles of Barnabas and Clement; and unless we close our eyes to the evidence, we cannot fail to recognise between them and the epistles of the apostle a great difference in this respect. It would be easy to establish the same fact in regard to the theology of the epistles of Ignatius. But discussions of this nature may here be put aside. These authors are for us witnesses to be consulted regarding what was said and believed in

---

[1] *Epist. Barn.* ch. 16.
[2] Ignat. *ad Phi ad.* ch. 7.
[3] Reuss, *History of Christian Theology,* E.T. Vol. II., B. vi.

their time by themselves, by the churches in whose midst they lived. In this capacity they must be heard, whatever be the value of their theology. I believe that their evidence justifies me in saying, that towards the year 130 the writings of the apostles, while continuing to be diffused through Christendom, and already serving directly or indirectly for the instruction of the faithful, did not yet form a special collection intended to be used along with the Old Testament in the periodical and regular readings; that tradition was valued and employed with the same amount of confidence; and that, where scriptural, inspired authorities were to be quoted, they were selected outside of what we now call the New Testament, and this was done without any very exact conception of a canon, without any very prudent choice of texts, and without showing any very close attachment to the letter.

CHAPTER III.

FIRST BEGINNINGS OF A COLLECTION OF APOSTOLIC WRITINGS.

By formulating this absolutely negative result, I place myself in opposition to the traditional opinion, that a canon of of the New Testament—*i.e.*, a collection more or less complete and official of apostolic writing—existed from the end of the first century. I must, therefore, before going further, examine the proofs advanced in favour of this pre-supposition. The course of my narrative will furnish numerous other arguments in support of my views, and will bring out the causes which for a long time hindered the formation of such a canon, as well as those which finally led to it.

We can readily understand that at a later period, when all the churches had been for centuries in possession of the complete Bible, and there no longer existed any disputes regarding its various components and their right to form part of it—we can readily understand how men would easily persuade themselves that it had been so from the first. Just as the laws of optics annihilate, to the observer's eye, the distance which separates the more distant stars from those nearer, so did the ecclesiastical institutions which were successively established in the course of the first centuries, naturally appear, to the generations following (very indifferent to historical criticism), as if they were all contemporaneous in their origin, as if they all dated from the very foundation of the church. The more these institutions were held in respect, the greater was the inclination to attribute them directly and immediately to the will of the apostles. The rites, the liturgical formulas, the rules followed for the government of the church, the discipline, in short all the laws and customs to which the growing needs of an organism, becoming more developed and complicated, had given rise—all these were regarded, and are in part regarded still, as the work of these first leaders of Christianity. The canon of Scripture is no exception. If what was said on this question in the ninth century[1] is to be admitted as irrefutable evidence, we must in the same way accept the much earlier evidence regarding the mass, and many other forms of worship or hierarchical regulations—evidence found in writings composed for the very purpose of supporting them, and received on that account by the public of their time.[2] As to our special subject, I can even show how the pre-suppositions of the middle ages arose. They are at bottom closely connected with another very gratuitous opinion regarding the relation of our gospels to one another, and founded solely on exegetical conjecture. We find that, in the fourth century,[3] much attention was devoted to this relation, and that there finally arose a belief that John, writing last, wished simply to complete the narratives of the three others, and thereby attest them after having read them. This view rested on a very arbitrary and partly legendary chronology, and on a conception of the Fourth Gospel as unworthy as it was insufficient. But when John had once attained the honour of closing the first part of the canon of the New Testament, only one step more had to be made in order to assign to him also the work of making the official collection of the second part.

The modern authors who accept this tradition believe that they find more direct proof of it in some passages from the Epistle of Ignatius to the Christians of Phila-

---

[1] Photii *Codex*. 254.
[2] See, further, what I shall say regarding the Constitutions and apostolic canons.
[3] Euseb., *Hist. Eccles.* iii. 24. Jerome, *Catal.* ch. 9.

delphia. The passage in that treatise runs thus: "I stand by the gospel as by the flesh of Christ, and by the apostles as by the body (or college) of the presbyters of the church. I love the prophets also, because they hope in Christ, and they too have themselves proclaimed the gospel."[1] He is supposed here to be speaking of the Bible as containing the prophets, the gospels and the epistles. But even if the name of the gospel ought to be taken as recalling more especially the historical element of the Christian faith, which may be granted without difficulty, we are not bound to think of a written form of it; the singular, and the use of the same term in what is said of the prophets, are even expressly opposed to such a view. And in regard to the apostles here considered as a kind of directing council for the whole church, it is evident that the author did not mean to speak exclusively of those who had written books. All this is amply confirmed by another passage (ch. 9) where the same names again appear: "Christ is the gate by which the patriarchs, the prophets, the apostles, and the Church enter. The prophets foretold him, the gospel is the accomplishment." No one will maintain that the terms *gospel* and *apostles* must here relate to the books. In the same epistle, there occurs a passage which may appear more significant still:[2] "I have heard some say that they would believe in the gospel only in so far as they found it in the records; and when I told them that it was written, they replied to me that that was the very point to be proved. This is what I say to the people of that kind: "My records, my authentic

---

[1] Ignatius, *ad Philad.*, ch. 5. . . . προσφυγὼν τῷ εὐαγγελίῳ ὡς σαρκὶ Ἰησοῦ καὶ τοῖς ἀποστόλοις ὡς πρεσβυτερίῳ ἐκκλησίας κ. τ. λ.

[2] Ignat. *ad Philad.*, ch. 8: ἤκουσά τινων λεγόντων, ὅτι ἐὰν μὴ ἐν τοῖς ἀρχείοις εὕρω, ἐν τῷ εὐαγγελίῳ οὐ πιστεύω. [καὶ λέγοντός μου αὐτοῖς ὅτι γέγραπται, ἀπεκρίθησάν μοι ὅτι πρόκειται.] Ἐμοὶ δὲ ἀρχεῖά ἐστι Ἰησοῦς Χριστός, τὰ ἄθικτα [v. l. αὐθεντικὰ] ἀρχεῖα ὁ σταυρὸς αὐτοῦ κ. τ. λ. In place of the bracketted clause, the text of the second recension reads: τοῖς δὲ τοιούτοις ἐγὼ λέγω.

records, are Jesus Christ, His cross, His resurrection, etc." As records[1] are mentioned here, some have hastily taken this to be a palpable proof of the existence of the canon, of the official and complete collection of the New Testament. Some would even see in it a direct appeal to the exclusive authority of Scripture, an exaltation of Scripture over every other source of the knowledge of the gospel. On the contrary, the author looks at the fact and the cause from a quite different point of view, and the passage has another meaning altogether. Taking his stand on the Pauline theology, to which as a rule he remains more faithful than Clement and the pseudo-Barnabas, Ignatius declares his preference for immediate faith in Christ, for the faith based on facts, as opposed to that which needs to be supported by exegetical discussions. The adversaries whom Ignatius has in mind are evidently persons little inclined to believe, Judaisers for instance, against whom, after all, a strong and immediate conviction has more weight than a careful exegesis. This father then rejects or despises that very apologetic method which Justin Martyr extols as the only one of practical value.

In the lack of positive proof that there existed an official collection of apostolic books from the end of the first century, resort has been made in France[2] (for I do not know that in Germany such an argument has been brought forward or held valid) to a process of reasoning believed to be beyond dispute. There existed, it is said, a canon of the Old Testament; the books which composed it were held in the deepest respect, because they were unhesitatingly regarded as the result of direct inspiration, as the word of

---

[1] A various reading in the first phrase is ἀρχαίοις and the old translation runs :—*in veteribus*. But this does not agree with what follows, though in substance the interpretation is accurate.

[2] [And in Britain, as recent discussions have shown].—*Tr.*

God. *A fortiori*, all this must have been true of the writings of the apostles, *since* the revelation of the New Covenant was more excellent than that of the Old. This reasoning would be, though not altogether orthodox, at least quite legitimate, if the point were to give an account of the theological ideas and standpoint of our century, for which, in many respects, the New Testament is above the Old. But when the point at issue relates to the first or second century, the reasoning is unsound. No doubt the *Gospel* was placed above the *Law*, and Christ incomparably higher than Moses: of that there can be no question; but it did not follow that the few pastoral exhortations which certain apostles had committed to writing out of the great number they had preached, that the few narratives of the life and miracles of the Lord, which began to circulate in the churches along with the rich and abundant oral tradition from which they were fed daily and which told them as much and more—it did not follow, we say, that these various writings were sure to be placed above the books of the prophets. To these latter a special place and value were assigned in the minds of Christians, because from age to age they had been the record of the revelations bearing on the advent of Christ, which revelations the previous generation had at last seen fulfilled. So true is this, that by-and-by we shall find the Apocalypse the first among the books of the first Christian century to be elevated to the rank of writings specially inspired (in the theological sense of the word), because far more than all the others, or rather the only one of them all, it shared in that prophetic character which was then the sole title to what we would now call canonicity. As to the evangelical histories, we must keep this fact clearly in view, that the miraculous narratives in them were accepted by every one with the greatest eagerness, not because they were written, but because they had been heard, known, and believed long before they were written. The books in this category, so far from having the value of a unique and privileged source, only occupied as yet the rank of secondary evidence.

Moreover, we should take care here not to make mistakes regarding the value of words. Though, in placing myself at the standpoint of the period we are now studying, I claim for the prophets of the Old Testament an inspiration which fully justifies the exceptional position of their writings, I do not mean to say that there was any refusal to acknowledge the inspiration of the apostles. Only there was nothing exceptional in the latter. It might be regarded as relatively greater than that of many other Christians, or than most, or than all, if you will; but it was not different in kind. Had not Jesus promised the Holy Spirit to all his disciples? Does not the apostolic history affirm on every page that this promise was richly fulfilled? Had not the apostles, in their theoretical teaching, incessantly exalted this promise and this fact into a fundamental principle?[1] It matters not that the action of the Holy Spirit had been manifested sometimes by the sanctification of the will, sometimes by the illumination of the intelligence, because the spirit is the same in all these manifestations. And, to guide the judgment of the faithful concerning these, the apostles had nowhere made appeal to their own writings, but to a special gift of the same Spirit of God, that of discernment,[2] granted to several in the communities. When Paul is enumerating the *charisms* or free gifts of the Holy Spirit,[3] we would not be surprised to see him making special mention of the gift of writing, for, as we do not hear him preach, we admire

---

[1] Comp., for instance; John xiv. 16, xv. 26, xvi. 7-15; Acts ii. 14, ff, iv. 31, viii. 15 ff, x. 44, xi. 15 f., xv. 8, 28, etc.; Rom. viii. 9, 14; 1 Cor. iii. 16, vi. 19, vii. 40, xii. 3 f; 2 Cor. i. 22, iii. 17 f; Eph. iv. 30; 1 Thess. v. 19 f; 1 John iv. 2, etc.

[2] Διάκρισις τῶν πνευμάτων, 1 Cor. xii. 10; 1 Thess. v. 21; 1 John iv. 1.

[3] 1 Cor. xii.; Rom. xii.

especially that gift which he possessed more than any of his colleagues; and the fact that so few of the disciples applied themselves to this form of instruction proves that it was a vocation quite as special as that of the apostleship or the diaconate. And yet Paul is so little concerned about the fate of his epistles which were intended for his contemporaries, that in his enumeration he forgets this precious gift. But not only do the apostles speak of inspiration as universal and equal among Christians; their successors continually say the same. All the Apostolic Fathers speak of that full effusion of the Holy Spirit on all the faithful, and expressly claim it for themselves.[1] In our days, by the very means of that gift of discernment *of the spirits* which was promised us, we measure without effort the enormous distance that separates the immortal pages of Paul from the dull and absurd allegories of Barnabas and his silly tales about hyenas and weasels (Barn. ch. 8 f.); we do not for a moment think of placing in the same category the assurance of the future life, given to the Christian by his fellowship with the risen Saviour (1 Cor. xv. 12 ff.) and the proof of the resurrection drawn from the story of the phœnix-bird (Clement, *loc. cit.*, ch. 25); and we neither need nor wish to connect redemption with the red thread of the harlot of Jericho (Clement, ch. 12). But the discernment of spirits did not hold good at the precise time of which we are speaking. I affirm the contrary. It is sad to think, but none the less true, that the increasingly luminous halo with which the succeeding generations surrounded the venerated heads of the first apostles, was not the reflection of the completer illumination shed on men's minds by their writings, but a kind of optical effect increased by distance and chiefly produced by the light—

---

[1] Πλήρης τν. ἁγ. ἰσχύεις ἐπὶ πάντας, Clem. *ad Cor.*, ch. 2, 46: Barn., ch. 16: Θεὸς οἰκεῖ ἐν ἡμῖν. . . . ἐν ἡμῖν προφητεύων. Comp. ch. 9, 19. Ignat. *ad Philad.*, ch. 7. Polyc. ch. 9. Herm. *Pastor*, ii. mand. 3 etc.

dim to us, brilliant to them—of legends which were at times simple and graceful, at times coarse and absurd.

But to return, let me, before entering on the details, point out two general facts which must influence our estimate of the causes that may have hastened or delayed the formation of a canon of the New Testament. In the first place, it must not be forgotten that, at the opening of the second century, the Christian Church was still divided, or was already divided, into two camps which had almost no communion with one another, and whose differences had not yet been settled by any decision of men, nor by the slower but more decisive judgment of time and their own progress. So long as this state of things lasted, so long as neither of the two parties could declare itself to be the only true Church, the Catholic Church, there could be no thought of a universally recognised collection of the writings of the apostles. The Christians of the circumcision, remaining faithful to the law, and persisting in regarding it as obligatory, would not hear Paul spoken of as an apostle, and in general saw no necessity for extending the Holy Scriptures by adding works of a recent origin. They had been accustomed to hear the story of Christ's life read in a book which some attributed to Matthew and others simply called the *Hebrew gospel*; but this was a means of edification and nothing more.[1] I am willing to admit that this same gospel—and for the same reason also the Epistle of James —did not penetrate into the Pauline churches. Before any collection could be made which would embrace writings of these two shades of opinion, their differences had to be smoothed down, or the schism so widened that the most advanced and best inspired party might claim to be the only representative of the true Church of Christ. This important advance was made, imperceptibly and by the force

[1] See Euseb. *Hist. Eccles.* iii. 27. Irenaeus *Adv. Haer.* i. 26.

of circumstances, during the course of the second century—the chief cause being the resistance made to Gnosticism by the communities and bishops who were the heirs of the apostolic tradition. I shall presently have to show how this movement had an influence on the formation of the canon.

There is a second fact to which I direct the attention of my readers, as proving the non-existence of an official canon at the period we are considering. Let us suppose for a moment that the apostles, or the last survivor among them, did fix, close, and sign a collection of this kind, how, then, is it to be explained that afterwards and for centuries there existed in the Church, and among the most learned and exalted theologians, so much uncertainty regarding the canonicity of certain books? If John had promulgated this code, could the Greek churches have by turns venerated and rejected his Apocalypse? If Peter had already in his hands the complete collection of the epistles of Paul, could Tertullian have attributed to Barnabas the Epistle to the Hebrews, while Clement attributed it to Luke, and Origen cried, "God alone knows the author of it?" If a book had been included in the canon by the only competent authority, would it have been omitted afterwards by a doctor or a church without a cry of indignation being at once raised from all sides? What right would any one have had to increase the volume by new works? How could the numerous fabricators of apocryphal books have hoped to deceive the public, and how could the public have let itself be taken in by a fraud so patent? There is no room for hesitation. If it is true that the canon of the New Testament was not only fixed and closed at the death of the last apostle, but was also recognised and guaranteed by him or by his colleagues, then all the writings, regarding whose apostolic origin the Church had doubts afterwards, or which simply remained unknown to certain churches, are made suspicious in the highest degree by the very fact of that doubt or that absence; or rather, they have lost their claims to canonicity. For, if Providence commissioned the apostles themselves to make the canon, it must have remained the same as it came from their hands; they alone are its legitimate vouchers, just as, from the standpoint of orthodox Protestant theology, they alone are the privileged interpreters of the evangelic thought itself. One might go still further back and say: If the apostles themselves formed the canon, how does it happen that several of their writings have not come down to us?[1] To this question there is but one answer, an answer poor, desperate, compromising, but given more than once in our days, viz., that these writings were not inspired!

Let us now run over the authors and works or fragments of Christian literature belonging to the period between 130 and 180, so far as they have come down to us. It was an important period, for during it the Catholic Church severed itself entirely from Jewish Christianity on the one hand and philosophic syncretism (Gnosticism) on the other. Unfortunately this series of testimonies is neither numerous nor rich in facts. Still there is not one which does not make its little contribution.

The first author to be mentioned here is Papias, bishop of Hierapolis, of whose writings some very interesting fragments have been preserved by Eusebius.[2] In his work entitled *Exposition of the Words of the Lord*, he declares his desire to adhere rather to oral tradition than to books.[3] The historian quotes two passages regarding the origin of the gospels of Matthew and Mark, from which it is apparent

---

[1] 1. Cor. v. 9; Col. iv. 10, 16; Luke i. 1; 3 John, 9. Comp. Polyc. *ad Phil.*, ch. 3, and the interpreters of 2 Thess. iii. 17.

[2] *Hist. Eccles.* iii. 39.

[3] οὐ γὰρ τὰ ἐκ τῶν βιβλίων τοσοῦτον με ὠφιλεῖν ὑπελάμβανον ὅσον τὰ παρὰ ζώσης φωνῆς καὶ μενούσης.

that the two gospels known to Papias were not precisely the same as we now possess under these names. Eusebius further affirms that he had found some mention (or at least some traces), of an epistle by John and one by Peter. The historical notices therein contained do not always agree with the canonical narratives. For instance, the death of Judas is told in quite a different way from the same incident in Matthew and Acts.

We pass to the famous *Epistle to Diognetus*, which is frequently printed at the end of the works of Justin Martyr, and has by some critics been placed in the same rank as the writings of the Apostolic Fathers. Of all the writings of the second age, it approaches most nearly the apostolic teaching in tone and expression. We do not find in it any quotations, properly speaking, but we do find some scattered reminiscences, less of texts than of ideas, from the Sermon on the Mount, as well as from Paul and John.[1] These reminiscences attest a certain familiarity with these authors, but not the need of invoking their authority. Once, however, on the last page, a word is quoted textually from Paul with a formula which contains no theological element.[2] But special attention has been directed to a passage where, in speaking of the revealing Word and of the graces with which he has enriched the Church, the author says: "Thenceforth the fear of the law is sung, the grace of the prophets is recognised, the faith of the gospels is established, the tradition of the apostles is guarded, and the grace of the Church leaps for joy."[3] When we compare this passage with those of Ignatius examined above, a difference, apparently slight, but very significant, is observable. The gospels appear in the plural, and the word is here for the

---

[1] *Epist. ad Diogn.* ch. 5, 6, 9.

[2] *Ep. ad Diogn.*, ch. 12: ὁ ἀπόστολος λέγει, 1 Cor. viii. 1.

[3] Ch. 11: εἶτα φόβος νόμου ᾄδεται, καὶ προφητῶν χάρις γινώσκεται, καὶ εὐαγγελίων πίστις ἵδρυται, καὶ ἀποστόλων παράδοσις φυλάσσεται, καὶ ἐκκλησίας χάρις σκιρτᾷ.

first time used for books and not for the abstract, primitive notion. Along with the law and the prophets, we have the *gospels* mentioned here as a regular source of faith and Christian instruction. I draw attention to this point that the gospels were the first to attain this honour, and I only observe further that the text gives no help in forming an opinion as to the number and choice of those books. As to the apostles, allusion is made to their oral teaching and not to their writings. I have no wish to diminish the force of this testimony, though modern critics are inclined to consider the two last chapters as not authentic. In a history where exact chronology is impossible, some dozens of years of difference cannot cause any great difficulty.

Another author of this period, Hegesippus, of whom the historian Eusebius has preserved some fragments,[1] says, in speaking of his travels, that he had everywhere found the churches and the bishops continuing in the true faith as preached by the law, the prophets, and the Lord.[2] Further, it is said that in his writings there are to be found extracts from the Hebrew *and* Syriac gospel and from Jewish traditions. These notes sufficiently prove to us that the author, so far as apostolic books are concerned, possessed or used but one gospel. Of this gospel Eusebius knew nothing precise, and he speaks of it so as to betray his ignorance; but in any case it was different from those which were finally adopted by the Church. As Hegesippus nevertheless declared himself to be in communion of faith with the churches he visited, it follows that in his time a collection of canonical books had not yet become the test of orthodoxy.

Some pages further on,[3] Eusebius cites another author— Melito, bishop of Sardis, who also lived towards the middle

---

[1] Euseb. *Hist. Eccles.* iv. 22.
[2] ὀρθὸς λόγος. . . . ὡς ὁ νόμος κηρύττει καὶ οἱ προφῆται καὶ ὁ κύριος, *loc. cit.*
[3] Euseb. *Hist. Eccles.* iv. 26.

of the second century. Among his numerous works there was one on the Apocalypse of John. Whether this was a commentary or an essay, it was certainly the first instance of a study made of an apostolic work. But the curious fact should not pass unobserved that the Apocalypse was the first to be honoured in this way. This confirms what I said before regarding the conception, which the contemporaries of Melito had formed of inspiration, and it is not the only nor the most striking confirmation of my remarks. The same writer had also composed a work which, apparently, included a series of extracts from the Old Testament intended to support the Christian faith. Eusebius has transcribed the preface of this work, which contains an enumeration of all the books of the Old Covenant, and speaks of it in such a way as to show that Melito had no idea of any other collection of sacred books. Eusebius, who is so anxious to collect the opinions of the ancients in regard to the canon of the New Testament, would not have failed to direct attention to those of Melito, if he had found the least trace of them. It may be remarked in passing, that the catalogue above mentioned omits the book of Esther. As we shall see later on, this was neither the fault of the copyist nor unwitting forgetfulness on the part of the author.

In the few fragments preserved to us of Claudius Apollinaris,[1] bishop of Hierapolis and contemporary of Melito, there is some discussion of the controversy which had arisen in Asia Minor on the subject of Easter-day. Apollinaris was the first bishop of that country who maintained that Jesus, in the year of His death, had not eaten the paschal lamb but had been crucified on the day on which the Jews were eating it. His adversaries made ap-

---

[1] *Chron. Pasch.* p. 13. ed. Dindorf. [This is the form of the name in the oldest Greek MSS. but Latin writers commonly use Apollinarius]. Tr. —

peal to Matthew; but he declares that they are mistaken and that they have against them both the Law and *the gospels*. This last expression, unless it be extended to include works now lost, can only refer to that of John, for he alone of those now existing supports the opinion of Apollinaris. This shows that the gospels were in his time consulted on questions of ecclesiastical discipline, and that they had already come to be compared with one another.

A little later came Dionysius, bishop of Corinth,[1] the author of a great number of epistles addressed to various churches. In the analysis which Eusebius gives of them, we find a very interesting passage, extracted from a letter to the Romans, and telling that on that same day, a Sunday, they had been reading the letter which the Romans had just written to the Corinthians, and that they would not fail to read it subsequently for the instruction of the faithful just as they had read the epistle written formerly by Clement. This shows that, in this locality and probably elsewhere, the public readings included epistolary communications. I shall make no difficulty in granting that, if Clement of Rome was read at Corinth sixty years after his death, the Apostle Paul had the same privilege. This would be the most ancient testimony (though only by inference) to a periodical reading of the epistles. Still it is certain that those of the apostles were not the only ones thus used. In another place, Dionysius complains that his letters had been falsified by interpolations and abridgments, but adds that there was nothing astonishing in this, since some had dared to treat in the same fashion the evangelic writings (γραφαὶ κυριακαί). This last text permits the supposition that the gospels, or gospels known and read at Corinth in the time of Dionysius, were still undergoing al-

---

[1] Eusebius, *Hist. Eccl.*, iv. 23.

terations such as history proves to have been made in times earlier.

I might pass over in silence an anonymous fragment which Eusebius (*Hist. Eccles.* v. 16, 17), extracts from an extensive work against the Montanists. In all probability, the author wrote only towards the end of the century, at a time when opinions relative to the canon were already much more settled. But seeing that the author, whatever be said of him, says absolutely nothing on our subject, I have no wish to dispute the chronological place claimed for him. In his preface, this author declares that he hesitated some time before deciding to write his book, not that he distrusted his ability to refute the error or to bear testimony to the truth, but because he feared to incur from certain people the reproach of desiring to add new ordinances to the word of the new evangelic covenant, to which word nothing ought to be added, and from which word, nothing ought to be taken away by any one who wishes to live according to the gospel.[1] By rashly employing here the term *New Testament* instead of *New Covenant*, some were led to suppose that this passage directly proves the existence of the New Testament, in the modern sense, as a collection closed and complete from the middle (?) of the second century. But it is evident that, even if the author in speaking of the *word* of the New Covenant, had certain writings in mind, he does not in any way determine their number and form, and therefore does not help us a step further than we had reached without him. Besides I maintain that he is not speaking here of books but of the faith legitimately preached in the church that had been constituted according to authentic tradition. This faith he wishes to defend against the more or less eccentric innova-

---

[1] . . . μὴ τῇ δόξῃ τισὶν ἐπισυγγράφειν ἢ ἐπιδιατάττεσθαι τῷ τῆς τοῦ εὐαγγελίου καινῆς διαθήκης λόγῳ κ. τ. λ.

tions (some kind of revivals) which the Phrygian sect was making. This is proved by a remark which the same author makes further on. "The special kind of pretended prophecy to which this false prophet (Montanus) is trying to give currency, is found nowhere, and with no one *under the Old or the New Covenant*," and with reference to this, he cites a series of names of Christian prophets, both those belonging to the time of the apostles, such as Agabus and the daughters of Philip, and those belonging to the century following, such as Quadratus, together with some contemporaries. At the same time he makes use of a saying of *the Apostle*[1] to the effect that the gift of prophecy was to exist in the whole church, until the coming of the Lord. This latter passage proves two things:—first, that by New Covenant the author does not mean the book we call the New Testament, and, secondly, that the author, notwithstanding his anxiety not to encroach on the rights of the evangelic word, is not well acquainted with the written texts, or handles them very freely.

While we are gleaning among the accounts which Eusebius gives of the Montanists, I may say in passing that he also cites a certain Apollonius.[2] This Apollonius wrote in the same strain against this sect, and Eusebius notes in him, as worthy of remark, quotations from the Apocalypse and the assertion that Jesus had ordered the apostles to remain twelve years at Jerusalem.

But we have further to consult the authors whose works have been preserved to us in their entirety as well as divers documents of less extent but also entire. In the first place, there are the works of Athenagoras who died about 177; an Apology by him and a treatise on the Resurrection

---

[1] Where did the apostle say this? In spirit it is a legitimate inference from 1 Cor. xii. xiv; still the text does not furnish the exact words.

[2] Euseb., *Hist. Eccl.*, loc. cit., ch. 18.

still exist. From this treatise it is manifest that the author had read what Paul says in 1 Cor. xv.; once he quotes it;[1] but beyond this, the texts of the New Testament though very numerous on this subject, are not quoted and have not even influenced his style. In the Apology, phrases or expressions borrowed from St. Paul,[2] occur a little more frequently, but no quotations, while the author more often cites words of Jesus Christ whose tenor conforms generally to the text of the Sermon on the Mount. Still, among these textual quotations, there is one for which we would vainly search in our canonical gospels. The Lord is said to have given precise instructions as to the manner in which Christians were to give each other the fraternal kiss, that no guilty thoughts might arise and compromise their salvation.[3] The formulas of quotation are here so positive that it must be acknowledged that the author had a written text before him.

We possess, almost complete, an account of the persecution of the Christians in Gaul, under Marcus Aurelius; it is contained in a letter addressed by the churches of Lyons and Vienne to those of Asia Minor.[4] This letter may go back to the year 177 and possibly enough Irenaeus, who later was bishop of Lyons, may have had some part in the writing of it. However, as that is not certain, we can consider the letter by itself. Of all the literary monuments of that period, it contains most allusions to the apostolic books. We find in it phrases, evidently borrowed from Romans, Philippians, First and Second Timothy, First Peter, and Acts; further, a saying of the Lord which we know only from the Gospel of John, once even a direct and textual

---

[1] Κατὰ τὸν ἀπόστολον. *De Resurr.* 16 ; comp. also ch. 9 and 19.
[2] Romans, Galatians, First Timothy. Comp. Athen. *leg.* ch. 13, 16, 37.
[3] *Ibid.*, ch. 32 : πάλιν ἡμῖν λέγοντος τοῦ Λόγου . . . καὶ ἐπιφέροντος . . .
[4] Eusebius, *Hist. Eccl.* v. 1.

BEGINNINGS OF A COLLECTION OF APOSTOLIC WRITINGS. 45

quotation, described as from *Scripture*. Strange to say this quotation, which besides is loose in form, is taken from the Apocalypse.[1]

To the same period may be assigned the account of the martyrdom of St. Polycarp which is printed in the collections of the Apostolic Fathers.[2] It is not altogether free from critical suspicion, but I do not wish here to enter on a discussion immaterial to my present purpose. In it also are found phrases borrowed without acknowledgment from the books of the apostles, from Romans, First Corinthians, and from the gospel narrative; but in regard to the quotations from the last, we cannot exactly say whether the author had a written copy before him.

The account of the martyrdom of Ignatius printed in the same collection, is much more suspicious. It exists in as many as eight different forms, and Eusebius was not acquainted with it. I therefore mention it merely. In the least amplified edition, the Old Testament is sometimes quoted,[3] the New nowhere directly. We can see in it many traces of the Epistle to the Romans and of Paul's history as related in the Acts; but that is all.

We pass to one of the most read and most highly extolled works of the first centuries, the *Pastor* of Hermas. This book, which we shall by and by see raised to the dignity of canonicity, nowhere quotes directly the Old or the New Testament. Nevertheless, as a matter of course, many passages in it are influenced by biblical language; and, in regard to the New Testament in particular, there are not a few allusions to certain passages in the Synoptic Gospels, in

---

[1] . . . . ἵνα ἡ γραφὴ πληρωθῇ, ὁ ἄνεμος ἀνομησάτω ἔτι καὶ ὁ δίκαιος δικαιωθήτω ἔτι; comp. Rev. xxii. 11.

[2] Comp. Eusebius, *Hist. Eccl.* iv. 15.

[3] Among others the passage from Leviticus which the author may perhaps have taken or copied from 2 Cor. vi. 16. At all events, the γέγραπται refers to Moses.

the Pauline Epistles, and in the First Epistle of Peter. But the famous *sicut scriptum est*, the binding formula of quotation to which great importance is rightly attached, is never found on these occasions. On the other hand, it is employed to introduce a quotation from an apocryphal book.[1]

We come finally to the author who, among all belonging to this period, is the most important both for the history of theology in general, and specially for the history of the canon. This is Justin Martyr. I have reserved him for the end of this chapter, that I might connect him with the general results of our studies on the period he represents. The authentic works by him are not numerous, but they are far more extensive than all we have been reviewing, and at several points they touch on the history of the canon.

Of all his contemporaries, Justin depends least on tradition and uses most frequently and most regularly written records when he is discussing theological proofs. To his mind the ultimate test of evangelic truth is the argument drawn from the prophecies.[2] The prophecies are the most direct and indisputable indications of the action of the Word, which is the only source of truth for mortals; and this characteristic of prophecy is confirmed above all by its fulfilment. Hence Justin bases his apologetic and polemic arguments on the relation between the prophetic texts of the Old Testament (inspired by the Word) and the facts in the history of Jesus as stated in the *Memoirs* of the apostles. These two kinds of quotations, which are very frequently

---

[1] Hermas *Pastor* Vis. 2. ch. 3, *sicut scriptum est in Heldam et Modal*. This was the title of a book founded on an incident in the history of Moses (Numbers xi. 26).

[2] The miracles may be the effect of magic, the narrators may lie; ἀλλὰ τοῖς προφητεύουσι κατ' ἀνάγκην πειθόμεθα διὰ τὸ ὁρᾶν . . . . ἥτις μεγίστη καὶ ἀληθεστάτη ἀπόδειξις (*Apol.* i. 30, p. 72). How could we believe of one crucified, that he is the eldest son of the Eternal and the judge of the world, if we had not had the prophecies previous to his birth and did not see their fulfilment? (*Ibid.*, ch. 53, p. 88. Comp. *Dial. c. Tryph.* 32, p. 249.)

employed, are almost the only quotations to be found in him. The didactic books of the New Testament are not once mentioned throughout his writings, though it seems to me impossible to maintain that he was not acquainted with them. On the other hand, we find often enough phrases and ideas which recall, either the Gospel of John, or the Epistles of Paul and the Epistle to the Hebrews (but neither the Pastoral nor the Catholic Epistles). Above all, it is to be observed that the quotations from the Old Testament sometimes agree more closely with the text of Paul (whose name is never mentioned by the author[1])than with the text of the Septuagint.

Justin's apologetic method has as its corollary or rather as its basis, a very rigorous theory of inspiration. He is in truth, the doctor of the θεοπνευστία or *plenary inspiration*. From him comes the famous explanation which has had great success in the Church, that the prophets were to the Holy Spirit, what the flute is to the musician. "Inspiration," he says, "is a gift which comes from above to holy men. To receive it, they need neither rhetoric nor dialectic; they must give themselves up simply and purely to the action of the Holy Spirit that the divine bow, descending from heaven and playing on them as on a stringed instrument, may reveal to us the knowledge of heavenly things."[2] This definition has been very inappropriately understood to relate to every kind of biblical composition. It is important to remember that Justin applies it only to what can rightly

---

[1] It is to be noted that Justin attaches a theological value to the number of the *twelve* apostles (*Dial. c. Tryph.* ch. 42.) which is prefigured in the Old Testament and cannot therefore be changed. Further, in the same book (ch. 35), the author declares in the most emphatic terms that those who give permission to eat of the ἰδωλόθυτα are false prophets. Comp. Acts xv. 29; Rev. ii. 14, 20; with 1 Cor. viii. 4, x. 23 ff.

[2] . . . . ἵνα τὸ θεῖον ἐξ οὐρανοῦ κατιὸν πλῆκτρον, ὥσπερ ὀργάνῳ κιθάρας τινὸς ἢ λύρας τοῖς δικαίοις ἀνδράσι χρώμενον, τὴν τῶν θείων ἡμῖν ἀποκάλυψιν γνῶσιν (*Coh. ad Gr.*, ch. 8.)

be considered prophecy—*i.e.*, from his point of view, to the whole of the Old Testament,[1] and to anything, outside of that collection, which bore the same character. That is why neither the gospels, nor the epistles are ever quoted as inspired books. The latter are not quoted at all as I have just said; the gospels are appealed to as historical documents proving the fulfilment of the inspired prophecies. But beyond the Old Testament, Justin was acquainted with other prophetic books which he quotes as such and which he regarded as entitled to all the prerogatives of prophecy. Three of them he quotes by name. The first is the Apocalypse whose author, John, one of Christ's apostles received a special revelation regarding the millenial reign.[2] Then comes the Sibylline Books from which he borrows a good deal; he explains their metrical defects by the power of the inspiration which prevailed in them.[3] Finally, the book of a prophet now unknown, one Hystaspes who long afterwards was quoted by the later fathers, is expressly put on the same level as the Sibylline Books and the sacred authors of the Old Testament, "the devils alone being able to restore a law which forbade the reading of them, so profitable to men."[4] Let me add further, that Justin, consistently with himself, maintains that the Old Testament is to be regarded not as the property of the Jews to whom Providence intrusted it provisionally but as the property of the Christians,

---

[1] And not once to what we call the New Testament, which Justin never employs for theological *demonstration* neither as a whole nor in its parts. The words of Christ, of the Logos, do not need to be called inspired, because the Logos is himself the author of all inspiration. They are independent of the books containing them.

[2] *Dial. c. Tryph. ch.* 81.

[3] δυνατὴ ἐπιπνοία (*Coh. ad. gr.* ch. 16, ch. 37, 38. *Apol.* i. 20, 44). On the use which the Fathers make of the Sybilline oracles, comp. generally the article in Vol. vii. of the *Nouvelle Revue*, pp. 199 ff.

[4] *Apol.* i. 20, 44. I have explained this passage in the article quoted in the preceding note.

to whom it belongs both as a collection of books and as containing dogma.¹ Justin would have said, "*The Old Testament is the canon of the Christians*,"² if that term had been in use in his day. He goes a step further, and is the first among the Christian writers we know, to proclaim the inspiration of the Septuagint.³ From what I said in my first chapter it will be understood that this fact is of great importance for the sequel.

But the point most interesting for the history of the canon is to get acquainted with Justin's gospels, for, excepting the Apocalypse, they are the only apostolic writings expressly quoted by him, and he even speaks of them as books used in worship. "On the day of the sun (Sunday)," he says,⁴ "all those of us who live in the same town or district assemble together, and there is read to us some part of the memoirs of the apostles, or of the writings of the prophets, so much as time permits; then, when the reader has finished, the president gives an hortatory application, after which we rise for common prayer; afterwards bread, wine, &c., are brought." Here, then, according to an explicit testimony which may go back to the year 140, we find the gospels regularly read along with the Old Testament. For there can be no doubt that these *Memoirs* of the apostles are gospels and nothing else. Justin says so himself a few lines previous,⁵ and in such a way as to remind us that this word *gospels*, in so far as it is used of books, is a popular

---

¹ οὐκ αὐτοῖς ἀλλ' ἡμῖν ἡ ἐκ τούτων διαφέρει διδασκαλία.... αἱ τῇ ἡμετέρᾳ θεοσεβείᾳ διαφέρουσαι βίβλοι (*Coh. ad Gr.*, ch. 13).

² The Holy Spirit predicted by the prophets *all* that relates to Jesus Christ: τὰ κατὰ 'Ἰησοῦν πάντα (*Apol.* i. 61; comp. ch. 50).

³ θείᾳ δυνάμει τὴν ἑρμηνείαν γεγράφθαι. ... with the fable well known through the account of Aristeas. ταῦτα οὐ μῦθοι! (*loc. cit.*)

⁴ *Apol.*, i. 67: τὰ ἀπομνημονεύματα τῶν ἀποστόλων ἢ τὰ συγγράμματα τῶν προφητῶν ἀναγινώσκεται μέχρις ἐγχωρεῖ.

⁵ οἱ ἀπόστολοι ἐν τοῖς γενομένοις ὑπ' αὐτῶν ἀπομνημονεύμασιν ἃ καλεῖται εὐαγγέλια (*loc. cit.*, 66).

term, introduced naturally, when the preaching of the *gospel* (in the religious sense) became connected with reading to the people the facts of the history of the Lord. It must not for a moment be forgotten that the term, in this sense, is not found in authors previous to this period.[1] But the name *Memoirs*, which Justin gives to the gospels, is still more striking. The name was not absolutely new. Some time before, Papias, when giving an account of the composition of Mark's gospel, had twice used the same term, telling how that disciple used to collect from the preaching of Peter the historical elements which the apostle happened to mention (ὡς ἐμνημόνευσεν), and put them together in writing as well as he could reproduce them from memory (ὡς ἀπεμνημόνευσεν).[2] On the other hand, Origen, in order to explain in what sense the Epistle to the Hebrews might be attributed to St. Paul, says, that the thoughts belong to the apostle while the expression must have been given by some one who reproduced the thoughts from memory (ἀπομνημονεύσαντος).[3] Eusebius directs attention to the fact that Irenaeus speaks somewhere of the ἀπομνημονεύματα (memoirs, recollections, narratives) of an apostolic presbyter.[4] The significance of the term would therefore not be doubtful. It is evident that, to Justin's mind, it denoted something quite different from the writings of the prophets, which were inspired miraculously by the Holy Spirit, and in which neither the memory nor any other human faculty had any active part. Observe further that our author

---

[1] The last chapter of the Epistle to Diognetus would form the only exception, if it were older than Justin's *Apology*—which there is reason to doubt.

[2] Papias, *apud* Euseb. iii. 39. Comp. *Nouvelle Revue* ii. 61. In the *Clementine Recognitions*, Peter also is made to say (ii. 1), *In consuetudine habui verba domini quae ab ipso audieram in memoriam revocare.*

[3] Origen *apud* Euseb. vi. 25.

[4] Eusebius, *Hist. Eccles.* v. 8.

declares plainly that these Memoirs had no authority in themselves, but that Christians put faith in them *because* the prophets (of the Old Testament) ratified and sanctioned their narratives beforehand.¹ Prediction alone is the test of truth, because it alone is an exclusively divine manifestation, and Christ Himself ordains us to obey not human teachings, but that which prophets have announced and He Himself has taught.² Thus, whatever has not been said by Christ or a prophet, is human teaching.

This expression, *Memoirs of the Apostles*, occurs pretty frequently in Justin's writings, while he rarely uses the term, *gospel*. I have already shown that he employs this word in the plural; I may now add that, in all probability, he saw no need for resorting in addition to oral tradition. On the contrary, from the tendency and method of his theological labours, it must have been important to him to have always at hand written documents acknowledged to be authentic and sufficiently ancient. Hence he asserts that the Memoirs to which he appeals contain *all* that concerns the life of the Saviour,³ and that they were composed by the apostles and their companions.⁴ What gospels, then, were these? For eighty years German critics have been writing volumes on this question. Justin does not cite any proper name. Once, indeed, when telling that Jesus gave surnames to several disciples, among others to Peter, he says that this is told in HIS (αὐτοῦ) Memoirs.⁵ As Justin nowhere else speaks of Memoirs, or rather, of Recollections of Jesus

---

¹ Οἷς ἐπιστεύσαμεν ἐπειδὴ καὶ τὸ προφητικὸν πνεῦμα τοῦτο ἔφη (*Apol.*, i. 33; comp. *Dial. c. Tryph.*, ch. 119).

² Οὐκ ἀνθρωπείοις διδάγμασι κεκελεύσμεθα ὑπ' αὐτοῦ τοῦ Χριστοῦ πείθεσθαι, ἀλλὰ τοῖς διὰ τῶν μακαρίων προφητῶν κηρυχθεῖσι καὶ δι' αὐτοῦ διδαχθεῖσι (*Dial. c. Tryph.*, 48).

³ οἱ ἀπομνημονεύσαντες πάντα τὰ περὶ τοῦ σωτῆρος (*Apol., loc. cit.*).

⁴ ἃ φημι ὑπὸ τῶν ἀποστόλων καὶ τῶν ἐκείνοις παρακολουθησάντων συντετάχθαι (*Dial. c. Tryph.*, ch. 103). These last words remind us of Luke's preface.

⁵ *Dial. c. Tryph.* ch. 106. Comp. Mark iii. 16.

Christ (as Xenophon said, *Recollections of Socrates*), but of Memoirs of the Apostles, the pronoun here can only refer to Peter, the author of the book in question. A gospel of Peter existed in ancient times,[1] and not impossibly Justin had known and consulted it among others. At any rate, I would prefer this interpretation to that which makes it the Gospel of Mark, here attributed to Peter. But as in every other passage, without a single exception, he speaks of Memoirs *of the apostles* (in the plural), I should rather be inclined to correct the text and to restore the plural, which would suit exactly the rest of the phrase.[2]

Apart from all this, the question of knowing what gospels Justin had in his hands can only be settled by a study of the extracts of which he gives a very large number. Most of these extracts may, without much difficulty, be referred to our Synoptic Gospels, especially to Matthew and Luke,[3] provided that we do not insist on a perfectly and rigorously literal coincidence. It is no doubt true that even such a coincidence would not absolutely prove identity, because the other gospels which were in circulation at the time, or which had been in existence at a previous date, might have a great resemblance to ours. But since it is beyond dispute that these particular gospels were widely spread in the churches in Justin's time, I see no reason for hesitation in supposing that he was acquainted with them. As he made use of the gospels only to show the fulfilment of prophecy, he did not attach much importance to the letter; and the imperfect resemblance between his quotations and our canonical texts ought not of itself to determine our judgment. At all events it is remarkable that several of

---

[1] Origen, ad Matt. xiii. 54; Eusebius, *Hist. Eccles.* iii. 3, 25, vi. 12; Jerome, *Catal.* ch. 1, ch. 41; Theodoret, *Haeret. fab.* ii. 2.

[2] He changed the name of Peter, one *of the apostles*, which is also told in THEIR memoirs.

[3] There are also some reminiscences of John's text, but very few.

Justin's quotations, in which the text differs from ours, occur *word for word* in other works, such as the *Clementines*, regarding the sources of which critics are not more agreed. This coincidence would lead us to suppose that Justin's variations are not all to be attributed to defects of memory. Further, when Justin recurs several times to the same point in the evangelic history, he generally makes use of the same expressions. This fact seems to suggest that he depended on one written source, and consequently, if such quotations differ from our canonical texts, we are bound to infer that he used a gospel now lost. But putting aside these details to avoid everything which might have the air of over-subtlety and passing to more essential points, let us examine whether he mentions the same facts, and only those facts related in the canonical gospels. If the point had always been discussed in this way, it would have appeared less difficult. Let us look, then, at some of the historical facts which Justin speaks of having found in the Memoirs of the Apostles. We leave it to our readers to decide on their value and origin.

The genealogy of Jesus, which Justin recognises, is always that of his mother Mary. It is she who is descended from David and the patriarchs. Nothing is said about Joseph. Now our gospels only give genealogies of Joseph, and say nothing of Mary's family.[1] Every time that Justin speaks of the Magi, he makes them come from Arabia.[2] This, in substance, does not contradict Matthew's narrative; but I cannot help thinking that Justin had read this proper name in the source which he was fond of consulting. Jesus was born in a cave[3] near the village, because there was no room for him in the houses. This detail, which is unknown to

---

[1] *Dial. c. Tryph.* ch. 43, 100. Comp. Matt. i. 16; Luke iii. 23.

[2] *Dial. c. Tryph.* ch. 77, 78, 88, 102, 106, seven times.

[3] ἐν σπηλαίῳ (*Dial c. Tryph.* ch. 78).

our gospels, is also given elsewhere,[1] and has been retained in ecclesiastical tradition. When Jesus came out of the water, after having received baptism, a fire was kindled in Jordan.[2] The voice from heaven on this occasion uttered these words: "Thou art my Son; to-day have I begotten thee, according as David foretold."[3] Jesus wrought at the trade of a carpenter, and made ploughs and other agricultural implements. Quirinus is called the first procurator of Judea and not governor of Syria,[5] which is a great difference, and may to some extent lessen the difficulties of a well-known passage in Luke. The miracles of Jesus are regarded by the Jews as produced by magic, or as illusions.[6] At Gethsemane, the sweat fell in great drops from the brow of the Lord; but Justin does not give the special designation which is found in Luke, and regarding which there had already been so much discussion.[7] Contrary to the narrative of all our four gospels, he affirms that, when Jesus was arrested, *not a single man* came to His aid, and in proof of this he appeals to Ps. xxii. 11. This testimony, according to Justin's theory developed above, had of course more weight than modern narratives, unless it be supposed that Justin possessed a gospel in which the incident of Peter and Malchus was omitted.[8] All the disciples *abjured* their

---

[1] *Evang. Jacobi*, ch. 18; *Evang. infant*, p. 169, Fabr.; Origen, contra Celsum i. 51; Eusebius, *Vita Constant.* iii. 40.

[2] πῦρ ἀνήφθη ἐν τῷ Ἰορδάνῃ (*Dial. c. Tryph.*, ch. 88. Coll. Fabric., *Cod. apocr.*, iii. 654. *Sibyll.* vi., vii.; comp. *Nouvelle Revue* vii. pp. 235, 238).

[3] *Dial. c. Tryph.* ch. 88, 103; Psalm ii. 7; Clement of Alex., *Pæd.*, i. 6; Augustine, *De consensu evv.* ii. 14, are acquainted with this formula (see Luke iii. 22; Matt. iii. 17). It exists in Codex D.

[4] *Dial. c. Tryph.* ch. 88; comp. Mark vi. 3. Origen maintains (contra Celsum vi. 36) that this is not found in any canonical gospel.

[5] *Apol.* i. 34.

[6] μαγικὴ φαντασία (*Dial. c. Tryph.*, ch. 69. *Clementine Recognitions*, i. 58. Lactantius, *Instit. div.* v. 3).

[7] *Dial c. Tryph.* ch. 103. Comp. Luke xxiii. 44.

[8] οὐδείς, οὐδὲ μέχρις ἑνὸς ἀνθρώπου, βοηθῶν αὐτῷ ὑπῆρχεν (loc. cit.)

Master until after the resurrection.[1] This exaggeration, which is several times repeated, is unknown to our gospels. Instead of the story which the latter give about the corruption of the soldiers by the party of the Sanhedrin, Justin speaks of various attempts made by Jewish agents selected and sent through the whole land for the purpose of accusing the disciples of having removed the corpse, &c.[2] Finally, words of Jesus, which are not found in the canonical gospels, are recorded in several passages.[3] If these quotations do not compel us to attribute to Justin the knowledge and use of a gospel differing from those which the Church finally and exclusively adopted, it must, at the very least, be granted that he considered the extra-canonical tradition to be an authority equally worthy of respect, and that in any case the question had not yet emerged in his day of what was afterwards called the canon of the New Testament.

If now, after carefully weighing all the testimonies discussed in this chapter, I affirm that there is in them no trace of the existence of any official catalogue, however incomplete, of the books of the New Testament, I shall not incur the reproach of having based my arguments on the accidental silence of some few authors. So far as theory was concerned, the Christians were still able to do without such a collection, whether, like Justin, they found the force of Gospel in the mysteries of the letter of the prophets, or whether, like Ignatius, they felt it confirmed by the power of the spirit and by its own internal testimony.

---

[1] *Apol.* i. 50. *Dial. c. Tryph.*, 53, 106 : ἀπίστησαν ἀρνησάμενοι.

[2] *Dial c. Tryph.*, ch. 17, 108 ; Matt. xxviii. 12 ff.

[3] "Εσονται σχίσματα καὶ αἱρέσεις (*Dial. c. Tryph.*, ch. 35).—Ἐν οἷς ἂν ὑμᾶς καταλάβω, ἐν τούτοις καὶ κρίνω (*ibid.*, ch. 47).—Εἰ ἀγαπᾶτε τοὺς ἀγαπῶντας ὑμᾶς τί καινὸν ποιεῖτε; καὶ γὰρ οἱ πορνοὶ τοῦτο ποιοῦσιν (*Apol.* i. 15).—Ἰησοῦς ἐνδύσαι ἡμᾶς τὰ ἡτοιμασμένα ἐνδύματα ἐὰν πράξωμεν τὰς αὐτοῦ ἐντολὰς ὑπίσχετο (*Dial. c. Tryph.*, ch. 116).—Ὅτι δεῖ αὐτὸν παθεῖν. . . . καὶ πάλιν παραγινήσεσθαι ἐν Ἰερουσαλὴμ καὶ τότε τοῖς μαθηταῖς αὐτοῦ συμπιεῖν καί συμφαγεῖν κ. τ. λ. ; comp. Matt. xx. 17 ; Mark x. 32 ; Luke xviii. 31.

As to their practice, they sought edification in the reading of the apostolic books which they had in their hands; even at that date they caused them to be used for the instruction of the faithful, and that regularly. In regard to the gospels, this is a positive fact; in regard to the epistles, it is possible; but the choice of the books was not fixed and regulated by any authority. We have seen that apocryphal books, or at least books afterwards excluded from the canon, were quoted, lent, and officially read. The canon of the Old Testament is no more fixed than that of the New. Melito excludes Esther from it; Clement adds Judith. In several respects the prophets are preferred to the apostles; the latter are never regarded as holding the first rank. The miraculous inspiration of the Septuagint is insisted on far more emphatically than that of the writers of the first century, considered as such. In the opinion of the theologians, the Apocalypse excels all the other apostolic writings. Tradition disputes the place of the Scriptures or is held in equal respect. Through lack of a critical spirit and religious discernment, men, otherwise well-meaning, are the dupes of gross literary frauds. All these facts belong to an impartial history of the canon, and cannot be neglected if the history is to be something more than the expression of pre-conceived opinion.

CHAPTER IV.

HERESY.

In the two preceding chapters, I have carefully collected from the Christian authors before 180, all the facts bearing upon the use which the church at this period made of the apostolic writings, and the authority which it assigned to them. But as yet we have only consulted writers of one single category or of one single party, viz., those who knew and professed themselves to be the depositaries or direct inheritors of the authentic teaching of Jesus Christ and his first disciples. These writers, if regarded from the standpoint of the Church's later development, must indeed be held to have represented and preserved the true apostolic belief, to have been the orthodox party. But side by side with them, there were authors quite as numerous and of very various opinions, whose teaching was held to be more or less erroneous and was therefore combated with an increasing energy. The chief result of this struggle was to fix dogma more precisely, to separate more clearly what was thenceforth called Catholicism—*i.e.*, the Church universal and its creed—from heresy or dissent; for it should be observed that this term, *heresy*, according to its etymology, denoted at first every kind of division. It was only later, when dogmatic controversies had assumed a preponderating importance, that the word obtained the narrower meaning which finally prevailed.

The phases of this conflict between apostolic tradition or orthodox Catholicism and the various aberrations of heresy are well suited for casting some light on the history of the canon, or more correctly, they form a very essential part of it. The general mode of treatment, it is true, has been to take advantage of what are called the *testimonies* of the heretics, in order to prove that *even* they recognised the authenticity of the books of the New Testament and could not escape from their authority; and the conclusion has been drawn *a fortiori* that the orthodox church must have been in possession of a canon already formed and closed. This method of argument is very plausible so long as we are only establishing the great antiquity or authenticity of certain books, and of books about which there is no dispute, but it is not quite sound when it attempts to prove the existence of an official canon. It gives to certain facts a force which does not belong to them, passes over others in silence, distorts some by considering them from the standpoint of a different century, and consequently imposes on the historian the duty of putting them all in their true light.

And, in the first place, a clear distinction must here be drawn between two tendencies diametrically opposed to one another, and both widely separate from the Catholicism which began to grow up in the course of the second century. These two tendencies were Judaic Christianity and Gnosticism.

Judaic Christianity—*i.e.*, the Christianity which maintained the perpetual obligation of the Mosaic law (as it was understood and applied at the time of Jesus Christ)—was not, whatever may be said of it, a heresy in the sense of having sprung from a secession, from an orthodox church previously established. The books of the New Testament themselves show that this was not the case.[1] I am well aware that it neither understood nor exhausted the inner teaching of the Gospel; but as an expression of the conviction of the masses, it had the previous claim of antiquity and

---

[1] Reuss, *History of Christian Theology.* Books iii., iv.

might, if it pleased, make use of its claim to designate as heretics all those who did not adopt its fundamental principle.[1] This Judaic Christianity finally became heretical itself, not through any formal or official declaration of the so-called Catholic Church, but imperceptibly through the growing ascendency of the latter, in whose bosom the development of Christian life and theological science was richer, more rapid, more victorious. But during the whole of the period with which till now we have been occupied, it had not yet come to be considered or called heretical. On the contrary, the bond of a common origin which linked it with the Church universal was still very firm, and the example of such men as Justin and Hegesippus shows that the transitions from one shade of opinion to the other were sometimes not easily perceived nor easily defined. No doubt amongst the Judaising party, there were already rising tendencies and systems more or less removed from the simplicity of the teaching of the first age, and soon strange and compromising elements were added by some to a tradition which at first had only sinned by its poverty.[2] But these were exceptions, and most of the churches with this shade of opinion refused to be drawn away into such eccentricities. Now it is certain, as I have already had occasion to say, that, at this particular period, these churches not only had no official collection of apostolic writings, but that they did not use these writings, even singly, for their edification in public or private. All that we find in them is a written history of the Lord, a gospel (as was the phrase before the middle of the second century) which some possessed in an Aramaic form, others in Greek, which was sometimes attributed to Matthew, sometimes to Peter, some-

---

[1] τοὺς λέγοντας Ἰουδαίους εἶναι ἑαυτοὺς καὶ οὐκ εἰσίν (Rev. ii. 9).

[2] I have here specially in mind gnostic Ebionism, represented by the *Clementines*, a work of the second century. This work is directly opposed to Paul and its gospel quotations abound in elements outside of the canon.

times to the apostles in general,[1] which in matter and form resembled very much our three first gospels, but also contained so many divergences that they were remarked by a more critical or more exacting age.[2]

What do all these facts prove for the history of the canon? Shall we say that the Jewish Christians separated themselves from a church which was in possession of an official, or at least widely-used, collection of apostolic books; and that, for some reason or another, they rejected these books, and no longer made use of them after becoming familiar with them? Such an explanation would be very singular, and very much opposed to the nature of things. The nucleus of the collection which afterwards became official was, on the one hand, the Pauline Epistles, as might have been expected after my previous remarks; and, on the other hand, those evangelic narratives for which there was sufficient authentication. As to the latter, we have just seen that they were not everywhere the same, and that they varied in their fulness of detail; and regarding the epistles, no one will contradict me when I affirm that it was not in the churches of Palestine they were first collected. They were collected in Greece, in Asia Minor, in short, abroad; and the fact that they did not penetrate into the communities which followed the Palestinian tradition proves of itself that the canon, as it existed later, was not a heritage from the primitive Church, but was formed, diffused, and

---

[1] κατὰ Ματθαῖον, κατὰ Πέτρον, κατὰ τοὺς δώδεκα, καθ' Ἑβραίους, τὸ ἑβραϊκὸν, τὸ συριακὸν, etc.

[2] For these facts, which are now placed beyond all dispute, I refer to the works dealing with the history of the gospels. It is useless to transcribe here the numerous passages from Irenaeus, Jerome, Epiphanius and other Fathers, which speak of Jewish Christians and their Gospel. It must only be remembered that these Fathers looking from the standpoint of their period and of the Catholic theory of their time, are inclined to treat the Jewish Christians as dissenters. See Reuss, *Geschichte des N. T.* Sect. 198, 199, and especially Credner, *Beiträge*, vol. i.

propagated slowly, progressively, on lines parallel with the theological and religious movement of the time.

With the Gnostics, matters took a different course. In their case we have not to do with churches whose origin goes back to the cradle of Christianity, who were nourished, so to speak, by a purely local tradition, and who were little influenced by any results of the evangelic spirit produced beyond their own narrow sphere. On the contrary, we have to do with individuals, with philosophers, with founders of schools, who sought to secure the triumph of their hazardous and daring speculations on the most difficult problems of metaphysics over the traditional beliefs of the Jews and the Christians, which they thought too simple and insufficient. What was the origin of these men? Were they foreigners—*i.e.*, thinkers of pagan origin who acquired influence over the Church by some false appearances of a community of feeling—or were they Christians led astray by the ill-regulated demands of their reason, or dissatisfied with the too popular theology of the Gospel? Science has not yet succeeded in giving a definite answer to this question, though for my part I should be inclined to accept the former supposition. But as we are, after all, dealing with many different men, placed in very different positions and confining themselves to systems more different still, it would be well that their methods and results should not lead us to assign the same point of departure to all alike. At any rate, one fact is certain regarding them all: they all put forward theories of religious philosophy, fundamentally different from anything in the pastoral teaching of the Church which could rightly bear that name, or rather their doctrines were so utterly out of harmony with that teaching that, apart from all direct contradictions, they were clearly not so much theologians to be expelled because they had become heretical, as philosophers to be debarred from entering because they were still unbelievers. And yet they were anxious to enter, or, if you wish, to remain in, not certainly for the sake of any material advantages, but because Christianity, of all the religions and systems which their syncretism had used for building up new doctrines regarding the origin of evil, the relations of the infinite with the finite, and man's means of raising himself towards God—Christianity, I say, had furnished them with the most abundant and the most precious material, and at the same time the Church contained the audience most disposed to listen to them.

In this position how could these promoters of Gnosis—*i.e.*, of religious philosophy—succeed in getting support for their theories? The difference between these and the traditional beliefs circulating in the Church was too plain to give them any hope of imposing them on the public. The guides of the flocks, ever present and vigilant, could oppose them with contradictions, effectual as well as formal, whenever they ventured, if I may say so, to speak in their own private name. They had therefore to seek some starting-point outside, and there could be no doubt about their choice. The members of the Church who were making theology—*i.e.*, who were trying to demonstrate the evangelic faith traditionally taught—had recourse to the Old Testament, to prophecy, to the spiritualistic interpretation of the law. Now, Gnosticism, at least in its chief forms, was very pronounced in its antipathy to the law and all connected with it, regarding it as the product of a very imperfect or even lying manifestation. The Gnostics were fond of putting Christ into direct contradiction with the law. They were thus led naturally to seek in the words of the Lord, in His history, in everything that could be regarded as the reflection of His thought, the proof of this antagonism and the confirmation of their own theories. From ecclesiastical tradition they appealed to the facts on which it was itself based, while they explained the facts in a new way; they appealed to the texts which gave the most authentic and most immediate representation of these facts. These texts, no doubt, were not unknown to the churches; but up to this time such teaching had not been discovered in them; edification had been found in them; but they had not been made the object of a studied, scientific exegesis, because Christians already possessed with less trouble all that could be learned from them. The Apocalypse was the only exception, for reasons which every one will understand. The Gnostic philosophers were the first to apply this method to the gospels and the epistles; they were the first exegetes of the apostolic books. The Fathers who afterwards took up the struggle with Gnosticism are unanimous in directing attention to this fact.[1] It is not necessary for me to pause over the estimate of this exegesis, to describe its means and its tendency, to give examples of its defective and arbitrary results.[2] It is the fact itself, this particular kind of theological work, which interests us by its novelty. And this fact is all the more curious that the very existence of several parts of the New Testament was first revealed to us by these exegetical studies of dissenting philosophers. Thus the gospel of John, the *name* of which first occurs among the Catholic party in a writer whom I have not yet had occasion to name, in

---

[1] Only through them are we acquainted with it. Basilides wrote 24 books of ἐξηγητικὰ εἰς τὸ εὐαγγέλιον. Heracleon was the author of commentaries on Luke and on John. Fragments of various other authors are collected in Grabe, *Spicil.*, Vol. II. Fabric., *Bibl. gr.*, Vol. V., etc.

[2] Irenaeus, *Adv. haer.*, III. 12: *Scripturas quidem confitentur, interpretationes vero convertunt.* Tertull., *Praescr.*, 38: [*Valentinus*] *sensu expositione intervertit* . . . He did not falsify the texts, *et tamen plus abstulit et plus adjecit auferens proprietates singulorum verborum et adjiciens dispositiones non comparentium rerum.* Euseb. *Hist. eccles.*, iv., 29: χρῶνται εὐαγγελίοις ἰδίως ἑρμηνεύοντες τῶν ἱερῶν τὰ νοήματα γραφῶν κ. τ. λ. Irenaeus, in his first book, Origen in his commentary on St. John, and the ἱπτομαί added to the works of Clement of Alexandria, furnish numerous examples.

Theophilus of Antioch, about the year 180, had been commented on forty years before by a Gnostic author!

Here several interesting questions emerge, over which we must pause for a little. First of all, can we determine the list of the apostolic writings, which the various leaders of Gnosticism must have had in their hands, or which they recommended and expounded to their followers? Does our knowledge of them permit us to say that there already existed an official collection which they had simply to borrow from the orthodox Church?

The answer to this question is complicated rather than difficult, because every doctor held a different attitude towards the texts according to the nature of his system. But they had this in common, that the choice and use which they had to make of the apostolic literature were decided by their theories, exactly as was the case with the Catholics in more than one instance as we shall see. The scriptural labours of the Gnostics prove, in the first place, what hardly needs such proof, that the books they quote existed and were acknowledged to be the compositions of the apostles; they prove next a point which is no longer disputed, that these latter enjoyed universal respect in the sphere in which they had been acknowledged during their lifetime; but they prove further that the appeal made to their authority was subordinate to the interests of the doctrine which was to be established in each special case. Now, as the apostolic texts do not quite preach the Gnosticism of the second century, it is unnecessary to show that appeal was made to them only so far as they were believed to be of use in supporting the special point. The number of passages to be utilised in this way might be very great, whenever a certain amount of willingness and exegetical skill was applied; and above all when the method in general use among Jews and Christians, was to pay no attention to the context, and to make much of isolated phrases, scraps of phrases, or single words. But it was possible also to abstain from such abundance of quotations, and to keep to one or the other book as seemed to be most suited for the purpose. Thus one philosopher confined himself to the words of the Lord, who was regarded as the revealer of all the mysteries of the world,[2] and sought to extract these mysteries from preaching which, to common eyes, was purely moral and popular. Another, struck by the mystical and speculative spirit of the Fourth Gospel and recognising even in the author's favourite terms some colouring of his own gnosis, could not but find it very easy to bring the shades of opinion into more perfect harmony.[3] A third, much occupied with the antithesis between the Gospel and the Law, which he exaggerated to the extent of detecting the traces of an absolute metaphysical dualism, could not but lean exclusively on that apostle in whom he detected an analogous tendency, or at least a tendency less opposed to his own, while he rejected with disdain all writings which seemed to him tainted with Judaism.[4]

It would be impossible to explain these widely different proceedings, if, at this period, the canonical collection of the Church had been fixed and closed. We nowhere find the Fathers accuse a Gnostic of disputing the authenticity of some particular book; they merely state that he does not make use of it, that he does not recognise its authority.[5] But

---

[1] *Valentinus integro instrumento uti videtur* (Tertull., *Præscr.*, 38).

[2] εὐαγγέλιόν ἐστιν ἡ τῶν ὑπερκοσμίων γνῶσις (Basil. ap. Hippol., *Philos.*, p 243). Comp. note 1 on page 63.

[3] Heracleon *ap.* Origen. *in Jo., passim*.

[4] See, in regard to Marcion, the details in the pages that follow.

[5] *Cum ex scripturis arguuntur, in accusationem convertuntur ipsarum scripturarum quasi non recte habeant neque sint ex auctoritate* (Iren.. III., 2). —*Ista hæresis non recipit quasdam scripturas, et si quas recipit . . . ad dispositionem instituti sui intervertit; et . . . non recipit integras etc.* (Tert., *Præscr.*, 17).—(Apelles) τῶν εὐαγγελίων ἢ τοῦ ἀποστόλου τὰ ἀρέσκοντα αὐτῷ αἱρεῖται (Hippol., *loc. cit.*, p. 259) etc.

we have seen, and we shall see again, that this liberty existed also in the other camp, that it was still the common right of all. Wherever a more frequent use of apostolic texts is observed, so as to justify the statement that such a writer *appears* to make use of the *entire code*,[1] such a statement from the pen of a Catholic author of later date can only mean that the writer makes more numerous and less exclusive quotations than usual. This might be said of the short letter from the Christians of Lyons quite as much as of Justin's comparatively voluminous works.

But further, the authentic texts of the apostolic age did not always furnish, I need not say, the materials for the proof sought in them; more often still, it happened that these texts were in direct contradiction to the theories of the day. In such a case several expedients were used, simple enough if no official canon existed, but very hazardous, not to say quite impossible, if an official canon did exist. I said that the Gnostics applied their exegesis chiefly to the words of the Lord in order to deduce from them their own dogmas; but these words were either circulating still in a purely traditional form, or they were recorded in certain writings more or less different, more or less widely known, but not yet approved by any ecclesiastical authority and all used in the same fashion just as occasion demanded. Now there was nothing easier than to form new collections of this kind, either by making simple extracts from those they possessed, or by combining several books, or even by composing narratives under the direct influence of the ruling ideas of the system. There are well-known examples of each of these three methods.

As to the system of making extracts, it is well-known that Marcion, who was the most distinguished leader of this period, and whose importance is proved by the books written

---

[1] See the note of Tertullian on Valentinus (p. 65).

against his teaching long after his death, was accused by the Fathers of having mutilated the Gospel of Luke. I shall not dispute the fact, although we can no longer verify it, but I shall simply observe that his adversaries in any case put the matter in a wrong light. They write at a much later period when Luke's book was included in the ecclesiastical collection; they are indignant that Marcion should have left out some chapters or passages, and they call him a forger. But Marcion had no intention of making the people believe that his edition was that of Luke, and thus obtaining for it the sanction of an apostolic name. He did not call it by that name, he called it the *gospel* (*i.e.*, the history) *of Christ*; it was the summary of what he judged to be true and good in that history, a summary meant to serve as a basis for the instruction of his disciples. He might have composed a gospel more freely; he might have given an edition quite new, just as we take it upon us to edit manuals of biblical history for the young; he preferred to keep to a book already in existence, either because it was the only one he knew, or more likely because it was the one which seemed to have most of the spirit of the Pauline theology. And still finding in it elements which seemed to him to contradict the Pauline spirit, he simply suppressed them.[1] He was, no doubt, a heretic; but he was not a forger. What he did clearly proves that in his time the gospels were *still* compositions private in character and used at discretion, like all ordinary books,[2] and that they were *not yet instruments* (Tertullian's expression)—*i.e.*, official documents, authentic

---

[1] *Contraria quæque suæ sententiæ erasit . . . competentia reservavit* (Tert., *Adv. Marc.* iv. 6. We learn also from old writers that his disciples continued to make alterations on it.

[2] It is right to remember here that in the second century the apostolic texts were treated with some freedom even by Catholics. The history of the various readings is very instructive on this point. It was not till much later that scrupulous care was taken for the diplomatic preservation of the text.

writings in the juridical sense of that term.[1] Besides, Marcion was neither the first nor the only Gnostic teacher who acted on this principle, only the others were less influential, and less outcry was made about them. Thus the Fathers often describe copies of Matthew without the genealogy, or speak in general terms of violent alterations in the texts.[2] But we must guard against giving too much weight to their assertions, as they sometimes contradict each other, and in every place show that they had only a vague knowledge of the facts. Thus the same Epiphanius, who accused the followers of Cerinthus of mutilating a Matthew, speaks elsewhere of their gospel as if it had been fundamentally different from those of the Catholic Church;[3] while Irenæus, much earlier than he, tells us that this same sect preferred the gospel of Mark![4] What, indeed, are we to think of the testimony of these authors, when we see the most learned

---

[1] The critical examination of the statements in the Fathers (especially in Tertullian and Epiphanius) regarding Marcion and his gospel would lead me too far at present. I prefer to admit the principal assertion of these authors, that I may not seem anxious to escape from a serious difficulty. See further my *Geschichte des N. T.* § 246. The Fathers further accuse Marcion of having mutilated in the same way the epistles of Paul. If the fact is true, it must be explained in the same way as his treatment of the gospel. But here there is more positive reason for suspecting the accusation. Among the reproaches made against Marcion's text, there are a good many which simply prove that at that time there were various readings in the copies; and more than once, the reading of Marcion, condemned by the deeply prejudiced ignorance of his adversaries, is the very reading adopted in our best printed editions.

[2] Jerome, *Adv. Lucif.*, ii. 100 ed. Trib. *Ad eos venio hæreticos qui evangelia laniaverunt, Saturninum quemdam et Ophitas. . . . et Carpocratem et Cerinthum et huius successorem Hebionem* (!) *quemdam.*—Epiphanius, *Hær.*, 28, 5, in speaking of the party of Cerinthus, says: χρῶνται τῷ κατὰ Ματθαῖον εὐαγγελίῳ ἀπὸ μέρους καὶ οὐχ ὅλῳ.—Origen, *Opp.*, iv. 52. Ruæi. says of Apelles: *Evangelia purgavit.*—Epiphanius, *Hær.* 44, 4, apostrophises the same Apelles: εἰ ἐ βούλει λαμβάνεις ἀπὸ τῆς θείας γραφῆς, καὶ ἃ βούλει καταλιμπάνεις, ἆρα γοῦν κριτὴς ἐκάθισας κ. τ. λ.—Euseb., *Hist. Eccl.*, v. 28, etc.

[3] Epiphanius, *loc. cit.* xxx. 14.

[4] Irenæus, *Adv. hær.* iii. 11, § 7.

among them *inventing* the very heretics whom he accuses of rending the Scriptures?[1]

The second method of bringing the gospels known in the churches into agreement with the new and heretical doctrines professed, was to bring together suitable materials so as to form a new book, what we would now call a Harmony. It has often been conjectured that the book from which Justin made his numerous quotations was such a work, containing texts from our canonical gospels and fragments from another gospel now lost. But there is one composition of this kind whose existence is certain. Tatian, an Assyrian philosopher, who was converted to Christianity and became a disciple of Justin, but afterwards adopted a very rigid asceticism and became leader of the sect of the Encratites (as we would say, leader of a temperance society), composed a gospel which must have been arranged according to the method indicated.[2] It was still in existence in the time of Eusebius, who does not appear to have examined it closely, and who knew it under the name of *Diatessaron* (which means pretty much, book or summary *of four*). This name, which may not have been given by the author himself, since the work of Tatian was known to the public by other titles,[3] would naturally lead us to suppose that the book contained our four canonical gospels, combined into one narrative, as has since been so often done. But Theodoret[4] tells us that it was not a simple harmony, and that it omitted the genealogies and all the passages relative to the human sonship of the Lord; and if Epipha-

[1] See in the note above what Jerome says about a supposed Ebion, founder of the Ebionite sect !

[2] Euseb., *Hist. Eccl.* iv. 29 : συνάφειάν τινα καὶ συναγωγὴν τῶν εὐαγγελίων οὐκ οἶδ' ὅπως συνθείς.

[3] Epiph., *Haer.* xlvi. 1, says that it was also called the *Gospel of the Hebrews*. Victor of Capua, in his preface to the *Harmony of the Gospels*, calls it *Dia pente*. Comp. Fabric. *Cod. apocr.* i. 378.

[4] Theod., *Haeret. fabb.* i. 20.

nius is not wrong in bringing it into connection with what was called the Gospel of the Hebrews, it must undoubtedly have contained elements foreign to our four canonical books. At any rate, Theodoret found it widely current in his diocese, where even the Catholics (in the fifth century!) used it without suspicion, and made no difficulty about the simplification of the harmonised text;[1] their bishop took the trouble to collect about two hundred copies of it, which he put aside—*i.e.*, destroyed, in order to replace them by canonical gospels.

Finally, I said that certain Gnostics reached their end more directly by composing new gospels. That does not exactly mean that they always invented both the miracles and the discourses of Jesus Christ which they put into their books. The name I give to these compositions is justified if they were based partly on a tradition not yet fixed in writing. Of course this tradition might be open to suspicion, and I by no means profess to maintain the authenticity of the details which they thought fit to collect in this manner.

---

[1] ἀλλὰ καὶ οἱ τοῖς ἀποστολικοῖς ἑπόμενοι δόγμασι, τὴν τῆς συνθήκης κακουργίαν οὐκ ἐγνωκότες, ἀλλ᾽ ἁπλούστερον ὡς συντόμῳ τῷ βιβλίῳ χρησάμενοι (*loc. cit.*)

[2] Origen *in Luc. Opp.* iii. 933: *Ausus fuit Basilides scribere evangelium et suo nomine titulare.* Comp. Jerome, *Prooem. in Matth.* Eusebius (iv. 7) attributes to him τερατώδεις μυθοποιίας; but what Clement of Alexandria (*Stromata* i. 340, iii. 426; *Sylb.*) quotes from Basilides agrees with our texts. Valentinus also had his own gospel, *suum praeter haec nostra* (Pseudo-Tertull., *Praescr.* 49). His disciples called it the true gospel (*vv. veritatis*), and Irenaeus (iii. 11) designates it as *in nihilo conveniens apostolorum evangeliis.* But what Tertullian says of it (*loc. cit.* 38), as well as the little treatise of his disciple Ptolemaeus, which Epiphanius (*Haer.* 33) preserves to us, and the extracts printed at the end of Clement's works, hardly go beyond the canonical texts (see Reuss., *Geschichte des* N. T. §§ 245, 508). I may also mention here the gospel of the Egyptians, quoted frequently by Clement, Origen, and Epiphanius, and used in what is called the Second Epistle of Clement of Rome, a Catholic work. This book contained words of Jesus Christ which were undoubtedly apocryphal, but were sometimes reproduced without any suspicion.

It is proper here to remind my readers that in the second century there also appeared a great number of pseudonymous books—*i.e.*, books falsely attributed to authors of the first century. I have no wish at present to discuss this kind of literature; still it is important to remark that the very possibility of producing it with any chance of success proves that the church did not yet possess an official collection so distinct that exclusion from it was enough to condemn a book and stamp it as prohibited. This remark applies specially to a great number of apocryphal Acts of various apostles, mostly of Gnostic origin, wherein the plan, generally romantic and full of marvels, served to introduce their authors' doctrines, which were put in the mouths of the heroes. Such books (and the same may be said of many gospels) were much read by those who greedily accepted all stories of miracles; the only precaution taken was to suppress the heretical discourses. Mutilated or expurgated editions circulated without hindrance in the Catholic Churches. A great number of these Gospels or these Acts, called heretical or Gnostic by the Fathers, have come down to us, and have been printed in recent years. But in most cases, the heterodox elements have altogether disappeared. They were read in this form in the churches, conjointly with the canonical books, on saints' days (Joseph, Mary) and on the days of the apostles they celebrated.[1] We know further, that the apocalyptic form was sometimes also employed to introduce to the public doctrines opposed to ecclesiastical tradition, or merely the fancies, more or less inoffensive, of some excited brain. The epistolary form was less suited to this kind of theological industry; still it too was represented in the pseudonymous

---

[1] For all these matters, see my *Geschichte des N. T.* §§ 236, 279, where are given the patristic proofs for each detail.

library of the period, which was far richer than that of the apostolic writings.

Let us return to the history of the latter, and to the use made of them by the heretics.

There is still one most interesting fact to be pointed out to my readers. The first trace in all ancient Christian literature of the existence of a collection of apostolic books, is connected with the name of the heretic Marcion. I have already said that this Gnostic philosopher, occupied with the necessity for basing his system on apostolic texts in order to obtain acceptance for it, chose from among them those least unfavourable to his views, after altering them however (as it appears), and suppressing everything which did not agree completely with his theory. His collection consisted of two parts, which he called the *Gospel* and the *Apostle*.[1] The first division I have already discussed; the second included ten epistles of Paul. It would be wrong to call this a scriptural *Canon* in the sense which afterwards was current in the church, for Marcion was far from regarding Paul as an absolute authority. Still less should any great literary importance be attached to his collection, as if it proved anything whatever against the authenticity of the epistles not contained in it. Nevertheless this collection is very curious; for it is easy to see that it was made quite independently, and with no previous usage to determine its form. So much may be clearly inferred from the list of the epistles, as Marcion had classed them, according to the authors who mention it. He placed them in the following order: Galatians, Corinthians, Romans, Thessalonians, Laodiceans, Colossians, Philemon, Philippians. Epiphanius makes a great outcry about this arrangement, because in his time—*i.e.* in the fourth cen-

[1] Among the authors who can be consulted on this point, are specially Tertullian, *Adv. Marc.* v. and Epiphanius, *Hær.* 42.

tury[1]—another arrangement had been generally adopted. Much clamour was also made about the substitution of the name of the Laodiceans for that of the Ephesians. But these very peculiarities, which had no connection whatever with the author's theological prejudices, should direct our attention to the collection itself. When he put the name of Laodicea in the passage where we now read that of Ephesus, Marcion may have simply made a conjecture based on Col. iv. 16, a conjecture which many moderns, not Marcionites, have likewise adopted; but he may also have had in his hands a manuscript which did not contain the name Ephesus, such as existed in the time of St. Basil[2] and exists even yet at the present time.[3] At any rate as he had not the least interest in preferring one name to the other, it may be inferred that no constant tradition, no collection officially circulated, was in existence to determine his choice. The order adopted for the epistles is still more significant. This order is evidently based on the chronology. According to the general consent of modern criticism, Marcion was wrong about the epistles to the Thessalonians, but criticism supports him regarding all the others; and it must be agreed that in this he gave evidence of great exegetical sagacity, or that he received good instruction from others who before him had already been making similar researches. The order which was finally adopted in the Catholic Churches is not at all rational, for it consists in putting the longest epistles first and ending with the shortest, or in assigning their places according to the political importance of the cities. Now I ask which of the two arrangements is the earliest, that which shows so great

---

[1] It is not true that the order of the books of the New Testament was constantly the same in the local manuscript collections. I shall return to this point further on.

[2] Basil, *c. Eunom.* i. 224.

[3] The Vatican and Sinaitic MSS.

an understanding of real and living history and of its importance for the study of the texts, or that which betrays so profound an historical ignorance, such complete forgetfulness of the necessity of connecting the reading of the espistles with the memories of their origin, a deference for Rome, unknown in the early days of the Church, methods in short so poor and superficial? Let there be no mistake about my meaning. I do not maintain that in Marcion's time no Catholic Church had as yet any collection of epistles (I have even shown that the contrary is very probable); but I think that in all the extent of territory traversed by Marcion, no church, not even Rome, possessed THE collection which was afterwards inserted in the canon—*i.e.*, the collection complete, closed and arranged in the order which was finally adopted. I have even material proofs of this and to these I shall return by-and-by.

It is useless to prolong this discussion for which there would be no lack of materials, although we have them only at second hand and in a very fragmentary state, the authentic documents having long ago perished, with the exception of a very small number.[1] The result of our researches is clear enough, and it is this—that in a portion of the Church which was notable at this period, but of little importance for the future, the use of the apostolic writings was almost unknown, and was restricted to evangelic narratives which

[1] The summary here made of the results of the *testimony* of the heretics applies at the same time to the *testimony* of the pagans on which the English apologists of the last century laid so much weight, using it to refute the pagans of their time who denied the antiquity of the books of the N. T. This kind of defence is no longer necessary for rational people. Celsus (whose writings are preserved only in Origen's extracts) also attests that certain writings, gospels, and epistles, were in his day read and quoted in the Christian Church. His quotations prove equally the existence and propagation of books now non-canonical. Nowhere does he speak of a collection closed and official; and he even indicates, though he does not make war on the Gnostics, that the text of the gospels was undergoing alteration ($\pi o \lambda \lambda a \chi \tilde{\eta}$ $\mu \epsilon \tau a \pi \lambda \acute{a}\tau\tau\omega\nu$, Orig., c. Cels. ii. 27).

the Catholic Fathers of the next century found to be in part open to grave suspicion. The Gnostics, on the other hand, manifest great interest in these writings. They not only use them homiletically, but they also make commentaries, opposing them to the tradition of the Church against which they were making war. They go even so far as to alter their form to suit their polemics or their theories. For this purpose they also quoted apostolic tradition;[1] but they found it in the texts of the apostles interpreted in conformity with the words of the Lord, and not in the mouths of the bishops. It was by virtue of this latter form of tradition that Gnosticism was arrested on the threshold of the Church, and not in the least by an official collection of books of a canon of the New Testament, the very existence of which would have refuted their claims. For had there been a canon, the orthodox church would have had nothing to do but protest against the pseudonymous writings of the Gnostics; the recent origin of these books could have been demonstrated simply by comparing them with the authentic *instrument*. We have seen that the members and leaders of the churches, so far from proceeding in this way and repelling Gnosticism by the previous question, do not themselves adhere to any invariable list of writings reputed to be apostolic.

[1] (ἀποστολικὴ παράδοσις) ἣν ἐκ διαδοχῆς καὶ ἡμεῖς παρειλήφαμεν μετὰ καὶ τοῦ κανονίσαι πάντας τοὺς λόγους τῇ τοῦ σωτῆρος διδασκαλίᾳ (Ptolem., *Ep. ad Floram*, ap. Epiph., *Haer.*, 33.

CHAPTER V.

CATHOLICISM.

The use or the abuse of the names and the books of the apostles among the Gnostics of the second century might react in two ways, almost diametrically opposed, on the spirit and method of their adversaries. The most direct and, from a psychological point of view, the most natural effect, was to cause a more exclusive adherence to that source of Christian instruction which Gnosticism neglected or rejected—viz., tradition. This was not only supported by the very names to which heresy appealed, but it also presented a double advantage in that it was a uniform and self-consistent authority, and contained teaching which had always kept in the van of the development of Christian thought, and might therefore be easily applied to the debates of the day. Apart altogether from the results obtained by philosophical speculation which professed to base itself on texts, which results were open to suspicion from their diversity and their novelty, the labour necessary for attaining them, this exegetical study, so arduous, uncertain, and arbitrary, brought into relief the advantages of the earlier and more usual method pursued in the church. That method consisted in accepting simply and frankly whatever was transmitted from one generation to another by the mouth of the bishops. This did not hinder the homiletic use of the apostles' writings, which there was no intention of restricting; but it prevented the possible errors of a subjective interpretation, which could only be held within bounds by a positive and distinct rule. What I am stating here is no gratuitous supposition; it is a fact attested by all the organs of the rising Catholicism [1]—*i.e.*, of that universal Christian Church which, at the end of its victorious contest with Gnosticism, had put to flight not only a speculative philosophy which was fundamentally opposed to the gospel of the Bible, but also a Jewish prejudice, and had at the same time arrived at complete self-consciousness. In proof of this it would be sufficient to give a few out of many possible quotations, or I might do without proof altogether, since the Catholic Church has remained faithful to its principle down to our own time. The *rule of faith* which united and guided the Church consisted in believing and teaching the existence of one God who had made the world from nothing by His Son, the Word, who after having appeared to the patriarchs and inspired the prophets, had finally become flesh in the womb of the Virgin, that He might come to preach a new law and a new promise of the kingdom of heaven; and who, crucified, risen from the dead, ascended to the right hand of the Father, sends now the power of the Holy Spirit to direct believers, and will one day return to receive them into glory and to punish unbelievers with fire eternal.[2] That is the whole of Christianity, the rule, the *canon* of the Church.[3] It deals with principles and facts, not with books. No doubt there may be a desire for greater knowledge on more than one point; but, if the essential truth is known, it is better to remain in ignorance than to learn what ought not to be known. It is faith that saves, and not the study of the Scriptures. Faith adheres to the rule and arrives at its end by submitting to its law; study is a matter of curiosity, and the glory result-

---

[1] The name of the Church *Catholic* is found for the first time in the letter from Ignatius to the Church of Smyrna, and then in the letter from the same church written about the martyrdom of Polycarp. From this period onward, it was in general use.

[2] Tertull., *De præscr. haer.* ch. 13.

[3] *Regula fidei*, κανὼν ἐκκλησιαστικός.

ing from it is infinitely less important than salvation.¹ Thus, so far from making appeal to Scripture, or placing discussion on a ground where victory is always uncertain, the right way is to begin by asking where is the true faith by whom and to whom Christian teaching has been transmitted? Then only will it be seen where the true interpretation of Scripture and the true traditions are.² Beyond this, an exegetical debate will have no other effect than that of upsetting your stomach or your brain.³ The heretics will always be able to escape you if you try to refute them by scriptural proofs; there is only one sure means of vindicating the truth, and that is to consult tradition as it has been preserved in the churches by the bishops whom the apostles instituted, or by their successors.⁴ There are too many things in Scripture to which any meaning we please may be given; the comprehension of it must therefore be sought among those who received it themselves in an authentic manner from the hands of their predecessors.⁵

---

¹ *Ignorare melius est ne quod non debeas noris quia quod debes nosti. Fides tua te salvum facit non exercitatio scripturarum. Fides in regula posita est, habens legem, et salutem de observatione legis; exercitatio autem in curiositate consistit, habens gloriam solam de peritiæ studio. Cedat curiositas fidei, cedat gloria saluti* (Tertull., *loc. cit.* 14).

² *Ergo non ad scripturas provocandum est, nec in his constituendum certamen quibus aut nulla aut incerta victoria est . . . nunc solum disputandum est cui competat fides ipsa? a quo et per quos et quibus sit tradita disciplina qua fiunt Christiani? ubi enim apparuerit esse veritatem disciplinæ et fidei, illic erit veritas scripturarum et expositionum et omnium traditionum* (Tertull., *loc. cit.* ch. 19).

³ *Nihil proficit congressio scripturarum nisi ut aut stomachi quis ineat eversionem aut cerebri* (Tertull. *l. c.* ch. 16).

⁴ Τὴν παράδοσιν τῶν ἀποστόλων ἐν πάσῃ ἐκκλησίᾳ πάρεστιν ἀναγνωρίσαι τοῖς τἀληθῆ ὁρᾶν ἐθέλουσι, καὶ ἔχομεν καταριθμεῖν τοὺς ὑπὸ τῶν ἀποστόλων καταστα:'ντας ἐπισκόπους καὶ τοὺς διαδεξαμένους αὐτοὺς ἕως ἡμῶν (Iren., *Adv. haer.*, iii. 3.)

⁵ *Sunt multa verba in Scripturis divinis quæ possunt trahi ad eum sensum quem sibi unusquisque sponte præsumsit . . . ideo ab eo oportet intelligentiam SS. discere qui eam a majoribus secundum veritatem sibi traditam servat* (*Recogn.*, x. 42).

It is needless to multiply quotations on this point. The Protestant opposition of the sixteenth century of itself testifies that Catholicism remained only too faithful in its attachment to this principle of subordinating Scripture to tradition, and only too logically pushed it to all its consequences. Still it would be unjust, if we neglected to note another tendency which arose at the same time, and may also be regarded as a natural re-action against the presumptuous boldness of Gnosticism as well as the impoverishing stagnation of the Jewish-Christian spirit. The same theologians who pleaded so energetically for the privilege of tradition, were also the most eloquent panegyrists of the apostles, and the first to recognise in them explicitly a special and exceptional inspiration. It is not difficult to state the causes of this movement, which resulted in causing a great advance to be made on the question of the canon.

In the first place, according to a law of the human mind, the distance which separated the generation living after the middle of the second century, from the glorious period of the foundation of the church, increased the glories of that period to the imagination. The daily experience of the imperfections of the actual reality made the picture of the primitive state appear brilliant as an ideal; in face of more than one symptom of corruption, the communities of the first age seemed to be free from every fault; miracles, grown rare, and hardly known except by hearsay, shed a great lustre over the age in which they had been frequent; and the religious and dogmatic dissensions which agitated the churches and absorbed its best forces, caused many to turn with bitter regret to a time in which it was supposed these had been unknown.[1] Ah! if they had really read and

[1] Μέχρι τῶν τότε χρόνων παρθένος καθαρὰ ἔμεινεν ἡ ἐκκλησία, ἐν ἀδήλῳ που σκότει φωλευόντων εἴσέτι τότε τῶν παραφθείρειν ἐπιχειρούντων τὸν ὑγιῆ κανόνα τοῦ σωτηρίου κηρύγματος. Ὡς δ' ὁ ἱερὸς τῶν ἀποστόλων χόρος εἴληφει τοῦ βίου τέλος παρεληλύθει τε ἡ γενεὰ ἐκείνη, τηνικαῦτα τῆς ἀθέου πλάνης τὴν ἀρχὴν ἐλάμβανεν ἡ σύστασις κ. τ. λ. (Hegesippus, ap. Euseb., iii. 32.)

meditated on the epistles, as certain modern authors maintain they did, they would have found numerous proofs to the contrary, they would have seen exhortations, reproaches, acts of discipline, incessant discussions, just as there were a hundred years later; and, certainly, in our opinion, the generation which remained steadfast in its faith in spite of the coldblooded Roman laws and the insensate rage of a population drunk with blood, was not unworthy of receiving the heritage bequeathed to it by the simpler and sometimes less enlightened enthusiasm of its fathers. But custom and discussion had somewhat chilled its ardour; there was not the same ready devotion to chimerical hopes, and for that reason many loved to invigorate their moral forces by returning to the past. The more the heavenly Jerusalem once so eagerly expected faded away from the eyes of the Church, the more the colours that had been lent to it enhanced the remembrance of what once had been accomplished in the earthly Jerusalem, and of what had come forth from it for the salvation of the world.

If this was specially the view of the masses who rightly estimated their immediate surroundings though they were deceived by the perspective, we must not refuse praise to the leaders of the churches, to the theologians above all and writers, for the deference and respect which they as generally but more intelligently showed towards the memory of their illustrious predecessors. Not only were the apostles extolled as the founders of the churches which might already have been celebrating the centenary of their origin, had their rough fortunes given them leisure to think of chronology; not only were the names and persons of the apostles made resplendent by the reflected glory of the Lord; but all admiration was given to the literary monuments which some of them had bequeathed to posterity; a modest pleasure was felt in recognising the spirit that had dictated their writings; and with a complete abnegation of self-esteem, their admirers marked the distance which separated the glowing eloquence, the sublime teaching, the pregnant brevity of those few pages, from the colourless imitations of a more recent period, the authors of which would certainly be the first to acknowledge their barren coldness, their dull and wearisome prolixity. The difference was one that could not be overlooked, and literary instinct, quite as much as religious sentiment, was soon compelled to give a special place to such of the writings of the first generation of Christians as had fortunately been saved. The unfamiliar form of the Greek idiom which the apostles had used, so far from presenting any difficulty to writers who looked more to the subject-matter, gave a special outward distinction to these writings, and brought them into closer contact with the more ancient sacred literature which had been read only in that form. In the case of the most fertile author of the first century, and the most indefatigable missionary founder of churches, there was further a necessity for showing personal gratitude, which necessity was increased by the opposition his name and glory were always encountering from a considerable part of Christendom. Paul's importance was bound to grow in the eyes of the communities of Syria, Asia, Macedonia, Achaia, Egypt, and Rome, simply because in other spheres, narrower in a double sense, his memory and his preaching were sometimes passed over in affected silence, sometimes secretly or openly attacked. To the churches of these countries, he was the apostle *par excellence*, and if they had no intention of pushing their zeal to the extent of excluding other apostles who were extolled exclusively by the Jewish-Christians, at least not one of these apostles could, from a literary point of view, dispute with him the first place. This attitude of mind towards those who had inaugurated the great work, an attitude right enough in itself and universally upheld by succeeding generations, will appear to us all the more natural that it has been constantly assumed in similar circumstances towards the most distinguished teachers of the great periods of history. With what a halo these illustrious theologians, who were themselves so modest towards their predecessors, and whose authority is consecrated by the name Fathers as by a kind of proper name—with what a halo they are surrounded in the eyes of all those who have not broken with tradition! How often too have our reformers, in the midst of an age more inclined to discuss every title than to acknowledge any superiority whatever, not only been surrounded by a respect justly due to them, but also clothed with a decisive authority to which they were the last to lay claim! By the side of so many faults and so much vanity, this instinctive deference for true greatness, above all when it reacts on the will and is not falsified by the prejudices of dialectic analysis, is a happy and comforting trait in human nature.

I cannot pass over in silence another fact which may have exercised a certain influence on the formation of the idea of inspiration, I mean Montanism. The most salient feature of this special religious tendency was the exaggeration of that principle, the assertion of a unique claim on the part of some to the gifts of the Holy Spirit, above all to prophecy. If up to this time the action of the Holy Spirit on the inner life of the faithful had always been spoken of in such a way as to exclude no one, these claims to a privileged communication now taught Christians to distinguish between the ordinary and the extraordinary, between the natural and the miraculous; and further, as the pretended extraordinary inspiration of the new prophets, in its strange and disorderly manifestations, seemed like a caricature of what had been attributed to the ancients, Christians came to recognise in the inspiration of the prophets and apostles a phenomenon really special and unique. By rejecting Montanism not only in its errors but also in the evangelical part of its principles, the Church drew a line of demarcation round apostolic times, and expressed its opinion that these were distinguished from later times, not only by exceptional historical facts but also by religious and psychological facts peculiar to that period. The Gospel had not intended to restrict these facts to the first century; but sentiment, which does not permit of such distinctions, had gradually given place to reflection, and some external circumstance alone was needed to give the latter an occasion for formulating its categories and defining its laws.

Finally, there was still another and more direct way in which the methods adopted by the Gnostic philosophers increased the estimate of the writings of the apostles even within the pale of the Church. If the heretics claimed to found their doctrines on these writings, there was all the greater reason that the Catholics should study them from the same point of view, whereas, up to this time, they had been content to found their teaching on a tradition still pure and living. When the books were put forward to contradict or modify this tradition, and there was no room for doubting their authenticity, it was natural that the fact should be examined and the pretended difference verified. On the other hand, as the dissenting schools were also producing unknown or suspected books in support of their systems, the orthodox found it necessary to distinguish more clearly the two classes of works and assure themselves of their respective value. In these two directions, the great struggle fought in the domain of pure dogma had its results also in a more precise knowledge, a more profound study, a more careful examination of a literature which hitherto had only been employed to a limited extent, and could not but gain by being more fully known. It was also about this same time, according to history, that there began a universal propagation of the apostolic books, a greater activity on the part of individuals and churches in collecting and utilising them, whether in theological discussions, or in the readings made at public assemblies. This fact I am going to establish by an attentive analysis of the authors of the end of the second century and beginning of the third. I shall point out by turns what relates to the general point of view just noted as an advance in theological ideas, and what concerns the detail of literary and ecclesiastical facts.

The first author, in the order of time, who furnishes clear evidence of this advance, is Theophilus of Antioch. In the course of his *Apology*,[1] after speaking of the prophets of the Old Testament and of their inspiration, proved both by their foretelling the future and by their perfect agreement, and after *likening* them to the Greek Sibyl, he goes on elsewhere[2] to put the Gospels on the same level, expressly claiming for the latter the same inspiration as for the former. It is true that on this occasion the author is only making a comparison between texts from the prophets and axioms from the Sermon on the Mount in order to establish the unity and excellence of revealed morality, so that we might be tempted to refer the inspiration of which he speaks not so much to the evangelic *books* as to the person of the Lord who speaks in them. But in other passages he clearly attributes this inspiration, if not to the writings taken

---

[1] Theoph. *ad Autol.*, ii. 9: οἱ τοῦ θεοῦ ἄνθρωποι πνευματοφόροι πνεύματος ἁγίου. . . . ὑπ' αὐτοῦ τοῦ θεοῦ ἐμπνευσθέντες καὶ σοφισθέντες ἐγίνοντο θεοδίδακτοι. . . . ὄργανα θεοῦ γινόμενοι. . . . Καὶ οὐχ εἷς ἢ δύο ἀλλὰ πλείονες ἐγενήθησαν παρὰ Ἑβραίοις, ἀλλὰ καὶ παρ' Ἕλλησι Σίβυλλα, καὶ πάντες φίλα ἀλλήλοις καὶ σύμφωνα εἰρήκασιν. . . . (comp. ii. 33, 35).

[2] Ἀκόλουθα εὑρίσκεται καὶ τὰ τῶν προφητῶν καὶ τῶν εὐαγγελίων ἔχειν, διὰ τὸ τοὺς πάντας πνευματοφόρους ἑνὶ πνεύματι θεοῦ λελαληκέναι (iii. 12).

objectively, at least to their authors. Thus, some pages further on, he quotes a phrase from the first Epistle to Timothy with the formula: *the divine word*,[1] a formula which not only indicates the intrinsic value of the passage quoted, but ought certainly to remind us of its supernatural origin. Elsewhere,[2] when developing the doctrine regarding the hypostatic and creative Word, Theophilus analyses first in this sense the narrative of Genesis and then transcribes, as if to summarise and confirm his theory, the first lines of the Gospel of John. He thus considers the latter to be inspired though still distinguishing it from the *Holy Scriptures*, a term reserved for the Old Testament. This last distinction is specially interesting as marking the progressive development of theological ideas. It clearly shows how the notion of a privileged inspiration, by which the Apostles were elevated to the rank of the prophets, was gradually added to the very much earlier conception of the Holy Scripture— *i.e.*, of the Old Testament.

If the apology for Christianity addressed by Theophilus to the pagan Autolycus has furnished me with only a few texts relating to my special purpose, it is quite different with the two writers who closely followed him. They are much engrossed with the necessity for defending the pure gospel against heresy, and continually assert, as the basis and source of all legitimate Christian teaching, the collective, unanimous, and equal authority of the apostles and of tradition. These of course are Irenaeus and Tertullian, the true representatives of Catholicism in the ancient sense of that word, and, in some sort, the founders of it in theological literature.

It is altogether superfluous to collect from these authors passages proving that everywhere they make much of tradi-

---

[1] iii. 14 : ὁ θεῖος λόγος.
[2] ii. 22 : αἱ ἅγιαι γραφαὶ καὶ πάντες οἱ πνευματοφόροι, ἐξ ὧν Ἰωάννης λέγει κ. τ. λ

tion; that, according to them, the Spirit of God comes to individuals only by means of the Church in its corporate capacity, so much so, that it may be said not only that the Church is where the Spirit is, but also that the Spirit is where the Church is;[1] that the guardians of tradition, the regularly constituted heads of the various communities, principally of those founded by the apostles themselves and of Rome above all,[2] are also the best teachers of the truth;[3] that entire peoples may believe in Christ and carefully preserve the ancient tradition without the aid of paper and ink;[4] in short, that if by chance the apostles had written nothing, recourse would have to be made to the tradition of the churches founded by them, and this would be done without any danger of mistake.[5] It is therefore by a singular delusion that certain modern authors transform these Fathers into Protestant theologians, solely intent on the absolute and exclusive authority of the apostolic scriptures, and setting out from this gratuitous supposition, which is entirely contrary to the spirit and the texts of the period, infer the existence of a scriptural canon which had been for some time fixed and universally adopted.

Still, on the other hand, if Irenaeus and Tertullian felt before all the need of being consciously in communion with the earliest churches, of asserting the uninterrupted succession of the legitimate channels of tradition, and conse-

---

[1] Irenaeus iii., 24, § 1 : *Ubi enim ecclesia ibi et Spiritus Dei, et ubi Spiritus Dei ibi ecclesia. . . . cujus non participant omnes qui non currunt ad ecclesiam.*

[2] Irenaeus iii., 1, § 2; comp. Tertull., *Adv. Marc.* iv., 5. *De Praescr*, 36.

[3] Irenaeus iv., 26, § 5 : *Discere oportet veritatem apud quos est ea quae est ab apostolis ecclesiae successio;* comp. § 2.

[4] Πολλὰ ἔθνη τῶν βαρβάρων τῶν εἰς Χριστὸν πιστευόντων χωρὶς χάρτου καὶ μέλανος γεγραμμένην ἔχοντες διὰ πν. ἁγ. ἐν ταῖς καρδίαις τὴν σωτηρίαν καὶ τὴν ἀρχαίαν παράδοσιν φυλάσσοντες. . . . (Iren., iii. 4, § 2).

[5] *Ibid.*, §1 : . . . . οὐκ ἄρ' ἔδει πρὸς τὰς ἀρχαιοτάτας ἀποδραμεῖν ἐκκλησίας. . . . λαβεῖν τὸ ἀσφαλὲς καὶ ἐναργὲς ;

quently the authenticity of tradition itself, they were bound also, as I have already indicated, to assign a special value to the apostolic writings. These formed the first link in that long series of testimonies which constitute tradition; they were, so to speak, the surviving representation of its starting-point, and thus served to control and support all that had followed. Scripture and tradition, then, are two facts, two witnesses, two inseparable authorities. By following the rule of the Church, we make ourselves heirs of the apostles, and, through them, of Christ:[1] tradition interprets Scripture.[2] While, with the heretics, falsification of texts and alteration of docrines go side by side, in the Catholic Church the integrity of both is both a fact and a mutual guarantee.[3] The apostles knew everything, and have transmitted everything to us.[4] All the faithful have the Spirit of God, but all the faithful are not apostles. The Spirit, such as the apostles received, exists where there is prophecy, the gift of miracles, the gift of tongues.[5] In order to get acquainted with the truth, we must go back as far as possible, to the apostles themselves, and, that we may not fail of our purpose, we must keep to the churches founded by them, and to the apostolic writings preserved in these churches.[6] In

---

[1] *In ea regula incedimus quam ecclesia ab apostolis, apostoli a Christo, Christus a Deo tradidit. . . ego sum haeres apostolorum* (Tert., *Praescr* 37, comp. 20, 21).

[2] *Omnis sermo (credenti) constabit si scripturas diligenter legerit apud eos qui in ecclesia sunt presbyteri apud quos est apostolica doctrina* (Iren. iv 32, § 1; comp. the passages quoted at the beginning of this chapter). The necessity of this interpretation was founded, not on the imperfection of the Scriptures, but on the relative feebleness of men: *Scripturæ quidem perfectæ sunt quippe a verbo Dei et spiritu ejus dictæ, nos autem secundum quod minores sumus*, etc. (Iren. ii. 28, §§ 2, 3.)

[3] Tertull., *Praescr.* 38.

[4] *Ibid.* 22.

[5] Tertull., *Exhort. cast.* 2. This work, written from the Montanistic point of view, does not mean to restrict these privileges to the apostles only.

[6] *Si constat id verius quod prius, id prius quod ab initio, id ab initio quod ab apostolis, pariter utique constabit id esse ab apostolis traditum quod apud ecclesias app. fuerit sacrosanctum. Videamus quod lac a Paulo Corinthii*

this way the Gospel, which was preached at first with the voice, has, by the will of God, been committed to writing, that it might become the foundation and mainstay of our faith.[1] The teaching of the apostles is connected with that of the prophets, for the Lord, predicted by the latter and realising their predictions, gave to His disciples the mission of being the spiritual guides of the human race.[2] It is the same Spirit who announced the coming Christ by the mouth of the prophets, interpreted their oracles by the pen of the (seventy) ancients, and by the apostles declared that the times were accomplished.[3] Finally, the two collections are united, and, consequently, are placed on the same level under a common name.

This intimate and general agreement between tradition and Scripture which Irenaeus and Tertullian present to us as a fact and as a principle, is also in their eyes the supreme criterion of what was afterwards called the canonicity of each of the apostolic books—*i.e.*, of their claims to have a normal authority in the Church. No doubt nothing was more common at this period than to see certain documents alternately extolled or rejected, according as they supported or contradicted the favourite theories of theologians; and

hauserint, ad quam regulam Galatae sint recorrecti, etc. (Tert. *Adv. Marc.* iv. 5.) *Percurre ecclesias apud quas ipsae adhuc cathedrae apostolorum suis locis praesidentur, apud quas authenticae literae eorum recitantur,* etc. (Id. *De praescr*, 36.) This latter passage might tempt us to believe perhaps that the epistles were not yet read generally; but no doubt the author wishes only to indicate what is the guarantee of the authenticity of these writings.

[1] Irenaeus iii. 1.

[2] Ibid., i. 8: προφῆται ἐκήρυξαν, ὁ κύριος ἐδίδαξεν, ἀπόστολοι παρέδωκαν.—Tert., *Praescr.*, 36: (*Ecclesia*) *legem et prophetas cum evangelicis et apostolicis literis miscet.*

[3] Iren iii. 21, § 4. Let me observe, in passing, that inspiration is claimed for the Septuagint on the same grounds and to the same extent as for the prophets and the apostles.

[4] *Universae scripturae, et propheticae et evangelica* (Iren ii. 27; comp. Tert., *De praescr*, 14 *s.s passim*. *De resurr. carnis*, 22, 25, 27, etc.)

more than once I shall have to return to facts of this kind. But it was precisely against this subjective criticism that the authors I am analysing took up their stand. According to them, the churches which, from the earliest times, have been in possession of the writings of the apostles, are always a guarantee for their authenticity, and against their agreement there is no appeal.[1] It is true this did not prevent any book which presented itself under the name of an apostle but was not generally known from being examined from a dogmatic stand-point, in order to have its value determined.[2]

Besides these Fathers, who were thoroughly conservative and champions of tradition, we have others who were more influenced by the philosophical movement. But while these claimed for themselves the right of study and the glory of a science more advanced and more profound than that of the common herd, and therefore plumed themselves on the name of *Gnostics*, they none the less remained attached to the principles of Catholicism, both for the substance of their beliefs and for their standards of the truth. Thus in regard to the apostolic writings, they make declarations very similar to those I have just recorded. For the period which we are considering provisionally, the principal author to be consulted is Clement of Alexandria. If we do not find in him those energetic protestations which appear on every page of Irenaeus and Tertullian, at any rate he also

---

[1] Tert., *De præscr.* 36, quoted a little ago.—Id., *De pudic.* 10, in speaking of the *Pastor* of Hermas: *ab omni concilio ecclesiarum falsa judicatur.*—Id., *De præscr.* 28: *Quod apud multos unum invenitur, non est erratum. Audeat ergo aliquis dicere illos errasse qui tradiderunt.*

[2] Eusebius (vi. 12), relates a noteworthy instance. The bishop Serapion, a contemporary of Irenaeus, had found a pretended gospel of Peter in use in his diocese. At first he saw no harm in it and did not proscribe it; but when he discovered in it traces of Docetism, he put his church on their guard against this book, while he protested his attachment to Peter and all the apostles, Πέτρον καὶ τοὺς ἄλλους ἀποστόλους ἀποδεχόμεθα ὡς Χριστόν.

knows no other rule than the harmony of the Church with the apostles,[1] and the harmony of the apostles with the prophets.[2] With him, too, the frequent quotations taken from the epistles are expressly introduced as the words of the Holy Spirit, and the apostles are represented as possessing completely all the gifts which other believers receive only partially.

But it is important here to remember that the speculative school, of which Clement was one of the first and most brilliant representatives, finding itself hampered by the narrow limits of the traditional teaching, and at the same time obliged to prove its agreement with that teaching or with Scripture, revived the hermeneutic method of the profound and hidden meaning which had already corrupted the theology of the Jews and was thenceforth to invade that of the Christians. Everywhere parables, allegories, mysteries,[3] were discovered; and if in other places we see the beautiful thought of Jesus maintained, that the simple are best able to understand the gospel, provided they possess the necessary moral qualities, here we see theologians pride themselves on a special sagacity, look with pity on simple believers, glory in that wrongly applied saying of the

---

[1] *Strom.* vii. pp. 762 f. Ἡμῖν μόνος ὁ ἐν αὐταῖς καταγηράσας ταῖς γραφαῖς, τὴν ἀποστολικὴν καὶ ἐκκλησιαστικὴν σώζων ὀρθοτομίαν τῶν δογμάτων, κατὰ τὸ εὐαγγέλιον ὀρθότατα βιοῖ.

[2] *Strom.*, vii. p. 757: ἔχομεν τὴν ἀρχὴν τῆς διδασκαλίας τὸν κύριον, διά τε τῶν προφητῶν, διά τε τοῦ εὐαγγελίου, καὶ διὰ τῶν ἀποστόλων.—*Ibid.*, vi. p. 676: Ὁ κανὼν ὁ ἐκκλησιαστικὸς ἡ συμφωνία νόμου τε καὶ προφητῶν τῇ κατὰ τὴν κυρίου παρουσίαν παραδιδομένῃ διαθήκῃ.—*Ibid.*, iii. p. 455: νόμος καὶ προφῆται σὺν τῷ εὐαγγελίῳ ἐν ὀνόματι Χριστοῦ εἰς μίαν συνάγονται γνῶσιν. This last passage expressly says that this harmony exists in so far as the Scriptures are explained in the Christian sense, and this must be everywhere understood. This Christian sense was simply the traditional faith.

[3] Πᾶσα γραφὴ ὡς ἐν παραβολῇ εἰρημένη (*Strom.*, v. p. 575).—Οὔτε ἡ προφητεία οὔτε ὁ σωτὴρ ἁπλῶς τὰ θεῖα μυστήρια ἀπεφθέγξατο ἀλλ' ἐν παραβολαῖς. ... Ἐγκρύπτονται τὸν νοῦν αἱ γραφαὶ ἵνα ζητητικοὶ ὑπάρχωμεν. ... τοῖς ἐκλεκτοῖς τῶν ἀνθρώπων τοῖς ἐκ πίστεως εἰς γνῶσιν ἐγκρίτοις, τηρούμενα τὰ ἅγια μυστήρια παραβολαῖς ἐγκαλύπτεται κ. τ. λ. (*Ibid.*, vi. pp. 676 ff.)

apostle that knowledge is not possible to every one,[1] and pursue the noble and perilous aim of extending its domains.

Those whose faith was summarised in the few lines which finally became the universal *credo* and are known to us by the name of the *Apostles' Creed*, had doubtless no need to trouble themselves about exegesis for proving its authority; nor did their profession of respect for the apostles (as may well be supposed) contain any Protestant meaning of opposing their writings to ecclesiastical tradition. As to the philosophers, I mean the school of Alexandria and many other theologians who took part in scientific work in the development of theology, they no doubt professed an equal respect for Scripture, but they wrought constantly and with a very marked, but, in some respects,[2] regrettable success in transforming the teaching of the Bible and the teaching of the Church.

[1] *Strom.* vii. p. 763.
[2] It is needless to enter into the details of this special series of facts. Every one knows the wildness of patristic exegesis; what seems to be less known, or less remarked, is the quite as great and more guilty wildness of modern exegesis.

CHAPTER VI.

THE COLLECTIONS IN USE TOWARDS THE END OF THE SECOND CENTURY.

I HAVE now established this much that, before the end of the second century, Catholic theology had raised the writings of the apostles to the level of those of the prophets [1] in regard to their inspiration and authority; it remains now for us to examine what were the writings to which this privilege was accorded, and to draw up a list of them. This part of our work would be very easy, if there existed anywhere an official document, a synodal declaration of this period, or even a catalogue made by a known and trustworthy author, for this might have told us in few words what was the complete series of apostolic books adopted by the church. We possess indeed two texts which may and ought to be quoted here. Unfortunately neither of them belongs to Greek Christianity, and they therefore cannot be completely relied on for establishing its usages. Beyond these, we are confined to scattered, accidental passages in the authors of the time. By uniting these passages, by comparing them with one another, we may succeed, not in restoring the *canonical* collection of the New Testament as it existed at that time (for I shall prove

---

[1] And not as it is sometimes put in our day, the Old Testament to the level of the New. The inspiration of the prophets, as well as the privileged position which they and their books on that account held, was an undisputed fact in theological science and in popular belief; it was contested only by Gnostic Antinomianism. The prophets could not grow in dignity.—Tertull., *De pudic.*, ch 12 : *Nos in apostolis quoque veteris legis formam salutamus.*

that none existed), but in finding out what were the books read more or less generally to the people in their assemblies, and cited as authorities in the writings of theologians.

Of course I shall give special attention only to what concerns the writings of the apostles; still, to clear away every prejudice, I shall once more remind my readers that the Christian theologians of this period knew the Old Testament only in its Greek form (in the Septuagint), and consequently that they made no distinction between what we call canonical books (Hebrew) and apocryphal books (Greek). They quote both with the same confidence, with the same formulas of honour, and attribute to them an equal authority based on an equal inspiration.[1] As this fact needs no lengthy demonstration, I pass to my chief subject and summon the witnesses in order, as was done with preceding generations.

I shall not spend time in discussing Theophilus of Antioch, an author who must be put at the head of this new series for reasons already given. The few direct quotations found in his book have all been mentioned already. It may be added that there are also in his writings frequent reminiscences of Paul's epistles,[2] perhaps even of the Epistle to the Hebrews, and of the first of Peter, although these last amount only to the use of one word.[3] There are no traces of the Acts, nor of the Apocalypse, nor of the other Catholic epistles; on the whole, he is one of those who scarcely use the writings of the apostles except for rhetorical or homiletical purposes,

---

[1] See e.g. regarding *Wisdom*, Clement of Alexandria, *Strom.* iv. 515, Sylb. (ἡ θεία σοφία); *ibid.*, v. 583 (ὁ Σαλομών); Tertullian, *Adv. Valent.*, ch. 2 (*ipsa Sophia, non quidem Valentini sed Salomonis*); regarding *Ecclesiasticus*, Tertullian, *Exhort. cast.*, ch. 2 (*sicut scriptum est*); regarding the story of *Bel and the Dragon*, Irenaeus, iv. 5 (*Daniel propheta*); regarding *Baruch* Irenaeus, v. 35 (*Jeremias propheta*); Clement, *Paed.*, ii. 161 (ἡ θεία γραφή) etc. Regarding the theory, see Irenaeus, iii. 21, § 4, quoted above.

[2] Comp. e.g. i. 6, 14; ii. 16, 17, 22, 36; iii. 2.

[3] στερεὰ τροφή (ii. 25, Heb. v. 12)—ἀθέμιτος εἰδωλολατρεία (ii. 34, 1 Pet. iv. 3).

and in this respect he might have been ranked along with his predecessors. I shall, however, note this other fact that he is the first Catholic writer who speaks by name of the Apostle John as the author of the Fourth Gospel. Some modern critics have availed themselves of this circumstance to suppose that the book only dates from the middle of the century; but I have shown that for a long time previous the Gnostic teachers had made this gospel the subject of their speculative studies. The silence of the Catholic writers then arises from more causes than one, and the explanations I have given regarding the general progress of ideas ought to dispel all doubts on this point.

In chronological order we come now to a document much more important, because it is the earliest that contains a genuine catalogue of apostolic books. This is the celebrated fragment known by the name of the *Muratorian Canon*. Muratori was an Italian scholar. He had found in a manuscript of the eighth century, belonging to the Ambrosian Library in Milan, and formerly in the convent of Bobbio, a little treatise in very bad, or at least far from intelligible, Latin. Some lines of it were missing both at the beginning and the end, but the part preserved contained the names of the books which the Catholic Church (term in the text) is said to acknowledge as apostolic, and to which it appeals as an authority against the heretical books. Muratori had this fragment printed in his *Italian Antiquities of the Middle Ages*,[1] in 1740, and since that time several scholars have applied themselves to study it in its bearings on the history of the canon, and have made new collations of the manuscript. Most of these critics have made an outcry about the copyist's ignorance, the frightful barbarity of his Latin, his

---

[1] L. A. Muratori, *Antiquitates Italiae medii aevi*, iii. 854. See the fac-simile of the fragment in the work by the late S. P. Tregelles. *Canon Muratorianus.* Oxford, 1867, 4.

gross solecisms. Corruptions, omissions, faults of translation, have been seen in it to any extent; and some, making the most of all these faults as facts convenient to their purpose, have manipulated the text in an arbitrary fashion to obtain from it what they wished, to efface awkward statements and insert in it titles which were wanting. All this cannot be tolerated by good and healthy criticism. I admit that the copyist had before him an original which had in part become illegible;[1] but the greater part of its alleged faults in Latin may be regarded as caused by a pronunciation evidently local or provincial, and a very vulgar dialect. The great importance and the curious peculiarities of this document compel me to devote some time to its examination. I give a complete analysis, which is supported in the notes by the transcription of the text in its authentic form.

The list of the apostolic books included at first four gospels, and Luke and John are named as the authors of the last two. The writer of the treatise insists on the connection and conformity of these four books in regard both to the facts narrated and to the spirit that dictated them. That to begin with is a very important point. This number *four*, these gospels forming a collection by themselves and opposed to everything analogous which might exist in the literature of the time—these are facts quite new in the history of the canon, and their novelty is not due merely to the accidental silence of the earlier authors. On the contrary, my narrative has shown that the usages were very different, that there was no official decision or choice made regarding the source of the evangelic history in the previous period, when oral tradition was still contending for

---

[1] The text begins, after leaving a space blank, with some words relating, it would appear, to the gospel of Mark, and passes immediately to the *third* gospel.

the first place with the written texts, and favouring a freer use of the latter.¹

After the gospels, the author passes to the Acts of the Apostles. With regard to Acts, the Catholic Church recognises only one single work, that of Luke, beginning with these words: *Optime Theophile,* and narrating what had taken place in the presence of the author.² As the legend of Peter's martyrdom was at that time attracting much attention, as well as the tradition of a journey made by Paul to Spain, the author expressly adds that it is not found in Acts, but elsewhere.³ Observe that this is the first direct mention of the book of Acts in all ancient literature.

In the paragraph devoted to the epistles of Paul, the author fixes their number and order, and adds various observations which we must not neglect. I place the entire

---

¹ As this first part cannot give rise to any doubts, I do not copy the text of it.

² Luke's work being anonymous, the author of course transcribed the first words in order to indicate it sufficiently. Further, it is clear from what he says of it how far the readers at this period were from being critically exact. No one now-a-days will admit that Luke was everywhere an eye-witness.

> . . . *acta autem omnium apostolorum sub uno libro scribta sunt lucas obtime theofi le comprindit quia sub praesentia eius singula gerebantur sicut et semote passionem petri evidenter declarat sed profectionem pauli ab ur be ad spaniam proficescentis* . . .

³ Is this an allusion to Luke xxii. 33, or perhaps even to John xxi. 18? Or have we here some notice of a lost book? As to the journey to Spain, it seems to me rather that there is a negative wanting in the text, or that the author had Rom. xv. 24, in mind. In this latter case, a member of the phrase would be wanting altogether, which appears to me very doubtful. The original bears some traces of correction, but as these have no influence on the points important for us, I shall not discuss them.

passage before my readers.[1] "The Epistles of Paul," it is said, "themselves declare for whom they were intended, whence and with what purpose they were written. Thus, to the Corinthians, the apostle forbids the schism of heresy, then to the Galatians, circumcision; on the Romans he inculcates the order of the scriptures of which Christ is the chief (*i.e.* he unfolds to them the general plan of revelation); all this is developed at length, and I shall have to speak of it in detail." Then, passing to another idea, the author continues: "Though Paul, following the example of his predecessor John,[2] wrote by name only to seven churches—viz.,

> [1] . . . . *epistulæ autem pauli quæ a quo loco vel qua ex causa directe* sint volentibus intellegere ipse declarant primum omnium corintheis scysme heresis interdicens deinceps callactis circumcisione* romanis autem ordine scripturarum sed et principium earum esse christum intimans. . .† prolexius scripsit de quibus sincolis neces se est ad nobis desputari cum ipse beatus apostolus paulus sequens prodecessoris sui johannis ordinem nomisi nomenatim septem ecclesiis scribat ordine tali a corenthios prima ad efesios seconda ad philippinses tertia ad colosensis quarta ad calatas quinta ad tensaolenecinsis sexta ad romanos septima verum corentheis et thensaolicensibus licet pro correbtione iteretur una tamen per omnem orbem terræ ecclesia deffusa esse denoscitur et johannis enim in a pocalebsy licet sebtem ecclesis scribat tamen omnibus dicit verum ad philemonem una et ad titum una et ad tymotheum duas pro affecto et dilectione in honore tamen ecclesiæ catholice in ordinatione eclesiastice descepline sanctificate sunt.* . . . .

* It is to be remembered that ancient orthography put e for æ and that m and n are often indicated by strokes (here omitted) over the preceding vowels.

† There seems to be a word wanting here.

[2] This idea, that Paul must have written to as many churches as John (in the Apocalypse) is passed from one author to another down to the end of the Middle Ages. Note that John is represented as writing first, though

the Corinthians, Ephesians, Philippians, Colossians, Galatians, Thessalonians and Romans (there are two epistles to the Corinthians and to the Thessalonians, because of reprimands that had to be made), still it is known that there is but one single Church spread over the whole earth. In the same way John, while addressing only the seven churches in the Apocalypse, has them all in view. As to epistles to Philemon, Titus and Timothy, which were written by the apostle from motives of friendship, they became sacred when ecclesiastical discipline was organised." This means no doubt that these epistles, which were private in their origin, became public and official documents because the Church drew from them the principles of her government. Two things must strike us here. One is the very peculiar order in which the epistles are enumerated. Nowhere else do we find this order; and as it is impossible to see any principle in it whatever, chronological or otherwise, I cannot help supposing that the author had in his hands a collection that had been formed in a purely fortuitous manner—*i.e.* just as the copies of each epistle had been obtained. At any rate tradition had little influence over it, and with this text before us, it can no longer be said that Paul's epistles were collected from the very first—*i.e.*, from the time of their composition or at least soon after, that they might be handed down to posterity in the form of a complete collection. Then also we see here for the first time that theology, while still recognising the primitive destination of each letter, expressly regards them as the common possession of the church, not only because the whole Church may profit by them, but also because the sacred writers had this universal destination directly in

he is generally placed at the end of the century. This proves that at first it was remembered that the Apocalypse had been written before the ruin of Jerusalem and not under Domitian, as is maintained by those who do not understand it.

view. It is easy to understand that this point of view had to be adopted generally and explicitly before the scriptural canon of the New Testament could be formed.

After enumerating the Pauline Epistles accepted by the Church, the author names several other writings which the Church rejects,[1] but which, if I rightly understand him, were all circulating under the name of that Apostle. He specially mentions an epistle to the Laodiceans and another to the Alexandrians. It is quite possible that even in the second century there may have been some idea of repairing by an apocryphal compilation, the loss of a letter to the Laodiceans, of which loss there was believed to be an indication in Col. iv. 16; but it is beyond all question that this compilation was not the document which still exists under that name in Latin and which will be noticed later. As to the letter to the Alexandrians, no other ancient writer speaks of it. Modern critics are inclined to see in it the Epistle to the Hebrews, which our text passes over in silence. Certainly if the latter epistle was written to any particular community, there are a thousand reasons for thinking of the Church at Alexandria more than any other. Still, as it is anonymous, the question arises how our author could have spoken of it as fabricated under Paul's name. That would be intelligible only if the copies of his time had borne that name, which is not found in our ordinary manuscripts. Further, only a prejudiced and very superficial reader could see in it any trace of Marcion's heresy.[2] However that may be, the

[1] . . . . fertur etiam ad laudecenses alia ad alexandrinos pauli no mine fincte ad hæresem marcionis et alia plu ra quæ in catholicam eclesiam recepi non potest fel enim cum melle misceri non con cruit. . . . .

[2] It has been proposed to read: *ad hæresem Marcionis refutandam*, or to put a comma before these words, so as to make them say this: besides the epistles to the Laodiceans and to the Alexandrians, *others* fabricated to favour Marcion, in short other books still (perhaps Acts of Paul).

author declares that he wishes to have an apostolic collection pure and without alloy; he not only seeks out the authentic books, but also eliminates with care the false merchandise; he does not wish to mingle gall with the honey.[1]

The few lines devoted to the epistles usually called Catholic present several difficulties.[2] Still it is evident that the author is not acquainted with the Epistle of James, nor with the two of Peter; in addition to that of Jude he only names two of John. But there are three words in the text which invite criticism. In the first place, what does this expression mean: there is *indeed* in the Catholic Church an epistle of Jude and two of John? Are we to suppose that the author alludes here to some opposition made to these epistles, or does it mean that he himself doubts their authenticity? In this case his remark would be connected with the last phrase where mention is made of the Wisdom of Solomon, written, he says, by friends of that king in his honour. But what is this book doing here? Ought we perhaps to change the text and read: (*ut* for *et*) these epistles are called by the names of Jude and John, *just as* Wisdom is named after Solomon—*i.e.*, these apostles, to say truth, did not write them with their own hand? Finally, what are we to make of that impossible word: *superscrictio?* Are we to read *superscripti* (the aforesaid John) because he has already been under discussion, or *superscriptione—i.e.*, if we adhere to the superscription, the title? This is far from

---

[1] The poor play on words (*fel cum melle*) seems of itself to prove that we possess the document in the original, and not as a translation from Greek.

[2] . . . . *epistola sane jude et superscrictio johannis duas in catholica habentur et sapientia ab amicis salomonis in honorem ipsius scripta.* . . . .

[3] By this name, the author appears to have meant to designate either the (apocryphal) Wisdom, or Proverbs, which were also at times designated in this way. The Jewish doctors did not regard Proverbs as composed by Solomon himself (see ch. xxv., xxx., xxxi.)

probable since the author has already spoken of one at least as an authentic writing. All the same, it is clear that it is very difficult to say exactly what was his meaning; but this does not authorise the rash changes in his text by means of which attempts have been made to insert the epistles passed over.[1]

I direct special attention to the omission of the *two* epistles of Peter. This forms another argument to be urged in favour of the hypothesis that this canon was composed in the Latin Church, and not in the Greek Church, though many scholars now-a-days regard it only as a bad translation of a Greek original. We have one other Latin witness who confirms us in believing that even the first epistle of Peter penetrated but slowly into the West.

Finally, the series of apostolic books ends with the Apocalypses of John and of Peter, of which the author says that they alone of all the Apocalypses then existing were received in the Church. He remarks, however, in regard to the Apocalypse of Peter, that some refuse it the honour of being used officially in the Church.[2]

Such is the famous Muratorian Canon, about which there has been so much writing and discussion for the last twenty years. The text clearly is not free from errors; but there is no trace of lacunæ or of corruptions such as would permit

---

[1] Some think themselves justified in taking these *two* epistles of John to be the second and third (which many early writers did not consider to be apostolic), because the first epistle was mentioned before along with the Gospel. But in the previous passage, the author does not enumerate it in the series of the sacred writings; he only appeals to it to prove (i. 1.) that the Gospel was written by an eye-witness. Here he returns to it in the order of the books. Another explanation to which I shall have to return would be given by saying that the first and second epistles were, by a misconception, joined into one. See p. 105.

[2] . . . . . *apocalapse etiam johannis et petri tantum recipimus quam quidam ex nostris legi in ecclesia nolunt.* . . . . .

us now to make alterations on it for the sake of some book not mentioned in it. It gives the names of four gospels, of Acts, of thirteen Pauline epistles, of three other epistles and two Apocalypses, and it does so with a dogmatic purpose, to form what was afterwards called the *canon*—*i.e.*, the list of authoritative books. It remains for me to inquire concerning its date and origin. To these two questions the answer cannot be doubtful. After speaking of Apocalypses declared to be canonical, the author names still another, the *Pastor* of Hermas, which he says had been written recently, *in our time*, while Pius occupied the episcopal chair of Rome.[1] This Pius, the first of the name and brother of Hermas, was bishop about the year 156. As it is said that the *Pastor* was read in the churches, a custom recommended by our author, though he refused it a place either among the prophets whose canon was closed or among the apostolic writings, some time must have elapsed between the publication of Hermas and the composition of the document before us. Hence the date generally accepted lies between 180 and 190. Further, the language, the rejection of the Epistle to the Hebrews, or at least the silence observed regarding it, everything down to the mention of the city of Rome and its bishop, betrays a Latin and probably African pen. One point more: it is very important to remark that the author does not express his own individual views, but sets before us the usage established in his ecclesiastical sphere. On the

---

[1] . . . . *pastorem vero nuperrime temporibus nostris in urbe roma herma conscripsit sedente cathe tra urbis romae pio episcopo fratre ejus et ideo legi quidem eum oportet se pu plicare vero in ecclesia populo neque inter profetas completum numero neque inter apostolos in finem temporum potest.*

other hand, he sets it before us only as a witness, and his treatise is not an official document.[1]

I pass now to Irenaeus. He nowhere gives the names of the books contained in his apostolic collection, but his scriptural quotations are so numerous that by scrutinising them we can, without risk of error, reconstruct that collection. As Irenaeus was a native of Asia, was full of respect for Rome, and was bishop of Lyons, it may be boldly affirmed that in certain respects his testimony is of greater weight than that of his contemporaries, whose ecclesiastical horizon was much more limited. Hence Eusebius even made this Father the subject of a work such as I am about to undertake; but he left it very imperfect.[2] I maintain that Irenaeus had before him the four gospels, the Acts, thirteen epistles of Paul, one of Peter, two of John, and the Apocalypse of John; consequently, with the exception of three books (Jude and the Apocalypse of Peter, on the one hand; the epistle of Peter, on the other), precisely the same list as is presented to us in the African treatise published by Muratori. Still, this list calls for some observations in detail.

In the first place, I insist on this fact, already mentioned on a former occasion but now placed beyond question for the history of the canon, that in the time of Irenaeus the Church Catholic had ceased to consider any but our *four* gospels, or, rather, one single gospel in four forms.[3] This fixing of the number and selection is final; it even became so much a matter of principle—I would almost say an article of faith—that theological scholasticism was already trying to find a reason for it: not in historical recollections, nor in

---

[1] The document closes with some lines relating to heretical books which have not come down to us. The numerous and gratuitous conjectures about the name of the author are of no interest.

[2] Eusebius, *Hist. eccl.* v. 8.

[3] τὸ εὐαγγέλιον τετράμορφον, Irenaeus, iii. 11, § 8.

a literary criticism of which nobody had any idea, but in a class of facts quite foreign to the question. There are four gospels because the Church represents the world, and, just as the world has four cardinal points whence four winds blow, so the gospel ought to be for the Church a quadruple column breathing both incorruptibility and life. The gospels are further represented by four cherubim: that of John, which begins with the generation of the word, has for its emblem the lion; that of Matthew, which begins with the genealogy, corresponds to the human figure; that of Luke, which begins with Zacharias the sacrificing priest, suggests the ox; that of Mark, finally, which ends in prophecies, is like the eagle.[1] That we may not have to return to it, I may say once for all that contemporary and later authors no longer show any variation from this fixing of the four gospels.[2] This theological idea of one single gospel narrated under four forms or having four faces, explains the true meaning of the title which our gospels bear in Greek and in Latin, as well as in several modern versions. This title nowhere suggests the idea of a composition at second hand, as if the proper name were not the writer's but the name of a guarantee or primitive witness.[3] But the proper and original meaning of the word *gospel* is still reflected in this

---

[1] Irenaeus, *loc. cit.*—As is well known, this symbolism was afterwards inverted without thereby becoming more spiritual. It has continued to be one of the favourite forms of traditional symbolism. Later exegetes exerted themselves to endow theology with other parallels of the same kind. The four gospels are the four rivers of paradise, the four elements of the universe, the four sides of Noah's ark, the four rings of the ark of the covenant, the four constituent parts of man's body, the four letters of Adam's name, etc. (Jerome, *praef in Matth.*; Pseudo-Jerome, *Expos.* iv. ev.; Athanasius, *Syn. S. S.* ii. 155; Alcuin, *Disp. puer.*, ch. 8, etc).

[2] Clem. Alex., *Strom.* iii. 465; Tertull., *Adv. Marc.* iv. 2ff; Origen, *apud* Eusebium vi. 14; Jerome, *Praef. in Matth.*; Jerome, *Praef. in ev. ad Damasum*, etc.

[3] εὐαγγ. κατὰ (secundum, according to) Ματθαίον, etc.

formula, while in common usage the name was already coming to signify a book and to be used in the plural.

I must now make some remarks on the epistles quoted by Irenaeus. Of the Pauline epistles, there would be wanting, it must be confessed, the Epistle to Philemon; but I do not for a moment hesitate to suppose that this silence arises solely from the fact that Irenaeus had no occasion to quote it, every other explanation being improbable. As to the Epistle to the Hebrews, which is nowhere quoted in his great work, I may for it refer to a passage in Eusebius, where he speaks of having found it quoted in a small work of Irenaeus now lost. The allusions which some profess to find in the texts we can verify are imaginary,[2] or, rather, their very insignificance and the absence of all direct quotation from an epistle so rich in theological ideas, prove indirectly that the bishop of Lyons was not acquainted with it, or did not acknowledge it. The Epistles of John present a curious fact. The first is quoted very explicitly in a passage[3] in which considerable extracts are made from it; but Irenaeus always speaks of it in the singular, as if there existed only one to his knowledge. Among these extracts, nevertheless, there are some belonging to the second epistle, and these extracts are introduced with the very same formula—in the *aforesaid* epistle, in *praedicta epistola*. It must be concluded from this that in the copy which Irenaeus possessed,[4] the text of the two epistles was not separated, but apparently formed one whole. Some have been in-

---

[1] Eusebius, *Hist. Eccl.* v. 26. Comp. Photius, *Cod.* 232.

[2] Irenaeus, iii. 6, § 5, *Moses fidelis famulus* is taken from Num. vii. 7; and ii. 30, § 9, *God created the universe by His powerful word* does not even correspond with Heb. i. 3, and is a thought so familiar to the theology of the second century, that no special quotation was needed for expressing it.

[3] iii. 16, § 5 ff., *in epistola sua*, ἐν τῇ ἐπιστολῇ. Comp. i. 16, § 3.

[4] And perhaps in others. See above what was said on the same subject in connection with the Muratorian Canon (p. 101).

clined to find a trace of the Epistle of James in a passage where Irenaeus calls Abraham a friend of God;[1] but this surname was not invented by James. It is found elsewhere in ancient literature, and notably in a passage in Clement of Rome, the substance of which has passed as it stands into the argument of Irenaeus; this argument, in other respects, being quite different from that of James. The latter reference seems to me all the more natural that we find elsewhere[2] the epistle of Clement praised at great length by our author. Finally, with regard to Peter, Irenaeus knew positively only his first epistle, from which he borrows some phrases, but which he very rarely quotes in any direct way.[3]

I have found in Irenaeus only two extra-canonical quotations introduced with the consecrated formula, *Scripture* (γραφὴ, *Scriptura*). One is connected with the epistle of Clement; the other, which is more express, with the *Pastor* of Hermas.[4] We know that these two writings were held in considerable esteem, very much circulated and publicly read for the edification of the faithful. Thus the power of practical and traditional usage was strong enough, even with this Father, to break through the line of demarcation, which was too recently drawn to adjust itself everywhere to the exigencies of the system.

The celebrated contemporary of Irenaeus, Tertullian, presbyter of the Church of Carthage, is quite as important for my history, though on other grounds. I was able to consider the Bishop of Lyons as a witness to ideas and usages adopted, not only in his immediate surroundings, but also in the distant countries with which he had main-

---

[1] iv. 16, § 2.   Comp. James ii. 23 ; Clem., *ad Cor.* 10.
   Irenaeus, iii. 3, § 2.
[3] iv. 9, § 2.   *Petrus in epistola sua.*
[4] Comp. note 2 on this page and iv. 20, § 2.

tained very direct relations. In this respect, Tertullian occupies a more modest place. He simply tells us what the Church of Africa knew, believed, received; I make no claim that he should speak for the Greeks. On the other hand, his scientific method makes him a very valuable witness, because his quotations from Scripture do not occur sporadically, occasionally, without order and succession, as with Irenaeus; but, when he is discussing a special point of ethics or dogma, he loves to pass in review the various parts of Holy Scripture from one end to the other according to the order of the books, that he may obtain from them the proofs of his assertions. We can therefore easily ascertain the state of the sacred collection as he had it, whereas, in other writers, the silence observed regarding a book may be attributed to chance, and even textual quotation may be sometimes insufficient to establish the canonical value of the source from which it is drawn. Here we have to do with actual dogmatic proofs, and no hesitation can be permitted when dealing with a method so strict and so careful to distinguish (as was said above) inspired and privileged writings from those which were only used popularly and occasionally.

Thus, in his polemic work on the Resurrection of the Flesh, after treating his subject according to the teachings of the prophets,[1] he declares (ch. 33) his purpose of passing to the gospels, and, in fact, he there collects all the passages suitable for throwing light on the thesis he is defending. He connects with them (ch. 38) a text from the Apocalypse, which he introduces as taken from the volume of John; whether it be that the identity of the authorship had suggested this order or that in his collection the Apocalypse

---

[1] We must not let ourselves be deceived by appearances when in this first part of the book we see from time to time comparisons between the prophetic books and the apostolic books.

did actually come next to the gospels.[1] Then he passes (ch. 39) to the testimonies of the apostolic *documents*. This term he applies in the first place to Acts, from which he borrows some passages, and next to the epistles of Paul, which furnish him with a long and copious series of passages. Nothing is wanting except some of the Pastoral Epistles. Finally, in ch. 62, the author closes the discussion with a saying of Christ. It is impossible not to be struck by the fact that not one of the Catholic Epistles is quoted directly or indirectly, although he would not have failed to find in them texts supporting his dissertation.

In another work on Chastity, where he protests energetically against the indulgence shown to sins of the flesh and the readiness with which they are pardoned even in the Church (Tertullian starts here from the rigid standpoint of Montanism), he follows the same method exactly. He begins by declaring that he intends to seek out his proofs in the Old and New Testaments (ch. 1); he does not, however, linger long over the former, which might furnish him with moral precepts but with few rules of discipline, and hastens to pass on (ch. 6) to Christ and the apostles. He discusses the bearing, first of some parables, then of some acts of the Lord (ch. 11) which seem to favour indulgence; finally, he comes (ch. 12) to the apostolic *document*, in which, as above, the Acts stand foremost, and next to them the epistles of Paul. Everywhere he lays stress on the texts which favour austerity, and tries to weaken the meaning of those opposed to it, *e.g.*, the pardon granted to the incestuous person at Corinth. Finally, he devotes a long chapter (19) to John, who this time is mentioned last. He not only discusses passages taken from the Apocalypse, but also, and in detail, the First

---

[1] For all questions of this kind, and the meaning of the technical terms connected with them, I refer my readers to the following chapter.

Epistle. After that he sums up as if he had completed his analysis of the apostles (ch. 20). But he is willing to go further, and produces the *subsidiary* testimony of a companion of the apostles—a man who ought to possess a certain authority, since Paul praises his self-denial as equal to his own—viz., Barnabas. From him there has come down an epistle "to the Hebrews," which the Churches generally prefer to the *Pastor* of Hermas—that apocryphal work cited by the champions of immodesty.[1] And he quotes the famous passage of Heb. vi., which has been such a stumbling-block to ancient and modern orthodoxy, and which was Luther's chief reason for rejecting the epistle. This book of Tertullian presents to us therefore several phenomena which it may be very useful to point out. His *apostolic document*, in addition to the gospels, evidently included Acts, the epistles of Paul, and the Apocalypse, to which was added the first epistle of John,[2] but nothing more. The epistles of Peter are not found in it any more than in the Muratorian Canon, and it is no mere matter of chance that all these documents belonging to the African Church are agreed on a point so remarkable. We see besides that this Church attributed the Epistle to the Hebrews to Barnabas, and that Tertullian has no idea that it might be Paul's; he is not acquainted with any tradition naming Paul as the author. Finally, we ascertain that, in addition to the documents analysed by our author as having undisputed authority, he speaks also of other books *received* by the Churches, but received in another sense—viz., as means of edification, as useful and

[1] Volo tamen ex redundantia alicuius etiam comitis Apostolorum testimonium superducere, idoneum confirmandi de proximo jure disciplinam magistrorum. Exstat enim et Barnabae titulus ad Hebraeos, adeo satis auctoritatis viri ut quem Paulus juxta se constituerit in abstinentiae tenore . . . . (1 Cor. ix. 5) . . . . et utique receptior apud ecclesias ep. Barnabae illo apocrypho Pastore moechorum.

[2] I would see no difficulty in adding also the second, in accordance with the remark already made in regard to Irenaeus (p. 105).

valued books, but quite distinct from those belonging to the sacred volume.

Let us further consider for a moment a third treatise by Tertullian, entitled *Concerning Flight in Persecution*. Here, too (ch. 6-9), we meet with testimonies from the New Testament in the same order and with the same number of parts: first, the Lord in the Gospels, then the apostles—*i.e.*, the history of the Acts, the epistles of Paul, the Apocalypse, and the first epistle of John. How are we to explain this consistency, this uniformity of exclusion in the choice of the texts, if the author's collection contained more books?

We have just seen, however, that Tertullian also speaks of books in a second category, and that he included among these the Epistle to the Hebrews and the *Pastor* of Hermas, the latter work, to which he himself was strongly opposed, being greatly liked and circulated in his day. But these were not the only books of this kind. He is acquainted also with the epistle of the *apostle Jude*,[1] which might have rendered him great service in his work *De Pudicitia*, had he considered it canonical. He quotes it only once in order to corroborate his own highly favourable opinion of the book of Enoch, which he extols as a prophetic *Scripture*, earlier than the Deluge. He seeks further to explain its miraculous preservation, as the Jews, according to him, rejected it only because it preaches Christ, and, to crown all, he applies to it the famous passage in 2 Tim. iii. 16, in order to justify his predilection. And still he knows quite well that this book does not belong to the canon of the Old Testament. Here then we have at once two deutero-canonical books. But only in one of the numerous works of Tertullian (*Scorpiace adv. Gnosticos*, ch. 12 ff.) do we find the Epistle of Peter mentioned, both by the name of its author, and as an *epistle to those of Pontus;* and criticism

[1] *De habitu muliebri*, ch. 3.

is still in doubt regarding the authenticity of this treatise, suspecting it to be a translation from a Greek original. But whether or not this suspicion is correct, whence comes this singular reserve regarding a book which offered so many texts for use, and which had for a long time been circulated and received in the churches of the East? There is but one reply: this epistle was not known in the West till later, and was not included in the oldest collections made for ecclesiastical use. That is why the Muratorian Canon does not speak of it at all, why Irenaeus quotes it so seldom, and why Tertullian does not rank it among the apostolic *documents*, quoting it but once in all his writings. As for the Epistle of James, Tertullian knows nothing and says nothing about it, and, in an author who is by no means sparing in proper names and direct quotations, some indirect allusions, for that matter purely imaginary, do not make up for such a silence.[1]

I shall not leave Tertullian without noticing a literary fact which is of some importance. He read the writings of the apostles in a Latin translation, and not in the original. This translation, of which he was not the author, had been in existence for some time, and had been used in the churches of Africa, perhaps even in other churches for anything we know. But if we are thus led to date this collection back at least to the period 160-180, it is not wonderful that it did not contain a very large number of books. If it be true, as we cannot reasonably doubt, that the collection was formed by exchange or communication among the

---

[1] These pretended allusions do not bear a moment's serious examination. The most striking, apparently, is that in which an apostle is mentioned who had said: *non auditores legis justificabuntur a Deo, sed factores* (*De Exhort. Cast.*, ch. 7); but this apostle is Paul (Rom. ii. 13) and not James (i. 22). As to Abraham, the *friend of God*, I refer my readers to the corresponding remark on Irenaeus (p. 106). Besides, the treatise containing this allusion (*Adv. Judaeos*, ch. 2) is an apocryphal compilation.

ancient churches, the slower propagation of certain books has a very natural explanation. And is it an impossible supposition that, when the first collection had been made at a certain time, the writings known only later should have remained outside of the collection, though authentic and cordially welcomed? Is not this the very basis of the history of the canon for the next two centuries? The difficulties, contradictions, impossibilities arise only to those who suppose that the apostles themselves formed and closed a scriptural code.[1]

Let us now pass to the East and see what we can learn regarding that region from the third great theologian of the close of the second century, Clement of Alexandria. On the whole it may be said that his *canon*—*i.e.*, the collection traditionally used in his church—is very nearly the same as that of the Latins; but, in addition to this collection, a Christian literature of the second rank, more abundant than in the West, is frequently quoted, and with much favour. This second class specially demands our attention.[2] Regarding the first, it is enough to say in passing that it included the four Gospels, Acts, and the thirteen epistles of Paul, two epistles of John,[3] one of Peter, and the Apocalypse of John.

The works of Clement have not all come down to us. There is one in particular whose loss we must regret—viz., the *Hypotyposes*, if it be true that that book contained a

---

[1] I leave untouched the question so warmly debated, whether there were more than one ancient Latin translation. The numerous publications, recently, of fragments of ancient Latin versions previous to that of Jerome, seem to me to have decided the matter, and at the same time to confirm the supposition that these versions were at first only partial.

[2] Eusebius had already observed this comparative abundance, and he directed attention to it in the passage where he speaks of Clement (*Hist. eccl.*, vi. 13, 14).

[3] Quite distinct from one another. He quotes the first with the formula: ἐν τῇ μείζονι ἐπιστολῇ.

succinct analysis of all the canonical scriptures.[1] But this assertion does not seem to deserve credit; for the last ancient author[2] who speaks of it, after having really read and studied it, protests against the heresies he had observed in it, and declares that they are explanations of Genesis, Exodus, the Psalms, the epistles of Paul, the Catholic Epistles, and Ecclesiasticus. Still these explanations must have been very unequal in length; for, according to the collected fragments of them, six books out of eight must have been devoted to the Pauline Epistles alone: the first book could then have treated only of the Old Testament, and as to the last, which seems to have been preserved in a Latin edition,[3] it embraced the four (or five) Catholic Epistles then known.

In regard to the Epistle to the Hebrews, we know from Eusebius that Clement held it to be a writing of the Apostle Paul, in the sense that Paul had composed it in Hebrew and Luke had translated it into Greek. Indeed, in his writings which survive, Clement quotes it without hesitation under Paul's name. This then was his own personal opinion, and also, no doubt, that of those around him. It is none the less true that the hypothesis of a Hebrew original is untenable, that the reasons given for the absence of the author's name are absurd,[5] and that the very arguments, when joined to the contrary tradition of the Latins, prove that

---

[1] πάσης τῆς ἐνδιαθήκου γραφῆς ἐπιτετμημένας διηγήσεις (Euseb., *loc. cit.*)

[2] Photius, *Cod.* 109.

[3] *Adumbrationes Clementis presbyteri in Epp. Petri* [i.], *Judae et Johannis* [i., ii.], *in Opp.* ed. Potter. This perhaps is the work which Cassiodorus (*De. div. lect.*, ch. 8) says he caused to be done, taking care to erase from it everything offensive. *Aliqua incaute locutus est quae nos ita transferri fecimus in latinum ut exclusis quibusdam offendiculis purificata doctrina ejus securior* (sic) *posset hauriri.* Only in place of Jude he mentions James, which may have been simply an inadvertence.

[4] See espec. *Strom.* iv. pp. 514, 525; vi. p. 645.

[5] Euseb. vi. 14.

in reality no one knew anything positive regarding the origin of the book.

The Epistle of James is nowhere quoted, and, as to the allusions to it which some find, I have only to repeat what was said on the preceding occasion. That of Jude is named on several occasions.

The most curious phenomenon in our Alexandrine philosopher is the stress he lays on the inspiration of those very books, belonging to what we have called the second category, in other words, not included in the collection generally used in the Church. I note here the *Pastor* of Hermas,[1] the Epistle of Barnabas (of course the epistle which commonly bears that name, and which most modern critics regard as a work belonging to the end of the first or the beginning of the second century, but do not attribute to a companion of Paul);[2] the epistle of Clement of Rome to the Corinthians,[3] with which we have already met as a book for edification; even books positively apocryphal, but occasionally employed, and furnishing at times somewhat long extracts, such as the Apocalypse[4] and Preaching of Peter, the Gospel of the Hebrews and that of the Egyptians, the book called *Traditions of the Apostle Matthias*,[5] and a pretended work of Paul, in which the Sibylline books and the prophet Hystaspes,[6] without counting a mass of anonymous quotations which we are no longer able to verify, but which must have been taken from various lost gospels. These quota-

---

[1] Θείως ἡ δύναμις ἡ τῷ Ἑρμᾷ κατὰ ἀποκάλυψιν λέγουσα φησί (*Strom.*, i. 356; comp. ii. 360, 384; iv. 503).

[2] Βαρνάβας ἀπόστολος (*Strom.* ii. 373, 375; comp. 389, 396, 410; v. 571, 577; vi. 646).

[3] *Strom.* i. 289; iv. 516 (ἀπόστολος); vi. 647.

[4] Euseb. *Hist. Eccl.* vi. 14; comp. *Epit. Theod.* p. 806.

[5] *Strom.* i. 357; ii. 380; iii. 436; vi. 635 f., 678. The Gospel of the Egyptians, though carefully distinguished from the four others, is nevertheless cited as ὁ κύριος (iii. 452, 453, 465).

[6] *Strom.* vi. 635.

tions we have already met with in the various Greek fathers.[1] Clement, in introducing such quotations, employs without hesitation the term, *Scripture*.

Nevertheless, the testimonies I have collected and analysed in the two last chapters give great probability, if not complete certainty, to the following suppositions. In the last quarter of the second century, the theological idea of the privileged authority of the apostles, as founders of the Church and writers, had as a fact caused a distinction to be drawn between their books and all the other writings which had for a longer or shorter period been circulating in Christendom, and were used for the edification of the faithful, partly in public readings. This distinction was based on the apostolic dignity of the authors and was guaranteed by tradition. But this rule was modified or made precise by several subordinate considerations. Thus, two gospels were received which had not been written by apostles, for the simple reason that they had long been consecrated by public use, and that common opinion placed them in close relation with certain apostles. The book of Acts was added for the same reason, all the more that it formed one whole with the third gospel.[2] Besides these historical books, there was the Apocalypse of John, which was the first of all apostolical writings to be regarded as inspired. Finally, there were the Epistles, especially those of Paul, which were distinguished both by their number and by the lasting interest shown in them by the churches which that apostle had founded. They formed the nucleus of the second part

[1] See, for example, *Strom.* i. 354; iv. 488; v. 596; vi. 647, &c.

[2] Still, as this book did not come under either of the two chief divisions of the collection, it must have been recommended by other arguments. *Quam scripturam qui non recipiunt, nec spiritus sancti esse possunt qui necdum spiritum sanctum agnoscere possint discentibus missum, nec ecclesiam defendere qui, quando et quibus incunabulis institutum est hoc corpus, probare non habent* (Tert., *Praescr.* ch. 22).

of the collection, and it was among the Pauline churches, as opposed to Jewish Christianity, that this collection arose. Further, there were two epistles of John[1] and one of Peter. What we call the third of John and the second of Peter were still unknown at the period indicated; at least no trace of them is to be found in the authorities we are able to consult. Finally, the epistles of James and Jude were not contained in this apostolical collection, their authors being generally held to be the brothers of Christ, and, by that title, distinguished from the Twelve. Still we saw that the epistle of Jude was held in much greater favour than that of James, for it seems to have spread more quickly; whereas we have ascertained that in the West, at least in Africa, even the epistle of Peter received but tardy recognition. But we have also seen that, in addition to this collection, sacred and in some respects privileged from the theological point of view, popular teaching and even learned discussion drew material from other sources. There was no official law on this point, but a simple tradition which left each Father of the Church more or less at liberty. Thus, Clement could make abundant use of apocryphal literature, while Tertullian, situated at a distance from this doubtful abundance, imposes great restraint on himself, without altogether resisting the attractions of books that excited his sympathy or curiosity.[2]

[1] This number may very well have been the result of an error. *See* above on p. 105 and Note 1 on p. 101.

[2] I might quote other texts to prove that in the second century the distinction between the authentic works of the apostles and other books of suspected origin was not established so clearly as it was afterwards. But it is superfluous to insist on an incontestable fact.

CHAPTER VII.

BIBLIOGRAPHY.

UNDER this title I shall bring together certain facts exclusively literary, and these will complete what I have to say on the history of the Christian canon at the end of the second century. Hitherto we have been discussing the theological principles which led to its formation and the elements of which it was composed. We have no acquaintance yet with the collection as a literary whole. On this point there are still some very interesting, and in certain respects very significant, notices to be gleaned among the authors already analysed.

First of all, we must get rid of the idea that the different books of what we now call the *New Testament* formed at that time a single volume—a compact whole, so to speak. The material conditions, the state of the art of writing, and the means then at the disposal of the Christians, made this impossible; and historically, they were too near the sources of the collection to have lost already the remembrance of its formation. Now, it must be remembered that at first two distinct collections were formed, independent of one another, that of the gospels and that of the Pauline epistles. Of these two collections the former was used at an earlier date than the other for regular and public reading. The adoption of the second, which already existed separately and was thenceforth employed for the same purpose, was almost contemporaneous with that general ecclesiastical movement which resulted in the formation of what was called Catholicism, the Church Catholic, the Church distinct from the Jewish-Christian communities which wished to remain stationary, and from the Gnostic schools which strove to drag it out of the sphere marked for it by the authentic tradition of preceding generations.

Further, the writers we have been studying last were still aware of the existence of two different collections, and distinguished them by different names, which are in part purely conventional, and afford all the more certain proof of my thesis. The first, containing the evangelical narratives, was called simply the *Gospel*; the other, containing the epistles of Paul, was called the *Apostle*, a term which was not changed or enlarged till the addition of Acts and some other epistles had rendered it absolutely necessary.[1] Tertullian, the lawyer-theologian, introduced and popularised the term evangelic and apostolic *instrument*—i.e., document, charter, official decree, brief of proofs and illustrations—and thus succeeded in giving a very distinct and brief indication of the special value of these books as legal and public writings.[2] This division was even regarded as analogous to the form and traditional designation of the Old Testament (Law and Prophets).[3] I need hardly observe that the use of the singular, *the apostle*, could only be explained by the fact mentioned above—i.e., that the Pauline epistles alone appeared in the second part of the collection as it at first existed. We can see from the

---

[1] τὸ εὐαγγέλιον—ὁ ἀπόστολος (Clem., *Strom.*, vii. 706.) *Evangelium Domini —Apostoli literæ* (Tertull., *De bapt.*, ch. 15.) τὰ εὐαγγελικὰ—τὰ ἀποστολικά (Iren., i. 3, § 6.) *Evangelicæ, apostolicæ literæ* (Tert., *De præscr.*, 36; comp. *Adv. Prax.*, 15.)—The author of the dialogue *De recta in Deum fide* (*Opp. Orig.*, vol. xvi.) introduces a personage who maintains (p. 309): ἡμεῖς πλέον τοῦ εὐαγγελίου καὶ τοῦ ἀποστόλου οὐ δεχόμεθα. The meaning of this last term, applied to Paul exclusively, could not be doubtful.

[2] *Instrumentum evangelicum, apostolicum* (Tert., *Adv. Marc.* iv. 2. *De pudic.* 12). *Instrumentum Moysi* (Tert., *Adv. Hermog.* 19.) *Instrumentum propheticum* (Tert., *De resurr. carn.* 33). *Instrumentum Joannis, Pauli* (Tert., *De resurr. carn.* 38, 39). *Instrumentum Actorum* (Tert., *Adv. Marc.* v. 2).

[3] Clem. Alex., *Strom.*, vi. 659: Νόμος καὶ προφῆται—Ἀπόστολοι σὺν τῷ εὐαγγελίῳ.—This parallelism in substance and form is called μουσικὴ συμφωνία.

very terms employed by Tertullian, and quoted in the note on page 118, how this second part was gradually extended and increased. To the single *instrument of the Apostle* there were added other instruments with equal claim, that of John (the Apocalypse and the First Epistle) and that of Acts, and all these materials made up the *instrument of the apostles*, composed of the books of various authors.

But things did not stop there. The difference to be made between the Scriptures which had already belonged to the Synagogue and those which had sprung up within the Church, was naturally more marked than that which existed between the respective elements of each of the two principal parts. Special names were therefore needed to recall this more fundamental division. Thus the Old Testament, as a whole, was designated according to an ancient usage, sometimes by the name of the *Law*, sometimes by that of the *Prophets*. As for the New Testament, the term *Gospel* or *Apostles*[1] was used indifferently, and this usage being introduced freely and gradually, we frequently find passages where apparently three co-ordinate parts are spoken of.[2] The theological notion to which this double series of *instruments*—i.e., of written and official documents—referred was older than Christianity itself; it was the notion of the double alliance of God with His people, already conceived by the prophets,[3] reproduced explicitly by Jesus,[4] and included in the teaching of the apostles as one of its fundamental ideas.[5] The only innovation to be noted here is that Latin theology, influenced by an inexact trans-

---

[1] Tertull., *Adv. Marc.* iii. 14: *Lex et Evangelium; Adv. Hermog.*, 45: *Prophetae et apostoli.*

[2] Clem. Alex., *Strom.*, iii. 445: νόμος καὶ προφῆται σὺν τῷ εὐαγγελίῳ; v. 561: τὸ εὐαγγέλιον καὶ οἱ ἀπόστολοι ὁμοίως τοῖς προφήταις κ. τ. λ.

[3] Jeremiah xxxi. 32.

[4] Matt. xxvi. 28: καινὴ διαθήκη, *novum testamentum* (for *novum foedus*).

[5] 2 Cor. iii. 6 f; Gal. iv. 24 f; Heb. viii. 8, ix. 15, etc.

lation of the Greek word, gave predominance to a term of jurisprudence which was foreign to the thought of the original, and which soon became the equivalent of the term before in use,[1] although the remembrance of the primitive value of these diverse expressions was not at once lost.[2] Later this remembrance was lost, and the name *Testament* for the collection itself was finally consecrated in such a way that the older and more logical terminology disappeared.[3]

The order in which the various books contained in the two collections of the New Testament were arranged, was not everywhere and always the same. This fact is of little importance in itself; still it may serve to prove that the collection was not made at a very early date and by a superior ecclesiastical authority, but, successively, according to necessities and means and no doubt in several places at once. It would be difficult otherwise to explain how the lists came to vary in this respect.

As to the four gospels the canon of which was the first to be closed, the order of the books as we have it now in all our editions, was fixed from the second century,[4] but it was not the only one in use. For, if the place assigned to each evangelist at first was determined by the supposed chronological sequence of the dates of their gospels, it was perhaps more natural still that care should be taken of the respective dignity of the authors in such a way as to give the apostles the precedence over their disciples.[5] The latter arrangement, in which John follows Matthew and Mark

---

[1] *Instrumentum, vel, quod magis usui est dicere, testamentum* (Tert., *Adv. Marc.* iv. 1). *Novum testamentum* (Tert., *Adv. Prax.* 15). *Utrumque testamentum* (Tert., *De pudic.* 1).

[2] *Totum instrumentum utriusque testamenti* (Tert., *De pudic.* 20).

[3] *Scriptura omnis in duo testamenta divisa est* (Lactant., *Inst. div.* iv. 20.

[4] Muratorian Canon; Iren., iii. 1. § 1. Clem. and Orig., *apud.* Euseb., vi. 14, 25. Jerome, Vulgate, etc.

[5] *Constituimus evangelicum instrumentum Apostolos autores habere . . . et Apostolicos, cum Apostolis et post Apostolos . . . Nobis fidem ex Apostolis*

comes last, was preferred, as it appears, by the Latin Church. At least the oldest Western MSS. follow it implicitly. It is also the order of the Gothic version, and down to the ninth century it was preserved in the Greek copies. A modification of it was introduced in another series of documents in which Mark stood third and Luke last, and this order predominated in the East till the fifth century, so much so that some modern critics have preferred it for their editions of the Greek New Testament.

The thirteen Epistles of Paul do not always follow each other in the same order as I have already had occasion to remark in speaking of Marcion and the Muratorian Canon. Still, notwithstanding the diversity of the lists preserved for us by the Fathers or in the manuscripts, a certain uniformity is observable in so far as they are nearly always arranged so as to form three groups, the members of which are kept distinct. The first group is composed of the Epistles to the Romans, the Corinthians and the Galatians, and these always stand first in the collection; the second group includes the five short epistles addressed to various churches, Thessalonians most frequently coming last in it, sometimes first[2] or third.[3] Finally, the last group embraces the epistles addressed to individuals, and in regard to this I have already noted some variations. It is not yet time to speak of the place to be given to the Epistle to the Hebrews, since it did not form part of what was called the *Apostle* at the end of the second century.

Johannes et Matthaeus insinuant, ex Apostolicis Lucas et Marcus instaurant (Tertull., *Adv. Marc.*, iv. 2).

[1] *Codices Vercellensis, Veronensis, Brixianus, Corbeiensis, Cantabrigiensis Palatinus* [For some account of these MSS. of the old Latin versions, see Smith's *Dict. of the Bible*, iii. 1692 f. and Scrivener's *Plain Introduction*, pp. 256 f.]

[2] *Codd. Decret. Gelasii*, various readings.

[3] Augustine *apud* Cassiod. *Divin. lect.*, ch. 13.—The Albigensian Version, Lyons MS.

In regard to the Catholic Epistles, the question is more complicated. When once their number had been brought up to seven, there was first this great diversity in the arrangement that the East assigned the first place to James and the West to Peter; then the others were placed in every possible form of mathematical combination and permutation by the various authors and churches, which is one more proof that the collection was closed gradually and that opinion was fluctuating. At the same time these are facts of no importance to us at this moment. For the period under consideration, there can be no question about fixing the rank of these epistles, for the simple reason that they were not yet in a collected form. We found Tertullian attaching the Epistle of John to the Apocalypse; we found in the same writer, in Irenaeus and in Clement, scattered quotations taken from the Epistles of Jude, of Clement, of Barnabas, from the first of Peter, and the second of John, which books undoubtedly did not form with one another one single collected work. I readily admit that each of these Fathers placed entire confidence in the writings of which he thus made use, and accorded to them the same authority. I believe simply that they possessed these epistles only as isolated writings,[1] and that copies of the Scriptures which did not include them all, perhaps even those which did not include any one of them, were not generally regarded as incomplete. It is no less probable that these diverse epistles, admitted in greater or less number into the sacred collection, were finally added to it under a special name.

This special name, which I have already employed, has been variously explained. The term *catholic* is undoubtedly opposed to *heretical*;[2] but in this sense it would not have

---

[1] That is a plain inference from the incontestable fact that each Father cites different epistles.

[2] Euseb., *Hist. eccl.*, iii. 3, iv. 23, without distinguishing between the **apostolic books and others**.

been reserved for the epistles in question to the exclusion of those of Paul. For the same reason, it cannot be taken here as meaning writings *received* by the Churches or recognised as sacred Scriptures.[1] The true signification of the word is indicated by the etymology alone. They are letters with a general destination, a characteristic all the more strongly marked as the Pauline epistles were all addressed to special churches or persons. Thus, the First Epistle of John is named the *catholic*, to distinguish it from the two others which are addressed to single individuals.[2] The same designation was used for the letter written by the apostles from the conference at Jerusalem,[3] and for that of Barnabas.[4] In all these cases, the historical sentiment predominated over every other consideration. Not till later did the name *Catholic Epistles* become merely a conventional term for the non-Pauline epistles inserted in the Canon.[5] In this sense the two short Epistles of John presented no difficulty. The same fact also explains why the Epistle to the Hebrews never figured in the number of Catholic Epistles, among which it should have been placed from its nature and title. When it was admitted into the canon, it was everywhere received as a Pauline epistle; and it was not admitted till a date at which the terminology was definitely fixed, as I have just said. Still the primitive meaning of the word was never completely lost.[6] The name *Catholic Epistles* was not adopted by the Latin

---

[1] Euseb., ii. 23, even speaks of Catholic Epistles which were not received.

[2] Dionys. Alex. *apud* Euseb., vii. 25. Orig., *passim*.

[3] Acts xv. Clem. *Strom.*, iv. 512..

[4] Origen, *Contra Celsum*, i. 63.

[5] Euseb., ii. 23; vi. 14.

[6] Leontius *de Sectis* (Sæc. vi.), ch. 2: καθολικαὶ ἐκλήθησαν ἐπειδὰν οὐ πρὸς ἓν ἔθνος ἐγράφησαν, ὡς αἱ τοῦ Παύλου, ἀλλὰ καθόλου πρὸς πάντα.—According to a Scholiast, the Epistle of James is put first ὅτι τῆς τοῦ Πέτρου καθολικωτέρα ἐστίν (*Cotelerii PP. ap. præf. in Barn.*)

Church, which preferred to call them *canonical epistles—i.e.,* recognised as apostolic. This term, to which I shall have to return, prevailed at the period during which the seven epistles were received into general use.[1]

But this digression has made us lose sight of the chronological order of the facts; I hasten to resume the thread of my narrative.

[1] Cassiod, *Div. lect.*, ch. 8. Pseudo-Jerome, *Prolog. in Epp. can.*

CHAPTER VIII.

THE THIRD CENTURY.

THE question of the Canon did not make much progress in the course of the third century. The collection, which generally included four gospels, the Acts, the Apocalypse, thirteen epistles of Paul, and the epistles of Peter and of John, as already mentioned, was in some localities enlarged by the addition of several other writings, formerly neglected or put in the second rank; but no official decision was anywhere given in the direction of fixing definitely the choice and the list of the sacred books, and even the number of testimonies at our disposal for simply ascertaining the state of things at this period is very limited. This proves that the theologians of the day did not consider the question so pressing as we are inclined to suppose. Besides, most of the testimonies to be quoted from this period are private judgments, individual opinions, as was the case also in the previous period, at most, only valuable information as to which books were received in certain localities. We must be specially on our guard against supposing that these opinions always exercised a direct and prevailing influence on ecclesiastical usages. I have already stated, on the strength of the express words of Tertullian, that in this century there was no official declaration proceeding from a central authority (which did not exist), and that therefore the recognition of the apostolic writings and the order of those included in the usual collection were fixed by the traditional custom of the principal, and particularly of the most ancient churches. The critical or scientific studies of the learned, so far as any were carried on, were of very little weight. From the principal churches, the metropolitan, the collection naturally passed into all the churches of one particular province, and thus without difficulty considerable uniformity was established among them.

This uniformity could not but show itself most of all in places where the apostolic writings were known and used only through a translation. I cannot be far wrong in saying that the need of a translation would be nowhere felt before the period when the nucleus of the collection had already been formed in the Greek Church, and for its use. It would be a singular thing that the Latin or Semitic Churches should, in this respect, have anticipated the Greeks, who were the depositaries and guardians of the books of the apostles; besides it would be contrary to all we know of the propagation of the Gospel at that period, since contemporary writers affirm that it was propagated by the ministry of the living word, and that the Scriptures came later.[1] I maintain, therefore, that the first translations made for the foreign churches, which had for a longer or shorter period been in existence, must have always included a certain number of books connected with one another by usage, and that the very idea of a special collection, closed and definite, must have been formed more readily and more distinctly in the minds of the Latin and Semitic Christians, who, from the very first, received an entire collection of holy books, than in the minds of the Greeks, among whom time was needed to efface the remembrance of the slow and gradual formation of the collection. To convince ourselves of the correctness of this observation, we have only to consider the difference in standpoint and reasoning between Clement and Tertullian—the difference observable in the numerous extracts already given from these two writers. Hence it is not by mere chance that the earliest

[1] Irenaeus, *Adv. haer.*, iii. 4.

attempt to form a complete and methodical list of the writings in the evangelical collection was not made in the Greek but in the African Church, and dates from a period which cannot be much later than that of the first Latin translation itself. That is a second fact in strict accordance with what was stated above, and confirming in all respects my theory.

At the other extremity of the Christian world, in the interior of Syria, where Greek civilisation had not succeeded in crushing the national genius, we meet with another translation into the vulgar tongue, which we must consider for a little. The precise date of its origin can hardly be determined. The Syrians themselves attribute it to an apostle;[1] but no dependence can be placed on such legends. The common opinion of modern orientalists assigns it to the end of the second century, or to the first half of the third. The date of its origin is not of so much importance, when I can affirm that for hundreds of years the Syrian churches were content with this work, although it was incomplete as compared with the final form of the Greek New Testament.[2] For this version, which soon acquired in the country and its schools an official authority, differs in several points from the collections we have hitherto been considering, whether of the Greek theologians or the Latin churches. On the one hand, it does not contain the Apocalypse; on the other, it adds to the Pauline epistles the Epistle to the Hebrews

[1] The supposition that the idiom of this version is exactly that spoken by Jesus Christ may be pardoned in fathers more pious than learned; it does not admit of more serious discussion.

[2] In the Old Testament the Syriac Version (*Peschito*) is limited to the Hebrew canon, arranged, however, in a peculiar fashion. Job comes immediately after the Pentateuch; Ruth stands between Canticles and Ecclesiastes; the latter is followed by Esther, Ezra, and Nehemiah; the minor prophets are inserted between Isaiah and Jeremiah. The collection ends with Daniel. At a later time, however, editions were published with various modifications.

as fourteenth and last, and puts the two epistles of Peter and John before that of James. There are here three innovations which demand closer consideration. The one that surprises us least, and is most easily justified, is the addition of the Epistle of James. We understand that in the East, in the neighbourhood of Palestine, in a sphere where Jewish Christianity might exercise a certain influence, this ancient work commended itself to special attention, whereas the churches under Pauline influence might neglect it, or even ignore its existence. It is to be observed, nevertheless, that its reception into the canon seems to have been due to an oversight, or, at least, to be connected with a mistake regarding the person of the author. The special title which precedes the volume of the Catholic Epistles, in the ancient Syriac version, expressly says they were written by the three disciples who were witnesses of the Lord's Transfiguration on Mount Tabor. Now, without insisting on the point that the precise designation of the place is purely legendary, it is a fact that the James, who was there present, was the son of Zebedee and the brother of John, and in no case could he be the author of this epistle, no matter what opinion we adopt regarding the person of its author, or the number of apostolic personages bearing the name of James. Still, this shows that in the Church of Syria also, there was no intention of putting anything in the sacred collection except works belonging to immediate disciples of the Lord. For the same reason, the Epistle to the Hebrews figures here only because it was attributed to the Apostle Paul, and not as an anonymous but authentic monument of the teaching of the first century. I go further, and say that the insertion of these two epistles seems to prove of itself, notwithstanding the lack of all direct evidence, that they were received on an equal footing, and read in the Greek churches of Syria at the time when the Syriac version was made. It is not at all probable that the collection contained in this version was formed in an independent manner, or even in contradiction to the usages among the nearest neighbours. This ought to be true, particularly of the Epistle to the Hebrews, any knowledge of which, especially in regard to the author's name, could come only from the Greeks. The omission of the Apocalypse leads me likewise to maintain that the re-action against this book had already begun among the Greeks at the date of the Syriac translation, or, at least, that the Eastern Churches no longer regarded it as a book suitable for the edification of the people, although the theologians favourable to Chiliastic views continued to set great store on it. In any case, these facts justify the chronological place I have adopted for the document under discussion. If its origin were placed much earlier, the hesitations, the contradictions, the silence which I have elsewhere noted in regard to the books in question, would be inexplicable.[1]

Among the Fathers of the third century to be consulted, there is not one that can be compared to Origen, either for the number of interesting facts furnished by him or for the confidence inspired in us by his vast erudition. Still the most striking features in the mass of facts furnished by him are the uncertainty of the results, the want of precision in his point of view, and the facility with which he passes in turn from scientific discussion to popular usages. That is already visible in what he says of the Old Testament. It will be remembered that the Greek Church was not at that time very sure of its choice between the Hebrew canon and the Septuagint. The learned Origen does not put an end

---

[1] The canon of the ancient Syriac version is not known simply by the existing MSS., which might be incomplete ; it is expressly recognised and confirmed by the Syrian authors of the centuries following.

to this uncertainty. When enumerating the books of the Old Testament,[1] he fixes their number at twenty-two, which is the number of the letters of the Hebrew alphabet, and this suggestive parallel is repeated again and again by later authors.[2] But the order of the books is evidently of Greek origin, and foreign to the official form of the Hebrew canon. Chronicles, Ezra, and Nehemiah are added to the other historical books, and these in turn are separated from the Prophets by Psalms and the three books bearing Solomon's name; Daniel figures between Jeremiah and Ezekiel, while Job and Esther come last. Further, when naming Jeremiah, the author expressly mentions his epistle, which gives ground for supposing that he acknowledged the canonicity of the Greek form of that prophet's book as well as of the books of Daniel and Esther. As to the apocryphal writings proper, he names in the passage quoted only the books of the Maccabees, which he distinguishes from all the others as not belonging to the catalogue of the twenty-two.[3] But we possess in the works of Origen two other writings containing much information on this point. His friend Julius Africanus writes him a letter regarding the story of Susanna, calling it a pure fable as it is not found in the Hebrew text, and declaring that nothing should be recognised as an integral portion of the Old Testament except what had been translated from that original.[4] Origen, in a very lengthy reply, maintains the opposite thesis, and defends the authenticity and even the inspiration of that story, as well as of the story of Bel and the Dragon, the Song of the Three Children, the

---

[1] *Selecta in Psalmos*, *Opp.*, xi. p. 378, ed. Lomm. The whole passage is transcribed by Eusebius, vi. 25.

[2] The enumeration itself is incomplete since the copyist has omitted the book of the twelve minor prophets.

[3] ἔξω τούτων ἐστὶ τὰ Μακκαβαϊκά (*loc. cit.*)

[4] ἐξ ἑβραίων τοῖς ἕλλησι μεταβλήθη πάνθ' ὅσα τῆς παλαιᾶς διαθήκης φέρεται (*Ep. Afric. ad Orig.*, ch. i. *In Orig. Opp.*, xvii. p. 18.)

additions to the Book of Esther, and lastly, Judith and Tobias. He professes that the Jews might possibly have mutilated the text, and concludes by saying that the usages of the Synagogue should not prevail over those of the Church which makes no difficulty about using these books.[1] This then was the traditional custom which to Origen could not but be an authoritative rule in conflict with historical science. After this it will not be surprising to find him elsewhere quoting the Wisdom of Solomon, Ecclesiasticus,[2] and the books of the Maccabees, as the *Scriptures*, the Word of God,[3] and making frequent reference to them. Origen went further. He used even to admit that, outside of the Bible in books really apocryphal,[4] there were inspired passages which the apostles with their own inspiration could easily discern and reproduce, while other Christians, no longer enjoying that gift, would do better to avoid these books. By way of proof he cites some passages from the New Testament, for which we search the Old in vain,[5] and he has not even a suspicion that the apocrypha, circulating in his time and containing these passages, may have themselves borrowed them from the apostles.

The same phenomenon of a science, uncertain of its grounds and incessantly conflicting with an imperious tradition or with practical convenience, also appears in what Origen tells us of the order of the apostolic books. When dealing with the different statements found in his numerous works

[1] *Orig. ad Afric.*, ch. 13, *loc. cit.*, p. 42 : Ἰβραῖοι τῇ Τωβίᾳ οὐ χρῶνται. . . ἀλλ' ἐπεὶ χρῶνται τῇ Τωβίᾳ αἱ ἐκκλησίαι, ἰστέον κ. τ. λ.

[2] *Qui liber apud nos inter Salomonis volumina haberi solet (Homil.* 18 *in Numer.).*

[3] θεῖος λόγος, *scripturæ* (*De princip.*, ii. 1, § 5. *Homil. in Lev.* I. T. vi. ; *in Jo.*, ch. 19; *in Matt.*, *Tract.* 31 ; *Contra Celsum*, iii. 72 ; viii. 50. *Philocal*, ch. 22.) See in general the *indices* to his works.

[4] ἐν ἀποκρύφοις, *in secretis.* See *Prolog. in Cantic.*, *Opp.* xiv. 325. *Comm. in Matt.* iv. 238 f. ; v. 29.)

[5] Matt. xxiii. 37, xxvii. 9 ; 1 Cor. ii. 9 ; 2 Tim. iii. 8 ; Heb. xi. 37 ff ; Acts vii. 51 f.

or preserved to us by Eusebius,[1] some have formed a theory that he contradicted himself at various epochs of his life, or even that those writings which no longer exist in the original were altered in translation. All things considered, there is no need of such expedients to understand his conclusions. Everything is explained and reconciled, if we keep sight of what I have so often repeated—viz., that the canon of the New Testament was not closed in Origen's time, and that, along with the most entire submission to traditional authority when sufficiently established, there was room for independence in all questions not yet decided by custom. Let us turn our special attention to these questions. Thus, in regard to the Gospels, it is hardly necessary to prove that Origen in the most explicit manner declares the four generally received to be the only ones which can be and ought to be considered as inspired; he founds his statements on the text of Luke's preface and on the authority of the church, which has made its choice among the great number that had come into existence.[2] Thus, too, the Acts written by Luke, and the thirteen Epistles of Paul which have long been gathered in one volume, need no longer to be mentioned, now or afterwards, as integral parts of the *Scriptures posterior to Jesus, and believed in the churches to be divine*.[3] For that matter all

---

[1] Euseb., *Hist. eccl.*, vi. 25.

[2] *Homil.* i. in *Luc.* (*Opp.* v. 87): *Ut sciatis non solum quatuor evangelia sed plurima esse conscripta e quibus haec quae habemus electa sunt et tradita ecclesiis ex ipso proœmio Lucae cognoscamus. . . . Hoc quod ait: "conati sunt," latentem habet accusationem eorum qui absque gratia Spiritus sancti ad scribenda evangelia prosilierunt. Matthaeus, Marcus, Joannes et Lucas non conati sunt scribere sed Spiritu sancto pleni scripserunt . . . Ecclesia quatuor habet evangelia, haereseis plurima . . . Quatuor tantum sunt probata . . . In his omnibus nihil aliud probamus nisi quod ecclesia, i.e., quatuor tantum evangelia esse recipienda.* Comp. i. in *Joh.*, ch. 6 (*Opp.* i. p. 13).

[3] *Contra Celsum*, iii. 45: The theological proof is given ἀπὸ τῶν παλαιῶν καὶ ἰουδαϊκῶν γραμμάτων οἷς καὶ ἡμεῖς χρώμεθα, οὐχ ἧττον δὲ καὶ ἀπὸ τῶν μετὰ τὸν Ἰησοῦν γραφέντων καὶ ἐν ταῖς ἐκκλησίαις θείων τινῶν πεπιστευμένων.

these books are designated by a common and distinctive name, which puts them in the same rank as those of the Old Testament. They are the books of the *Covenant*, or, as Tertullian would have said, the books of the *Testament*.[1] The use of the singular in this formula has special significance, because it removes the last trace of any difference between the two parts of the sacred collection.[2] The terms *canon, canonical*, terms of which I have already made occasional use by anticipation, did not yet exist apparently in a literary sense. By the *ecclesiastical canon*[3] was still meant the traditional rule, the established and regular usage.

But I am in haste to come to facts more unexpected. To begin with, Eusebius has preserved to us a very curious passage regarding the Epistle to the Hebrews. According to him, Origen said:[4] "The style of this epistle does not bear the characteristics of Paul's ordinary diction. Paul acknowledges himself to be no practised writer, whereas this is classical in style, as all competent judges will agree. On the other hand, no one can fail to see that its thoughts are admirable and in no respect inferior to the apostolic writings which are generally recognised. I am therefore of opinion that the ideas are the apostle's, but that the form of their expression is due to some one who reproduced them from memory. Hence, if any church holds it to be Paul's, that church does not err, for the ancients had some grounds

---

[1] τὰ ἐν τῇ διαθήκῃ βιβλία, αἱ ἐνδιάθηκοι βίβλοι. They are the same to which he also gives the name ὁμολογούμενα, *i.e.*, the books which all the churches agree in accepting.

[2] This unity is expressly set forth (ἡ παλαιὰ διαθήκη ἀρχὴ τοῦ εὐαγγελίου) i. *in Jo.*, ch. 15.

[3] κανὼν ἐκκλησιαστικός (Euseb., vi. 25).

[4] Euseb., *loc. cit.*: ὁ χαρακτὴρ τῆς λέξεως . . . . οὐκ ἔχει τὸ ἐν λόγῳ ἰδιωτικὸν τοῦ ἀποστόλου. . . . ἀλλὰ ἐστὶν συνέσει τῆς λέξεως ἑλληνικωτέρα. πᾶς ὁ ἐπιστάμενος κρίνειν φράσεων διαφορὰς, ὁμολογήσαι ἄν. πάλιν τι αὖ ὅτι τὰ νοήματα τῆς ἐπιστολῆς θαυμάσιά ἐστι, καὶ οὐ δεύτερα τῶν ἀποστολικῶν ὁμολογουμένων γραμμάτων.

for transmitting it to us as that apostle's. Nevertheless, God alone knows who wrote it, and on this point tradition mentions sometimes the name of Clement of Rome, sometimes that of Luke."[1] Clearly Origen here has had before him several opinions somewhat opposed to each other, and he is seeking to harmonise them in a more or less plausible, but quite arbitrary manner. The Epistle to the Hebrews, which in the West was attributed to Barnabas, was regarded in the East sometimes as written by Paul, sometimes as a work by one of his friends or disciples, sometimes even as a translation made from a Hebrew original. The Alexandrine scholar is not aware of the first opinion; he tacitly rejects the last, though it was that of his illustrious master, Clement; he cannot rely on the Eastern tradition, which had arisen simply from conjecture; finally, his critical sagacity does not permit him to assign it to Paul. But the high admiration entertained by him for a book, which more than any other of the first century consecrates the theological and exegetical method which he makes the basis of all his studies, suggests to him a new theory. This hypothesis, made at a venture, seemed to reconcile the hesitations of criticism with the instincts of a popular opinion that was favourable to it, and was beginning to gain ground. In the works remaining to us, Origen makes very frequent use of the Epistle to the Hebrews, and cites it sometimes with Paul's name, sometimes without it. In one passage,[2] he distinguishes it from the books *manifestly* canonical, and speaks of its author as an unknown person, at the same time adding that it could be proved to be by the apostle, though many persons disputed the fact.

[1] .... τὰ μὲν νοήματα τοῦ ἀποστόλου, ἡ δὲ φράσις καὶ ἡ σύνθεσις ἀπομνημονεύσαντός τινος τὰ ἀποστολικὰ καὶ ὥσπερει σχολιογραφήσαντος τὰ εἰρημένα ὑπὸ τοῦ διδασκάλου κ. τ. λ.

[2] *Epist. ad Afric.*, ch. 9. The facts given regarding the death of the prophets by him who wrote the Epistle to the Hebrews (ὁ γράψας), ἐν οὐδενὶ τῶν φανερῶν βιβλίων γιγραμμένα.

Eusebius has also preserved another passage of Origen regarding the epistles of Peter and John, wherein, for the first time, there is some discussion of the two writings attributed to these apostles, which I have not yet mentioned. "Peter," it is there said, "on whom the Church of Christ is built, left one single epistle which is generally acknowledged, perhaps a second, for this is doubtful. John (besides the Gospel and the Apocalypse) left also a very brief epistle, perhaps a second and a third, for all are not agreed about their authenticity."[1] These three epistles are nowhere quoted in the Greek works of Origen; when he speaks of the first of Peter, he calls it simply *the epistle* (in the singular, without a figure)—the Catholic Epistle,[2] although the second is no less entitled to this epithet. But, in the Latin texts, we find allusions to this second epistle, and even direct quotations.

The epistles of James and Jude, too, are quoted with some hesitation. The former is introduced as a work *considered* to be by James,[3] and the author is described as a brother of the Lord,[4] which description, according to the ideas of the time, distinguished him from the Twelve. In the same way, Jude is very explicitly called a brother of the Lord, and distinguished from the apostles; and for this reason his epistle, though recommended as full of celestial grace and quoted several times, is not included among the writings whose authority is indisputable.[5] Here, too, the name of *apostle* is given to James and Jude in those works

---

[1] Euseb., *loc. cit.*: Πέτρος μίαν ἐπιστολὴν ὁμολογουμένην καταλέλοιπεν. ἔστω δὲ καὶ δευτέραν· ἀμφιβάλλεται γάρ. . . . Ἰωάννης. . . . ἐπιστολὴν πάνυ ὀλίγων στίχων. ἔστω δὲ καὶ δευτέραν καὶ τρίτην· ἐπεὶ οὐ πάντες φασὶ γνησίους εἶναι ταύτας.

[2] For instance: *In Joh.*, tom. vi. ch. 18. *In Psalm* 3 (*Opp.* xi. 420).—*In Matt.* vol. xv. ch. 27, there must also be read ἀπὸ τῆς Πέτρου ἐπιστολῆς.

[3] ἡ φερομένη Ἰακώβου ἐπιστολὴ (xix. *in Joh.*, ch. 6).

[4] Tom. x. *in Matt.* ch. 17.

[5] εἴ τις πρόσοιτο τὴν Ἰούδα ἐπιστολὴν (tom. xvii. *in Matt.* ch. 30). Comp. tom. x. ch. 17; xiii. 27; xv. 27).

of Origen, which have been preserved only in a Latin translation. I do not on this account attempt to suggest that the translator knowingly and wilfully altered the text, though such a supposition is warranted by what we know of him. It is enough to say that, in Origen's opinion, the writings of the brothers of Christ, as well as some other epistles not yet consecrated by general and undisputed usage, might be used perfectly well for the edification of the faithful and for the requirements of theological discussion, along with the writings already included in the usual collection, although science could still draw a distinction between the two categories of books. This explains how, in certain of Origen's works, more practical in their tendency and existing only in translation, we find an enumeration either of eight apostolic writers, or of twenty-seven books of the New Testament. Thus, in his thirteenth homily on Genesis, when speaking of the pits dug by the servants of Abraham and Isaac, he compares the former to the authors of the Old Testament, and the latter to the four evangelists and the apostles, Peter, Paul, James, and Jude. Thus, too, in his seventh homily on Joshua, the same personages sound the trumpet to overthrow the walls of the mystical Jericho, a symbol of paganism, and in such fashion that Peter and Luke hold two trumpets, John five, and Paul fourteen.

Our theory removes other difficulties arising from the supposition that Origen placed on the same level all the writings we have just been discussing. If he had done so, his canonical collection would have been not only (as is believed) quite as complete as the others, it would have been still fuller; for he complacently quotes several other books, using the same formulas, sometimes pious, sometimes hesitating. Thus the Epistles of Clement and Barnabas do not appear to him less worthy of attention than they

[1] For instance: *De Princ.* iii. 2. *Comm. in Rom.* iv. 8, v. 1.

did to his predecessors. He identifies the former of these authors with a personage recommended by Paul, and in this fact finds an additional motive for attributing to it a certain authority;[1] the second is even quoted, along with Luke and Paul, in support of a theme under discussion. But above all he extols the *Pastor* of Hermas on many occasions and has no doubt of its inspiration, though he regrets that every one is not of his opinion.[2] He is not equally convinced of the reality of the claims of the Gospel of the Hebrews, or the Acts of Paul; still he understands that others may value these books, and of this circumstance he avails himself to quote them in their turn.[4] Nor are these quotations unimportant, such as we are making daily; he attributes to them an authority which, if not absolute (for that belongs only to the homologumena), is at least relatively superior to every other. Origen knows very well how to distinguish from these books others which deserve no credence and usurp titles not belonging to them. Thus, for example, he discusses very sensibly the value of a book called the *Preaching of Peter*, which was in circulation in his time, and he refuses to recognise any authority in its teaching.[5] While speaking of this work, he is even led to make a scientific classification of the works which might

---

[1] Vol. vi. *in Joh.*, ch. 36.

[2] *Contra Cels.*, i. 63.

[3] *Quæ scriptura mihi valde utilis videtur et ut puto divinitus inspirata* (*Comm. in Rom.* Book x. ch. 31). Τιρομένη ἐν τῇ ἐκκλησίᾳ γραφὴ οὐ παρὰ πᾶσι δὲ ὁμολογουμένη εἶναι θεία (*in Matt.* vol. xiv. ch. 21). *Qui a nonnullis contemni videtur* (*De princ.* iv. 11). Comp. *Hom. 1 in Psalm* xxxvii. *Hom. 8 in Num.* *In Luc. hom. 35. Opp.* v. p. 218.

[4] ἴ τις παραδέχεται (*Hom. in Jerem.* xv. 4). ἴ τῳ φίλον παραδέχεσθαι (vol. xx. *in Joh.*, ch. 12. Comp. *De princ.*, ii. 1, § 5).

[5] κήρυγμα Πέτρου, *doctrina Petri* (*De princ.*, preface, § 8). *Respondendum quoniam ille liber inter ecclesiasticos non habetur et ostendendum quia neque Petri est ipsa scriptura neque alterius cuiuspiam qui Spiritu Dei fuerit inspiratus.*

claim to serve as a rule for the church. He distinguishes them into three categories: those that are authentic (legitimate), those that are suppositious (bastard), and those that are partly both (mixed), *i.e.*, that may have, in spite of their general apocryphal character, elements of a value incontestably superior.[1] Authenticity, or legitimacy, as may be seen, is not taken here in an exclusively literary sense.

The School of Alexandria of which Origen was the most learned and most brilliant representative, was in an embarrassing position in regard to a book of which no special mention has been made in these last pages. We have seen that at a very early period the Apocalypse was held in special, even exceptional, regard; that, as a prophetic book, it was the first of all the writings of the first century to be ranked by theology with the inspired Scriptures. This exceptional position was retained by it so long as Chiliasm, or the belief in the coming of the thousand years' reign of the elect, prevailed in the church and was admitted by the principal theologians. But towards the end of the second century a reaction had set in against this belief, which had grown more and more materialistic, and the Alexandrine Fathers in particular laboured for the spread of more spiritual views regarding the general essence of Christianity, and specially regarding the last things. The Apocalypse, which was eminently favourable to the views already current, must have given them trouble, and, as traditional opinion seemed to put its claims beyond all attack, the Alexandrines had recourse to an interpretation which caused the eschatological predictions to disappear, leaving only allegorical pictures of the present state of humanity or of the church. Origen most of all gave support to this kind of interpretation which soon prevailed in the church.[2] Still

---

[1] Ἐξιτάζοντις περὶ τοῦ βιβλίου πότιρόν ποτι γνήσιόν ἐστιν ἢ νόθον ἢ μικτόν (vol. xiv. *in Joh.*)

[2] See Origen, *De princ.*, ii. 11, § 6. *In Matt. Opp.*, iv. 307.

the new method met with opposition, and an Egyptian bishop, named Nepos, published a volume of criticism against the Allegorists[1] which made much noise, as it frankly reasserted the literal meaning of a book which up to that time had been so highly prized by Christians. The most learned of Origen's disciples, Dionysius, bishop of Alexandria, made extraordinary efforts to remove this opposition; he held public conferences with the partisans of Chiliasm, and wrote besides a treatise "*On the Promises*,"[2] of which Eusebius has preserved several very interesting fragments. Among other points, we find in them that Dionysius, while professing respect for a book which others before him, he says, had rejected as unworthy of an apostle and had attributed to a heretic, tries to establish a doubt regarding the person of the author. He alleges various reasons for not identifying its author with the author of the Fourth Gospel and of the Epistle, and he concludes that probably another apostolic personage of the name of John, either Mark or rather a certain presbyter of the Church of Ephesus whose tomb was still to be seen in that city, wrote this Apocalypse. He does not, however, dispute its inspiration. I shall not discuss here the value of the arguments of Dionysius, which recall those adduced by Origen in support of his theory regarding the Epistle to the Hebrews; I shall insist only on the one fact of the sudden change of opinion in regard to the Apocalypse, and of the effect which this change produced on its canonical authority. There is here every proof that it fell into neglect and disesteem, so soon as the current began to withdraw from the hopes that had formerly excited the visionary enthusiasm of the first generations. The book was bound to follow the fate of the ideas consecrated in it, and the allegorical interpretation, the busi-

---

[1] Ἔλεγχος ἀλληγοριστῶν *ap.* Euseb., *Hist. eccl.* vii. 24.
[2] περὶ ἐπαγγελιῶν (Eusebius, *loc. cit.*)

ness of scholars only, could do no more than hinder the people from turning away from the prophet when they had ceased to believe in the prophecy. But if this were the case, as no one can doubt, what is to be said of the basis on which finally the choice of the church rested when forming its sacred canon? On the one hand we have Origen recommending the inclusion of an epistle that was still doubtful, because its contents seemed to him excellent, while at the same time he confesses that he does not know who wrote it, and that the elegance of its style makes it impossible for him to attribute it to an apostle. On the other hand we have Dionysius advising the exclusion of a prophecy which had long been received, but was opposed in the letter to his theology, while he seeks for it a perhaps imaginary author who is to be responsible both for the solecism in form from which he wishes to relieve the apostle and for those peculiarities in the subject-matter with which he is unwilling to burden his own conscience. But I hasten to add that the fate of those books did not depend on the individual opinion of our two learned theologians. They themselves felt the pressure of an opinion more generally entertained, before lending to it the support of their own personal authority, which was no doubt very powerful. We may conclude from all this that the tradition which, as we have seen, predominated in the formation of the canon of the New Testament, did not rest necessarily and everywhere on primordial guarantees, on the testimonies of the first age; otherwise these fluctuations of opinion would be inexplicable, and ecclesiastical usages could not have been modified from time to time in accordance with systems, nay, according to the taste of a particular age or school.

The Greek Church of the third century furnishes us with scarcely any more texts to be consulted on the history of the canon. A hundred years after Origen we shall find things just where we left them. I simply remark that the testimonies, commonly fragmentary, which have come down to us from this period prove that the Epistle to the Hebrews appears to have been accepted without difficulty in the East as a work of Paul; at least, there is no trace of any opposition on the point. Still, I shall not leave the Eastern Church and pass to the no less interesting details furnished by the Latin authors, without calling the attention of my readers to a book which in its first form must belong to this same period, and which, for more than one reason, still presents matter of great historical interest. This is the famous compilation known under the name of the *Apostolic Constitutions*, a vast collection of laws and ordinances touching the government of the Church, worship, discipline, and similar subjects, intermingled with moral teachings. The apostles appear in it as a kind of legislative body, speaking in their collective name, and ruling with a sovereign authority all that concerns the wants and duties of the Christian commonwealth. It is, in truth, the earliest ecclesiastical code, and its importance is hardly lessened by the pretentious form in which it is drawn up. Modern scholars are generally agreed in assigning the principal part (Books I.-VI.) to the third century, while they make the appendices (Books VII., VIII.) a hundred years later. The passages therefore in this work, which relate to the history of the canon of the New Testament, ought to be mentioned here. In the first place, let me quote the place which the apostles claim for themselves in the economy of Providence. "Every generation," they say,[1] "has had its prophets who interpreted the will of God, and were the means of his call to repentance: before the deluge, there were Abel, Shem *(sic)*, Seth, Enos, and Enoch; in the time of the deluge, Noah; in the time of Sodom, Lot; after the cataclysm, Melchisedec, the patriarchs, and Job; in

[1] *Const Apost.* ii. 55.

Egypt, Moses; among the Israelites, in addition to the latter, Joshua, Caleb, and Phinehas, and others; after the Law, angels and prophets; then, further, God himself by his incarnation in the Virgin; a little before His coming, John, the forerunner; finally, after His Passion, we, the Twelve, and Paul, the chosen vessel. Witnesses of His presence παρουσίας), with James, the brother of the Lord, and seventy-two other disciples and the seven deacons, we heard from his own mouth, etc." Among the injunctions laid upon the Church, there is that of reading the Scriptures. Thus it is ordained[1] that during the night preceding the Passover Sunday there shall be read the Law, the Prophets, and the Psalms until cock-crow, then the baptism of catechumens shall take place, and the Gospel be read (τὸ εὐαγγέλιον). In another passage[2] a complete enumeration is made of these Scriptures :—" The reader, placed in an elevated chair, shall read the books of Moses, Joshua, Judges, Kings, Chronicles, and the Return,[3] further, those of Job, Solomon, and the sixteen prophets. At the end of every two pericopes[4] another shall intone the Psalms of David, and the congregation sing the responses. After that there shall be read our Acts and the epistles of our fellow-worker, Paul, which he addressed to the churches by direction of the Holy Spirit; then a deacon or a presbyter shall read the Gospels which we, Matthew and John, have transmitted to you, and which the fellow-workers of Paul, Luke and Mark, have left to you." It will be observed that no mention is made here of any one of the Catholic Epistles or of the Apocalypse. This fact of itself, alone, authorises us in assigning an early date either to the composition of the book itself, or to the usages

[1] *Const. Apost.* v. 19.
[2] *Const. Apost.* ii. 57.
[3] Ezra and Nehemiah.
[4] ἀναγνώσματα. It is evident that here only *readings* or extracts are under discussion.

which it consecrates. In another passage[1] the faithful are put on their guard against the pseudepigrapha. It is not to the names they bear, it is said, that we must give heed, but to their contents and spirit. Finally, in a passage of the appendix,[2] where he is speaking of the enthroning of the bishop, Peter prescribes also the reading of the Law, the Prophets, the Epistles, the Acts, and the Gospels, without entering into the details. We shall hardly go wrong if we see in these summary enumerations an index of the number of the volumes of which the sacred library was composed, and the care bestowed on reading a portion from each volume. This supposition is further confirmed by the venerable usages of the Catholic Church and of the Lutheran Churches.[3]

I shall be able to pass rapidly over the Latin authors of this century, for to them the canon of the New Testament seems to have remained in its primitive simplicity, and almost in the same state as we saw it in the Muratorian Canon. The most salient feature is the tenacity with which the West refused to recognise the Epistle to the Hebrews as the work of Paul. This unanimous refusal is supported much later by an author all the more worthy of credit that he is himself of a different opinion.[4] The fact is proved in particular for the Roman presbyter, Caius, and for the Italian bishop, Hippolytus, who has grown so famous in our days,[5] but whose works are lost. In a fragment of Victorinus, bishop

---

[1] *Const. Apost.* vi. 16.

[2] *Const. Apost.* viii. 5.

[3] I say nothing here of other passages (i. 5, 6 ; ii. 5) where the O. T. is more particularly spoken of ; a distinction is there established between what has a permanent value and what only concerns the Jews.

[4] Jerome, *De Viris Ill.*, ch. 59 : *Apud Romanos usque hodie quasi Pauli ap. non habetur.* Comp. Euseb,, *Hist. eccl.,* iii. 3, vi. 20. Placed at a greater distance and having no doubt a less complete acquaintance with the literature of the West, the latter expresses himself in a less decided fashion, παρὰ Ῥωμαίων τισί.

[5] Jerome and Eusebius, *ll. cc.*

[6] Steph. Gobarus *ap.* Photius, *Cod.* 232.

of Petabium, in Pannonia,[1] the number of the churches to which Paul is said to have written is expressly limited to seven, as to a sacred number. In the works of Lactantius there is no trace of the Epistle to the Hebrews. Later, when opinion had changed, attempts were made to explain this dislike of the early fathers to the epistle, by saying that the orthodox theologians were prejudiced against this epistle by the abuse which the heretics made of it. The Arians, it is said, appealed to the passage in iii. 2; the Novatians, who denied repentance to the renegade *(lapsi)*, availed themselves of vi. 4 and x. 26.[2] But in what remains to us of Novatian himself,[3] no use is made of the epistle, and if its authenticity and authority had been acknowledged previously, it is far from probable that the orthodox fathers would have sacrificed it, simply to get rid of an exegetical argument which was inconvenient to them.

The most celebrated and the most important Latin author of the third century, the Bishop Cyprian of Carthage, will also give us most complete information on the state of the canon. In the Old Testament, he makes no difficulty about using the apocryphal books Tobias, Ecclesiasticus, Wisdom, the Maccabees, and he quotes them as inspired writings. As to the New Testament, the elements of which it is composed appear to him to be determined beforehand by mystical reasons. The gospels are four in number, like the rivers of Paradise;[4] Paul and John wrote each to seven churches as was prefigured by the seven sons spoken of in the song of Hannah.[5] The first of Peter and the first of

---

[1] *De fabrica mundi*, ap. Cave, *Hist. Lit.* 1720, p. 95 : *postea (non nisi) singularibus personis scripsit ne excederet modum septem ecclesiarum.* Comp. the same. *In Apoc.*, p. 570, ed. Paris, 1654.

[2] Ambrose, *De Poenit.* ii. 3. Philastr., *Haer.* 89.

[3] Gallandi, *Bibl. P.P.*, vol. iii.

[4] Cyprian, *Epp.*, 73.

[5] Id., *De Exhort. mart.*, ch. 2. *Adv. Jud.*, i. 20. Comp. 1 Sam., ii. 5.

John are the only Catholic Epistles known or quoted by Cyprian.

I may add further that the Latin theologians were far from sharing that kind of antipathy against the Apocalypse which, as we have just seen, sprang up and gained ground in the bosom of the Eastern Church during this same century. I quoted just now the testimony of Cyprian on the point. Hippolytus,[1] Victorinus,[2] Lactantius, as partisans of Chiliasm, professed great veneration for this book, and this opinion was so predominant among the Latins that, as we have seen elsewhere, Lactantius exalts in the most emphatic manner the Sibylline prophecies, and does not hesitate a moment about placing them on a level with inspired writings. The only author who is an apparent exception, is the presbyter Caius, an adversary of Chiliasm. According to Eusebius (*Hist. eccl.*, iii. 28), Caius accused the heretic Cerinthus of having deceived the world by producing under the name of a great apostle, pretended revelations communicated by angels. This passage has often been interpreted as if it applied to the Apocalypse of John, which Caius would thus seem to have rejected and treated as an apocryphal work. But this is not stated explicitly, and above all Eusebius does not appear to have understood him in this fashion. The *great* apostle might very well be, either Paul or Peter; at least this epithet was not given to John in the early church.

---

[1] He had written a defence of the Gospel and the Apocalypse of John (*Opp.* ed. Fabricius, p. 38. Jerome, *De Vir. ill.*, 61. Andreas, *Prolog. in Apoc.*).

[2] Jerome, *l.c.*, 18. The traces of Chiliasm have disappeared from his commentary in the recension which has come down to us.

CHAPTER IX.

THE FOURTH CENTURY—STATISTICAL RETROSPECTIVE.

We have now come to the epoch in which Christianity, having gained a decided victory over the old religion of the empire, and having no longer anything to fear either from a distrustful policy or from popular antipathy, was free to develop and organise itself in all directions according to its spirit and its needs. What use did it make of this freedom of movement which up to this time had been unknown? We do not find that any advantage was taken of it for remodelling social institutions that had sprung up and developed in difficult times and under the blows of persecution. It was left to time, to the instincts of future generations, the exigencies of circumstances, the convenience of governments or individual interests, to modify these institutions, complete them, or adapt them to the genius of each epoch or country. That which predominated from the first day of the emancipation, so to speak, from the day after the last judicial murder; that which occupied first the cultivated minds that could lead the way in thought, and then the masses; that which for centuries absorbed almost all the religious activity of the church, enslaved all its powers and finally exhausted them, was speculation, the infatuation for transcendental questions, the demand for defining metaphysical notions, for analysing them and drawing inferences from them; in a word, for changing religion into theology and theology itself into a matter for the learned and for dialectics. This has a bearing on our special history inasmuch as all this work was begun, continued, and, so to speak, accomplished, at least in its most important and most decisive parts, without the Church being in possession of a clear and precise theory regarding the standard of dogmatic truth, or of an official collection of the sacred books carefully limited and generally recognised. Not but that there were certain writings of the Old and New Testaments regarding whose authority all were agreed, and against which there could not be raised the least doubt, the least contradiction; but the number and the list of these books were nowhere definitely determined; and, besides, there was a crowd of others whose claims were not verified, which were used neither uniformly nor generally, and held a vague and fluctuating position between sacred and profane literature, a position that might at any time embarrass science and disconcert the faithful.

For the historian, this fact alone is enough to prove that the formation of the sacred collection was a matter of local custom, unconscious tradition, practical needs, relations more or less intimate, more or less accidental between the various churches. It was in no sense whatever an inheritance from the apostolic age, complete and guaranteed from the first, and running no risk of alteration in its form or materials.

But it is not my duty here to interpret the facts; I have only to recount them and let them speak for themselves. What the modern historian can establish by the study of early writers and the analysis of the literary documents of the first centuries—viz., the absence of any clearly defined canon of Scripture at the Council of Nicæa, and the variations of opinion regarding the various parts of our existing collections—all this was established through the same methods by the contemporary historian, who had himself been struck by the facts to which I now call attention, with this single difference that he had them before his eyes, while modern science has had to begin by discovering them anew.

Eusebius of Caesarea (for my readers will have divined that I wish to devote this chapter to him) was the most erudite of the theologians of his day. If he leaves much to be desired as an exegete or an apologist for Christianity, he had, on the other hand, one quality which was wanting in all his predecessors as in all his contemporaries, the instinct for historical research. I use the word *instinct* purposely. His ecclesiastical history is an invaluable collection of materials, the fruit of the most meritorious labour; but it is nothing more. And we have reason to congratulate ourselves on this, for his notes acquire all the more interest and value that he is clearly incapable of blending them into a true pragmatical history of the Church. What renders them most of all precious to us, is the very marked attention which he directs to all that concerns the history of the Christian Bible. He read a prodigious number of authors, for the most part now lost, and in the extracts he gives from their writings he never fails to note the use they made of Scripture, the list of books which they quote in passing or fully discuss, the judgments they pronounce on them. What is the reason of this anxiety? If we were still in possession of all these authors, would we not have more pressing questions to address to them on the problems specially which occupied the age of Eusebius, the problems of dogmatic and speculative theology? But, unless I am strangely deceived about the state of things at the beginning of the fourth century, it will not be difficult to explain why the bishop took so much care to register these numerous individual *testimonies*. Their relative value was all the greater that there nowhere existed any official declaration having an absolute value, no canon of a synod, no collective agreement among churches or bishops, no letter from a pope or mandate from a patriarch, and, above all, no apostolic decision. Of all these there is not the shadow of a trace in this long series of literary notices, so painfully, so conscientiously amassed by a man who, after all, had not sought them from any vain curiosity, but with the distinct purpose of reaching something certain. And, when all is done, the most positive result to which he comes is still uncertainty, and an uncertainty so great that he gets confused while making a statement of it. This may be seen from the analysis of his summary.

He returns to this subject in several passages of his third book, to one of which, the twenty-fifth chapter, we must devote some attention. I am going to transcribe it entire and study it carefully, so as to institute a comparison between its parallel texts. Let me begin by saying that Eusebius, in the absence of any official list of the canonical writings of the New Testament, finds it the simplest way to count the votes of his witnesses, and by this means to distribute all the apostolical or pretended apostolical books into three categories:—(1) Those on whose authority and authenticity all the churches and all the authors he had consulted were agreed; (2) those which the witnesses were equally agreed in rejecting; and (3) an intermediate class regarding which the votes were divided. This division is certainly very far from being scientific; as a matter of theory and dogma, it is even absurd; but it is very practical, and, above all, it is one to inspire us with great confidence, whereas a more rigid and dogmatic classification might have seemed to us to be more the work of the theologian than of the historian. Further, the very terms used by Eusebius to designate the different classes of books are so far from being precise and clearly defined that they continually confuse the discussion, or rather the report he makes of the state of things. From his historical point of view, he wishes to call the books of the first category the *homologumena*,[1] or books universally

[1] Ὁμολογούμενα, ἀναντίρρητα, ἀναμφίλεκτα, ἰνδιάθηκα. This last term is untranslatable. Still, though a synonym with the three others, it clearly

recognised; those of the second (*i.e.*, of the intermediary class) the *antilegomena*,[1] or contested books. But with these terms, which are perfectly clear and natural, he continually mixes others borrowed from a different order of ideas, and these other terms have contributed not a little to mislead modern scholars in the interpretation of his texts. I am thinking here chiefly of an expression which we have already met in Origen, but to which Eusebius gives a slightly novel meaning. He uses, the term νόθα, *bastards*, (*apocrypha*), not exactly for fictitious writings, *pseudepigrapha*, works bearing falsely an author's name, nor, again, for books which are to be rejected from a dogmatic point of view, but simply for works which do not bear, so to speak, the stamp of canonical legitimacy, which are not warranted by the mass of votes as are those of the first class. I beg my readers to take note of this, and to remember, when reading the translation I am going to give of the texts from Eusebius, that this term *illegitimate*, with its derivations, does not imply in the author's thought any reproach of literary falsification or dogmatic heresy, but simply states that there was no general ecclesiastical adoption of the writings, and that consequently they either were, or ought to be, held inferior.

The following is the chief passage in which Eusebius sums up the facts he has been able to establish by his literary researches[2]:—"Now that we have come to this

---

says something more. It not only affirms the unanimity of their reception or use, but, no doubt, implies also the theological idea of a normal rule. I shall translate it in this sense: *books of the Covenant, i.e.*, containing the testimonies or authentic documents of Revelation. But, as this privileged character given to certain books rested exclusively on a very ancient tradition, it is understood that as a general thesis, it could only be attributed to the homologumena.

[1] ἀντιλεγόμενα, γνώριμα τοῖς πολλοῖς.
[2] Eusebius, *Hist. eccl.*, iii. 25: Εὔλογον δ᾽ ἐνταῦθα γινομένους ἀνακεφαλαιώσασθαι τὰς δηλωθείσας τῆς καινῆς διαθήκης γραφάς. καὶ δὴ τακτέον ἐν πρώτοις τὴν ἁγίαν τῶν εὐαγγελίων τετρακτύν. οἷς ἕπεται ἡ τῶν πράξεων τῶν ἀπ. γραφή, μετὰ δὲ ταύτην τὰς

point in our narrative, it seems to us fitting that we should give a list of the Scriptures of the New Covenant regarding which there has been discussion. In the first rank we must place the sacred quaternion of the Gospels; it will be followed by the book of the Acts of the Apostles; after this we must rank the Epistles of Paul, and next to them we must receive that which is known by the name of the first of John, and likewise the Epistle of Peter. To these must be added, if it be thought right, the Apocalypse of John, to which we shall return. These are the books which stand in the class of those universally acknowledged. In the class of contested books, which, however, are recognised by most, it is usual to place the Epistle of James, the Epistle of Jude, and those which are named the second and third of John, whether they come from the evangelist or some other person of the same name. Among the illegitimate books we must rank the Acts of Paul, what is called the *Pastor*, the Apocalypse of Peter, the epistle attributed to Barnabas, and the work entitled *Institutes of the Apostles*; further, as I said, if it be thought right, the Apocalypse of John, which some reject, as I said, while others include it

Παύλου καταλεκτέον ἐπιστολάς αἷς ἑξῆς τὴν φερομένην Ἰωάννου προτέραν καὶ ὁμοίως τὴν Πέτρου κυρωτέον ἐπιστολήν. ἐπὶ τούτοις τακτέον, εἴγε φανείη, τὴν ἀποκάλυψιν Ἰωάννου . . . καὶ ταῦτα μὲν ἐν ὁμολογουμένοις. τῶν δ' ἀντιλεγομένων, γνωρίμων δ' οὖν ὅμως τοῖς πολλοῖς, ἡ λεγομένη Ἰακώβου φέρεται καὶ ἡ Ἰούδα, ἥτε Πέτρου δευτέρα ἐπιστολὴ καὶ ἡ ὀνομαζομένη δευτέρα καὶ τρίτη Ἰωάννου· εἴτε τοῦ εὐαγγελιστοῦ τυγχάνουσαι, εἴτε καὶ ἑτέρου ὁμωνύμου ἐκείνω. Ἐν τοῖς νόθοις κατατετάχθω καὶ τῶν Παύλου πράξεων ἡ γραφή, ὅ τε λεγόμενος ποιμήν, καὶ ἡ ἀποκάλυψις Πέτρου, καὶ πρὸς τούτοις ἡ φερομένη Βαρνάβα ἐπιστολή, καὶ τῶν ἀποστόλων αἱ λεγόμεναι διδαχαί· ἔτι δὲ, ὡς ἔφην, ἡ Ἰωάννου ἀποκάλυψις, εἰ φανείη, ἥν τινες, ὡς ἔφην, ἀθετοῦσιν ἕτεροι δὲ ἐγκρίνουσι τοῖς ὁμολογουμένοις. ἤδη, δ' ἐν τούτοις τινὲς καὶ τὸ καθ' Ἑβραίους εὐαγγέλιον κατέλεξαν. . . . ταῦτα μὲν πάντα τῶν ἀντιλεγομένων ἂν εἴη. Ἀναγκαίως δὲ καὶ τούτων ὅμως τὸν κατάλογον πεποιήμεθα, διακρίναντες τάς τε κατὰ τὴν ἐκκλησιαστικὴν παράδοσιν ἀληθεῖς καὶ ἀπλάστους καὶ ἀνωμολογημένας γραφὰς καὶ τὰς ἄλλας παρὰ ταύτας, οὐκ ἐνδιαθήκους μὲν ἀλλὰ καὶ ἀντιλεγομένας, ὅμως δὲ παρὰ πλείστοις τῶν ἐκκλησιαστικῶν γιγνωσκομένας· ἵν' εἰδέναι ἔχοιμεν αὐτάς τε ταύτας καὶ τὰς ὀνόματι τῶν ἀποστόλων πρὸς τῶν αἱρετικῶν προφερομένας. . . . ὅθεν οὐδ' ἐν νόθοις αὐτὰ κατατακτέον, ἀλλ' ὡς ἄτοπα πάντη καὶ δυσσεβῆ παραιτητέον.

amongst the books universally acknowledged. Finally, some place in this category the Gospel acccording to the Hebrews, which the Jewish-Christians use by preference. All these books may be ranked in the class of those which are disputed. But we have been obliged to draw up the catalogue carefully, taking pains to distinguish the Scriptures that are true and authentic according to the traditions of the Church and are universally received, from the others which are not considered to be books of the Covenant, but are disputed, though known to most ecclesiastical authors. In this way we can draw a clear line between these books and others produced by heretics under the names of various apostles, such as the Gospels of Peter, of Thomas, of Matthew, or the Acts of Andrew, John, etc., books to which no writer belonging to the legitimate succession in the Church has ever deigned to appeal, and which betray their apocryphal and heretical origin as much by their strange style as by doctrines opposed to the true faith. They should not be ranked even among the illegitimate books, but should be rejected as absolutely absurd and impious."

This passage is exceedingly instructive, and we must pause over it for a little. In the first place, it is clear that I was right in saying that the author distinguishes three categories of books. Those who persist in discovering four are misled by a prejudice founded on modern habits of thought. Eusebius expressly says that he wished to draw up the *double* catalogue of the *homologumena* and the *antilegomena*, which have this in common that their credit is established in the churches, though in different degrees, by the votes of the doctors, and this he did that he might be able to distinguish them from the heretical books which are unworthy of any such honour. It is only by making this *absolute* separation from the last class, that he finds himself able to direct attention also to the *relative* difference between the two first.

This difference, I repeat, does not depend on the tendency more or less orthodox of the teaching, on which point there would certainly have been no compromise, nor on the author's personal opinion regarding the apostolic authenticity of each writing, but solely on the reception, more or less general, which these writings had in the churches, or rather on the testimonies, more or less unanimous, which the historian found in previous authors. Eusebius explains himself after the same fashion in two other passages. Thus, in a passage where he is speaking of Peter, he distributes the writings bearing the name of that apostle into the three categories as indicated above, the first epistle being acknowledged and undisputed, the second disputed; while the Acts, the Gospel, the Preaching, etc., are not reckoned at all among catholic works, as no ecclesiastical author grants them his suffrage.[1] Then he continues[2]:—" In what follows I shall take care to indicate the authors of each age who make use of any disputed book, and to report what they say both of the books of the Covenant or Scriptures universally received as well as of those which do not belong to these classes." Elsewhere he says, when finishing the part of his work relating to the apostolic age proper:— "That is what has come down to us relative to the apostles and their time, as well as to the Holy Scriptures which they left to us; to the books, which, though disputed, are nevertheless consecrated to public use in most of the churches; lastly to those which are absolutely apocryphal and contrary to the true apostolic faith."[3] Everywhere there are three classes

[1] I must return later to what this passage (iii. 3.) also says of the Apocalypse of Peter.

[2] Euseb., *Hist. eccl.*, iii. 3: προϊούσης δὲ τῆς ἱστορίας προὔργου ποιήσομαι ὑποσημήνασθαι τίνες τῶν κατὰ χρόνους ἐκκλησιαστικῶν συγγραφέων ὁποίαις κέχρηνται τῶν ἀντιλεγομένων, τίνα τε περὶ τῶν ἐνδιαθήκων καὶ ὁμολογουμένων γραφῶν, καὶ ὅσα περὶ τῶν μὴ τοιούτων αὐτοῖς εἴρηται.

[3] *Ibid.*, iii. 31: . . . . ὧν τε καταλελοίπασιν ἡμῖν ἱερῶν γραμμάτων, καὶ τῶν ἀντιλεγομένων μὲν ὅμως δ' ἐν πλείσταις ἐκκλησίαις δεδημοσιευμένων, τῶν τε παντελῶς νόθων καὶ τῆς ἀποστολικῆς ὀρθοδοξίας ἀλλοτρίων.

and not four. The modern critics who have preferred this last number have been misled by the use which Eusebius makes of the word *illegitimate,* used by him as synonymous with *disputed,* ἀντιλεγόμενος. There has been unwillingness to recognise this fact, which, however, has been already established by the first passage copied above, and which will be amply confirmed by the details to which we are now coming.

Let me first direct attention to this very curious fact that Eusebius absolutely does not know what to do with the Apocalypse of John and the Epistle to the Hebrews. As to the former, we saw that he first places it among the books universally received, adding, however, this singular phrase: *if it be thought right;* then, some lines lower, he returns to it and places it among the illegitimate (disputed) books, adding a second time his expression of doubt. There is in this a want of precision and logic, I had almost said, a striking absurdity, which would be inexplicable if we did not know that in regard to this book there had arisen a conflict between ancient custom and recent tendencies, between the favour of primitive times and the disfavour of contemporaries. When applied to this sudden change of opinion, the classification of the historian was insufficient. We must not reproach him with calling the same book at once disputed and undisputed, since there prevailed unanimity and disagreement, adoption and rejection, in two different and successive periods. And as he knows too well that this change in regard to the Apocalypse is only the consequence of another change which had taken place in the current of religious ideas, he does not venture to pronounce a decided opinion, but leaves his readers free to follow their own personal sympathies.

As to the Epistle to the Hebrews, Eusebius is in a similar, though less embarrassing position. His general catalogue does not name it in any of the three categories. As it is impossible to suppose that a writer of the fourth century should have been able to avoid considering it, we may rightly infer that in this passage he includes it without special mention among the Epistles of Paul, the number of which he does not specify. As an actual fact, their number is elsewhere given as fourteen, and that in terms showing that the author entirely adopts this calculation. Still he adds: "It is right at the same time to mention that several reject the Epistle to the Hebrews, on the ground that it is disputed by the Church of Rome as not Pauline." Here it is at once evident that Eusebius agrees with the Greeks who in his time commonly attributed this epistle to the apostle Paul, and for this reason he has no hesitation in ranking it among the undisputed books. He mentions the opposition of the Latins without attaching any great weight to it in the balance of his criticism. In another place, however, his impartiality makes him rank it among the disputed books, between Wisdom and Ecclesiasticus on the one hand, Barnabas, Clement and Jude on the other[2]. His personal opinion is that Paul wrote it in Hebrew and that Clement translated it into Greek;[3] he professes to prove this by the similarity between the style of the anonymous epistle and that of the bishop of Rome, in which, he adds, there are many phrases borrowed from the former.

The Epistles of James and Jude were, in the passage quoted above, reckoned among the disputed books. This description is repeated several times regarding the latter.[4]

---

[1] *Ibid.*, iii. 3: τοῦ δὲ Παύλου πρόδηλοι καὶ σαφεῖς αἱ δεκατέσσαρες. ὅτι γε μὴν τινὲς ἠθετήκασι τὴν πρὸς Ἑβραίους, πρὸς τῆς Ῥωμαίων ἐκκλησίας ὡς μὴ Παύλου οὖσαν αὐτὴν ἀντιλέγεσθαι φήσαντες, οὐ δίκαιον ἀγνοεῖν.

[2] *Ibid.*, vi. 13: . . . ἀπὸ τῶν ἀντιλεγομένων γραφῶν· τῆς τε λεγομένης Σολομῶντος σοφίας καὶ τῆς Ἰησοῦ τοῦ Σιράχ, καὶ τῆς πρὸς Ἑβραίους ἐπιστολῆς, τῆς τε Βαρνάβα καὶ Κλήμεντος καὶ Ἰούδα.

[3] *Ibid.*, iii. 38.   [4] *Ibid.*, vi. 13, 14.

Both are mentioned further in another passage which we cannot overlook. After narrating at length the history and martyrdom of James, the brother of the Lord, Eusebius adds,[1] "It is to him that the first of what are called the Catholic Epistles is attributed. It should, however, be known that it is illegitimate. Only a few ancient authors mention it, as well as that other which bears the name of Jude and also stands among the Catholic Epistles. Still we know that both are used along with the others in most churches." This passage is specially interesting because it furnishes us with the last piece of evidence that the terms *illegitimate* and *disputed* have with Eusebius exactly the same meaning. He does not mean to say that the Epistle of James is a work forged, or heretical, or unworthy of being read by the faithful; on the contrary he attests that it was read and recommends it; he expresses no doubt regarding the person of the presumed author, but he knows that all the churches do not regard it as a book of the first rank, no doubt because it is not by one of the twelve, and he mentions this lack of the highest *legitimacy*.

In this same class of books of a second rank, Eusebius also put, as we saw, the Epistle of Barnabas, the *Pastor*, the Acts of Paul and the Apocalypse of Peter. Elsewhere he adds to these the Epistle of Clement. All these writings, I repeat, have their place in this list by the same title as the five disputed Catholic Epistles. I have just quoted a passage in which the Epistles of Barnabas and Clement are enumerated among the disputed books, between the Epistle to the Hebrews and the Epistle of Jude.[2] In the same place this classification is repeated almost in

---

[1] *Ibid.*, ii. 23 : οὗ ἡ πρώτη τῶν ὀνομαζομένων καθολικῶν ἐπιστολῶν εἶναι λέγεται. ἰστέον δὲ ὡς νοθεύεται μέν. . . . ὅμως δὲ ἴσμεν καὶ ταύτας μετὰ τῶν λοιπῶν ἐν πλείσταις δεδημοσιευμένας ἐκκλησίαις.

[2] vi. 13 (see Note 2 on the preceding page).

THE FOURTH CENTURY—STATISTICAL RETROSPECTIVE. 157

the same terms.¹ Elsewhere he even says, when speaking of Clement: "There remains of him a great, admirable epistle, written in name of the Church of Rome to the Church of Corinth, and universally acknowledged. "We know that it has from an early date been publicly used in most churches and is so still in our day."² Here, then, is the same Epistle of Clement raised to the rank of the undisputed writings;³ there were so many opinions in its favour, and such was the general use made of it ecclesiastically in the fourth century. The Acts of Paul are described, in a very favourable manner, as not undisputed.⁴ As to the *Pastor*, it should be known, says Eusebius, that it meets with opposition: it cannot therefore be placed among the undisputed books; others, however, consider it indispensable for elementary teaching. For this reason it is used in the churches, and I see that several very early authors make use of it.⁵ The only point on which Eusebius contradicts himself, is regarding the Apocalypse of Peter which he puts sometimes among the disputed books, sometimes among the heretical books;⁶ and even here he is only repeaitng the divergent opinions of his predecessors without reconciling them.

What now is the conclusion to be drawn from all these facts? Are we to place in our canon of the New Testa-

---

¹ vi. 14. Clement of Alexandria in his *Outlines* (Ὑποτυπώσεις) passes in review all the canonical Scriptures, not neglecting the disputed books: μηδὲ τὰς ἀντιλεγομένας παρελθών, τὴν Ἰούδα λέγω, καὶ τὰς λοιπὰς καθολικὰς ἐπιστολὰς, τήν τε Βαρνάβα καὶ τὴν Πέτρου λεγομένην ἀποκάλυψιν.

² iii. 16: Τούτου τοῦ Κλήμεντος ὁμολογουμένη μία ἐπιστολὴ φέρεται μεγάλη τε καὶ θαυμασία. . . . ταύτην ἐν πλείσταις ἐκκλησίαις ἐπὶ τοῦ κοινοῦ δεδημοσιευμένην πάλαι τε καὶ καθ' ἡμᾶς αὐτοὺς ἴγνωμεν.

³ iii. 38: . . . . τοῦ Κλήμεντος, ἐν τῇ ἀνωμολογημένῃ παρὰ πᾶσιν.

⁴ iii. 3: οὐδὲ μὴν τὰς λεγομένας αὐτοῦ πράξεις ἐν ἀναμφιλέκτοις παρείληφα.

⁵ *Ibid.*: ἰστέον ὡς καὶ τοῦτο πρὸς μὲν τινῶν ἀντιλέλεκται, δι' οὓς οὐκ ἂν ἐν ὁμολογουμένοις τεθείη. ὑφ' ἑτέρων δὲ ἀναγκαιότατον οἷς μάλιστα δεῖ στοιχειώσεως εἰσαγωγικῆς κέκριται. ὅθεν ἤδη καὶ ἐν ἐκκλησίαις ἴσμεν αὐτὸ δεδημοσιευμένον. κ. τ. λ.

⁶ Compare the passages quoted above, iii. 3 and vi. 14.

ment the Acts of Paul and the Epistle of Clement, or are we to reject the Epistle of James and the Apocalypse? By no manner of means. But the statements of Eusebius, so positive, so impartial, so rich in facts which without him would have been lost, show us plainly that the Church in the middle of the fourth century did not yet possess any official canon, clearly defined, closed and guaranteed by any authority whatever; that usage, differing in different localities, nay, according to individual tastes, was still the decider of many questions; and neither the literary authenticity, nor the name of the authors, alone guided custom or determined whether a book was to be received or rejected. Let me make my meaning clear. So far from refusing to certain books the glory of having had a place formerly in the collections commonly used or the right of having a place there still, I maintain that in the time of Eusebius these collections were in part much more extensive than they are in our day.

For this statement I can produce documentary evidence. The Codex Sinaiticus, which is reckoned the oldest MS. existing of the Greek Bible, includes in the Old Testament the Apocrypha, and in the New Testament the Epistle of Barnabas and the *Pastor*. The Codex Alexandrinus in the British Museum likewise contains an Old Testament complete, and in the New Testament Clement of Rome.[1] These are documents which may go back to the age of Eusebius, and, if they are not to be considered so old, they would furnish still better proof of the persistence of certain customs so different from ours. It must not be forgotten above all that these fine copies in large size on parchment were not made for in-

---

[1] There exists no other ancient MSS. containing the N.T. complete. The Codex Vaticanus is incomplete from the beginning of the ninth chapter of the Epistle to the Hebrews; the Pastoral Epistles and the Apocalypse are wanting in it, and it is impossible to say whether all these books, or perhaps more, were contained in it when complete.

dividuals, but for use in churches. Here is another proof better still. The Codex Claromontanus, now placed in the National Library at Paris, and including the *thirteen* Epistles of Paul, written by a hand belonging to the seventh century, presents at the end of the text the copy of an old complete list of the books of the Old and New Testaments, with the number of lines in each book, what was then called a stichometry.[1] In the Old Testament, the historical books, enumerated in their usual order down to Chronicles, are followed by the Psalms and the *five* books of Solomon,[2] then by the sixteen prophets, the *three* books of the Maccabees, Judith, Ezra,[3] Esther, Job, and Tobias. When dealing with such a confused medley, we cannot but acknowledge that the church in which or for which the collection was made up in this fashion, had no idea of the original diversity of the books which are here enumerated promiscuously. The New Testament first presents to us the four gospels (the number is expressly given) in the following order:—Matthew, John, Mark, Luke; then come the Epistles of Paul (no number indicated) to the Romans, two to the Corinthians, to the Galatians, to the Ephesians, two to Timothy, to Titus, to the Colossians, to Philemon, two to Peter. This last piece of information is evidently due to the carelessness of the copyist, who continued mechanically the preceding formula. The omission of the Epistles to the Philippians and to the Thessalonians can only arise from a similar cause. Then follow the Epistle of James, three of John, the Epistle of Jude, the Epistle of Barnabas, the Revelation of John, the Acts of the Apostles, the *Pastor*, the Acts of Paul,

---

[1] The same list is also found in the Codex Sangermanensis which is now at St. Petersburg, but which is only a copy of the Codex Claromontanus. It is reproduced by Coutelier, in his edition of the *Apostolic Fathers* i. p. 6, R. Simon, *Hist. du Texte du N. T.* p. 423, and other authors.

[2] Including, as is well known, Wisdom and Ecclesiasticus.

[3] Under this name is always included the book of Nehemiah.

and the Revelation of Peter. These three last books are exactly those which we saw Eusebius place among the disputed books along with James, Jude, etc. As to the Epistle of Barnabas, we cannot doubt that we have here our Epistle to the Hebrews, which used to bear that name in the African Church, and which would otherwise be omitted in this list. The Codex is Græco-Latin, and belongs to the West. A later hand has added the text of the Epistle to the Hebrews after the catalogue which we have been discussing.

But let us leave the manuscripts, though they are sometimes more important and more eloquent witnesses than the Fathers themselves; I shall return to them in connection with the period of the Middle Ages. We are not yet done with Eusebius. The history of this author presents a curious fact. About the year 332, the Emperor Constantine, wishing thoroughly to organise the Christian worship in his capital, applied to the bishop of Cæsarea, asking him to get fifty copies of the Bible made by practised scribes and written legibly on parchment. At the same time the emperor apprised him in a letter still preserved to us,[1] that everything necessary for doing this was placed at his command, among other things two public carriages. Eusebius, tells how he acquitted himself of his commission by sending to the emperor magnificent volumes composed of double sheets in sets of three or four, and that he received the thanks of the prince. Two public carriages for fifty Bibles! that gives us some idea of the dimensions of the work, and confirms what I said above regarding the number of the volumes which were to be found in a complete collection. The simplest calculation leads me to think that these were complete Bibles, the Old Testament being included. The emperor asks for fifty σωμάτια of the Holy Scriptures; this

---

[1] Eusebius, *Vita Const.*, iv. 36, 37.

word should not be translated *volumes* (otherwise the carriages must have been miserable vehicles), but *sets of volumes*, copies complete and properly arranged. At this point, however, an interesting question arises, the most important of all, and to this the text of Eusebius gives no reply. The emperor asks for fifty copies of the Holy Scriptures, " those which you acknowledge to be the most necessary to be put together and used, in the opinion of the church " (or, regard being had to the church).[1] Thus Eusebius will be free to put what books he thinks necessary into these sets. Now, if such a liberty could be granted to a simple scholar by a sovereign who had lately found at Nicæa how difficult it is to maintain agreement among theologians, and who would certainly not lightly run the risk of a new quarrel in his own capital, it is evident that every one more or less must have had this liberty, no competent authority having ever decided the questions regarding the canon. But the astonishing part of it is that this same Eusebius, who took care to tell us at some length about the fluctuations of opinion in regard to certain books apostolic or supposed to be so, and who, in that same passage, amuses himself by speaking to us of his double sheets in sets of three or four, has not a word to say to us regarding the choice he made on this great occasion. For we cannot but see that this choice must have fixed the component parts of the collection, at least within the bounds of the patriarchate of Constantinople —*i.e.*, in the most important part of Christendom. Fifty magnificent copies, all uniform, could not but exercise a great influence on future copies. But, I repeat, Eusebius does not tell us what he caused to be put in them. Did he abide by the principle of following the unanimity of opinion, of restricting himself to the undisputed books ? Or did he

---

[1] Eusebius, *l. c.* : . . . . . τῶν θείων δηλαδὴ γραφῶν, ὧν μάλιστα τήν τ' ἐπισκευὴν καὶ τὴν χρῆσιν τῷ τῆς ἐκκλησίας λόγῳ ἀναγκαίαν εἶναι γιγνώσκεις.

make the limits of the collection wider, while he preserved established usages, traditional customs (as the text of the emperor's letter seems to insinuate)? We do not know. There is no doubt that he admitted the Apocrypha of the Old Testament and the Epistle to the Hebrews; but what about the Apocalypse, with which almost no one at that time in the East would have anything to do? And what about the "beautiful and admirable Epistle of Clement, universally received by the churches?" In any case, the silence of Eusebius on this fundamental point does not arise from the New Testament of that day being a *set* of books strictly defined, as it is in our day. It would be explained more naturally in this way, that if the commission given by the emperor and executed to his satisfaction was a fact very honourable for the illustrious bishop who was hardly considered by his colleagues to be of strict orthodoxy, the details of the execution might not be to every one's taste, and it would be better to pass by anything which might give rise to cavilling.

CHAPTER X.

ATTEMPTS AT CODIFICATION—THE EASTERN CHURCH.

THE critical work of Eusebius, which we have been analysing, has proved to us that there was no official decision about the apostolic books, and no uniformity in the usage of the churches towards the middle of the fourth century. It has also shown us that there was a growing necessity for coming to some definite understanding on a point so fundamental. Thus, we are not surprised to see the most illustrious theologians of the second half of this same century make reiterated efforts to put an end to all uncertainty and to fix opinion on certain points of detail, regarding which doubt was ceasing to pay respect to long-standing usage. Here we enter on the most interesting period of the history of the canon; for we find here very numerous and express testimonies, together with catalogues of the sacred books, which more and more approach those that have been adopted in modern churches. But these documents themselves demonstrate that the end they proposed was not reached, that the unity was not obtained, that the principles followed were divergent, that, in more than one respect, the theory of the schools conflicted with the practice of the churches, in short, that science had not succeeded in endowing Christendom with an exact scriptural code. The study of the texts will fully justify the title I have given to this chapter; it will bring to our notice a series of attempts, the very number of which proves a fact which modern apologetics seek in vain to disguise—viz., that, at a period so far removed from primitive times, there was no longer any means of doing better. These observations are all the more important that the testimonies to be collected will be no longer like those of preceding generations, occasional allusions or heterogeneous facts, but judgments purposely delivered, opinions taking the attractive form of dogmatic thesis, or even regulations sanctioned by the common suffrages of persons invested with a public authority. I shall bring together, in one chapter, the testimonies of the Easterns; another will contain those of the Latins; a third will be devoted to a systematic recapitulation of these elementary facts, the explanation of the terminology connected with them, and an estimate of the general results.

Let us begin with the most celebrated theologian of the fourth century, the bishop Athanasius of Alexandria († 372). From what we know, he appears to have been the first prelate who took advantage of his position at the head of a vast and important diocese to settle the question of the biblical canon. It was an ancient custom for the Egyptian patriarchs, at the beginning of each year, to publish the ecclesiastical calendar—*i.e.*, to settle the date of Easter, on which most of the other festivals depended, and on the same occasion to address to the faithful pastoral letters, or, as we would now say, episcopal charges. In one of these epistles,[1] which was written for the year 365, if the number it bears in the manuscripts (39) refers, as is supposed, to the year of the author's pontificate, he deals with Scripture, and gives the complete list of the books composing it. He begins by setting forth the utility and necessity of such a list, when numerous heretical books were circulating in the Church; and, to excuse his boldness,[2] he quotes the example of the evangelist Luke, who decided to narrate the history of the Lord, because others had attempted to introduce suspicious matter into it. It needed boldness therefore to

---

[1] Athanasius, *Ep. festal.* *Opp.* ed. Montfaucon, ii. 38 f.
[2] χρήσομαι πρὸς σύστασιν τῆς ἐμαυτοῦ τολμῆς τῷ τύπῳ τοῦ εὐαγγελιστοῦ Λουκᾶ κ. τ. λ.

ATTEMPTS AT CODIFICATION—THE EASTERN CHURCH. 165

draw up a catalogue of the holy books. That single word reveals these facts to every one who does not obstinately close his eyes to evidence—viz., that the catalogue was not up yet drawn up officially, and that it was not easy to draw it so as to please all the members of the Church. But let us look at the catalogue itself. In the Old Testament, Athanasius reckons twenty-two books, according to the number of the letters of the Hebrew alphabet. Through Origen we are acquainted both with this number and its curious explanation; but, in spite of a coincidence which could not be fortuitous, the catalogue of the patriarch differs from that of the professor, both in the order of the books and in the books themselves. With Athanasius, Job is put between Canticles and Isaiah; Daniel comes after Ezekiel; the book of Ruth is counted as an independent work, distinct from Judges. On the other hand, the book of Esther is deliberately omitted altogether. As this omission is contrary to the usages of the Synagogue and cannot be founded on a point of dogma, it must be concluded that it was due to some ancient custom, whose influence the patriarch did not think it right to resist. We shall find that he was not the only one of his century who held the same opinion, and, as we have already seen, Melito, Bishop of Sardis, had two centuries before expressed a similar opinion, both for himself and for those around him. Such an opinion could only have been founded, at first, on the absolute difference between the spirit of this book and that of the Gospel. Finally, it is almost superfluous to note that Athanasius attributed canonicity to the Greek texts of the books of Daniel, Jeremiah, and Ezra, without giving any heed to the differences between the Septuagint and the original. That would be certain, even although the text of his charge did not say so in so many words.[1] But the point

---

[1] Ἱερεμίας καὶ σὺν αὐτῷ Βαρούχ, θρῆνοι καὶ ἐπιστολή.—The epistle of Jeremiah which the ancients regarded as a separate work, forms with us the last

which gives special importance to this document is, that in the New Testament he enumerates all the twenty-seven books which we now include in it, and excludes every other book. The seven Catholic Epistles are attached to Acts; the Epistle to the Hebrews is inserted between the second to the Thessalonians and the first to Timothy; and the Apocalypse is reinstated in its ancient rights and honours. Besides this collection of writings, called divine on the faith of tradition and recognised as the only source of salvation and of the authentic teaching of the religion of the Gospel,[1] Athanasius notes certain other books inferior in dignity and used habitually in elementary instruction. In this latter class he places Wisdom, Ecclesiasticus, Esther, Tobit, Judith, the *Pastor*, and the *Apostolic Constitutions*. I shall have to return to this classification and to the theological terms which are used to distinguish its component parts.[2]

As the document we have just been studying is a pastoral charge, and not a critical dissertation, the author brings no proof to support his decisions. He himself calls them bold, and they are indeed bold, especially as regards the number of the Catholic Epistles. If he makes appeal on this point to the traditions of the fathers, he goes much beyond the testimonies of history, which a short time before had been so carefully collected by his learned theological antagonist, Eusebius. But my readers now know them too well for me to need to return to them. Let it be enough to show that the individual opinion of the patriarch of Alexandria was far from becoming the general law of the Church. The liberty, or rather the uncertainty, continued afterwards as before.

chapter of the book of Baruch. But in the Greek Bibles it is separated from this by Lamentations.

[1] παραδοθέντα πιστευθέντα τε θεῖα εἶναι βιβλία. . . . ταῦτα πηγαὶ τοῦ σωτηρίου. . . . ἐν τούτοις μόνοις τὸ τῆς εὐσεβείας διδασκαλεῖον εὐαγγελίζεται.

[2] I shall not stop here to consider another text printed in the works of Athanasius, the *Synopsis S.S.* which belongs to a much later date.

We see this in a contemporary of Athanasius, Gregory of Nazianzus († 390), who was no less illustrious as a theologian, and no less attached to the Nicæan orthodoxy. He, in turn, sees the necessity for drawing up a catalogue of the biblical books, and, whether it was that the subject seemed to him worthy of it or that he wished to aid the memory of his readers, he put it into verse.[1] So far as concerns the Old Testament, he agrees with Athanasius—twenty-two books, twelve being historical, five poetical, and five prophetical. Esther is wanting. In the New Testament there is just this little difference that the seven Catholic Epistles come only after the fourteen by Paul; but what is more important, the Apocalypse is omitted, and omitted designedly. For, after having named the Epistle of Jude and in the same verse, so that there is no room for suspecting an omission on the part of the copyist, he declares that these are all and that beyond these books there are none legitimate.[3] Still, it is to be observed that this exclusion implies no unfavourable judgment regarding the book considered in itself. Indeed, we find elsewhere in the works of the same Father, though very rarely, some quotations from the Apocalypse, and in the work now under discussion he calls the author of the Fourth Gospel the great herald who has traversed the heavens,[4] a name which of course marks him as the author of the Apocalypse. The legitimation refused to this book is therefore not the authenticity in the literary sense of the word, but the privilege of being ranked among those writings which were to regulate ecclesiastical teaching.

In the editions of Gregory's works there is another piece

---

[1] Gregor. Naz., *Carm.* 33. *Opp.* ed Colon. ii. 98.

[2] These not being enumerated, we do not know in what place he put the Epistle to the Hebrews.

[3] Ἰούδα δ' ἐστὶν ἑβδόμη. Πάσας ἔχεις,
εἴ τι τούτων ἐκτὸς οὐκ ἐν γνησίοις.

[4] κῆρυξ μέγας οὐρανοφοίτης.

of verse called *Iambics to Seleucus*, which relates to our subject. Modern criticism attributes it to a friend of the preceding writer, to Amphilochius, Bishop of Iconium in Asia Minor (towards 380). Its author enters into more details of literary history, and, if the poetry does not gain thereby, that fault is amply atoned for in our eyes by the facts with which the text supplies us. Amphilochius, too, belongs to that phalanx of Greek Fathers who, in regard to the Old Testament, stoutly held out against the admission of the six books (Wisdom, Ecclesiasticus, Judith, Tobit, and the Maccabees) wholly foreign to the Hebrew canon, though this did not prevent them from receiving all the others, notably Daniel and Jeremiah, in the amplified recension of the Septuagint. He also mentions expressly the exclusion of Esther in terms which show that he approves of it, and that this was the opinion of most.[1] The list of the books of the New Testament presents several details worthy of remark. John is named the fourth among the evangelists according to the chronological order, while the author assigns him the first rank because of the elevation of his teaching. The Acts of the Apostles by Luke are styled catholic, no doubt to contrast them with the numerous apocryphal and heretical Acts which were then in circulation. After them come the fourteen Epistles of Paul, the Epistle to the Hebrews being the last, and the author defending it against its detractors.[2] There remain[3] the Catholic Epistles, which some say are seven in number, others three; those of James, Peter, and John, one of each. The author does not add a word to decide the question. He

---

[1] τούτοις προσεγκρίνουσι τὴν Ἐσθὴρ τινές.
[2] τινὲς δέ φασι τὴν πρὸς Ἑβραίους νόθην, οὐκ εὖ λέγοντες· γνησία γὰρ ἡ χάρις.
[3] εἶεν τί λοιπόν. . . .
[4] τινὲς μὲν ἑπτά φασιν, οἱ δὲ τρεῖς μόνας χρῆναι δέχεσθαι. . . .

does the same with the Apocalypse, though, after having mentioned the difference of opinions on this book, he says that most are for rejecting it.[1] The most curious feature is that, having thus stated the doubtful right of several books to be included in the sacred collection, the poem ends with this incredible phrase: "This is perhaps the most exact list of the inspired Scriptures,"[2] a phrase which by its hypothetical form furnishes the last proof that his list is not founded on any official or generally acknowledged rule.

There is another contemporary who treats the question of the canon in honest prose, and, what is more important, as a chapter of popular theology. I refer to Cyril, Bishop of Jerusalem († 386).[3] In his *Catecheses* there is a passage on our subject which deserves to be read, and I place its substance before my readers. The author begins by establishing the intrinsic unity of all Scripture and recommending the exclusive reading of the *homologumena*.[4] Passing to the Old Testament, he relates at length the legend of the seventy-two interpreters shut up in as many separate chambers, and each in seventy-two days completing the translation of the whole sacred code of Israel, their translations agreeing in every single word. Having thus proved the inspiration of the Septuagint, the author proceeds to

[1] τὴν δὲ ἀποκάλυψιν Ἰωάννου πάλιν
τινὲς μὲν ἐγκρίνουσιν, οἱ πλείους δέ γε
νόθην λέγουσιν. . . .

[2] . . . . οὗτος ἀψευδέστατος
κανὼν ἂν εἴη τῶν θεοπνεύστων γραφῶν.

[3] Cyrill. Hieros., *Catech.* iv. p. 67.

[4] He appears, however, to take this word in a larger meaning than Eusebius, because it is in close connection with a new terminology, to which I shall return. If I am not deceived, the words *antilegomena* and *apocrypha* mean the same thing with him; they do not imply any literary (critical) reproach, but exclusion from the catalogue of normative writings: Ἐπίγνωθι παρὰ τῆς ἐκκλησίας ποῖαι μέν εἰσι τῆς παλαιᾶς διαθήκης βίβλοι, ποῖαι δὲ τῆς καινῆς καί μοι μηδὲν τῶν ἀποκρύφων ἀναγίνωσκε. ὁ γὰρ τὰ παρὰ πᾶσιν ὁμολογούμενα μὴ εἰδώς, τί περὶ τὰ ἀμφιβαλλόμενα ταλαιπωρεῖς μάτην;

enumerate the twenty-two books which their work contains, and which the Christian disciple ought not to put on a level with the Apocrypha. The enumeration itself shows us once more, as with the Fathers previously analysed, a Hebrew canon in a Greek recension—*i.e.*, the exclusion of the six books already mentioned, which are absolutely foreign to the Hebrew canon, and the reception of the Greek additions with which the Bible of Alexandria had enriched some others.[1] These twenty-two books thus translated, and these only, the disciple is to read; they are read by the Church and have been handed down by the apostles and the ancient bishops, to whom the present generation owes respect and deference. Cyril attempts also a new division of the Old Testament: (1) *Five* books of Moses, to which are added Joshua, Judges, and Ruth, as sixth and seventh; (2) *five* other historical books, Samuel, Kings, Chronicles, Ezra, and Esther; (3) *five* books in verse; (4) *five* prophetical books, headed by that of the Twelve. I shall return elsewhere to this manner of reckoning. In the New Testament, the author does not attempt to reduce the catalogue to a significant number. In this respect he is not more advanced than his predecessors, who certainly would not have failed to discourse regarding the number, if that had been already fixed. He limits himself therefore to analysing the collection into its chief elements, without entering on the details: four Gospels, the Acts, seven Catholic Epistles, fourteen Pauline. All the others are to be placed apart in a second rank.[2] Here, then, the Apocalypse is formally excluded; the disciple ought not to read it; for, adds the author, what is not read in the assemblies, ought not to be read in private. We

---

[1] Ἱερεμίου μία μετὰ καὶ Βαρούχ καὶ θρήνων καὶ ἐπιστολῆς.—These various witnesses do not make separate mention of the story of Susanna, of Bel and the Dragon, simply because these additions were integral parts of the book of Daniel.

[2] τὰ δὲ λοιπὰ πάντα ἔξω κείσθω ἐν δευτέρῳ.

might be tempted to believe that Cyril forbade the Apocalypse only to the young because it was hardly suited to their knowledge; but such cannot have been his motive, for his *Catecheses* also include the eschatological dogmas, and in the fifteenth, for instance, where he is treating of the Antichrist and where the Apocalypse ought to have furnished him with the most direct texts, he expressly declares, without naming that book, that he is borrowing from Daniel and not from the Apocrypha. I repeat that in this designation of a book which others put in the canon, he does not touch on the question of authenticity, but he refuses to it the normative character of scriptures divinely inspired.

Though all these Fathers contradict Athanasius on the subject of the Apocalypse, it might be said that they represent churches very remote from that of Alexandria, and that the influence of the Egyptian patriarch did not extend beyond his own diocese. This would make no difference to my assertion since the very point I maintain is that no agreement existed among all the churches. But I go further, and say that there was no agreement even in the city where Athanasius had his see. In an exegetical work on the seven Catholic Epistles, a work now extant in a Latin translation, Didymus, director of the school of Alexandria († 392), pronounces formally against the canonicity of the Second Epistle of Peter.[1] In order to understand rightly the terms he uses, they must be re-translated into Greek, which is not difficult. It is then evident that the author does not mean to speak of a literary falsification, but simply of what Eusebius had called the non-legitimacy (*falsata* = νοθεύεται); the epistle was in use in the church (*publicatur* = δεδημοσίευται), but had no canonical and normative authority for theological teaching. That is one more

[1] *Non est ignorandum præsentem epistolam esse falsatam quae licet publicetur non tamen in canone est* (Didymi Alex. *opp.* Col., 1531, fol. civ.)

proof that the two categories of books supposed to be apostolic were not separated by any definite selection.

We come now to Epiphanius, Bishop of Salamis in Cyprus († 403), one of those Fathers who were most careful about their orthodoxy and most anxious to take note of all the heresies. In his works he recurs several times to the number of the sacred books, and, at first sight, it might be supposed that, in his opinion at least, the question was one definitely settled with something like arithmetical precision. Thus, in his treatise on *Weights and Measures*,[1] he goes into ecstasies over the mysteries of that famous number 22 with which we are acquainted. There were twenty-two works by God during the six days of creation, twenty-two generations from Adam to Jacob, twenty-two letters of the alphabet, and twenty-two *sextarii* in a *modius*. Therefore, there are also twenty-two books in the Old Testament, or rather there are twenty-seven, because the Hebrew alphabet contains five letters that have two forms. The order in which Epiphanius gives these books should interest the critics who believe that the Christian Bibles were stereotyped from the apostolic age: Pentateuch (5), Joshua, Job, Judges, Ruth, Psalms, Chronicles (2), Kings (4), Proverbs, Ecclesiastes, Canticles, Twelve Prophets, Isaiah, Jeremiah, Ezekiel, Daniel, Ezra (2), Esther. These are made into twenty-two by counting Chronicles, Kings, and Ezra, each as one. We have still Lamentations left, it is true; the author does not know what to make of it, and mentions it at the end as an additional book. As he has thus succeeded, well or ill, in carrying the number of the books of the Old Testament from twenty-two to twenty-seven, without giving up the mystic privileges of the former of these figures, we would naturally expect to see him adopt the same figure for the New Testament. But in the case of the latter,

[1] Epiphan., *De Pond. et Mens.* ap. Le Moyne, *Varia Sacra.*, p. 477.

Epiphanius seems to attach no importance to such a calculation, or rather, as I have already indicated, the number was not settled in the church, and could not therefore be made the subject of mystical speculation. This is evident in another passage where his text presents a strange enough anomaly: "The man," he says,[1] "who is regenerated by the Holy Spirit and instructed in the apostles and prophets, ought to have perused history from the creation of the world down to the time of Esther, in the twenty-seven books of the Old Testament reckoned as twenty-two, and in the four gospels, and in the fourteen Epistles of St. Paul, and in the Catholic Epistles of James, Peter, John and Jude, which preceded them, and which are united to the Acts of the Apostles belonging to the same period,[2] and in the Apocalypse of John, and in the Wisdom of Solomon and of the son of Sirach (*i.e.*, Ecclesiasticus), in a word, in all the Holy Scriptures." I admit that Epiphanius included in his collection the seven Catholic Epistles, though he does not say so; I do not at all maintain that he put Wisdom and Ecclesiasticus in the New Testament;[3] but I cannot without remark pass from this singular addition of two "divine books," which are nevertheless out of place and unclassed in the passage where they are mentioned. If they deserve such a description, why do they not appear in their proper place? If not, why are they named at all?

[1] Epiphanius, *Haeres.*, 76. *Opp.* tom. i. p. 941, ed. Petav.

[2] καὶ ἐν ταῖς πρὸ τούτων καὶ σὺν ταῖς ἐν τοῖς αὐτῶν χρόνοις πράξεσι τῶν Ἀποστόλων. This does not mean that "the Acts were written previous to, or about this period," as some have believed it possible to translate it, but that the Catholic Epistles form *with* the Acts a volume which is placed in the general series *before* the volume of the Epistles of Paul, and that the book of Acts contains the narrative of facts contemporaneous with the composition of these epistles.

[3] It is none the less curious that he here insists on the fact that the Catholic Epistles form with Acts one whole. Is it perhaps that he may get a total number which presents a mystical meaning? I leave to any one who pleases the task of going over calculations so superfluous.

The sequel of my discussion will throw some light on a fact apparently inexplicable. Let me at present simply affirm that Epiphanius had no firmly settled opinion regarding the nature and value of the Apocrypha of the Old Testament (as we now call them) and of some other books;[1] in other words, that his mathematical and mystical tendencies could not bring him to any precise result.

But if the leaders of orthodoxy were so far from being fortunate in this work which is supposed to have been very simple, how many difficulties had to be encountered by those who were not so much influenced by popular practice! I am thinking now of the theologians of the School of Antioch, of men who, in the eyes of modern science, were infinitely superior to most of their contemporaries in all that concerns biblical studies. Even yet their sound exegesis, guided by a rare historical instinct and a sympathetic intelligence with the true needs of the Christian public, may be used with profit, while no sensible interpreter now dreams of drawing inspiration from the allegorical eccentricities brought into fashion by Origen. Unfortunately the works proceeding from this school are in great part lost; we know its opinions only in a fragmentary way, and through the reports of ignorant and prejudiced opponents. Thus the celebrated Theodore of Mopsuestia (†428), who in his time received the honourable surname of the *Exegete*, is accused by them not only of having interpreted Scripture in a poor and paltry fashion (which means that he clung to the proper sense of the text and despised the sterile abundance of mystical allegories), but also of having rejected some books from the number *divinely prescribed*.[2] He rejected,

---

[1] Wisdom and Ecclesiasticus are, from their doubtful value, called ἀμφίλικτα (*Haer.* 8, tom. i. 19). The *Apostolic Constitutions* are a word of God, θεῖοι λόγοι (*Haer.*, 80); doubtful, but not without value, ἐν ἀμφιλέκτῳ ἀλλ' οὐκ ἀδόκιμοι (*Haer.*, 70).

[2] Leont. Byzant. *Contra Nestor. et Eutych.* iii. (sec. vi.): *Theodorus*

it is said, the Epistle of James and other Catholic Epistles, the titles of the Psalms, Canticles, Chronicles, and Job. It is evident that in this case the accusers did not even understand the opinions they were attacking. In regard to Job, Theodore seems to have considered the framework of this book as a poetic fiction and not as genuine history; his interpretation of the Psalms seems to have led him to regard the inscriptions they bear as open to suspicion; and in both cases he gave proof of a sagacity far from common in his day. The rejection of Canticles leads us to suppose that he gave a purely literal interpretation of it, the result of which could not have appeared to him to be for the edification of the Christian Church. Chronicles also may have appeared to him unsuitable for edification, both on account of their interminable lists of proper names, and their useless repetition of facts already given in Kings. In other words, his decisions were not those of a critic disputing the antiquity of these books; he was rather a practical theologian, estimating them according to the needs of the church. As to the particular Catholic Epistles which Theodore excluded from the collection, there were many even in the opposite camp who were allied with him on that point.

In his own camp he had on his side a colleague still more illustrious than himself. This was the man to whom his church and posterity have given the highest eulogiums and honours, John Chrysostom, the great orator, the popular exegete *par excellence* († 407). In none of his works, which are almost all on practical and popular theology, do we find any trace of the Apocalypse or of the four smaller Catholic Epistles.[1] Among his works there has been printed an

... *audet contra gloriam Spiritus sancti, cum omnes scripturas humiliter et demisse interpretans, tum vero a numero ss. Scripturarum divine praescripto et indicato eas separans.*

[1] In the 6th homily on Genesis (p. 40, Montfaucon) some have supposed that 2 Pet. ii. 22 was quoted; but the passage refers to Prov. xxvi. 1 1.

anonymous and incomplete treatise, entitled *Synopsis of Holy Scripture*.[1] This treatise the learned Benedictine editor thinks himself able to attribute to Chrysostom, for reasons sufficiently probable. It contained, to begin with, a very detailed analysis of the contents of the whole Bible. Of this there has only been preserved the greater part of the Old Testament, and nothing of the New. Tobit and Judith are put between Esther and Job, as is generally the case in Catholic bibles. After Job come Wisdom, Proverbs, then after a blank, Ecclesiasticus and the Prophets. It is evident therefore that the author adheres purely and simply to the canon of the Septuagint, and that, in this respect, he is less scrupulous than most of the fathers we have consulted in this chapter. It is all the more interesting to find him having scruples regarding the New Testament. His analysis is preceded by an introduction presenting a general view, literary and historical, of the Bible. This introduction ends with an enumeration of the books of the New Testament. They are the fourteen Epistles of Paul; the four Gospels, two being by John and Matthew, disciples of Christ, two by Luke and Mark, the one a disciple of Paul, the other of Peter; then the book of Acts and the three Catholic Epistles.[2] An old scholiast has added on the margin of the MS., "Observe that he does not speak of the Apocalypse."[3] The conclusion from all this is that, at the end of the fourth century, the collection used in the diocese of Antioch—*i.e.*, in the Greek Church of Syria—was exactly the same as that which had been in use two hundred years before, and with which we are acquainted through the ancient Syriac version. For there can be no doubt regarding the *three* Catholic Epistles—they are the epistles of

---

[1] *Opp.* ed. Montfaucon, vi. pp. 308 f.

[2] It even says : καὶ τῶν καθολικῶν ἐπιστολαὶ τρεῖς (p. 318), a turn of expression which indicates the decided exclusion of other Catholic Epistles.

[3] σημείωται ὅτι οὐ μνημονεύει τῆς ἀποκαλύψεως.

James, John, and Peter. In the same volume of Chrysostom there is a homily which Montfaucon does not venture to attribute to him, though he believes it to belong to the same school of Antioch. When making a quotation from the first Epistle of John, the homily says that this epistle is received in the Church and is not apocryphal, whereas the second and third are not recognised as canonical by the fathers.[1] Let me quote further a passage from Chrysostom, showing that he too valued the sacred books, not by the theories of theologians, but by the salutary teaching the masses might derive from them. In his ninth homily on the Epistle to the Colossians, where he is exhorting his hearers to read the Holy Scriptures, he says: "Buy these books, which are the medicine of the soul; if you wish no other, at least buy the New Testament, the Apostle, the Acts, the Gospels."[2] The *Apostle, par excellence,* is he on whom the orator was at that moment preaching and whose glory eclipses the names of the other authors of epistles. According to the received reading, Chrysostom would seem to have spoken only of the Gospels and the Acts as books absolutely necessary and to have passed over all the epistles in silence, even those of Paul.

The last writer of this school whose works we possess was Theodoret († 450). He knows no other reason for excluding the Epistle to the Hebrews than Arianism, and he supposes that the canon has been mutilated by heretics.[3] This instance shows how completely previous facts had been forgotten, and how unanimous the orthodox Eastern Church had become in thinking favourably of that epistle.

---

[1] τῶν ἐκκλησιαζομένων οὐ τῶν ἀποκρύφων μὲν ἡ πρώτη ἐπιστολή. Τὴν γὰρ δευτέραν καὶ τρίτην οἱ πατέρες ἀποκανονίζουσι (Chrysost. *Opp.*, vi. 430).

[2] *Opp.*, xi. 391: κτᾶσθε βιβλία φάρμακα τῆς ψυχῆς. εἰ μηδὲν ἕτερον βούλεσθε τὴν γοῦν καινὴν κτήσασθε, τὸν ἀπόστολον, τὰς πράξεις, τὰ εὐαγγέλια. Montfaucon prints τῶν ἀποστόλων τὰς πράξεις, but the omission of St. Paul in a homily on a text from that apostle would appear to me quite as singular as that construction.

[3] Theodoret, *Prooem. in Hebr., Opp.* iii. 541, ed. Hal.

Up to this point I have been collecting the testimonies of the principal Greek Fathers of the second half of the fourth century. We have seen that these testimonies do not at all agree with one another, neither regarding the canon of the Old Testament nor regarding the elements of which the sacred collection of the New Covenant ought to be composed. In other words, we have seen that regarding several writings, the general opinion was not at all fixed. But, after all, these testimonies are from simple individuals who are expressing their own personal views, and who, notwithstanding the high consideration they enjoyed, cannot throw a decisive weight into the scale of history. We possess other documents of a more general character: on the one hand, translations of the Bible which, as I have already remarked, could not but be made from collections complete and exactly determined; on the other hand, decisions of councils or other declarations in a form more or less official. Let us see if these documents establish, any more than the texts just analysed, that uniformity of the scriptural canon of which traditional science speaks, and for which we have been seeking in vain up to this point.

The national Church of Syria continued to use its translation called the *Peschito*, consecrated by long-continued usage. It did not contain, as is well known, the Apocalypse and four Catholic Epistles; but we have just seen that the Greek Christians in Syria were equally content with this less extensive collection. This does not mean that the five antilegomena were unknown in Syria; we know the contrary by the works of the most celebrated Syrian theologian of this period, Ephraim († 378). He makes use of them, and his example is one more proof that the line of demarcation between the various classes of books was uncertain and fluctuating here as elsewhere.

The same fact is revealed, but by totally different symptoms, in the Aethiopic Church in Abyssinia, to which country Christianity had penetrated towards the period of the Nicæan Council, and where the Christians soon possessed a Bible in the national tongue. No complete manuscript of it now exists, but, from the numerous mutilated copies which have been examined and from the text of the canons that formerly regulated this church, it is clear that in it were read not only all the books which the Church of Egypt, the metropolitan of the Church of Abyssinia, received in the time of Athanasius, but also the apocrypha of the Old Testament and a certain number of pseudepigrapha—*e.g.*, the book of Enoch mentioned in the Epistle of Jude, the fourth book of Ezra, the vision of Isaiah, &c. The originals of these works are now lost, but they have been in part preserved through this very Aethiopic translation. There are even manuscripts existing in which it is plain that Enoch and Job preceded the Pentateuch, simply because these two patriarchs are more ancient than Moses, and the position given to the former of these two books seems to imply a presumption of its canonicity. In a list of the holy books (included in what are called the Apostolic Canons,[1] as they are received in the Aethiopic Church), their total number is carried up to 81, of which 46 are for the Old Testament (the Apocrypha all included), and 35 for the New. This latter number is explained by the addition of the eight books of the *Apostolic Constitutions*, and at the same time betrays the Greek origin of the catalogue. The division into eight books does not appear in the Aethiopic version of the *Constitutions*.[2] I shall close this long series of testimonies by

---

[1] See further on p. 182.

[2] As to the Armenian literature, of which I ought at this point to say something, I do not know it sufficiently well to say what was the primitive canon of the churches of that nation. The editions printed in our time might well be more or less directly dependent on the Vulgate. Still, so far as I have been able to compare them, they present some peculiarities worthy

bringing before my readers two very interesting texts which can both pretend to a kind of official authority.

There is first the famous sixtieth canon [1] of the Council of Laodicea, commonly but wrongly regarded as the definite rule on the subject of the canon for the Eastern Church. This Council of Laodicea is uncertain in date, but plausible arguments place it in 363. It was a simple provincial synod which had no pretention to make laws for the universal Church; and, if its canons were afterwards adopted outside of its province and included in the collections of ecclesiastical rules, this was not in the least owing to the official position of their first authors. The fifty-ninth of these canons of Laodicea forbids in the church the use of psalms composed by private individuals (modern hymns as compared with those of David) or of non-canonical books. The canonical books of the Old and New Testaments are alone to be employed in liturgical usage.[2] Then follows a sixtieth canon giving the list of these canonical books, and giving it evidently as complete and official. It is true that the authenticity of this canon has been much doubted in our day; and certainly if exterior proofs—*i.e.*, proofs drawn from manuscripts and quotations—were alone to decide this question, we would perhaps be bound to cease assigning this text to the Laodicean Fathers. But I confess that this question of authenticity concerns me very little. The

---

of remark. They include three books of the Maccabees, inserted among the other historical books; they change the order of the prophets; they put the Epistle to the Hebrews before the Pastoral Epistles, and add at the very end Ecclesiasticus, a second recension of Daniel, the Prayer of Manasseh, a third epistle to the Corinthians, and the legend of St. John. It may be that some of these works formerly occupied a more honourable place.

[1] The name *canons*, as every one knows, is given to the laws and regulations emanating from councils or other ecclesiastical authorities. The simultaneous use of this term in two different senses cannot here give rise to any confusion.

[2] ὅτι οὐ δεῖ ἰδιωτικοὺς ψαλμοὺς λέγεσθαι ἐν τῇ ἐκκλησίᾳ οὐδὲ ἀκανόνιστα βιβλία ἀλλὰ μόνα τὰ κανονικὰ τῆς καινῆς καὶ παλαιᾶς διαθήκης.

list itself is positively very old; it is identically the same with that given by Cyril of Jerusalem, so that, if it must be assigned to a later date, it might always be said that its editor took it from a Father contemporary with the Council. It is all the more important to lay stress on this fact, since the fifty-ninth canon itself, whose authenticity is unquestioned, reproduces a principle which, as we saw, was also formulated by Cyril and most energetically recommended. From all this, I do not hesitate to say that the sixtieth canon of Laodicea, authentic or not, expresses regarding the sacred collection an opinion belonging positively to the fourth century and adopted by several Greek Fathers of different countries; in the Old Testament, twenty-two books without the Apocrypha;[1] in the New Testament, twenty-six without the Apocalypse. And this omission of the Apocalypse is by no means a simple measure of pedagogic precaution, indicating that this book is not of a nature to be read in public. If the text of the sixtieth canon is authentic, its silence regarding the Apocalypse excludes that book from the number of canonical writings; and if it is not authentic, so that the classification given in the fifty-ninth article does not apply to it,[2] we know none the less from Cyril what meaning we must attach to it.

The second collection of ecclesiastical regulations, old enough to be discussed in the present chapter and containing a text relative to our subject, is that which the Greek Church has received under the name of *Apostolic Canons*, and which traditional opinion declares to be of a very early date. Among the arrangements contained in this canon, there may

---

[1] It is understood that in the case of Jeremiah, Daniel and Esther, we have to do with the Greek recension, for the text says formally: Ἱερεμίας καὶ Βαρούχ, θρῆνοι καὶ ἐπιστολή. See the note on the canon of Athanasius, p. 165.

[2] It would be so quite as much from the standpoint of any one who added Article 60.

no doubt be some very ancient; still, as a collection, they were probably not in existence before the fifth century, and were then added as an appendix to the eight books of the *Constitutions*. In the recension adopted in the East, there are eighty-five articles.[1] The following concern us here. The sixtieth pronounces the deposition of any one who should publicly use in the Church pseudepigrapha and impious books. The eighty-fifth recommends to all, both clerical and lay, the books of the Bible as venerable and sacred, and gives a complete catalogue of them. In the Old Testament the order is the same down to Esther as with us; then come *three* books of the Maccabees,[2] Job and the others in the received order, with no other apocryphal books. At the end of the Old Testament it is said; " Further you will add, for the instruction of youth, the Wisdom of the very learned Sirach.[3] Our own books (it is the apostles who are speaking) —*i.e.*, those of the New Testament, are: four gospels, fourteen epistles of Paul, two of Peter, three of John, one of James, one of Jude, two of Clement and the *Constitutions*, which I, Clement, dictated to you bishops in eight books, but which must not be used in public before every one, as they contain mystical things.[4] Finally, the Acts of ourselves, the apostles."

At first sight, this list seems singular enough; but on closer examination, it can be explained without much difficulty, and even the date of its composition may be approximately determined. At bottom, it is the list which we have seen more than once in the course of the fourth century: the Old Testament without the Apocrypha, the

---

[1] The Latin recension of Dionysius Exiguus includes only the first 50.
[2] Some MSS. also mention Judith after Esther.
[3] ἔξωθεν ὑμῖν προσιστορείσθω μανθάνειν ὑμῶν τοὺς υἱοὺς τὴν σοφίαν τοῦ πολυμαθοῦς Σιράχ.
[4] An allusion to the parts of worship in which the catechumens did **not** take part.

New without the Apocalypse. At the same time, I am much inclined to believe that this article has been altered several times. The Maccabees may have found an entrance contrary to the opinion of the first editor, as is the case very probably with the book of Judith which is added in some manuscripts. Still, we saw that Origen, while putting aside the other apocrypha, expressly mentions the Maccabees as a kind of complement of the Old Testament. Ecclesiasticus in like manner is recommended by Athanasius and Epiphanius; the former of these Fathers (who adds to it also the *Constitutions*) assigns it a place analogous to that reserved for it here. Finally, in regard to the epistles of Clement, we have also met with them in the Codex Alexandrinus, which must have been written, like this article of the Apostolic Canons, in the course of the fifth century at the very latest.

My readers will demand no other proofs before accepting this fact which I have advanced—viz., until after the fourth century, the Eastern Church, though speaking of a scriptural canon, though feeling the need of it both for science and popular instruction, though making efforts to establish it by means of its theologians, legists, and synods, did not succeed in producing absolute uniformity on this point among the doctors and the dioceses, or in fixing a sure and invariable line to separate the inspired canonical books from those of a quite different value. If all the attempts I have recorded fell short of their end, and if, after all, there was agreement towards the end of the second century only regarding what had been already sanctioned by usage, it is because the canon, whether in the earliest times or later, was formed only by this ecclesiastical usage, in part local and accidental, and was not formed according to scientific principles and methods, nor by the ascendency of one primordial and pre-eminent authority. Hence, the greater the distance from the point of departure, the less possible it was to efface the divergences of opinion. The generations preceding having pronounced no supreme decree, the generation of Athanasius came too late to gain universal currency for the decree which it *dared*[1] to formulate.

[1] ἡ ἐμαυτοῦ τόλμη (Athanas. *Ep. fest.*, *l. c.*)

CHAPTER XI.

CONTINUATION—THE WESTERN CHURCH.

LET us see now whether the Latin Church was more fortunate or better advised than her elder sister at this period when, more than at any other, literary glories were blazing on the theological horizon at the two extremities of the Christian world. The West had less science, fewer resources, perhaps even less interest in concerning itself with this question from the dogmatic point of view; but on the other hand it was more inclined to consider the question from the standpoint of ecclesiastical discipline and more capable of settling it as a matter of administration, being still very much under the influence of imperial traditions in government. If, then, it had come to a definite solution, this would prove not so much the intrinsic value of the rule adopted, as the imperious necessity for solving the question, and the powerful means used for that end. If, on the contrary, that end was not attained, the opinion expressed at the close of the preceding chapter will receive the most striking confirmation.

I begin with Hilary of Poitiers (†368), who forms, so to speak, the intermediate link between the two churches, his speculation and exegesis connecting him in a very marked way with the East. In the Prologue to his Commentary on the Psalms, he gives a list of the books of the Old Testament, copied literally from the text of Origen which we have analysed;[1] the same analogy to the alphabet, the same order of the books, the same omission of the Apocrypha, the same express mention of the letter of Jeremiah. There

---

[1] Hilarii Pict., *Prol. in Ps.* § 15. Comp. Euseb., vi. 25.

is, however, at the end a curious addition. To these twenty-two books, he says, there are added Judith and Tobit, in order to make up the number of the letters of the Greek alphabet. Very probably the Bishop of Poitiers was not the first to make this discovery, especially as he takes care to add that the Roman alphabet stands midway between the two others. But it would be a great mistake to infer from this that he at least held this number to be fixed and the canon of the Old Covenant to be defined in limit. The other apocrypha are in his eyes not less the works of the prophets, the Scriptures to be quoted on the same level as the other Scriptures.[1] As to the New Testament, some importance should certainly be attached to the fact that all the Fathers, Hilary as well as those of the Eastern Church, abstain from mentioning any fixed number for this collection, as they do for the Old Testament. Why do they not appeal to the twenty-four letters of the alphabet, by counting Corinthians, Thessalonians, and Timothy as single epistles, as is done with certain Hebrew books, or by doing the same with the Catholic Epistles? There is but one answer; but it is enough: no number was fixed officially. In this case the abstention is all the more remarkable that Hilary might have brought out the perfect harmony between the two collections, since his canonical collection of the New Testament only contained twenty-two books, like that of Origen, and there is not in all his writings the least trace of the five disputed Catholic Epistles. When it is remembered that this author lived more than a century after the celebrated professor of Alexandria, in totally different surroundings, at a period when the current collection had been enriched by some books in many dioceses, is it

---

[1] For Wisdom, see *De Trin.*, i. 7; *Psalm* 135 § 11; for Ecclesiasticus, *Prol. in Ps.* § 20; for Susanna, *Psalm* 52 § 19; for 2 Maccabees, *Psalm* 134 § 25; for Tobit, *Psalm* 129 § 7.

not astonishing that he should have been able to adhere to an authority so ancient and so distant, without giving heed to what was going on near him? Like Origen, he assigns the Epistle to the Hebrews to Paul[1] contrary to the general usage of the Latins; like Origen, he is acquainted with but two Catholic Epistles as forming part of the canon, contrary to the usage of all the churches of his time. I leave to my readers the task of drawing from these facts the logical and legitimate conclusions; but the facts seem to me to condemn the thesis I have been contending against, and to demonstrate that at this period the collection was not closed and fixed. Hilary, observe, was one of the pillars of orthodoxy.

I pass now to an Italian author, Philastrius of Brescia († towards 387). We have from him a list of 150 heresies, from which list we obtain very instructive information regarding the state of the canon in the West towards the end of the fourth century, and also unfortunately regarding the profound ignorance which from that time began to manifest itself even among the leaders of the church. In § 88,[2] he takes occasion to speak of a "heresy called apocryphal (:), *i.e.*, secret, a heresy which accepts only the prophets and the apostles, but not the canonical writings, *i.e.*, the law and the prophets, viz., the Old and New Testament."[3] To make some sense out of this rigmarole, we must change the text and suppose that the author said or meant to say that these heretics read only books *pretending* to be prophetic and apostolic, pseudepigrapha. Or perhaps he had heard some vague talk about sects rejecting the Mosaic law, and, for want of positive knowledge, reported the fact badly.

---

[1] *De Trinit.,* iv. § 11.

[2] Edition of Fabricius, 1721. The numbers vary in the editions.

[3] *Haeresis est etiam quae apocrypha, i.e. secreta dicitur, quae solum prophetas et apostolos accipit, non scripturas canonicas, i.e., legem et prophetas, vetus scilicet et novum testamentum.*

Further on he adds that "the apostles and their successors have decreed[1] that no one in the Catholic Church should read anything but the Law, the Prophets, the Gospels, the Acts, the thirteen Epistles of Paul, and seven others added to the Acts." Clearly in this Philastrius was copying a catalogue of Eastern origin, and even his assertion that he is transcribing an apostolic decree rests on an illusion till then foreign to the Latin Church but formulated in express terms in Greece or Asia, as I have shown at the end of the preceding chapter. The only circumstance which might justify a doubt on this point is the omission of the Epistle to the Hebrews, and it must be admitted that in this the author wrote under the influence of the established usage of his country. He says in continuation: "The hidden— *i.e.*, apocryphal—writings are to be read by the perfect for moral edification, but not by every one, because the unintelligent heretics have made in them all kinds of additions and mutilations."[2] This last phrase gives us the measure of the *intelligence* of the Bishop of Brescia himself, and shows us how useless it is to resort to critical conjectures in order to prevent him from saying things without common sense. For never had it occurred to any one in the Church to recommend the reading of the books of the heretics for forming the morals of the perfect, while forbidding them to those who are not perfect. Philastrius has evidently fallen here into the strangest confusion. The Greek Fathers had recognised in the apocrypha of the *Old Testament* (Ecclesiasticus, Wisdom, Tobit, etc.) a relative value and permitted them to be used in instruction, while refusing at the same

---

[1] *Statutum est ab apostolis et eorum successoribus non aliud legi debere in ecclesia catholica nisi legem et prophetas et evangelia et actus et Pauli tredecim epistolas et septem alias*, etc.

[2] *Scripturae autem absconditae, i.e., apocryphae etsi legi debent morum causa a perfectis, non ab omnibus legi debent, quia non intelligentes multa addiderunt et tulerunt quae voluerunt haeretici.*

time to put them on the level of canonical books. He, on the other hand, though believing himself to be reproducing their opinion, is thinking of the pseudonymous Acts of Andrew, of John, of Peter, etc., whose miraculous results he willingly accepts as suitable for edification, while he rejects the doctrines inserted in them by the heretics.

Having thus established the true meaning of this paragraph of our author, let us see what he says elsewhere on the same subject. If hitherto it has been possible for us to believe that he observes a prudent reserve regarding the apocrypha of the Old Testament and makes the example of the Greeks his rule, copying them without understanding them, we shall soon discover that such is not the case. These books are in his eyes writings inspired like the others; they were written by prophets, Solomon among others;[1] and Philastrius on this point does not depart from the usage of the Western Churches in the form in which I shall afterwards state it. There is the same confusion in regard to the New Testament. A little ago the Apocalypse did not appear in the number of the books declared to be canonical by *the apostles and their successors*, because the Eastern Fathers, from whom this notice is borrowed, held that opinion at this period. But § 60 reproaches the heretics for rejecting the Gospel and Apocalypse of John, and this last book is employed as canonical in the course of the work.[2] It is clear that everywhere a distinction must be drawn between Philastrius the editor and Philastrius the compiler. He copies more or less exactly texts of Greek origin without even observing that they contradict himself. The Epistle to the Hebrews, which was likewise omitted in the preceding text, is frequently quoted in other passages

---

[1] See *e.g.*, regarding Wisdom, *Haer.*, 26, 95, 108, 110; for Ecclesiasticus, *Haer.*, 26; for 2 Maccabees, *Haer.*, 18; for pseudo-Daniel, *Haer.*, 96.

[2] See *e.g.*, *Haer.*, 42.

as an apostolic writing.[1] He even devotes to it a special paragraph where his confusion of ideas is again manifest; not knowing how to strike his course in the controversy between the Greeks and the Latins, he transcribed alternately notes borrowed from both. His text runs thus:[2] "There are persons who do not acknowledge the Epistle to the Hebrews to be by Paul, but say that it is by the apostle Barnabas or by Clement, Bishop of Rome; others attribute it and also the Epistle to the Laodiceans to the evangelist Luke. They wish, indeed, to read the writings of the blessed apostle; and, because some people badly advised have made certain additions to it, it is not read in the church. It is much read by some; but to the assembled people only his thirteen epistles are read, sometimes that to the Hebrews. Its elegant style and rhetoric have caused some to say that it is not Paul's; and it is not read because it is said in it that Christ was made, as well as on account of what is said about penitence, etc."[3] What are we to think of this passage, and how are we to give to it any sort of intelligible meaning? I shall not stop to ask how Philastrius can rank as heretics all the Fathers who have uttered one of the above-mentioned hypotheses regarding the Epistle to the Hebrews, just after declaring that the apostles and their successors gave official recognition to only thirteen epistles by Paul. A contradiction so glaring is explicable only in a writer whose whole work consists in

---

[1] *Haer.*, 117, 122, 127, 134, 144, 150, etc.

[2] *Haer.*, 89. *Haeresis quorundam de ep. Pauli ad Hebraeos.*

[3] *Sunt alii quoque qui ep. P. ad H. non adserunt esse ipsius sed dicunt aut Barnabae esse Ap. aut Clementis ep. alii autem Lucae ev. ajunt epistolam etiam ad Laodicenses scriptam. Scripta b. Apostoli quidem volunt legere. Et quia addiderunt in ea quaedam non bene sentientes inde non legitur in ecclesia. Etsi legitur in quibusdam non tamen in ecclesia legitur populo nisi tredecim epp. ejus et ad Hebraeos interdum. Et in ea quia rhetorice scripsit sermone plausibili, inde non putant esse Apostoli. Et quia factum Christum dicit in ea inde non legitur, etc.*

accumulating from all quarters scattered notices which he heaps together in his miserable compilation without trying to bring them into harmony, perhaps without knowing Greek enough to understand them, and certainly without knowing Latin enough to make himself understood. But I shall ask a bishop who counts heresies by the dozen, where he learned that people badly advised have made additions to the Epistle to the Hebrews? What are these additions? And when did the church ever renounce one of its sacred books, because an outsider was supposed to have somewhere altered a copy? Or is it possible to imagine that heresy had ever succeeded in falsifying them all? But what am I saying? If the church no longer wished to read this epistle to the people because there were passages in it apparently favourable to heresy,[1] then it was the Catholics and not the heretics who thus excluded it from the canon. It may be seen from these considerations what kind of witness we have here, and we might have spared ourselves the trouble of subjecting him to a preliminary examination, if some of his modern critics did not make him the subject of a critical and philological skill worthy of such a model.

The two authors we have just been consulting were evidently under the influence of the Greeks in the opinions they express regarding the extent of the biblical collection. Only Hilary represents a more ancient phase of traditional opinion than does Philastrius, who besides understands nothing of the divergences he finds, and is acquainted neither with their origin nor bearing. We come now to a

[1] The author alludes to iii. 2 and vi. 4, which might be said to be written in the sense of the Arians and Novatians. If he asserts that the epistle, in the opinion of certain people, contained a passage suspected of Arianism, we should remember that at the same period it was said in the East that the Arians alone rejected this epistle because it was too openly against them. These contradictions arise from the habitual practice of attributing to a heresy every difference in literary judgments, the origin of which was no longer known.

third Latin author, who was equally familiar with the ideas of the East where he had lived for a long time, but was more desirous of positive facts, and adopted the views prevalent in his time. Toranius Rufinus, presbyter of Aquileia († 410), reproduces, all but exactly, what we have already found in Athanasius: in the Old Testament the Jewish canon, including Esther; in the New Testament the complete series of the books now placed there, with the seven Catholic Epistles, the Epistle to the Hebrews, and the Apocalypse. In the next chapter I shall have to give some attention to his ideas and dogmatic definitions regarding the sacred books. At present I simply state that in drawing up this catalogue, he appeals to no official authority, no standard and authorised edition, but only to the tradition of the Fathers.[1] We have sufficient information regarding the value of this tradition which, even in the time of Rufinus, was far from being fixed on all points.

I have just been proving that the East had a certain influence on the opinions of the Latin authors of whom I have been speaking. But, in general, the West was separated from the East on several very important points in its ecclesiastical and liturgical traditions regarding the use of the Bible. At first, the Latin churches did not share in that kind of repulsion for the Apocalypse which we have noted among the Greeks; then they were not willing, or they did not know how, to make any distinction between the different elements of which the Old Testament was composed (primitive Hebrew canon and additions of the Septuagint), as their Latin Bible did not furnish them with the means; finally, the Epistle to the Hebrews, added to the Greek collection at the beginning of the third century,

---

[1] Rufini *Expos. in Symbol.*, ch. 37 : *Quae sunt N. ac V. T. volumina quae secundum majorum* TRADITIONEM *per ipsum Sp. S. inspirata* CREDUNTUR *et ecclesiis Christi tradita, competens videtur in hoc loco evidenti numero, sicut ex patrum monumentis accepimus, designare.*

was hardly known in Italy, in Africa, in Gaul, where it was introduced with much greater difficulty than certain other epistles formerly less widely circulated, because it was anonymous, and the volume of Paul's epistles had for centuries been closed and known.[1] This last fact is so well established that I do not think it necessary to collect all the testimonies proving it for the fourth or fifth century. I prefer even to remind my readers that this exclusion was not universal. Besides the writers already named, there may be quoted others who admit the Pauline origin of the epistle—*e.g.*, Lucifer of Cagliari, and Ambrose of Milan; while Zeno of Verona, the deacon Hilary of Rome, Optatus of Milevis, and others less known, represent the majority. Their dissension, which is of no importance so far as the authenticity or origin of this epistle is concerned, is of great importance for the history of the canon.

It is this same difference between the Greeks and the Latins which engrosses and embarrasses the two most celebrated theologians of this period in the Western Church, Jerome and Augustine. Their testimony is specially interesting, because while we read it we cannot help thinking that they are making, so to speak, an inventory of the opinions and usages of their time, as Eusebius had done at another period, and that the results they give are what might be called the last utterance of tradition. We shall see that the generations following *down to the sixteenth century* understood their testimony in this way. Let us therefore give most careful attention to what they say.

In the works of Jerome there are several catalogues of the sacred books, two being complete and embracing the whole Bible. The first is the famous Epistle to Paulinus,

---

[1] *Latina consuetudo non recipit*, etc. (Jerome, *In Isai.* iii., 6). *Multi latini dubitant*, etc. (Id. *In Matth.* xxvi.) *Apud Romanos usque hodie quas Pauli ep. non habetur* (Id. *Catal.*, 59. Comp. *In Zach.*, viii., etc.)

printed as a prologue in all the old editions of the Vulgate; the second is his preface to the translation of the four books of Kings. There is besides a recension of the New Testament in the first chapters of his *History of Ecclesiastical Writers*. Use might be made also of numerous passages in his other works. To make the matter clearer, I shall treat separately the different questions here presented.

The preface to Kings enumerates the books of the Old Testament in general, according to the Jewish custom: five books of the Law, the first and the last prophets to the number of eight, and nine hagiographa—in all twenty-two. Only, to get this number, he had to join Ruth with Judges, and Lamentations with Jeremiah. Hence Jerome says that, if they are left in their place in the last volume, there will be a total of twenty-four books, which may be accepted because there are also twenty-four elders round the throne of God in the Apocalypse. Still the order of the hagiographa is different from that in our Hebrew Bibles, and we do not know whether it was altered by Jerome himself, or stood thus in the copies of his time. The catalogue in the Epistle to Paulinus differs from all the others we know, and is a fresh proof that the old Bibles had no fixed order. Job precedes Joshua in it; the prophets come immediately after Kings; next to them come David and Solomon, Esther, Chronicles, Ezra, and Nehemiah. As five of these books are double, they represent the five final letters of the Hebrew alphabet and complete the number of twenty-seven. This puerile desire for mystical analogies constantly reappears, and I direct attention to it once more to establish the fact that the canon of the New Testament was not solid enough in its basis to permit such ingenious analogies. The most interesting point of all in these two catalogues is, that they are positively based on the tradition of the Synagogue. As Jerome had studied the Hebrew text, an accomplishment of which no other Father since Origen could boast, the fact is beyond doubt. Elsewhere he declares formally that Wisdom, Ecclesiasticus, Tobit, Judith, are not in the canon.[1] But he cannot withdraw himself altogether from the customs of his Church, and his attachment to tradition is more powerful than his scruples as a scholar, his devotion greater than his logic. Thus, in his preface to the book of Tobit, he says:[2] "The Jews have *excluded* it from the list of the Holy Scriptures, and have reduced it to the rank of the hagiographa.[3] Now they reproach me for having translated it, against their principles, in a Latin Bible. But I have preferred to displease the Pharisees and yield to the invitations of the bishops," who evidently asked that the book should not be left out. The preface to Judith runs thus: "With the Jews this book is ranked among the hagiographa, and its authority is considered to be insufficient for settling controverted points. *But* as the Council of Nicæa reckoned it among the Holy Scriptures, I have yielded to your invitation, etc." I suppose no one will be angry with Jerome for having made it a point to agree with the Nicæan Fathers in everything; and, if we cannot but suppose that he was mistaken about that council's opinion, it would nevertheless be a fact that he did not refuse Judith a place in the canon of the Bible. I do not intend to avail myself of these two texts for drawing any inference that Jerome mixed the Apocrypha with the other books of the Old Testament. On the contrary, I know the care he takes in his translation of Daniel and Esther to separate the two component elements by marks

---

[1] *Prol. galeat.*, p. 13. *Præf. ad Salom.*, p. 18. *Opp.* tom. III. ed. Francf.

[2] *Quem Hebræi de catalogo div. S.S. secantes his quæ hagiographa memorant manciparunt . . . sed melius esse judicans displicere Pharisæorum judicio et episcoporum jussionibus deservire, institi ut potui.*

[3] Just now the *hagiographa* were Job, Psalms, Solomon, Daniel, etc. !

and critical notes. But I was anxious to prove that the line of demarcation is always fluctuating, and that a writer so solicitous as the illustrious monk of Bethlehem of running counter to no opinion which could call itself orthodox, was led from time to time to make concessions in two opposite directions. The matter had not been settled in a supreme court, and there was a risk of compromising oneself whatever one said.

In regard to the New Testament, the dedication to Paulinus enumerates all our twenty-seven books, the Acts coming after Paul's Epistles. It is not so much an historical and literary introduction as a piece of somewhat high-flown rhetoric, and yet Jerome speaks in it as if the canonicity of the Epistle to the Hebrews were very doubtful.[1] From what we have established above, the phrase he uses (that this epistle is *excluded from the number* by most churches or theologians) can have no other meaning than that indicated. Still, when he comes to write the simple prose of the literary scholar, he makes more critical reserves. He knows and writes that the authorship of the second epistle that bears Peter's name is disputed *by most*;[2] and, when he adds that this arose from the difference of style, he thereby reveals not so much the motive for excluding it, as the expedient invented by the defenders of its authenticity. He himself professes elsewhere that this difference arises from the apostle having used in turn various secretary interpreters,[3] thus insinuating at one stroke and with inconceivable levity that we possess only translations, or even editions, made freely according to general directions from the

---

[1] *Paulus Ap. ad* SEPTEM *ecclesias scribit; octava enim ad Hebraeos a* PLERISQUE *extra numerum ponitur.*

[2] *Catal. Vir. Ill.*, ch. 1 : *Secunda a plerisque ejus esse negatur, propter styli cum priore differentiam.*

[3] *Ex quo intelligimus pro necessitate rerum eum diversis usum esse interpretibus (Epist. ad Hedib.* qu. 11 : *Opp.* iii. 102).

Bishop of Rome.[1] He knows likewise that the Epistle of James was considered to have been written by another in that disciple's name (whom he makes a cousin of the Lord in order to put him in the number of the Twelve, contrary to the general opinion of the first centuries); but he adds that in time it gained a footing.[2] He reports that the Epistle of Jude is rejected by most because it appeals to an apocryphal testimony; nevertheless, he says, it was already at a very early period reckoned among the Holy Scriptures.[3] Let us note this word *plerique*, the most, which so constantly recurs with him. It clearly reveals to us a fact which we ought not to neglect. If we reckoned only the authors whom we can still consult, the term in question would hardly be justified; on the other hand, it is far from probable that there were so many opponents or critics among the authors now lost. But Jerome's expression will be fully explained, if we suppose that most of the churches had a collection less complete than that known to our witnesses, who were all more or less occupied with theological quarrels. It seems to me that the books which were not included in the collection at the time when it was formed— *i.e.*, at the end of the second century—must have had great difficulty in gaining an entrance everywhere even in the most remote churches. The successive increase, in turn attempted, patronised, or resisted by various scholars, must long have remained a question for the school and study, and cannot easily have penetrated to the masses and popular usage. If this view of the case be not an illusory conjecture, Jerome's *plerique* gives us more reliable informa-

---

[1] For Jerome also *knows* that Peter was for twenty-five years Bishop of Rome. It is an integral part of his *testimony.*

[2] *Catal.*, ch. 2 : *Quae et ipsa ab alio quodam sub nomine ejus edita asseritur, licet paulatim tempore procedente obtinuerit autoritatem.*

[3] *Ibid.* ch. 4: *Quia de libro Enoch qui apocryphus est assumit testimonium a plerisque rejicitur ; tamen autoritatem vetustate et* usu *meruit.*

tion about the canon of the fourth century than all the catalogues I have hitherto copied.

But let us continue our examination of Jerome. This is what he says regarding Paul:[1] "He wrote nine epistles to seven churches, besides to his disciples, two to Timothy, one to Titus, and one to Philemon. The epistle, entitled *to the Hebrews*, is considered not to be his because of the difference in style, but to be by Barnabas, according to Tertullian, or by Luke, according to others, or by Clement of Rome, who was supposed to have committed the apostle's thoughts to writing." Jerome, for his own part, adopts the least tenable hypothesis of all, that of a Hebrew original and a translation made by another hand. Moreover, when he comes to speak of this epistle, he usually introduces it with a doubtful formula.[2] This is true even in the passage where he most frankly expresses his desire to see it received in the West as it was in the East, and where he naively invites the Greeks and Latins to adopt each other's *antilegomena*, setting his own syncretism before them as an example. This passage is so very curious that I must ask my readers to think over it. It shows how carelessly critical opinion was formulated, since the author has no fear of falling into the most flagrant contradictions (*all Greek authors attribute it to Paul, though most believe it to be by Barnabas or Clement*), of affirming things which

---

[1] *Catal.*, c. 5.

[2] *Comm. in Tit.*, i. and ii.; *in Ephes.*, ii.; *in Ezech.*, xxviii. etc.: *si quis vult recipere; in Amos*, viii.: *sive Pauli sive alterius esse putas; in Jerem.*, xxxi.: *quicunque est ille qui scripsit.*

[3] *Ep. ad Dardan., Opp.* iii. 46 : *Illud nostris dicendum est hanc ep. non solum ab eccl. orientis sed ab omnibus (?) retro graeci sermonis scriptoribus quasi Pauli ap. suscipi, licet eam* PLERIQUE (!) *vel Barnabae (? !) vel Clementis arbitrentur* ET NIHIL INTERESSE CUJUS SIT *cum ecclesiastici viri sit et quotidie lectione eccl. celebretur. Quod si eam latinorum consuetudo non recipit inter SS. canonicas, nec Graecorum eccl. apocalypsin eadem libertate suscipiunt, et tamen* NOS *utraque suscipimus* NEQUAQUAM HUJUS TEMPORIS consuetudinem sed veterum auctoritatem sequentes.

we know positively to be imaginary, and insinuating that the churches of his time *abandoned* the healthy tradition of the Fathers, because they do not accept a proper name which he himself declares to be, after all, a matter of indifference. I insist on all these details in order to make it manifest that in no case was the fourth century fit to finish a critical task which the second had had to leave incomplete.

The following is a last note of Jerome on the Epistles of John :[1] "He wrote one single epistle, which is acknowledged by all the learned men of the church. The two others which begin with these words, etc. . . . are attributed to a presbyter John, whose tomb is still pointed out at Ephesus." I do not lay much stress on this hypothesis; I do not know a single ancient author who gave it out before Jerome; but I see in it a new confirmation of what was advanced above. The fact of the omission of the two short epistles which bear John's name is established for certain by Jerome's note; but, while this omission arises, in my opinion, from their not appearing in the primitive canon, Jerome and perhaps others wish to explain it as the sequel of a conjecture already made by Dionysius of Alexandria in regard to the Apocalypse. But this opinion of the scholars of the time, however incontrovertible, would certainly not have been a cause of exclusion. We have hardly ever seen any book excluded from the canon which once had a place there; but I have sufficiently shown how difficult it was to obtain an entrance for any who were not in it from the beginning.

Thus Jerome, in spite of the most strongly avowed intention of giving to the Bible of the people an authentic

[1] Catal., ch. 9: *Scripsit unam epistolam quae ab universis ecclesiasticis et eruditis viris probatur. Reliquae autem duae. . . . Joannis presbyteri asseruntur* (comp. ch. 18)—In another place (*Ep. ad Evagr., Opp.* ii. 220) he makes no difficulty about attributing these epistles to the evangelist.

and readable text, and also a unity of design—Jerome, the learned philologist, the diligent compiler, the indefatigable visitor of foreign countries and curious libraries, has only succeeded in showing how far removed his age was from this unity, and in furnishing to the centuries after him the means of perpetuating the uncertainty and of never forgetting the divergences of tradition and of ecclesiastical customs. We shall now see how far his illustrious contemporary, the Bishop of Hippo, was more successful, Augustine, the man of theory, the theologian *par excellence*, whose genius paved the way for the reform of the sixteenth century, and still rules, in certain aspects, the teaching of the schools. With him, the need of putting an end to these eternal hesitations about certain parts of the canon was much more imperious, the authority of any decision much more absolute, the interest in the work of criticism much feebler, and the means of carrying it on much more insufficient than with Jerome. But, for want of historical investigations, he had to recommend and assert two means of arriving at the end—dogmatic rule and the intervention of authority. On this ground we shall see him at work.

It would not be difficult to gather from the numerous works of Augustine phrases equally doubtful regarding the books on which opinions varied—*e.g.*, reserves made regarding the value of the Apocrypha of the Old Testament,[1] or the Epistle to the Hebrews.[2] But the very rareness of such passages in these vast folios, where biblical texts are quoted

---

[1] *Contra Gaudent.*, i. 31 : *Hanc Scripturam quæ appellatur Machabæorum non habent Judæi . . . sed recepta est ab ecclesia non inutiliter si sobrie legatur vel audiatur.*—*Civ. Dei.*, XVII., 20 : *Salomonis tres libri recepti sunt in auctoritatem canonicam . . . alii duo . . . propter eloquii similitudinem ut Salomonis dicantur obtinuit consuetudo ; non autem esse ipsius non dubitant doctiores. Eos tamen in auctoritatem maxime occidentalis antiquitus recepit Ecclesia.*

[2] *De pecc. mer.*, i. 27 : *Ep. ad. Hebræos nonnullis incerta ; magis me movet auctoritas eccl. orientalium quæ hanc quoque in canonicis habet. Expos.*

in thousands, proves how little the author concerned himself about critical questions, and we ought not to stop at isolated and inconsequent words, when we find elsewhere an exact and systematic exposition of the author's own conviction. We understand that he may have found an occasional pleasure in showing casually his acquaintance with the state of such questions. There exists in his dogmatic works a very explicit and complete passage which relieves us from making any troublesome search for such facts as shall enable us to form an opinion regarding the substance of his thought of the extent of his Bible. This passage stands in the second book of his *Christian Doctrine*.[1] He treats there of biblical studies, recommending them very strongly, and giving instructions at once sensible and spirited, not such as his own exegesis, unfortunately, would lead us to expect. The following is the part which concerns us at present: " The most intelligent investigator of the divine Scriptures is the man who first reads over only the books that are called canonical, even though he does not yet understand them perfectly. Once instructed in the true faith, he will read the others with more security, and will no longer run any risk of being led astray in his weakness by the wanderings and lies of the imagination."[2] Here at the very outset there is an important point to be noted. It is very evident that in Augustine's eyes all the divine Scriptures are not canonical Scriptures, since he recommends the reading of the latter first of all and the reservation till a later time of

in Rom., § 11 : *Nonnulli eam in canonem S. S. recipere timuerunt ; sed quoquo modo se habeat ista quæstio cætt.*—*Adv. Julian.*, iii., 85 : *Fidelis fidei prædicator qui scripsit ep. cætt.* Comp. *Civ. Dei.*, xvi. 32.

[1] *De Doctr. Chr.* ii. 12 f. This part of the work, it is important to observe, was written before the Council of Carthage, 397.

[2] *Erit divinarum scripturarum solertissimus indagator qui primo totas legerit notasque habuerit, etsi nondum intellectu jam tamen lectione, duntaxat eas quae appellantur canonicæ. Nam cæteras securius leget fide veritatis instructus cætt.*

those books of the divine Scriptures which are not canonical. In a different form, it is the same fact as that we have so often met with already, the existence of two collections, the one more exclusive, the other more copious. The only difference to be marked here is that the term *divine books* or *scriptures* is very positively given to the latter collection. Divine and canonical are therefore not quite synonymous, and we see from this first step that Augustine is siding both with the liberty which reigned in practical usage and with the doctrinal demands of the school. But this very distinction argues a more exact consciousness of the theological point of view, and necessitates a more or less precise principle for directing the choice of the faithful. Let us hear what he says further: "In order to know what are the canonical Scriptures, you must follow the authority of the greatest possible number of Catholic Churches, especially of those which were founded by the apostles and had the honour of receiving the epistles. Those received by all the churches will therefore be preferred to those received only by some. Of these latter, those will be preferred which are received by the greatest number and by the most considerable churches, to those which possess only the fewest and least important suffrages. If we were to find some patronised by the majority, while others were patronised by a respectable minority, in that case, no doubt very rare, I believe their value would be the same." I might have fine sport in criticising such a method of verifying the canonicity of

[1] *In canonicis S.S. ecclesiarum catholicarum quam plurium auctoritatem sequatur, inter quas sane illœ sunt quæ apostolicas sedes habere et epistolas accipere meruerunt. Tenebit igitur hunc modum in SS. canonicis ut eas quæ accipiuntur ab omnibus ecclesiis catholicis præponat iis quas quædam non accipiunt; in eis vero quæ non accipiuntur ab omnibus præponat eas quas plures gravioresque accipiunt, eis quas pauciores minorisque auctoritatis ecclesiæ tenent. Si autem alias invenerit aspluribus alias a gravioribus haberi, quanquam hoc facile invenire non possit, aequalis tamen auctoritatis habendas puto.*

the holy books; it is enough for me to say that it was impracticable. No simple believer ever had the means of gathering, counting, and weighing thus the suffrages of all the churches in Christendom, an Italian or an African, still less than others, since all the witnesses quoted by Augustine were in Greece and Asia, unless he were thinking by preference of Rome itself. I might add that those who try to set up against me the authority of the Bishop of Hippo, prudently suppress the better part of his text, and take care themselves not to proceed in the same way. We have only to remember that his principles issue in that famous saying which is diametrically opposed to the basis of all Protestant theology: "I would not believe in the Gospel, if the Catholic Church did not guarantee to me its authenticity."[1] But I have other reflections to make which go more directly to the heart of the question. There are then canonical Scriptures which are preferable to others? There are some which are not admitted by all the churches? There are some which are patronised only by a respectable minority? But if all this is to have any meaning, does not the illustrious bishop here make, without wishing it, a double admission, very inconvenient for his Protestant admirers? On the one hand, he admits this cardinal fact that the canon was neither closed nor uniform, and that it included, in its more extended forms, components having very various authority; on the other hand, he declares that this authority is not at all in the books, that it is not a privilege attached to their origin, but depends on the chance they have had of being circulated in the churches, of being received by a larger or smaller number of communities. And, as the text itself shows that he was speaking more especially of the epistles, Augustine evidently cannot deny that several of these, even in his day, were far

---

[1] *Contra ep. Manich.*, c. 5: *Ego evangelio non crederem nisi me catholicæ ecclesiæ auctoritas commoveret.*

from possessing all the suffrages of the churches. That being so, it is of little importance to us to know his own opinion, because he declares himself that it is not a question of history, or internal criticism, or individual appreciation, but of statistics. And this was how the science of the canon stood with a writer who was undoubtedly the greatest theologian of the early Church.

After considering the theory, let us look now to the application. We are bound to suppose that Augustine himself performed the statistical work he recommends to others. Indeed, he adds to what we have just been reading, a complete catalogue of all the books of his Bible; he introduces it even with the remark that it is the collection from which the choice will have to be made;[1] but he concerns himself little with the *greater or less* authority of the various canonical Scriptures, as depending on the number of testimonies in their support. He speaks as if he were absolutely ignorant of the state of things in the Eastern Churches. We conclude from it that in Augustine's opinion this difference had no practical bearing. The theologian could and should make distinctions; the pastor and the preacher had no need of them. His list is as follows: there are first two series of historical books in the Old Testament, the one from Genesis to Chronicles, forms a chronological whole; the second, very different in this respect, contains books having no connection with one another, and standing in no chronological order:[2] Job, Tobit, Esther, Judith, the Maccabees, Ezra. Then come the Prophets, a book of David, three of Solomon; "for the two others, Wisdom and Ecclesiasticus, are said to be Solomon's, only because of a certain resemblance;[3]

---

[1] *In quo istam considerationem versandam dicimus.*

[2] *Quae neque huic ordini neque inter se connectuntur.*—I abstain from all comment.

[3] *De quadam similitudine Salomonis esse dicuntur, qui tamen, quoniam in auctoritatem recipi meruerunt, inter propheticos numerandi sunt.*

though they are to be counted among the prophetic books, because they have merited to be *received as authoritative,*" which means, received as canonical. The list ends with the minor and greater prophets, and the total of the books of the *canon* of the Old Testament is brought up to 44.[1] This is exactly twice the number given by "the majority and the most venerable of the Fathers;" but, according to Augustine, it is that of the Church[2] and only Jews can have any other. In his New Testament he had all the twenty-seven books which stand in our Bibles. It is true that the Epistle of Jude is wanting in the list as given in the editions of Augustine; but that may be only an old error of the copyist.

Practice was decidedly more powerful than theory. The need of fixity, generally felt as it appears, caused several African synods to turn their attention to the canon. Even in 393, before Augustine became bishop, the bishops assembled at Hippo had had to draw up a list of the holy books; but the acts of this council, in their present form, seem open to criticism.[4] This is of little importance, since from the year 397 and under Augustine's direct influence, a synod of Carthage took up the matter anew and consecrated what had been previously adopted,[5] by deciding that in the assemblies of the Church, only canonical books should be read under the name *Divine Scriptures.* An exception was made in favour of the Legends of the Martyrs. The list of the canonical books attached to this decree includes the Old Testament from Genesis to the Psalter, then *five* books of

---

[1] *His quadraginta quatuor libris V. T. terminatur auctoritas.*

[2] Comp *Retract.*, ii. 4.

[3] *Civ. Dei* xviii. 26: *Liber Judith, quem sane Judæi in canone non recipere dicuntur. Ibid.,* 36: *Machabæi, quos non Judæi sed ecclesia pro canonicis habet* (comp. xvii. 20, and *Contra Gaud.* i. 31. quoted above.)

[4] *Concil Hippon.,* ch. 36, *ap.* Mansi, iii. 924.

[5] *Concil. Carthag.* iii. 47. *ap.* Mansi, iii. 891.

Solomon, the Prophets, Tobit, Judith, Esther, Ezra, and two books of the Maccabees; in the New Testament, four gospels, the Acts, *thirteen* Epistles of Paul, another by the same to the Hebrews, two of Peter, three of John, one of James, one of Jude and the Apocalypse. Finally, it was decided that the Church across the sea (Rome) should be consulted about this list. Several points for reflection are here presented. In the first place, the synod no longer admits that there are divine Scriptures which are not canonical and thus gets rid of the subtle and embarrassing distinction made by the author of *Christian Doctrine*. That was simpler at any rate. Augustine had also slipped into his list a little remnant of erudition when he said that Wisdom and Ecclesiasticus were said to be Solomon's only because of a certain resemblance;[1] the Fathers of Carthage quite simply put *five* books of Solomon. That too was simpler. But it was more difficult to decide about the Epistle to the Hebrews. Within the memory of man the Africans had only had thirteen Epistles of Paul. Augustine, more learned than the others, warmly recommended a fourteenth. It may be seen from the text quoted above what a strange formula was employed to arrange the matter to everybody's satisfaction. As to the confirmation from beyond the seas, it never came, because at Rome the Legends of the Martyrs were not read. Perhaps there were other reasons; but the very fact that the Holy See was consulted proves of itself that the canon was not fixed, and that the canon of the Italian churches was not even known at Carthage!

Still the Africans were not alone in seeking to get out of a position in which they were always speaking of canonical books without knowing exactly what they were. The un-

---

[1] Later (*Retract.*, ii. 4) he even acknowledges that he had since learnt that Solomon was not the author of Wisdom.

certainty was such that one of the greatest bishops of Gaul, Exsuperius of Toulouse, applied to the Pope to know what he was to do in this matter. Innocent I. (405) allowed himself to be much pressed, as the answer was not easy and the see of Rome had no interest in bringing the dispute to an end, and finally decided to send a list.¹ This list agrees in the main with that of Carthage, but it gives the series of the books quite differently from first to last and altogether suppresses the objectionable formula about the Epistle to the Hebrews.² Thus the variations are reproduced *ad infinitum* throughout all this history, and, unless we say the Pope had not opened his Bible, we must conclude that the Roman collection had been formed differently from that of Africa.

However that may be, the letter of Innocent was not known in the latter country. In 419 a new Synod of Carthage again took up the question of the canon, reproduced its old list (with this single change that in place of saying 13+1, it was now understood to be better to say 14), and again decreed that the Bishop of Rome should be asked to confirm a canon which was said to have been received from the Fathers.

---

¹ Innoc. *Ep. ad Exsuper. Tolos. ap.* Mansi, iii. 1040.

² Moses, Joshua, Judges, Kings, Ruth, Prophets, Solomon (five books), Psalter, Tobit, Job, Esther, Judith, Maccabees, Ezra, Chronicles, Gospels, Paul (14 epistles), John, Peter, James, Jude, Acts, Apocalypse.

³ *Concil. Carth.*, v., ch. 29 ; *ap.* Mansi iv., 430.

CHAPTER XII.

THEORY AND TERMINOLOGY.

ALMOST all the works which treat of the history of the canon stop at the point we have now reached, at the end of the fourth century. It is supposed that, as the Councils of Laodicea and Carthage sanctioned and published official lists of the holy books, there was nothing more, henceforward, to be said. I am of a totally different opinion. It is easy to prove that the debate was not terminated by these Synods—especially as they were only provincial assemblies and contradicted one another in the most flagrant manner—that the uncertainty, the divergences, the investigations, the attempts at codification continued to the fifth century and in the centuries following, to the two extremities of the Christian world, with means of enquiry more and more insufficient, with decreasing chances of success, and, unfortunately, also with an increasingly perceptible lack of intelligence for the subject-matter of the question and for its theological bearing. But, before continuing my narrative, I have still to present a series of more general observations on the fourth century.

Let me for a moment grant, with the majority of my predecessors, that at the end of this century the canon was so well fixed that the generations following had only to accept it tranquilly and, after no great lapse of time, might even have convinced themselves of its being fixed from the very first, as many French and English theologians in our day still suppose. Yet even on this hypothesis, it must be acknowledged that the decision of Laodicea is quite different from that of Carthage. The two Synods lay it down as a principle that only canonical writings are to be read in the Church; but the lists they give differ from one another. In the East the Apocalypse is excluded; in the West it is inserted. In the West the Old Testament is composed of all the writings contained in the Septuagint, without any distinction of origin; in Asia the six books totally unknown to the Synagogue are rejected, while others are received in a recension which in part was very different from the Hebrew original. Is all this the consequence of an arbitrary selection, or is it the result of critical study? This question is not to be settled by a single yes or no; it demands serious examination.

Among the facts I have been bringing out hitherto, the one which has recurred most constantly and which must have struck my readers most, is not the variation in the lists, but the lack of clearness in the very conception of the canon; in other words, it is the uncertainty of the theological idea of the collection of the sacred Scriptures. As this fact cannot be explained in accordance with the principles prevailing in Protestant schools, it is judged inadmissible. Consequently many authors seem not to know that the canon has its history; and they continually confound two, or even three, questions radically different—viz., the origin and authenticity of each book in the Bible from a literary point of view, the intrinsic value of the book from a theological point of view, and the formation of the collection of books. This last question alone engages us here: it is a question of history and nothing more. It is not my part to teach what idea we should form of inspiration, what rank we are to assign to the prophets or to the apostles. Dogmatic theology defines that inspiration; faith determines that rank according to the religious elements it finds in the sacred books. We wish simply to see how the Bible we now possess was formed; and since it certainly did not fall from the sky complete, as Mussulman doctors say of their Koran, science has the right and the duty of inquiring into its origin. Up to this point the following are the results established in our investigation.

When Christian preaching began, the Old Testament, as it existed in the Synagogue, was used by the Church, not only as a book of edification in the practical and popular sense of that word, but also as a code of revelation, as the Word of God in an absolutely special and privileged sense, though from the first a certain divergence in the theological ideas regarding it manifested itself. For, while some (the Jewish Christians) continued to insist on its legal character, others preferred to recognise in it a prophetic character, and, in regard to the direct application, to recognise this solely. But in spite of this diversity of sentiments, the volume was for the entire Church that which it had been for the Synagogue, the book which was read before the assembled community, the text on which the faithful meditated for their spiritual direction, the source from which they drew their knowledge of the ancient revelations, and the proof of what had been revealed through the apostles. It was a book standing by itself, entirely distinct from every other book. This state of things underwent a certain change only at the time when, and in the countries where, the Hebrew original had to be replaced by translations. These translations not only gave certain books in a new and very much altered form, but also included books not found in the primitive collection. In proportion to the learning of those who used them, this difference was observed and commented on, or neglected and ignored, and imperceptibly two, or even three, recensions were in common use at the same time in the churches. As philological and historical knowledge gradually disappeared, the majority soon lost sight of these diverse elements. In the West, in Ethiopia, in

Armenia, in all the countries where the Scriptures existed only in the form of a translation, only the most learned paid any heed to the diversity, and then not with the purpose of introducing any reform, but to invent some plausible justification for existing usages. In other places, a minority, better placed or more instructed, were anxious to separate, at least in theory, the books of Greek origin from those which had formed the Hebrew canon; but these latter even were accepted in the amplified Greek form, because the philological means of re-establishing the primitive text did not as a rule exist. Jerome was almost the only scholar who imposed such a task on himself, and his success in it was of no public advantage. His Latin translation, used even now in our day, distinguishes the two elements by critical notes, but does not eliminate anything. There were, therefore, as I said, two editions of the Bible of the Old Testament, the one more extensive than the other; and it is quite clear that in practice—*i.e.*, in ecclesiastical readings, in the instruction of the people, in sermons and catechisings—the elements peculiar to the one edition were used with no less confidence than those common to both. Even theology, whether dogmatic or polemical, did not always observe the line of demarcation very strictly; science alone traced the line, and it had to do so without disturbing the traditional order. We shall see by-and-by how this came about.

In regard to what we now call the New Testament, the history is more complicated and much less understood. By a natural enough illusion, it has been supposed that, as there was, at the beginning of the church, an Old Testament quite complete and acknowledged, there must also have been a New Testament, the very name of the first supposing the immediate addition of the second. It has then been hastily concluded that the last surviving apostle at least must have collected his own works and those of his colleagues in order to endow the church with an authentic and official body of texts, equal or even superior in dignity to the books of the prophets. A conscientious examination of the facts and the testimonies has shown us that this was not the course of events. According to the apostles themselves, the New Covenant was to be directed and vivified by the Spirit, while the Old was founded on the letter. In any case, the *Scripture* (*i.e.*, the Old Testament by itself), for a long time after the apostles, was the basis of the evangelic teaching. This evangelic teaching was propagated by simple oral transmission, and was held to be sufficiently guaranteed by the succession of the bishops which could be traced back even to the disciples of the Lord. This teaching, moreover, was so simple that it was summarised in a formula which our children still learn by heart, and to it there were added practical exhortations and consolations of hope, the common heritage of all the faithful. Still, all these elements of Christian instruction rested on historic facts, on the coming, death, and resurrection of Christ. The narration of these facts formed an essential part of the teaching. Christians soon came to seek for such narratives, and to read them together. Thus a general and public use began to be made of certain books proceeding from the circle of the first disciples, and this use was so solidly confirmed by its abundant results, that soon steps were taken to prevent the insertion of any suspected book among the documents bequeathed by the first generations. After the middle of the second century, the church had fixed its choice and marked out four gospels among the large number already in circulation. At quite as early a period, the hortatory letters of the most respected doctors or bishops were read in several churches; efforts were made to procure and collect them. It was natural that in Greece and

Asia Minor the name and writings of Paul should receive most attention. Accordingly we find that about the time indicated there was already in existence a collection of Paul's epistles. When the circumstances of the faithful became more trying and more filled with temptation, it was all the more important to reanimate their courage by the contemplation of the first origins of the church and by the powerful eloquence of the founder of so many communities. Other apostolic writings were soon added to these first elements. Writings were discovered and put into circulation, writings which hitherto had been left in obscurity or used only by the individuals possessing one of the few copies. Nevertheless it was not till the first half of the third century that all the existing literary productions of high Christian antiquity came into general knowledge.

But before this epoch, two things had already appeared which exercised a very marked influence on the destinies of the New Testament. In the first place, the custom of making public and regular readings from the writings of the apostles was introduced long before the collection was in any degree complete, and hence the collections in the various churches soon differed from one another. Some were not acquainted with the writings which were admitted in other places; others refused to admit books not known to them from the first, preferring to keep to those already received among them and consecrated in their eyes by long custom; others received these additions, but in varying proportions; others finally, and these were the most numerous, assigned them a secondary place. If it be remembered how far the Church in the first centuries was from having a centralised organisation, and how freely and independently local customs could develop themselves, no one will be surprised at this diversity. Besides, it embarrassed Christian life and popular teaching so little, that it might have existed unnoticed, had not scientific theology been bound to consider it. But at the very time when these readings from apostolic writings became regular, and began to form everywhere an integral part of worship, some progress in theological ideas had taken place. By the very struggle which the Church had had to wage against Gnosticism, it had learned to appreciate more accurately the distinction between its own creed and this exotic philosophy, and to base its own traditional teaching more firmly. It was not long in assigning to its first masters a privileged place, ranking them among the prophets. Their writings necessarily shared in this same honour, and were put on a level with the inspired books of Moses and his successors. A code of the New Covenant was at last added to that of the Old.

From this point of view it was a matter of great importance to draw a distinct line, marking off the books that were to enjoy this prerogative. If the idea of such a canonical collection had existed from the first century, perhaps it would not have been very difficult to form it in such a way as to secure its remaining thenceforth invariable. But a hundred years later, the time had passed for this. The usage of the readings had consecrated writings which had not been composed by apostles properly so called : other books which might claim such a title—at least in the opinion of more than one theologian—had not had the advantage of being known soon enough or widely enough, to obtain general acceptance without very great difficulty. As theology could not establish a rule to decide the choice, or rather as it was entirely dependent on a tradition which had arisen and gained strength in complete independence of all theological formula, theologians had soon to face numerous difficulties as my analysis of the testimonies of the two latter centuries has established on every page. Theory aspired towards a rigorous selection, and from its own point of view was perfectly right, for it was a matter of much moment to purify from all alloy the texts which alone were to have an indisputable authority in the ever-widening discussions of theological questions. Practice sought to utilise everything suitable to its purpose, and was particularly afraid of divesting itself of any one means of action—*i.e.*, of any book used in popular instruction, which, perhaps, was not of the number of those extolled by theory, but had the immense advantage of being already familiar to the class least easy to initiate in abstract theories. This explains why so many Fathers and excellent theologians did not hesitate to eulogise the *Pastor* of Hermas, Ecclesiasticus, Tobit, and other writings of a similar nature.

This also explains the difference between the rules of Laodicea and Carthage. The bishops of Asia had regard to theory, the interests of the school, the rules of dogma and faith, the theological code; their decision is only a link in the long chain of dogmatic decisions formulated by Eastern councils. The bishops of Africa had regard to practice, the ecclesiastical code, the interests of worship and popular instruction, respect for established forms, which they were unwilling to sacrifice to a necessity purely scientific; their decision falls into the category of the disciplinary statutes for which the West all along had a great legislative aptitude. The former were unwilling to admit anything which had not positive proofs of canonical dignity and divine origin; the latter were unwilling to exclude anything sanctified by usage. The former were afraid to burden themselves with any addition open to suspicion; the latter, to impoverish themselves without plausible motive, by rigorously applying a principle which was not at all familiar to them. To this principle they did homage, almost against their will, when they accepted an epistle still unknown to most of the churches.[1]

---

[1] I have already quoted several passages from Augustine, clearly showing

I have just been characterising the two points of view by reducing them to their simplest expression; but I have not meant thereby to convey that the two parties were always clearly aware of the true origin and nature of this divergence. Both professed to settle the *canon*—i.e., the normal collection of the Scriptures; and by using the same term with a different connotation, they introduced great confusion into all that was said on this important subject. This confusion manifests itself so soon as the necessities of dogmatic theology take their place beside the traditional customs of the Church, and my readers have been able to convince themselves by every page of my narrative that the efforts made on all sides to reach a solution of the question, a definite catalogue of the holy books, always came to nothing because it was impossible to evolve from the debate one chief principle to which every other might have been sacrificed. The theologians, on the contrary, were at pains to find middle terms which would satisfy everybody and everything, but they only made the confusion greater than before.

We have seen that Eusebius, in drawing up his statistics of the New Testament, concerned himself only with the use made of each book in the various churches. His division into homologoumena and antilegomena rests only on this external principle of distinction, and the dogmatic question plays as small a part in it as the question of authenticity. The Acts of Paul belong to the antilegomena on the same grounds as the Epistle of James; the uncertainty of his process is even so great that the Apocalypse and the

that this was the point of view among the Latins. I give another, which is very much to the point. Hilary of Arles had been astonished that the Bishop of Hippo should cite the authority of the Wisdom of Solomon, the Gallic theologians being at that time more familiar with the ideas of the Greeks than were the Africans. Augustine replies: *Non debuit repudiari sententia libri Sapientiæ qui meruit in ecclesia Christi tam longa annositate recitari et ab omnibus cum veneratione divinæ auctoritatis audiri* (Hilar. *ap.* Aug. *Ep.* 226, *et De prædest.* i. 27).

Epistle to the Hebrews are put in both classes. But the generation of Greek theologians who adorned the second half of the fourth century were too much engaged in the discussion of dogma to be content with such an unscientific method. We find, therefore, in them a series of terms hitherto unknown, or at least unfamiliar to their predecessors, of terms which henceforth were to have their place in the language of the school and the Church. I have had to use them by anticipation, and I was able to do so without fear of being misunderstood; but it is proper to pause here and estimate their true value.

Of all these terms the most famous and the most important is the word *Canon*, which I have put in the title of this work. This word, in addition to its theological value, has received various dissimilar meanings in the applications of common life, which applications are all justified by its etymology. With the Greeks[1] it meant originally a cane, a stick for measuring or determining a straight line; in the figurative sense, it denoted every kind of rule—*e.g.*, in the mathematical sciences, in philology, and even in the sphere of moral ideas. Later, the grammarians and critics of Alexandria understood, by this technical term, the series of authors who were to serve as models, or standards for purity of language, or, as we would now say, who were to be considered classic. In the New Testament, the word is also employed sometimes in the sense of a rule, a principle,[2] perhaps even a line of demarcation or direction.[3] Among ecclesiastical authors it is used somewhat frequently in the same sense, especially when they are speaking of religious and dogmatic truth. The rule, which was to guide men in the search for this truth, and more particularly in the

---

[1] Comp. Stephani *Thesaur. l. gr.* ed. Paris s.v. κανών.
[2] Gal. vi, 16; comp. Phil. iii, 16, where the reading is uncertain.
[3] 2 Cor. x, 13; comp. Clem. *ad Cor.*, 41.

comprehension of the Scriptures, was ecclesiastical tradition,[1] just as the Scriptures in their turn were to serve as a rule for the teaching of the Church;[2] and the perfect agreement of these two authorities was the supreme rule, the true *ecclesiastical canon*.[3]

It is under this meaning, too, that the question arises of *canonical books*, or a *scriptural canon*. Only modern writers are not agreed regarding the manner in which these expressions were derived from the primitive conception, some seeing in it by preference, if not exclusively, a dogmatic purpose, others restricting its value to a purely literary significance. I must say frankly that there seems to me to be an error here on both sides, inasmuch as the interpreters of patristic theology have in general thought there existed only one single meaning of the word, whereas in truth the two elements are represented in it, and take the first rank by turns, just as each author's point of view was more or less scientific, his language more or less popular. It is a fact that the expression *canonical books*[4] is frequently taken in the dogmatic sense, as denoting writings which are to regulate teaching, because they are the fruit of a special inspiration, and the Church therefore regards them as having a standard authority. Only it is not very clear, whether this adjective is to signify that these books *contain* the canon, *i.e.* the rule of faith itself, directly; or whether,

---

[1] ἐχομένοις τοῦ κανόνος τῆς Ἰησοῦ Χριστοῦ κατὰ διαδοχὴν τῶν ἀποστόλων οὐρανίου ἐκκλησίας (Origen., *De princ.*, iv. 9).

[2] Chrysost., *Homil.* 58 *in Genes.*, *Opp.*, iv. 566: κανὼν τῆς θείας γραφῆς opposed to οἰκεῖοι λογισμοί. Isidor. Pelus., *Epp.*, iv. 114: τὸν κανόνα τῆς ἀληθείας, τὰς θείας φημὶ γραφάς, κατοπτεύσωμεν. Iren., iii. 11, *regula veritatis*.

[3] κανὼν ἐκκλησιαστικός, a term which we have already found in Clement and Eusebius with different applications. It must not be forgotten that the use of the term *canon* has never been restricted to the Bible. There were canons of councils, canon law, the canonical life, canons of cathedrals, etc. All these expressions have at bottom the same origin and are derived from a primitive meaning anterior to our canon of Scripture.

[4] βιβλία κανονικά, *libri canonici, regulares*.

as others think, and as seems most reasonable, it indicates that they *form* the canon, *i.e.* the collection of books which is to furnish the standard. This latter explanation seems to me preferable, because the adjective *canonical* always reminds us of a plurality[1] of writings possessing authority as a collective whole, and I do not know a single text where this interpretation proves insufficent. Further, it leads us by a very natural transition to the purely literary significance of the term. For it cannot be denied that by *canon* the Fathers very often understand the collection itself, or even the simple catalogue of the books forming it. It is evident then that the dogmatic sense is not attached to the word, but forms part of its connotation. Thus, at the end of the enumeration of the biblical books, made in Article 85 of what are called the Apostolic Canons, it is said: "These are the provisions to be observed in regard to the two canons;"[2] thus too, at the end of the poem of Amphilochius, we read these words: "This is what may be considered as the most exact canon (catalogue) of the inspired Scriptures." The common point in the two acceptations of the term is no doubt the suggestion of a theological standard, but it is still more the notion directly contained in the word, of something definite, determined in number as in quality.[3] That also explains to us why this term is not found before the second half of the fourth century; Eusebius even does not appear to have known it.[4] The Greek Fathers of that

---

[1] Thence, too, the phrase: *non in canone est* (Didym. alex. *l.c.*), synonymous with: *in catalogo SS. divinarum* (Jerome, *Praef. in Job*).

[2] ταῦτα περὶ κανόνων διατετάχθω (*Can. Ap.*, 85.) See above, p. 181.

[3] βιβλία οὐκ ἀόριστα ἀλλ' ὡρισμένα.—*certo canone comprehensi libri* (Pseudo. Athan., *Synops. S.S. Opp.*, ii, 96).

[4] Unless use be made of the passage in vi. 25, where he says that Origen recognises only four gospels, following in that respect the ecclesiastical *canon*. I believe, however, that in this place the word only means a traditional rule. The term *canonizatae scripturae* is found in Origen (iv. 239. Lomm.), but it is due entirely to the translator.

epoch were far more occupied than any of their predecessors, with the necessity of determining the privileged books, and drawing up a catalogue of them. The previous attempts of this nature were only rare exceptions, and there was no imperative necessity for a special technical term.

In ordinary language the second of the two acceptations of which I have just been speaking, naturally became the more popular, and finally formed by itself the notion of the canon. In this sense was formed the verb *canonise*—i.e., to insert a book in the catalogue of the canonical writings, to place it in the regulating and standard collection.[1] It is superfluous to quote texts here in support of my statement; more than enough will be found in the extracts from the Fathers, contained in the two preceding chapters.

Still the same Fathers to whom we owe, if not an unvarying definition of the *canon*—i.e., an unvarying list of the books reputed to be canonical—at least a clearer notion of *canonicity*—i.e., of the specially divine character of these books; these same Fathers, I say, were not able, and in fact were not willing to take from the hands of the faithful, or the library of their own churches, all the non-canonical writings which were used in public reading or for the edification of the community. They attempted therefore to place these in a category by themselves, or, as was also said, in a second canon—i.e., in a collection of less authority, of inferior dignity. These formed a collection of books not to be studied with the desire of deriving from them the rule of faith and teaching, but to be read for religious edification and moral training, a collection of books intended not for the dogmatic investigations of scholars, but for the practical teaching of the church. The Greeks, more exacting on this

---

[1] βιβλία κανονιζόμενα, κεκανονισμένα, libri intra canonem conclusi, in canonem recipere (Athan., *Ep. fest.*, l. c., Isidor. Pelus, *Ep.* i. 369. Rufin. *in Symb.*, c. 37. August. *in Rom.*, § 11, etc.)

point than the Latins, were unwilling to grant the favour of such a reading to any but catechumens,[1] a restriction which they did not succeed in establishing generally. In this category were placed (1) the six books of the Old Testament not found in the canon of the Synagogue, especially the two Wisdoms. Of these the one bearing the name of Jesus, son of Sirach, was so much in fashion in the early church, that to this day, in Latin, French, and English, it is called Ecclesiasticus—*i.e.*, the book of the church, the book of edification *par excellence*.[2] These books are useful, it is said, but have no authority in matters of faith, and are not deposited in the *Ark of the Covenant*. Athanasius also ranks the book of Esther in this category. But no Greek Father ever placed in it the additions to Daniel and Jeremiah, which in the Greek text form integral parts of the work of these prophets. (2) The antilegomena where they had not already attained the honours of canonicity. Thus, *e.g.*, if the Catholic Epistles had not been read in an increasing number of churches, no one would ever have thought of putting them in the canon. It was the same with the Apocalypse.[3] (3) A certain number of other books, the official use of which died out after the

---

[1] See, *e.g.*, the definition given by Athanasius, *l. c.*: ἐστὶ καὶ ἕτερα βιβλία τούτων ἔξωθεν, οὐ κανονιζόμενα μὲν τετυπωμένα δὲ παρὰ τῶν πατέρων ἀναγινώσκεσθαι τοῖς ἄρτι προσερχομένοις καὶ βουλομένοις κατηχεῖσθαι τὸν τῆς εὐσεβείας λόγον. Comp. what was said in chap. x., regarding Cyril of Jerusalem. Rufin., *l. c.*: *Sciendum quod et alii libri sunt qui non canonici sed* ECCLESIASTICI *a majoribus appellati sunt. . . . quos legi quidem in ecclesia voluerunt, non tamen proferri ad auctoritatem fidei confirmandam.*—Βιβλία ἀναγνωσκόμενα (Athan., *l. c.*), ἐν δευτέρῳ (κανόνι), Cyril of Jerusalem, *l. c.*

[2] Jerome, *Praef. ad Salom.*: *Sicut Judith et Tobia et Machab. libros legit quidem ecclesia sed ea inter canonicas SS. non recipit, sic et haec duo volumina (Sap., Sir.) legit ad aedificationem plebis, non ad auctoritatem dogmatum confirmandam.*—Epiph. loc. cit.: αὗται χρήσιμοι μὲν εἰσι καὶ ὠφέλιμοι ἀλλ' εἰς ἀριθμὸν ῥητῶν οὐκ ἀναφέρονται, διὸ οὐδ' ἐν τῇ τῆς διαθήκης κιβωτῷ ἀντέθησαν.

[3] τὰ λοιπὰ ἔξω ἐν δευτέρῳ (Cyrill., *Catech.*, *l. c.*).—*Apocalypsis in ecclesiis legitur, neque enim inter apocryphas SS. habetur sed inter ecclesiasticas* (Jerome, *In Psalm.* 149).

fourth century—*e.g.*, the epistles of Clement and Barnabas, the *Pastor*, the *Apostolic Constitutions*, and some other literary productions posterior to the apostolic age, regarding which I refer my readers to the notices extracted from Eusebius, Athanasius, and other authors. (4) Homilies of celebrated Fathers, letters from other communities and their bishops,² and legends of martyrs, the very name of which recalls that custom.³

Of course such a distinction, though justified in the eyes of the theologians, was above the capacity of the people in general. The texts read in religious solemnities could not but be of equal value to most of the audience, and scholars must have tried in vain to make the simple faithful retain more or less subtle classifications, the meaning of which escaped them. But there was still another inconvenience. If, before this division into two classes, the learned had not been able to agree on a uniform catalogue, it was much worse when there were two. So far from the way being paved for the final settlement of the superior canon, the confusion had only been doubled. We found several Fathers, including Jerome the most learned of all, taking up by turns the two points of view, and ranking the same books sometimes in the second canon, sometimes in the first or rather in one single canon, sometimes leaving the readers to decide for themselves. As soon as the churches could recognise their position, they made efforts to get out of it. The double classification, good in theory, was abandoned in practice. In the East the faithful were told to read only what was canonical. In the West everything that was read to the people was called canonical.

I have still to explain a term quite as frequently em-

---

¹ Jerome, *Catal.*, 115.
² *Epistola communicatoria*, κανονικὰ γράμματα (Euseb., vii. 30.)
³ Euseb., iv. 15, v. 4. *Concil. Carth.*, iii. ch. 47. Augustine, *passim*.

ployed as that of *canon* and its derivatives, but more variable in its signification and hence more difficult to define. It is the word *apocryphal*. Now-a-days this word is commonly used (outside of theological discussions) in the sense of fictitious, lying, and it is certain that the Fathers sometimes used it also in this acceptation, as synonymous with pseudepigraphic (bearing a false title[1]); but it is quite as certain that this acceptation is neither the only one, nor the most ancient, nor that which was definitely adopted into theological language. In Greek, the word signifies what is hidden, secret; hence the Latin theologians simply speak of *secret* books where the Greeks spoke of apocryphal books.[3] And here we must at once reject the explanation given by Augustine,[4] an explanation satisfactory neither to philologist nor historian. He thinks that the term apocryphal was given to the books whose authors where unknown (hidden). There is no doubt that attention was paid to the name of the authors, only in so far as it was important to verify fictitious titles. In my opinion the term apocryphal applies first of all to the contents of the books, to contents which were hidden, mysterious, inaccessible to the ordinary intelligence, or rather which had to be concealed from simple, feeble minds, from those whose faith and morals might be shaken by reading them. Clement of Alexandria uses it in the first sense when he says that the disciples of Prodicus boast of possessing apocryphal books of their master,[5] and so Gregory of Nyssa and Epiphanius when they see in the Apocalypse an apocryphal—*i.e.*, mysterious and obscure—

[1] Cyril of Jerusalem, *Catech.*, iv. 36.

[2] Luke xii. 2; comp. viii. 17. Mark iv. 22. Col. ii. 3.

[3] Βιβλία ἀπόκρυφα, *libri secreti*. See the passages from Origen and his translator in chap. viii. p. 131.

[4] *Quorum origo non claruit patribus* (*De civit. Dei*, xv. 23). Comp. *Gloss. ad decret. Gratiani dist.* 16: *sine certo auctore*.

[5] *Strom.*, i. 304: βίβλους ἀποκρύφους αὐχοῦσι κεκτῆσθαι.

writing.[1] Origen uses it in the second sense when he says[2] that the story of Susanna exists in Hebrew, but that the Jews, desirous of concealing from the people everything hurtful to the honour of the chiefs and judges, suppressed it in the book of Daniel, though it has been preserved in the apocrypha. The meaning here cannot be questioned; for the author is contrasting these apocryphal books with the books well-known, and he says further[3] that to this day the Hebrew original ranks among the forbidden works. He says, moreover, that it is otherwise with Judith and Tobit, which do not appear even in the Jewish apocrypha.[4] According to this, an apocryphal book is a work which the persons charged with the direction of the flock, do not permit to be read in the Church,[5] while the books read in the assemblies are called public or published works,[6] a term we have met with several times in the Fathers. Of course, from this point of view the works of the heretics were the apocryphal books *par excellence*, since they are to be hid rather than read.[7] Also we often find the term *apocryphal* taken to be synonymous with corrupting, perverse, dangerous,[8] and for this reason the apocrypha form a third class in addition to the canonical and ecclesiastical books, as in the catalogue of the festal epistle of Athanasius.

Still, among Latin theologians the term apocryphal is

---

[1] Greg. Nyss., *Or. de ordin.*, ii. 44: 'Ἰωάννης ἐν ἀποκρύφοις δι' αἰνίγματος λέγει.—Epiph., *Hær.*, 51: διὰ τὰ βαθέως καὶ σκοτεινῶς εἰρημένα.

[2] περιεῖλον ἀπὸ τῆς γνώσεως τοῦ λαοῦ, ὧν τινα σώζεται ἐν ἀποκρύφοις (Orig. *ad Afric.*, c. 9).

[3] *Ibid.*, c. 12: τὸ ἑβραϊκὸν ἐν ἀπορρήτοις κείμενον.

[4] *Ibid.*, c. 13: οὐδὲ γὰρ ἔχουσιν αὐτὰ καὶ ἐν ἀποκρύφοις ἑβραϊστί.

[5] Rufin., *in Symbol*, *l. c.*: *quos in ecclesia legi noluerunt.*

[6] βιβλία δεδημοσιευμένα, *publicari*, to be read in the church (Didym., *l. c.*).

[7] ἀποκρυφῆς μᾶλλον ἢ ἀναγνώσεως ἄξια (Synops. *S. S. in Opp. Athan.*, ii. 55).

[8] βλαβερὰ (Cyril., *l. c.*). φθοροποιὰ (Constit. ap., vi. 16). αἱρετικὰ (Athan., *Ep. fest.*, *l. c.*). Comp. Iren., i. 20. Tertull., *De anim*, c. 2. Orig., *Prol. in Cant.*: *Appellantur apocrypha propterea quod in iis multa corrupta et contra fidem veram inveniuntur.*

employed in quite a different sense. They oppose it purely and simply to the term *canonical,* so that it is synonymous with ecclesiastical;[1] and that is why to this day we speak of the Apocrypha of the Old Testament, without meaning thereby to say that Wisdom and Ecclesiasticus are dangerous or heretical books.[2] In another aspect we have seen above that the same authors maintain the distinction between the Apocrypha and the ecclesiastical books. I am right, therefore, in saying that the very efforts made to reach a more precise theory of the canon and more rigorous definitions, were a continual source of new confusion. To be certain of this, we have only to read the explanation which Isidore of Seville gives of the term under our notice, an explanation combining without criticism the heterogeneous elements of all the previous definitions.[3] In support of my assertion, I might further quote numerous passages from Latin authors of the same epoch; but I think the fact sufficiently established by the testimonies already placed before my readers. Besides, the history of the Middle Ages,

---

[1] Jerome, *Catal.* 6 : *Barnabas composuit epistolam ad aedificandam ecclesiam quae inter apocryphas legitur.*—Id. *Prolog. in Reges* (after enumerating the Hebrew books): *quidquid extra hos est inter apocrypha ponendum.*

[2] The term thus took a somewhat vague signification, and we cannot always be sure whether or not it contains an allusion to heretical books.— Jerome, *Ep.* 7 *ad Laetam : Caveat omnia apocrypha et si quando ea non ad dogmatum veritatem sed ad signorum reverentiam legere voluerit sciat non eorum esse quorum titulis praenotantur multaque his admixta vitiosa et grandis esse prudentiae aurum quaerere in luto.* Does this apply to the Apocrypha of the Old Testament, or did Jerome think that a woman may find specks of gold even in the mud of heresy? Comp. a similar passage of Philastrius, above in chap. xi. (p. 188).

[3] Isidor. Hispal. *Etymol.*, vi., 2 : *Apocrypha autem dicta i.e., secreta, quia in dubium veniunt. Est enim occulta origo nec patet patribus, ex quibus usque ad nos auctoritas veracium scripturarum certissima successione pervenit. In iis apocryphis etsi invenitur aliqua veritas, tamen propter multa falsa nulla est in iis canonica auctoritas, quae recte a prudentibus judicantur non esse eorum credenda quibus adscribuntur. Nam multa sub nominibus prophetarum et apostolorum ab haereticis proferuntur,* etc.

which has very wrongly been neglected by those writing that of the canon of the Scriptures, will furnish me with one occasion more for proving this absence, both of a theological theory distinctly formulated for guiding the choice of the books, and of a definite and invariable official catalogue of the books themselves.

The mention of the Middle Ages, just made by anticipation, and the implied engagement to continue my narrative beyond the point at which most authors stop, suggest another reflection which I may suitably insert in this place. As a general rule, those who collect from the writings of the Fathers, passages relative to the books of the apostles, do so with the intention of proving the authenticity of these books, so that they are really not writing a history of the formation of the New Testament during the first centuries, but rather a demonstration or external proof of the correctness of the collection as it now exists. I willingly admit that science undertakes this latter task; I grant even that it is not without its utility, though I do not share the illusions of those who expect from it a final solution of all critical questions. The testimonies nearest to the apostolic age, so far as any exist, are too incomplete, too indefinite to satisfy all requirements; and those which do not sin in these ways are too distant from the primitive period to have absolute value. Even if such value were assigned to them, they are always of a nature to leave doubts on many points. If modern criticism has conceived more or less serious doubts regarding the authenticity of certain books of the New Testament, formerly regarded as homologoumena, still it ranks them among the productions of an age anterior to that in which the positive testimonies of the Fathers begin. As to those regarding which the most suspicious criticism has not dared to raise doubts, the conviction of their apostolic origin rests on grounds of authority quite different from that of a semi-fabulous tradition or the rhetoric of some authors wholly unaccustomed to historical studies. But further, supposing even that these testimonies are never wrong regarding the names of the authors, or have never given different names for one and the same book, does it follow that they are equally sure in regard to all the other historical questions which present themselves in connection with these writings? Must we accept all the chronological, geographical, or linguistic conjectures invented by their unsound exegesis? The Epistle to the Galatians will then have been written at Rome, the Apocalypse at the end of the century, the Fourth Gospel by a centenarian Apostle, the Gospel of Matthew in Hebrew? I see no difference between these questions and those above, and I do not see why the conscientious historian, finding himself obliged to reject as inadmissible the traditional solutions given to the one, should profess an implicit faith for those recommended by the other. If he is prudent, he will accept them only so far as they are warranted by facts.[1] Considering this so-called external proof from whatever point of view I will, I regard it, therefore, as extremely feeble, insufficient, and open to suspicion, and I have not paid much attention to it either in this present work or elsewhere. Let us not ask the Fathers for things they cannot give us, and, above all, let us be distrustful of ourselves in weighing their testimonies; we are only too much inclined to exalt their authority when they speak in conformity with our own views, while we affect not to listen to them whenever they doubt or hesitate, or are not agreed with one another or with our preconceptions. The only thing we can ask of them in perfect security, the only thing, too, that they can give in any satisfactory measure, is the information which will acquaint us with the state of opinion and usage in the

---

[1] The original French is *sous bénéfice d'inventaire*, equivalent to the phrase in Roman law *sub beneficio inventarii*.

various localities and at the various times represented by them. By limiting ourselves to researches of this kind, we shall not narrow in the least the field of science, and we run much less risk of going wrong.

I have another no less important remark to make, which may reassure those who might be disposed to fear that I hold too cheaply what in their eyes (but not in the opinion of Protestant theology) is the most solid foundation for the authority of the apostolic writings. I have just been calling the above process of quoting the Fathers illusory and uncertain; to what would it come if it were consistent with itself and were applied with sincerity? Those who extol it are wont to make a great display of proofs on behalf of the documents which least need proof, and when, in regard to those that do not need proof, they find themselves obliged to express opinions that may become compromising, they can only neutralise these opinions by exaggerating or weakening the strength of each particular testimony, according as it is favourable or unfavourable to the thesis they wish to maintain. Frequently, they resort to a suppression pure and simple of the testimonies that are inconvenient. That is not an historical method, nor is it sound criticism. I have done something very different. While traditional science, having in view the gropings of the fourth century in regard to the canonical collection, exerts itself to deny the most patent facts, for fear of sacrificing the only basis supposed to be solid for the apostolic authenticity of this or that book of the New Testament, I have confined myself to establishing that the collection was formed slowly in the course of time, and that the prolonged absence of several books is explained by reasons absolutely independent of their origin. The theory that the canon was composed by the apostles themselves, strews, as at random, doubt and difficulties all along the path of the history, while an unprejudiced study of the latter drives away the phantom of a wholly gratuitous hypothesis, and at the same time removes the greatest stumbling-blocks strewn along the route.

Whatever merit there may be otherwise in these remarks, they will do good in reminding our Protestant theologians that in any case the collection has been formed in accordance with a principle foreign to our Church. That principle is tradition, the succession and authority of the bishops. In the first centuries, so long as the Christian communities were independent of one another, local customs, arising from diverse and fortuitous circumstances, might vary in regard to readings for edification as they did in many other things. The unity of the Christian churches, founded on the hereditary bond which attached them to that of the Apostles,[1] had no need of any more material support, *e.g.*, a written and uniform code; and if, as times went on, we can congratulate ourselves on seeing everywhere the same nucleus of apostolic books, serving as a source of instruction to the faithful, this agreement even when established by the language of the school,[2] rested on no official decision whatever. Later, when the Church entered into closer connection with the empire, submitted to a more oligarchic constitution, and felt an increasing need for laying down rules, synods, and along with these, popes undertook to convert into law what had already been consecrated by custom. The diversity of custom necessarily prevented the law from being uniform, though uniformity is a thing which prejudice has first to invent in order to give itself the satisfaction of finding it

[1] *Ecclesiae universae quae apostolicis de societate sacramenti confoederantur* etc. (Tertull., *Adv. Marc.*, iv. 5). *Tot et tantae ecclesiae, una est. Illa ab apostolis prima ex qua omnes* .... *Omnes probant unitatem; communicatio pacis et appellatio fraternitatis, et contesseratio hospitalitatis: quae jura non alia ratio regit quam ejusdem sacramenti una traditio* (Id., *De Praescr.*, c. 20; comp. c. 32, 36).

[2] See above in chap. ix, p. 149, regarding the origin and value of the term *homologuomena*.

again in history. Thus, at all periods, under all regimes, for discipline as for dogma, hence also for the canon which is connected with both, tradition ruled the Church, inspired the doctors, opposed the strongest bulwark to heresy; tradition also undertook the task of directing the choice of the holy books. This choice, though its results have not been always and everywhere the same, may have been excellent, at least as good as was possible with the means and material at its disposal; but Protestant theology, which has no desire to elevate tradition, and professes in every other respect to insist on having it first verified, is bound to do the same with regard to the canon of Scripture; it is bound to seek out some other standard than the process which is the very thing to be verified.

But I may go further and explain, in a simpler and more rational way, the fact of these numerous variations, these unceasing hesitations, which I have shown to exist during the whole course of this long work. How came it that the early Church did not succeed in determining clearly what now seems to our Church a matter of prime necessity? To this only one answer can be given. At the time when it would have been the easiest thing in the world—*i.e.*, when the apostles and their first disciples were still alive—an official collection of their writings, a collection destined to serve as *law*, was not a matter of prime necessity. So far indeed was it from existing, that the absence of the thing and of the idea was noted as the characteristic sign of the new covenant of God with men, inaugurated by Christ and cemented by the Holy Spirit. Jesus himself, in response to those who asked of him a law, a rule of conduct, a positive direction, referred them to Moses and the prophets,[1] while at the same time he declared that the kingdom of heaven rested on a condition other than that of the authority of

[1] Matt. xix. 18. Luke xvi. 29.

their letter.[1] Paul in turn, developing the Master's thought, expressly opposed the spirit to the letter, the principle of the new economy to that of the old, life to death.[2] The apostles, when recommending and practising the reading of the prophets, in order to trace in them the admirable ways and purposes of Providence preparing the salvation of men, took care not to put themselves in the place of Him, of whom they were only witnesses. He had reserved for himself to abide in direct and immediate communion with all those who should henceforth come to him to cast on him their cares, the burden of their sins increased by the burden of legality. He wished to deliver them from the yoke of both, and he had promised to do so by one single means, by sending them his spirit, to instruct and sanctify them. Alas! humanity knew not how to understand this high vocation; it experienced again the need of institutions similar to those which had served to educate the people of Israel; but as centuries elapsed before the last trace of the spiritualism of the Gospel was effaced, which spiritualism had at last to be re-discovered anew in its literary remains, this fact proves how great was its primitive energy.

[1] Matt. v. 21 f.; xi. 11 f.; xix. 8 etc. Comp. John i. 17.
[2] 2 Cor. iii. 6 f. Comp. Gal. iv. 24 f.; Rom. viii. 15 f. etc.

CHAPTER XIII.

THE MIDDLE AGES.

I RESUME the thread of my narrative in order to conduct the readers who have been willing to follow me thus far, across a field which, as a rule, is less attractive in ecclesiastical literature, and has hardly been explored as yet in the interests of the history of the canon. For that matter, if the chief point were to collect opinions or count suffrages which had a certain weight in solving disputed questions, I might spare myself the trouble of disturbing the dust that covers the forgotten volumes of the authors of the Middle Ages. Experiencing no scientific need, such as that which engages us at this moment, they could not pretend to the privilege of instructing us on points regarding which we had hitherto been ignorant, and of dissipating doubts which their predecessors had not succeeded in silencing, or had even helped to produce. I shall therefore not consult them in order to learn from them what opinions we are to hold about the origin of any particular book about which there was dispute in early times; I consult them only about the state of the canon in their respective spheres; and I think not only that they are quite admissible as witnesses in this great debate, but also that their testimony is much more instructive than is supposed by those who through routine or ignorance neglect them. We have to deal with a period of decadence and barbarism, which saw all the institutions of antiquity—governments, laws, sciences, arts and letters—perish in succession, that on their ruins might be built the Christian Church as the last refuge for the old civilisation which was departing, and the cradle of a new and better civilisation.

This period is generally considered to be conservative and stationary on all points connected with religious beliefs; and, certainly, literary and historical criticism must have been the least anxiety of that golden age of legend and tradition, which felt neither need nor taste for criticism, still less possessed means or courage for exercising it. But just for that very reason, I attach a certain importance to the facts I am going to state. They will serve to verify the conclusions we have drawn from our previous researches.

I shall begin by placing before my readers a series of catalogues of the holy books, some composed by theologians of greater or less distinction in one or other of the churches, others proceeding from various authorities and invested with an official character.

The first document of this kind is known as the decree of Pope Gelasius I., who occupied the holy see in the last years of the fifth century (492-496). This decree is included in the code of the canon law,[1] and contains a long enumeration of all the writings which can and ought to have authority in the Catholic Church, especially those of councils and orthodox Fathers; to which is added the series of synods or authors considered heretical or open to suspicion. The origin and date of this document are not quite certain. There are manuscripts attributing it to Pope Damasus, a contemporary of St. Jerome; others bringing it down to the pontificate of Hormisdas (514-523). The first chapter, which contains the list of the biblical books, is wanting in many manuscripts, especially in those bearing the name of Gelasius, and may perhaps have been added at a later date. This same chapter also betrays its more recent origin by a circumstance which is directly interesting to us, and ought to excite our curiosity to the highest degree—I mean the numerous variations presented in the list of the Holy Scrip-

[1] Gratian., p. 1, dist. 15, 3. Mansi, vol. viii. 146.

tures, and proving conclusively how far the Latin Church, even at the beginning of the Middle Ages, was from having a uniform Bible.

The following is the substance of this pretended decree,[1] whose importance for our critical history is not lessened in the least by the doubts regarding its official value. The books of the Bible are divided into several categories, or, if you will, several volumes in the editions which have come down to us. There is first of all what is entitled *Ordo Veteris Testamenti*, which may also be taken to be the general title of the Old Testament, though it contains only the half—viz., the five books of Moses, the historical books from Joshua to Chronicles, the Psalter, three books of Solomon, Wisdom and Ecclesiasticus. These two last titles are sometimes wanting; on the other hand sometimes *five* books of Solomon are mentioned. Then comes the *order of the prophets*, in which the name of Baruch is sometimes joined to that of Jeremiah, and the series of the minor prophets is generally different from the Hebrew and existing recension. Finally, the Old Testament ends with an *order of the histories* which includes the books of Job, Tobit, Judith, Esther, Ezra, and the Maccabees, the order being invariable only for the first and the two last. So, too, in the *order of the Scriptures of the New Testament*, the list varies *ad infinitum* with the exception of the gospels, which always occupy the first rank.[2] The Epistles of Paul are very diversely numbered; that to the Hebrews usually occupies the last place, but there are also copies which speak of only thirteen epistles by Paul just as there are some which omit the Apocalypse. In the catalogue of the Catholic Epistles, the author of the last is regularly called Jude the Zealot, and

---

[1] Credner has a lengthened discussion of this decree in his *Beiträge zur Geschichte des Canons*, 1847.

[2] For example, Paul, Apoc., Acts, Cath.—Acts, Paul, Apoc., Cath.—etc.

the two short epistles of John are attributed in several copies of an author different from that of the first. Without pausing over the long list of apocryphal books rejected by the decree, I shall ask how such variations, at a date comparatively so recent, can be explained? Whence come these hesitations, these divergences, these literary notices even, which betray research made in earlier authors? The answer cannot be doubtful. These same doubts, these same hesitations, were found in the early writers that were most influential during the whole course of the Middle Ages, especially in Jerome. There they were discovered, and the authority of such a name prevented them from falling into oblivion. But only the complete absence of any definite and obligatory decision regarding the canon, and above all the secondary place given to the Scriptures after tradition, can explain to us why the Papacy itself did not consecrate an unvarying catalogue of the holy books, or did not even feel the need of attempting such a consecration. It is curious to verify the fact that the interest taken in collecting and preserving the rare fragments of tradition (for example, the conjecture about the two epistles of John the Presbyter) the bearing of which fragments was no longer seen, was still superior to that of the standard uniformity of the canon. This is seen especially in the second part of the decree which contains what might be called the earliest *index* of prohibited books. In it stand numerous titles of works which assuredly no one had ever seen at Rome, or which had at least been long out of circulation; but their names were still carefully registered, because they had been found in earlier documents. This ascendency of tradition is a fact of the highest importance in the history of the canon; it furnishes us with indirect or negative proofs in places where modern prejudice only sees inconsistencies.

[1] *Joannis apostoli epistola una ; alterius Joannis presbyteri epistolæ duæ.*

Another list of the biblical books, of much more uncertain date and origin, is the *Synopsis of Holy Scripture*,[1] printed in several editions of the works of St. Athanasius, but certainly not written by that author, and assigned by modern critics to a much more recent period, though it is difficult to fix it exactly. But, though no one can in these days appeal to this document as an authentic testimony of the fourth century, I shall take care not to neglect it. I believe it to be a kind of commentary or paraphrase made by some unknown person on the analogous text of the festal epistle of the illustrious patriarch of Alexandria. The catalogue agrees with that of the epistle in almost all the details, while at the same time it gives indications of a more modern point of view. Thus the twenty-two books of the Old Testament are reckoned exactly as in the old list (Ruth standing by itself and Esther being excluded) which constitutes a peculiarity remarkable enough to establish the relationship of the two documents. So, too, the author of the Synopsis appends to the list of the canonical books of the Old Testament a second series of books not canonical, but reserved for the reading of catechumens [2]—viz., the Wisdom of Solomon, Ecclesiasticus, Esther, Judith, and Tobit. That is textually the distinction drawn by Athanasius, only the latter also mentions the *Apostolic Constitutions* and the *Pastor*, which the former passes over in silence, probably because the church, as time went on, had abandoned the use of them. Our commentator adds a note to inform us that, according to early writers, the book of Esther is canonical among the Hebrews, while Ruth is counted as an integral part of Judges, so that even in the hypothesis of this second conjecture, the number 22 is retained which apparently was the great point. On the subject of the Apo-

---

[1] Σύνοψις ἐπίτομος τῆς θείας γραφῆς.

[2] οὐ κανονιζόμενα μὲν, ἀναγινωσκόμενα δὲ μόνον τοῖς κατηχουμένοις.

calypse which Athanasius includes in his list without remark, our author finds it necessary to add that it was received as the work of John the theologian, and admitted as canonical by early and inspired Fathers,[1] a note which implies the fact that other Fathers, perhaps not so early and at any rate otherwise inspired, did not share in that opinion. After giving a complete enumeration of all the biblical books, the author of the Synopsis takes them all up again in the same order that he may enter into more or less extended details by way of introduction. Then he adds a catalogue of antilegomena and apocrypha, which shows that he was drawing from different sources without using any criticism, and that his notion even of the canon could hardly have been farther from being precise and settled. Under the head of *antilegomena* he once more introduces Wisdom, Ecclesiasticus, Esther, Judith, and Tobit, and with them four books of the Maccabees, the Psalms of Solomon, the story of Susanna, the Acts of Peter, John, and Thomas; the Gospel of Thomas, the Apostolic Constitutions, and the *inspired extracts* from the Clementines,[2] which means no doubt an orthodox recension of that famous romance. The confusion of the author's ideas betrays itself most of all in the fact that he ends his list of the antilegomena with these words—*These are the books which are read.*[3] This would lead us to think that the terms *antilegomena* and *deutero-canonical* were with him synonymous; but he immediately adds that he has enumerated them only by way of memorandum, because they are more worthy of being hid than of being read.[4] I see no other way of harmonizing these contradictory statements than by saying that an ignorant

---

[1] διχθεῖσα ὡς ἐκείνου καὶ ἐγκριθεῖσα ὑπὸ πάλαι ἁγίων καὶ πνευματοφόρων πατέρων.

[2] τὰ Κλημέντια ἐξ ὧν μετιφράσθησαν ἐκλεγέντα τὰ ἀληθέστερα καὶ θεόπνευστα.

[3] ταῦτα τὰ ἀναγινωσκόμενα.

[4] ἀποκρυφῆς μᾶλλον ἢ ἀναγνώσεως ἄξια.

compiler collected them from various sources, without succeeding in reconciling them, perhaps without perceiving that they are irreconcilable.

Another text, curious in a different way, may serve to prove that well on in the sixth century, the criticism of the canon did not so much lack liberty in its methods as means for being profitable to science and the church. We possess a treatise on the Holy Scriptures by a certain Junilius, who was long supposed to have been an African bishop, but according to recent researches,[1] must have been a civil functionary high in place at the court of Constantinople. In this essentially dogmatic treatise, we find, among others, two singular enough classifications of the books of the Bible —the one based on their contents, the other on the degree of authority they are supposed to enjoy. According to the former, the author reckons four classes of books: (1) the historical books, Pentateuch, Joshua, Judges, Samuel, Kings, Gospels and Acts; to these books several add Chronicles, Job, Tobit, Ezra, Judith, Esther, and Maccabees; (2) the prophetical books; to this category the author refers the sixteen prophets properly so called, enumerating them in chronological order, and also the Psalter and the Apocalypse, regarding which last the Eastern Fathers had special doubts; (3) the proverbial books—*i.e.*, the Proverbs of Solomon and Ecclesiasticus; some add Wisdom and Canticles; (4) the books of simple doctrine (didactic books)—viz., Ecclesiasticus, fourteen Epistles of Paul, one of Peter and one of John, to which very many add five other epistles called canonical (Catholic). As to their respective value, these books have either complete authority, or medium authority, or no authority at all. To the first class belong those

---

[1] See Kihn, *Theodor v. Mopsuestia und Junilius*, Friburg 1880. The treatise of Junilius is known under the name *De partibus legis divinæ* (Gallandi, *Bibl. P.P.*, tom. xii). The true title is: *Instituta regularia divinæ legis.* Kihn gives a critical edition of it.

named in the first rank in each series; to the second, those marked as added by several; to the third, all the others.[1] It is difficult to say exactly of what books the author was thinking when speaking of the third class, all the more that he ranks it with the others under the general title of *divine* books. Still from a phrase just a little obscure, he seems to have had in view, among others, Wisdom and Canticles. The question naturally arises, whence can such a system of classification have come to an author of the sixth century, in whose surroundings ecclesiastical usages had long ago succeeded in implanting quite different principles. We know now that Junilius took his information from a source which we must connect directly with the ancient school of Antioch. The kind of disfavour with which he treats so great a number of biblical books, or, if you will, his bold and non-traditional mode of selection, cannot be the result of an historical or literary criticism; it must have been inspired by considerations of practical utility, such as formerly prevailed among the Greek theologians of Syria. To this sphere also we are directed by the exclusion of the Apocalypse, and some of the Catholic Epistles. Perhaps Junilius himself did not understand the bearing of his system. At any rate, he does not seem to have been afraid of provoking complaints on the part of his readers, though the question of the canon is said to have been definitely settled for them by public documents.

The East did, for some time later, preserve feeble remains or confused remembrances of the critical theories or traditions which had formerly been put in circulation by the learned lectures of Diodorus of Tarsus and Theodore of

---

[1] *Quomodo divinorum librorum consideratur auctoritas? Quia quidam perfectæ auctoritatis sunt, quidam mediæ, quidam nullius. Qui sunt perfectæ auctoritatis? Quos canonicos in singulis speciebus absolute enumeravimus. Qui mediæ? Quos adjungi a pluribus diximus. Qui nullius auctoritatis sunt? Reliqui omnes* (*l. c.* p. 81).

Mopsuestia. But serious studies had so much degenerated in a land falling into the saddest decay, that the last representatives of a once famous school were unable even to expound with clearness and moderation the critical theses they had inherited. We have a striking example of this in another author of the same epoch. Cosmas[1] (535), an Egyptian monk, who had formerly travelled much as a merchant, inserted in the fifth book of his *Christian Topography*, a catalogue of the Holy Scriptures, in which he simply passes over in silence the Catholic Epistles and the Apocalypse, while extolling the value of the Bible and the salutary effects of an assiduous reading of the sacred texts. As regards the Apocalypse, its omission would not give the author's compatriots much concern; it was different with the Epistles. Hence Cosmas saw himself obliged afterwards to justify their exclusion. He boldly affirms that the church in every age has regarded them as doubtful, and that not a single author has made account of them or included them in the canon. He cites to this effect, Irenaeus, Eusebius, Amphilochius, and other Fathers, even Athanasius, according to a doubtful reading of the text; he grants that some receive all these seven epistles, that the Syrians admit three, that others distinguish those which may have been written by apostles from those which were the work of certain presbyters, and at this point he recalls the story of the two Johns of Ephesus. But the very variety of these opinions appears to make him inclined towards a more radical criticism. The fact that people spoke of the first, the second, the third of John, seems clearly to indicate to

---

[1] Cosmas Indopleustes, *Topogr. chr. ll.* xii. ed. Montfaucon (*Coll. nov. P.P.*, tom. ii.), Book v. pp. 242, f.

[2] Id., *ibid.*, B. vii. pp. 290 f. : τὰς καθολικὰς ἀνέκαθεν ἡ ἐκκλησία ἀμφιβαλλομένας ἔχει· καὶ πάντες δὲ οἱ ὑπομνηματίσαντες τὰς θείας γραφὰς οὔτε τις αὐτῶν λόγον ἐποιήσατο, ἀλλὰ καὶ οἱ κανονίσαντες τὰς ἰδιαιτέρους βίβλους πάντες ὡς ἀμφιβόλους αὐτὰς ἴσασι . . .

him that there is but one author, the man to whom early writers positively assign the two latter—viz., the presbyter of Ephesus. He concludes that a good Christian ought not to rest his faith on books so doubtful, but only on those which are generally recognised as canonical, and teach all that it is useful to know.[1] There is no need here to direct attention to the author's exaggerations and errors; still less shall I proceed to conclude from his statements, that the seven Catholic Epistles were not very generally regarded as canonical in the age and country in which he lived. But I insist once more on this incontestable fact, that the canon was settled by custom and not by an act of authority, that it was not a dogma; for otherwise an opposition so decided and so unjustifiable as that of Cosmas, would certainly have raised a tempest and called forth disciplinary measures. Moreover, there is apparent in this author a special motive of antipathy against the Catholic Epistles. In his work he exhibits a particular theory of the world against which a passage from the second epistle of Peter (iii. 12) was urged. Not having learning enough to meet the objection by a critical examination of this epistle, he found it more convenient to reject the whole volume in which it was included, because he had heard certain rumours regarding its origin.

Still we shall not be so severe on the facile decision of Cosmas, when we remember that the seven Catholic Epistles only came into use at the public readings in the second half of the fifth century. The Egyptian bishop, Euthalius, seems to have divided them about 462 for the first time into sections or pericopes, to be read in due order at the usual assemblies of the faithful.[2] Up to this date, these epistles

---

[1] οὐ χρὴ οὖν τὸν τέλειον χριστιανὸν, ἐκ τῶν ἀμφιβαλλομένων ἐπιστηρίζεσθαι, τῶν ἰδιαθέτων καὶ κοινῶς ὁμολογουμένων γραφῶν ἱκανῶς πάντα μηνυόντων κ. τ. λ.

[2] *Euthalii episc. Sulcensis editio actuum et epp.* ed. Zacagni (*Collect. monum. vet. eccl.*, Rome 1698, tom. i.), p. 529 : τὴν τῶν ἀναγνώσεων ἀκριβιστάτην τομὴν ἡμεῖς τεχνολογήσαντες ἀνακεφαλαιωσάμεθα.

were not always put together in one volume, nor were they everywhere admitted into the ordinary course of official readings in the Eastern Churches, ancient usage maintaining its ground long after the time at which science had ceased to have doubts regarding any one among them. The work of Euthalius must have been called forth by a need more universally felt, but it may also have contributed to produce and extend that need.

I shall mention only in passing the catalogues of Leontius of Byzantium (560), and of Anastasius Sinaita, patriarch of Antioch (†599). The former is complete for the New Testament, and for the Old it adheres to the Hebrew canon, except that it omits Esther.[1] In this, the influence of Athanasius is traceable, or rather there is one more proof that the authority of a writer justly renowned in the orthodox church was the most decisive argument in such questions, and procured acceptance even for peculiarities which had completely passed out of knowledge. The catalogue of Anastasius reckons 60 canonical books in all, 34 for the Old Testament (without the Apocrypha) and 26 for the New (without the Apocalypse). That is the catalogue which was drawn up at Laodicea.

The same century furnishes us also with two illustrations from the Latin Church which must not be neglected, though the history of the canon has not much to gain from their testimonies. One of these is Cassiodorius, once minister and senator at the court of the King of the Ostrogoths; he died in 562 in a convent founded by himself at Viviers: the other is Pope Gregory the Great.

Among other books for the instruction of his monks, Cassiodorius wrote a treatise on the Holy Scriptures,[2] in which he inserts three catalogues of biblical books, differing

---

[1] Leont. Byz. *de sectis*, ch. 2. *ap.* Galland. tom. xii.
[2] M. Aurelii Cassiodori *de institutione div. litt. Opp.* ed. Paris, 1600, tom. ii.

more or less from one another, but, according to him, equally venerated by the Catholic Church.[1] The first is that of Jerome, who reckons 22 books for the Old Testament and 27 for the New, completing along with the Holy Trinity, the true author of these books and of the predictions contained in them, the total sum of 50, a mystic sign of the year of jubilee and therefore of the remission of sins. The second is taken from St. Augustine, who reckons 22 historical and 22 prophetical books of the Old Testament, and 27 books in the New, which, added to the Trinity, make up the perfect and glorious number 72.[2] The third is taken, it is said, from the Septuagint, or, according to a more rational if not more authentic reading, from an old translation, *i.e.*, from a copy which the author had beside him. By a singular inadvertence, Cassiodorius found in it only 70 books, though this Bible had been as complete as that of Augustine, because he had forgotten to transcribe the title of the Epistle to the Ephesians. But he is as far from observing this as from seeing what caused the great difference between the first and second catalogues, a difference which, apart from counting the books separately, arose from omitting or adding the Apocrypha of the Old Testament; still less does he take any pains to justify his total figure, in which he proceeds at once to recognise the seventy palm-trees of the station at Elim (Exod. xv. 27).

Gregory (†604) gives no catalogue; but from his various works there may be brought together notices of sufficient interest regarding the questions with which we are now engaged. Just as in regard to the text in the Bible he seeks to recommend Jerome's new translation, while dealing gently

---

[1] *Nunc videamus quemadmodum lex divina tribus generibus divisionum a diversis patribus fuerit intimata quam tamen veneratur et concorditer suscipit universarum ecclesia regionum* (*l. c.*, f. 384 v).

[2] *Cui cum s. trinitatis addideris unitatem fit totius libri competens et gloriosa perfectio* (*ibid.*, f. 386 r).

with the prejudices of those who adhered to the old version,[1] so his judgment is somewhat hesitating on the value of the Apocrypha of the Old Testament. When quoting Maccabees, for instance, he makes excuse for appealing to the testimony of a book not canonical, but published for the edification of the Church;[2] the authors of Tobit and Wisdom are sometimes quoted as *certain just or wise men*;[3] but in other passages when quoting them, he does not hesitate to pronounce the name of Solomon or the sacred term *Scripture*. As to the New Testament, we learn from him, and for the first time, that Paul wrote *fifteen* epistles, but that the Church adheres to the number fourteen,[4] because fourteen, broken up into ten and four, represents both the Law (the Decalogue) and the Gospel. This ingenious discovery was reproduced by many posterior authors. Gregory does not tell us here which is Paul's fifteenth epistle, but we shall meet with it again more than once in the sequel of this history.

In the works of Isidore of Seville (†636) there are three catalogues, identical in substance and complete so far as the traditions go, which were generally accepted by the Latin Church.[5] Still this celebrated bishop is too learned and too anxious to show his learning to efface all traces of the criticism of previous centuries. Thus in the Old Testament, the Apocrypha, with Esther, are put at the end as a fourth class, their authors being unknown; in the New Testament he runs together, without observing the contradiction, the two formulas which speak of Paul's fourteen epistles and of the

---

[1] *Novam editionem ediscero sed ut comprobationis causa exigit nunc novam nunc veterem per testimonia assumo ut quia sedes apostolica cui præsideo utraque utitur (Præf. in Job).*

[2] *Moral. in Job.*, xix, 17.

[3] *Quidam justus* (ibid., x, 6); *quidam sapiens* (ibid., v, 25; vi, 7; xix, 13).

[4] *Quamvis epistolas quindecim scripserit sancta tamen ecclesia non amplius quam quatuordecim tenet* (ibid., xxxv, 25).

[5] Isidori Hisp. *de offic.*, i. 12. *Etym.*, vi, 2. *Lib. proœmior. in V. et N. T. init.*

seven churches to which the apostle is said to have written. He mentions the doubts of the Latins regarding the Epistle to the Hebrews, and the opposition made to several of the Catholic Epistles;[1] but, when all is said, all the books enumerated, even those of the *fourth* class, are equally inspired, and their true author is the Holy Spirit.[2] The author's critical reserves are in truth nothing more than faint echoes of his readings in Jerome.

My readers will have observed that Isidore, while displaying his erudition in what concerns the Apocrypha of the Old Testament and the disputed epistles of the New, mentions no doubt regarding the Apocalypse. For this, there was probably a special reason; it is impossible to suppose that he was not acquainted with the fact. Indeed, we know that a council of Toledo in 633, at which Isidore was present, took up the book in question in order to decree its canonicity, and to pronounce excommunication against those who should refuse to receive it or to take from it texts for their preaching at a certain period of the year.[3] I assume that Isidore's silence in regard to this controversy was intended, that the decree might not be weakened by the untimely recollection of a greater freedom in other churches. But the decreee itself, with its quite unusual severity, seems to have

[1] *Ad Hebræos ep. plerisque Latinis incerta propter dissonantiam sermonis. Eandem alii Barnabam, alii Clementem conscripsisse suspicantur. Petri. . . . secunda a quibusdam eius esse non creditur propter stili distantiam. Jacobus suam scripsit epistolam quae et ipsa a nonnullis eius esse negatur. Joannis epistolas tres idem Joannes edidit quarum prima tantum a quibusdam eius esse asseritur (De Off., l.c.).*

[2] Wisdom was rejected by the Jews from the canon because of its Christological testimonies.

[3] Concil. Tolet., IV. ap. Mansi, X. p. 624, c. 17: *Apocalypsin librum multorum conciliorum auctoritas et synodica ss. praesulum romanorum decreta Joannis ev. esse perscribunt et inter divinos libros recipiendum constituerunt, sed quamplurimi sunt qui eius auctoritatem non recipiunt atque in eccl. Dei praedicare contemnunt. Si quis eum deinceps aut non receperit, aut pascha usque ad pentecostem missarum tempore non praedicaverit excommunicationis sententiam habebit.*

had an immediate connection with the anti-Arian reaction which had taken place among the Visigoths a short time before. The Gothic Bible did not apparently contain the Apocalypse; at least the remains of it permit this supposition. The Latin Catholics were naturally led to impose the orthodox Bible on the populations that had recently entered into the pale of the orthodox church, and to attach a comparatively exaggerated importance to points of difference. It is above all to be observed here that the Arian Goths also did not receive the Epistle to the Hebrews; but on this point the Latin Catholics were far from being radically opposed to them. In the West, it was still an open question. Besides, very little importance can be attached to anything Latin authors say on these points. Isidore, who only compiled books, may still pass for a learned man for his age; his successors cannot claim that modest merit. Thus the catalogues given by the bishops Eugenius and Ildefonsus of Toledo, the one in verse the other in prose, adhere to the most complete enumeration without adding any remarks either critical or polemical. The latter is even a literal copy from the passage of Augustine which I have already placed before my readers. Further, these Spaniards seem to have had a more decided interest in insisting on the limitation of the biblical canon. We know that in the fifth century, and probably later still, their country was inundated with apocryphal and heretical books,[2] *i.e.*, with legends of suspicious origin (Gnostic or Manichæan) which spread the poison of heresy by the very attraction of the marvellous

---

[1] We find, *e.g.*, in Cassiodorius (*l. c.* ch. 8.) that he was obliged to get Chrysostom's homilies on that epistle translated from the Greek, because there existed no exegetical work in Latin which he could put into the hands of his monks.

[2] Turribii episc. Astur. *Epistola de non recipiendis apocr. scripturis in Opp.* Leonis M. ed. Ballerin., i. 711. Leonis *Ep. ad eundem* (*ibid.*, i. 706).

stories, and with which the guardians of orthodoxy could find no other fault.

While the West saw theological science gradually reduced to the reading of some selected authors of the fourth and fifth centuries, or to extracts made from their works and variously modified, the East still maintained a last relic of activity, though it shared equally in the general decay. But in our special and restricted sphere, this slight difference hardly made itself felt. On the contrary, I have a fact of some importance to mention which proves sufficiently that a positive science of the canon did not exist even in the Greek Church, and that the regulations which professed to put an end to the eternal hesitations resulted, at the end of the seventh century, just as they did three centuries before, in perpetuating the hesitations, even in consecrating them. In 691 and 692, under the Emperor Justinian II., a council was held at Constantinople, in the part of the palace called Trullum,[1] the first œcumenical council which took up the question of the biblical canon, at least implicitly. By one of its first decrees, it determined the series of the authorities which were to make law in the Church. Among these authorities there are reckoned the 85 so-called apostolical canons; then a certain number of synods, notably those of Laodicea and Carthage; finally a great number of fathers, among others Athanasius and Amphilochius. Now it is unnecessary for me to remind my readers that, so far as the list of the biblical books is concerned, this sanctioned the most incongruous and contradictory opinions. All my readers know what a great difference there is between the list of Laodicea and that of Carthage, what difference there was between Athanasius and many Greek Fathers of his century quite as orthodox as he, what extra-canonical books were given to the church

[1] *Concil. Trullanum, ap.* Mansi, xi. 939.

by the ancient rules attributed to the apostles: in a word there is not a single one of all the writings regarding which there were various opinions in the preceding centuries, there is not one which this decision does not both admit and reject, declare canonical and exclude from the canon.[1] It might be said that the members of the council had not even read the texts thus sanctioned. The fact is, that the Bible and its canon did not engage their attention very much. The essential point for them was to determine orthodoxy and discipline on other points of more immediate importance in relation to their own times; a detail of so little bearing in practice could not attract the attention of those who were preparing the formulas to be submitted for the sanction of the assembly. If the Church of Rome rejected that council, it was certainly not on account of these difficulties, for they existed in her own midst; she had many other reasons for being discontented with its decrees.[2]

A decision like this, neither clear nor positive, was not one that would efface from later theological literature all the recollections of criticism, all the traces of a diversity which nevertheless was far from being in harmony with the spirit of a generation devoured by the need of religious uniformity. At least I can produce for the centuries following further material proofs of the fact which I have been anxious to establish throughout my narrative. The celebrated John of Damascus (†754), the first Christian theologian who tried to reduce the doctrines of the church

---

[1] The apostolic canons admit the seven Catholic Epistles, but they likewise admit the *Apostolic Constitutions*; while these latter exclude the seven epistles. As for the Apocalypse and the Apocrypha of the Old Testament, it is superfluous to pass in review the contradictory declarations.

[2] The second Council of Nicaea (787), chiefly occupied with the task of re-establishing the worship of images, subscribed to the decrees of the Council of Trullum without entering into a critical examination of them. It only proscribed the Epistle to the Laodiceans which had found a place in some copies of the Bible.

to a systematic form, naturally takes up the question of the canon in his great dogmatic work.[1] He divides the Old Testament into four Pentateuchs or groups of writings, each composed of five books: the Law, the Scriptures, the Poems, and the Prophets.[2] In this classification, Job, contrary to custom, is ranked among the poetical books; Ezra and Esther are relegated to an appendix; the Apocrypha, notably Wisdom and Ecclesiasticus, are not counted at all.[3] In the New Testament, he enumerates in continuation of the 27 canonical books, the 85 so-called canons of the Apostles, and even, according to a various reading, the two Epistles of Clement.

Half a century later, the patriarch Nicephorus of Constantinople (†828) inserted in his *Abridgment of Chronography*, a catalogue of the holy books, which is curious in more than one respect. His Old Testament is composed of 22 canonical books, among which stands Baruch (inserted under a special number between Jeremiah and Ezekiel), but not Esther. The New Testament reckons 26 books, without the Apocalypse. Then, under the title of *antilegomena*, come the Maccabees, Wisdom, Ecclesiasticus, the Psalms of Solomon, Esther, Judith, Susanna, Tobit, the Apocalypses of John and Peter, the Epistle of Barnabas, and the Gospel of the Hebrews. Finally, there comes a long list of apocrypha, among which may be noted the *Constitutions* the epistles of Clement, Ignatius, Polycarp, and the *Pastor*. This document is also included in the Latin translation of the *Chronography*, made towards the end of the ninth century by the Roman librarian, Anastasius. The title of

---

[1] Joannis Damasc. *De Orthod. Fide*, iv. 17.

[2] ἡ νομοθεσία or five books of Moses; τὰ γραφεῖα, Joshua, Judges, Samuel, Kings, Chronicles; αἱ στιχήρεις βίβλοι, Job, Psalter, Solomon; ἡ προφητική. See above (p. 170) the similar classification by Cyril of Jerusalem.

[3] ὑπάρετοι μὲν καὶ καλαὶ ἀλλ' οὐκ ἀριθμοῦνται οὐδὲ ἔκειντο ἐν τῇ κιβωτῷ, a phrase borrowed from Epiphanius.

each book is accompanied by a figure indicating the number of lines it contains. These figures are wanting only in the Catholic Epistles, where the translator took care to add them. This catalogue, however, does not appear to be the work of the historian who has transmitted it to us. It must be much more ancient, as may be seen by the critical results it represents, by the mention of several works which probably were not in existence in the time of Nicephorus (such as the Gospel of the Hebrews), as well as by the absence of any bibliographical note for the Catholic Epistles, a fact which can hardly be explained except by supposing an origin antecedent to the time when these epistles were generally included in Bibles. But even with this supposition, the document of which I am speaking has a peculiar interest for the knowledge of the state of the question of the canon in the time of Nicephorus. By inserting it in his work, the patriarch as much as says that he has no better list to give, and that he does not consider this list to be incompatible with the orthodoxy of the Church of which he is the head.

The feeble revival of literary activity in the West which characterises the Carlovingian epoch, furnishes us with hardly any new materials for the history of the canon. The theologians of Gaul and Germany knew only the translation of Jerome, and the catalogues they give are usually in agreement with the Vulgate. The most fertile exegete of the ninth century, Raban Maur, archbishop of Mayence (†856) gives a complete catalogue of 72 biblical books, at the same time mentioning the doubts of earlier writers regarding the antilegomena; but in this there is nothing very remarkable, for it is plain from the very first that all this critical science is literally borrowed from Isidore, beyond whom the researches of French learning hardly found it necessary or

---

[1] Rab. Maurus, *de Instit. cleric.* ii., 53 f.

prudent to venture. The old distinctions were no longer kept up.[1] In the same way, though his contemporary, the Bishop Aimon of Halberstadt (†853) is at pains to defend the canonicity of the Epistle to the Hebrews,[2] this does not mean that the epistle had met with opposition in the monasteries along the Saale; the author is only taking pleasure in the adornment of his work with some morsel of science picked up in the course of his reading.[3] Still I might quote examples of a more independent judgment. Thus the anonymous author of a work on biblical miracles[4] formally declares his desire to exclude the stories of Bel, the dragon, and the Maccabees, because they have no canonical authority. Thus, too, Notker Labeo, a monk of St. Gall (†912), applies this same criticism to the books of Esther and Chronicles.[5]

The name of Charlemagne himself may find a place in this history of the canon. The powerful emperor, who set much store on being the defender and bulwark of the Church, did not think it beneath his dignity to watch over the purity of the Scriptures,[6] which does not mean, however, that he engaged in the criticism of the canon. I have in another work[7] had occasion to prove that he was concerned only about the exactness of the Latin copies, which were growing more and more faulty through the ignorance

---

[1] *Hos (ll. apocr. V.T.) moderno tempore inter S.S. enumerat ecclesia legitque eos sicut cæteras canonicas* (Id., *Prol. in Sap.*)

[2] Haimon. Halb. *Hist. sacr.*, iii. 3.

[3] There exist many other lists in the authors of the ninth and following centuries, but it is useless to reproduce them here; they are only copies of one another.

[4] Anonymus Anglus, *de Mirab. S.S. in Opp. Augustin*, tom. xvi., ed. Bass., B. ii., 32 f.

[5] Notker Labeo, *de Viris Illustr.*, ch. 3: *Non pro auctoritate sed tantum pro memoria et admiratione habentur.*

[6] *Volumus et ita missis nostris præcepimus ut in ecclesiis libri canonici veraces habeantur* (*Baluzii Capitul. r. franc.*, i., 210).

[7] *Fragments relatifs à l'hist. de la Bible fr.* (*Revue de théol.*, first series, ii., pp. 65 f).

of the scribes.[1] As to the collection itself, it is to be believed that the emperor adhered to general usages. Moreover, Pope Adrian I. had sent him a collection of ecclesiastical laws, among which was also the letter of Innocent I. to Exsuperius of Toulouse. Of this letter I have already given the substance; it contained a complete list of the sacred books. It is true that a capitulary of Aix-la-Chapelle (789) is often quoted, wherein an appeal in regard to the biblical canon is made to the decision of the Council of Laodicea. This would practically mean that the Church of the French empire officially rejected the Apocrypha of the Old Testament and the Apocalypse. In this way it has been interpreted by several authors. But the results of modern criticism justify us in thinking that the appeal to the decree of Laodicea refers only to the prohibition against reading in church other books than those received as canonical, while the list itself, which now forms the sixtieth article of the acts of that Synod, was neither known to the composers of those of Aix-le-Chapelle, nor reproduced by them.

Before going further, let us glance at another class of documents more eloquent than the Fathers and more positive than the councils on questions relative to the canon:— these are the Bibles themselves which have survived from that period. I have already had occasion to point out the importance of their testimony; I am willing to grant that this importance diminishes in proportion as we advance towards modern times; still it will not be superfluous to say some words about it in passing. In speaking here of Bibles, I am using a term hardly suited to the facts. At least, there is scarcely anything but the Latin translation, of which there still exist some copies complete, or supposed to be complete, and belonging to a date before the eleventh

[1] *Igitur quia curæ nobis est ut nostrarum ecclesiarum status ad meliora semper proficiat . . . universos V. et N. T. libros librariorum imperitia depravatos correximus* (Capitul., l.c. p. 203).

century. In the Greek language (the Septuagint and the New Testament) there is not a single one beyond the three or four very ancient MSS. of which I have already spoken. But an examination of the detached parts which have come down to us, several belonging to the Carlovingian period, cannot fail to be very instructive. Thus it is very useful to note the fact that there exist twice as many copies of the Gospels (upwards of 500) as of the Epistles; that the Epistles of Paul, of which we possess about 260 copies, were transcribed much more frequently than the Catholic Epistles; that the Apocalypse was copied and consequently read and employed much more rarely than these last, not a hundred copies being in existence. These figures clearly show that the conception of the canon of the New Testament was not essentially a dogmatic fact (according to which all the parts of the text should have been regarded as equally sacred and necessary) but rather a point in ecclesiastical practice, subordinated to needs that were independent of the theories of the school. If the Apocalypse formed the only exception here, we might believe that copies were rare, solely on account of the disfavour with which criticism received that book in the East. But this very disfavour was based on prejudices not connected with historical science, and certainly in the contrary case, there would be no explanation for the comparative scantiness of the copies of the Pauline Epistles whose authenticity nobody doubted. Among the volumes containing these epistles, there are several which include only thirteen. Thus, to speak only of manuscripts anterior to the tenth century, the Epistle to the Hebrews is entirely wanting in Codex G (Dresden); it is given only in Latin, and not in Greek in Codex F (Cambridge); it is added by a much later hand in Codex D (Paris); it did not succeed in obtaining a settled place among the other epistles to which it was added; for it is put sometimes between Thessalonians and Timothy, sometimes after the Epistle to the Colossians, most frequently after the Epistle to Philemon, as an appendix added by way of afterthought to a collection already complete. This variation, apparently quite fortuitous, in the place assigned to it, is a sure index of the persistence of the traditional doubt. The numerous Latin manuscripts preserved to us have not yet been sufficiently examined in relation to the history of the canon; still I am in a position to mention some facts which prove that researches made in this direction would not be fruitless. Thus we often find that fifteenth epistle of Paul already mentioned, the Epistle to the Laodiceans, a little apocryphal document of unknown origin; it is a poor compilation of Pauline phrases, made solely with the purpose of filling up a supposed lacuna in apostolic literature.[1] It has no fixed place in the Bibles, standing sometimes after Galatians, sometimes quite at the end, often too before the Pastoral Epistles. From the Vulgate it passed into the German and Romance translations of the Middle Ages. I have met with it in the version of the Albigenses.[2] It was so generally considered to be authentic, to be an integral part of the Bible, that it was included in it at the time of the invention of printing and long afterwards. I might quote a series of editions, Latin, German and others, containing it, and the number of them is probably greater than I am aware of.[3] It is besides not the only book of this nature which was confounded with the Bible. In a MS. of the Dresden Library, the *Pastor* of Hermas is inserted between Psalms and Proverbs; the number of the books of the Maccabees is sometimes increased to four; the little work, called the

[1] Col., iv. 16.
[2] *Revue de Théol.* First series, v. p. 335.
[3] It exists in no Greek MS. Codex G of the Pauline Epistles ends with the title "*To the Laodiceans*," corrupted into πρὸς Λαουδακησας ἄρχιται ἐπιστολή; but the text is not there.

Prayer of Manasseh and unknown to the East, had the chance of continuing in its usurped place down to our own time.

In speaking of these manuscripts, I have already crossed the limit of the Carlovingian period from which previously the testimonies were gathered. There still remain to be gleaned some interesting details in the vast field of the period of scholasticism. As every one knows, that period is characterised by the total absence of historical studies and an excessive demand for theoretical subtlety, and for system-making. Still this characterisation is not enough here. Other elements are to be recognised in the spiritual life of the generations preceding the epoch of the Reformation. Exegesis there was none, or rather what bore that name was composed of mystical dreamings, allegorical interpretations applied by preference to the texts least fertile for Christian edification; and these lucubrations, sometimes ingenious and clever, often impregnated with a spirit of profound piety, but more frequently dull, far-fetched and absurd, came more and more to be regarded as the necessary accompaniment of a text, the students of which persuaded themselves that it had been written only to serve for such studies. The *gloss*[1] or comment, above all when made under a name known and venerated, when it took the decisive charms, so to speak, of a lexicographic assertion, became an integral part of the text, was confounded with it, first as a marginal note, then by various kinds of intercalations. Historic knowledge regarding the biblical books and their authors was nothing but a tissue of legends (many of which, be it said parenthetically, have passed into the science of French and English Protestantism), and spread all the more easily that the dominating tendency towards

---

[1] On the meaning and history of this term, see my article in Herzog's Real-Encyclopädie, Vol. v. pp. 192 f. sec. ed.

allegory went very well with the taste for the marvellous, the same poetic lustre being shed on these two elements apparently foreign to one another. In general, there no longer existed any distinction between what was canonical or apocryphal—or rather, one might be tempted to say, the legendary stories of the lives of biblical people were better known and more relished than the simple and sober narrative of the Gospel; the didactic books of the Old as of the New Testament had fallen into oblivion.[1] On the other hand, the books of ritual, which were indispensable to worship and were therefore more widely circulated and more popular than the Bible itself, became almost of necessity an integral part of the canon, since they were canonical in the primitive and fundamental meaning of the word, *i.e.*, they were fixed by ecclesiastical authority. The terminology itself introduced or consecrated this confusion; and public usage, which was every day bringing together the biblical texts and the formulas of the liturgy, gave to both the same rank.[2] Dom Mabillon found in the monastery of Bobbio a very old liturgical book containing a catalogue of the holy books in which the New Testament was reckoned as having 28 books; fourteen and seven epistles, the Apocalypse, Acts, the gospels, and a book *sacramentorum*—*i.e.*, the missal.

When the theological idea of the canon was so completely forgotten, there cannot be any great interest in gathering from the principal authors of the scholastic period, in-

---

[1] For further details, I may refer to what I have said in my *Fragments sur l'Histoire de la Bible fr.* (Revue de Théol., first series, iv.) and especially in my treatise, *Die deutsche Historienbibel vor der Erfindung des Bücherdrucks*, Jena, 1855.

[2] Aurel. Agricola *De Chr. eccl. politia*, ed. Ritter i. 156 : *Sacros libros appellamus illos qui canonicas continent V. et N. T. scripturas quæ in sacra liturgia leguntur. Hujus generis potissimum sunt evangelia atque apostolorum epp. et acta, tum ex V. T. prophetarum scripta. His addimus missæ canonem quem inter sacros libros merito recensemus.*

[3] *Mus. Ital.*, i. 396.

dividual opinions regarding the form and tenor of the sacred collection. Still, as my narrative is the first of its kind in France, I would rather run the risk of wearying my readers than of making any notable omission. Besides, the names to be cited are not unknown in the history of the Church and of literature. From the details I am going to give, it will be seen that the science of St. Jerome was quite enough still for the schools, only instead of being imperfect, insufficient as it had been formerly, it had, for a disinherited generation, become bold and superfluous.

Peter of Clugny (†1156) reckons 22 *authentic* books in the Old Testament, in addition to which there are six others he cannot pass over in silence; these, though unable to attain the same distinguished rank, have still deserved, by their excellent and necessary contents, to be received by the Church.[1] Hugo of St. Victor (†1141) speaks to similar purpose when he says of the Apocrypha of the Old Testament that they are read but not written in the canon.[2] As for the New Testament, he reckons in it eight books in two *orders* or series: on one side, the four gospels; on the other, the Acts, Paul, the canonical epistles, and the Apocalypse. He speaks further of a third *order* which includes in the first rank the Decretals, then the writings of the orthodox Fathers. This third class is evidently not formed according to the dignity of the books (since the two other classes make up the New Testament), but in order to draw a distinction between what is peculiar to the Christian Church and what it has in common with the Synagogues. At the same time he declares that the books of this third order are not assimilated to the canonical books, but to those which are simply

---

[1] Petri Cluniac. *Ep.* ii. B. i. : . . . . *restant post hos authenticos ll. sex non reticendi libri* (Wisd., Eccles., Judith, Tobit, Macc.) *qui, etsi ad illam sublimem præcedentium dignitatem pervenire non potuerunt, propter laudabilem tamen et pernecessariam doctrinam ab ecclesia suscipi meruerunt.*

[2] Hugon. a S. Victore *Elucidd. de S.S.* c. 6.

read.[1] John of Salisbury, bishop of Chartres (†1182), when recalling the various lists of Cassiodorius, declares,[2] that for his part, he adheres to Jerome as the author most worthy of faith in these matters. In his opinion, therefore, there are 22 books in the Old Testament; the Apocrypha (to which he adds the *Pastor*, telling us he never saw it) are not in the canon, though they are piously received as edifying to faith and religion.[3] When speaking of the New Testament, this author repeats all he had read in Jerome about the doubts of the ancients relative to the antilegomena, without, however, attaching more importance to them than we attach to other curiosities of tradition. But he reckons fifteen Pauline epistles, and on this point the opinions of his age prevail very decidedly over the claims of the learned monk of Bethlehem.[4]

Speaking generally, the science of those times was entirely second hand, and no great weight can be given to the appearances of criticism found here and there in authors who were mere compilers. The Church and its tradition were everything; individual knowledge was nothing; and we would do well to master this truth completely if we are to appreciate its inevitable consequences and guard against deceiving ourselves about the effects which would be produced if the same causes were again to come into operation. The great St. Thomas Aquinas,[5] no doubt, does not show his science in a very brilliant light, when he states that before the synod of

---

[1] The same distinction of the Apocrypha of the Old Testament is also made by Richard of Saint-Victor (*Exceptt.*, ii. 9.), by Pierre-le-Mangeur (regarding whom I may refer to my article in the *Revue*, vol. xiv.), and others. Still it is not the opinion of all authors.

[2] Joann. Sarisber. *Ep.* 172, *ad Henric. comit.*

[3] *Quia religionem et fidem aedificant pie admissi sunt.*

[4] *Quindecima quae ecclesiae Laodicensium scribitur, licet (ut ait Jeronymus) ab omnibus explodutur, tamen ab apostolo scripta est!*

[5] Thom. Aquin., *Prolog, in ep. ad Hebr.*

Nicaea some doubted whether the Epistle to the Hebrews was Paul's, as if the synod of Nicaea had had anything to do with the matter; but we must not exaggerate the importance of the definition given by the unknown author of a gloss inserted in the body of the canon law,[1] which gloss distinguishes in the Bible, books of different value. Ideas continued to be fluctuating, theories to be uncertain, for the simple reason that all practical interest in the question had died out.

While the science of the West, in so far as it existed, leans on Jerome (since it maintains after a fashion the distinction of the Apocrypha of the Old Testament), the science of the East prefers to adhere to the official authorities whose decisions it delights to recall, without removing their contradictions. Indeed, in the numerous commentators on ecclesiastical law,[2] there are not so much complete catalogues as indications of the texts that decide the question of the canon. These texts are especially the 85th of the Apostolic Canons, and the decree of the council of Constantinople (Trullanum, 692) and, subsidiary to these, Fathers quoted by that council, the synod of Carthage and sometimes the synod of Laodicea, but rarely its famous 60th canon which gives the list of the holy books, but appears not to have been known generally at this time. From what has been said of all these texts, it is manifest that, even apart from the one last mentioned, they were not at all agreed about the details. This simply proves that the authority of decrees when given, and that of the Fathers, were in fact more im-

---

[1] Decret. Gratiani, P. i. dist. 19 c. 6: *Potest esse quod omnes recipiantur, non tamen quod omnes eadem veneratione habeantur.*

[2] *E.g.* Zonaras, Alexius Aristenus, Theodorus Balsamon, Arsenius, Blastares, whose works are brought together in the collections of the canonists. The passages relative to our subject were first collected by Credner, *Geschichte des Canons*, p. 251 f.

portant than the question of the canonicity of any particular book. As the 85th canon serves here as basis and point of departure, the addition of the Apocrypha and the Apocalypse (this latter being omitted in that article), is sometimes mentioned as optional; the exclusion of the Epistles of Clement and of the *Constitutions* (which are included in it) is justified, either by the other texts, or by the heretical falsification the latter had undergone. But both exceptions are mentioned with profound indifference for the question itself, which the jurists left to the theologians, they in turn no longer paying any attention to it.

I shall cite further Nicephorus Callistus, an author of the fourteenth century who, in his *Ecclesiastical History*,[1] inserted an extended note on the biblical canon. It is clear from that note that he explicitly and unreservedly accepts the New Testament complete, with the 27 books as we have it. He has read Eusebius; he knows and reproduces all that was said before about the seven disputed books; but he thinks that the doubts regarding them have finally been dispelled, and he affirms that the Churches are unanimous on this point.[2]

Several symptoms, however, appear in the midst of that dark period, and announce a coming change in the direction of theological studies. The religious and literary movement which characterises the second half of the twelfth century, was not slow in reacting on the sphere we are now exploring. I do not think I am wrong in directing attention first to a feeble effort, made by a small number of theologians, to break through the narrow limits of Latin science, the common Bible and allegorical interpretation, that they might inquire a little into the form and meaning it had among the

---

[1] Niceph. Callisti *Hist. eccles.* ii. 45 f.

[2] ταῦτα μὲν εἰ καὶ ἀμφίβολα τοῖς πρότερον ἔδοξαν, ἀλλ' οὖν ἀπάσαις ἐς ὕστερον ταῖς ὑπ' οὐρανὸν ἐκκλησίαις τὸ ἀναντίρρητον ἐσχηκότα ἐγνώκαμεν.

Jews. The remembrance of the difference, as we have just seen, had never been completely effaced; but even those who assigned a special place to the six apocrypha were acquainted with the rest only in the usual form. Now it is interesting to establish the fact that a beginning was made of looking more to the primitive form of certain books, and soon also of using new lights for comprehension of the texts. Modest as it is, this opening of modern science deserves to be noted. It is perhaps connected with some more intimate relations between the Christian theologians and the learned exegetes of the Synagogue, who flourished at that time on both sides of the Pyrenees.

Thus we find in the works of Peter of Blois[1] (†1200) a catalogue of the books of the Bible, which not only takes into consideration the division of the canon of the synagogue (though the order of the hagiographa is different in the Hebrew Bible), but mentions also the title given to each book by the Jews. At the same time, the author is not sure of his facts, since he hesitates to detach Ruth and Lamentations from the books of Judges and Jeremiah, with which they are connected in the Latin Bible. He ranks in a fourth *order* the apocryphal books which the Jews exclude from the canon, while the Church of Christ honours them, and preaches from them as divine. It is obvious that the antipathy against the Jews contributed to maintain these apocrypha in the canon.[2] A similar catalogue is given by the Dominican, Hugo of St. Cher (†1263), in the prologue of his series of sermons on Joshua. I transcribe it in a note that my readers may at the same time have an idea of the form which science assumed in the hands of these powerful dialecticians, and of the literary taste with which their

---

[1] Petr. Blæsensis, *de divisione et scriptoribus ss. ll.*

[2] This catalogue by Peter of Blois is not the only one of the century which reproduces the Hebrew titles.

lucubrations were framed.¹ The list in it is arranged from the Hebrew canon, though there is no doubt that the author had his science at second hand, and was compelled to use a little liberty for the sake of versification, which all the same had not caused him very great anxiety. When he places the *Pastor* among the apocrypha of the Old Testament, the illustrious cardinal spares us the trouble of going into an ecstasy over his innovations; besides it is a peccadillo that will be pardoned to him much more readily than his unfortunate division of the Bible into chapters, by which he has gained an unhappy immortality.

In the following century, the Norman Franciscan, Nicolas de Lyra (†1340), is already availing himself of his acquaintance with Hebrew; but his merits belong more to the history of exegesis than that of the canon. The reserves he makes regarding the canon hardly surpass those of his predecessors in boldness.²

A century later (for progress was not very rapid in those days) came the Greeks, classical studies, the Platonic philosophy, the great movements of opposition to Rome, things which exercised more or less influence on the march of biblical studies. But the effects they produced fall only in part into the scheme of my narrative, and I prefer to speak of them in a special chapter.

> ¹ *Quinque libros Moysi Josue Judicum Samuelem*
> *Et Malachim ; tres præcipuos bis sexque prophetas*
> *Hebræus reliquis censet præcellere libris.*
> *Quinque vocat legem, reliquos vult esse prophetas.*
> *Post hagiographa sunt: Daniel David Esther et Esdras*
> *Job Paralipomenon et tres libri Salomonis.*
> *Lex vetus his libris perfecte tota tenetur.*
> *Restant Apocrypha: Jesus Sapientia Pastor*
> *Et Macchabæorum libri Judith atque Tobias.*
> *Hi quia sunt dubii sub canone non numerantur,*
> *Sed qui vera canunt ecclesia suscipit illos.*

² Nic. Lyr. *Postilla (passim)* in the prefaces to the Apocrypha: *Non sunt de canone sed per consuetudinem romanæ ecclesiæ leguntur.*

I shall conclude this present chapter by reminding my readers of a second symptom of awakening, more immediately fertile than that we have just been discussing. I mean the religious movements connected with the name of the Waldenses, Albigenses, and other sects who tried to free themselves from the yoke of Roman tradition. As this opposition was based on the Bible, at least in part (though not so much so as the Protestant historian would like to affirm), the dominant church found itself under the necessity of recurring to the Bible for its defence and polemics. As the first versions in the popular tongue owed the light to these tendencies, they occupy a very important place in the history of the Holy Scriptures.[1] At present I confine myself to reproducing briefly what is connected with the history of the canon. The Albigenses or Cathari, as dualists, rejected generally the Old Testament, whose origin they attributed to the evil principle (the devil); still from several contemporary testimonies it would appear that this opinion was not shared by all the members of the sect, and that some confined themselves to a selection which meant the rejection only of the Law and the historical books. The proofs of these facts will be found in my preceding works on the subject; it is superfluous to repeat them here. Besides, this wholly subjective and dogmatic criticism, exercised by men who had broken with the church, did not change the natural course of ideas, and could only prove one thing—viz., that in the most opposite camps the Bible had to bend to the exigencies of systems. The Cathari did not make their selection to secure the purity of the texts, but rather to favour their heretical theology; and they were in no position to reproach the Catholics with adding certain non-canonical books, for they themselves sought edification

---

[1] See my articles in the *Revue*, First Series, ii. p. 321; v. p. 321; vi. p. 65.

in reading Apocryphal books, such as the Vision of Isaiah.[1] As to the New Testament, we do not need to consult the early writers, since we possess still a complete copy of it in which the Apocalypse is placed between Acts and the Catholic Epistles, and the *fifteen* epistles of Paul at the end.[2] They had moreover a work attributed to the Apostle John. The text of this work has been re-discovered; it was of a nature to support their special dogmas.[3]

As to the Waldenses, I may simply repeat here what I have proved at length elsewhere—viz., that the common opinion which gives them the honour of having made a careful separation between the Apocrypha of the Old Testament and the canonical books, is false and erroneous on every point. It is founded on a pretended Confession of Faith, dated 1120, which is now known to be forged, at least antedated, and to belong at the earliest to the year 1532.[4] The Waldenses of the Middle Ages were acquainted and could be acquainted with the Vulgate only, as it was generally received in their time; it is even very doubtful whether they had a complete version of it. But of the four supposed Waldensian manuscripts of the New Testament, there are two which also contain Wisdom and Ecclesiasticus.

---

[1] Moneta, *Summa adv. Cathar.*, p. 218; *Dicunt prophetas bonos fuisse, aliquando autem omnes damnabant præter Isaiam cuius dicunt esse quemdam libellum in quo habetur quod spiritus Isaiæ raptus a corpore usque ad septimum cœlum ductus est in quo vidit quædam arcana quibus vehementissime innituntur.*

[2] In this order . . . Phil., Thess., Col., Laod., Tim. &c.

[3] Thilo reprinted it in his *Codex apocryphus*, p. 884 f.

[4] *Ara sensegon li libres apocryphes li qual non son pas receopu de li hebrios, mas nos li legen (enaima dis Hierome al prologe de li proverbi) per lenseignament del poble, non pas per confermar lauthorita de las doctrinas ecclesiasticas.*—For the proofs that this Confession of Faith is not authentic, see *Revue*, First Series iii. p. 326 f. I take this opportunity of saying that Mr. Gilly's work (*The Romaunt Version of the Gospel of St. John, with an introductory history of the Version of the Waldenses*) swarms from beginning to end with faults and errors.

In spite of these reserves, which I am bound to make for the sake of historical truth, it is none the less just to say that these religious movements, though powerless in changing the traditional form of the Bible and ignorant of any necessity of innovation in that direction, contributed much to pave the way for a more serious reform.

CHAPTER XIV.

THE RENAISSANCE.

From all the facts or testimonies with which the literature of the Middle Ages, and above all the period of the domination of scholasticism furnishes us, we have been able to draw these conclusions: that a vague remembrance of the uncertainty of the canon had been preserved in the schools, that the learned delighted to parade on occasion whatever shreds of historical knowledge they had been able to collect in their reading, but did not know how to use them in combating traditional opinions, or in making the least change in received usages. In fact, all the Latin Church received the Bible in the form in which it has been preserved to our day, and the Greek Church, which formerly had considered it important to give a more exclusively theological value to the notion of the canon, had insensibly come to be in harmony with the sister church as to the extent of the collection.

Still it will not be out of place to say once more that this result was brought about by usage, and not by any official and peremptory decision made by authority. On this point, things were no further advanced at the end of the fourteenth century than they had been at the end of the fourth; appeal was made at one and the same time to the rules laid down at Laodicea and Carthage, which contradicted each other, and to those of Trullum which assigned the same authority to them both. Exclusive use was made of the text of Jerome, who presented in a confused mass the elements of the double canon, and carefully distinguished between them in his prefaces. From the standpoint of a scriptural theology such as ours, such a state of things would have been intolerable. The reality of the fact, and the absence of all greater inconvenience which might have resulted from it, prove of themselves that the theology of the Middle Ages, or rather Christian theology at the time when official Catholicism was coming into existence, was not based on biblical teaching as such to the exclusion of all other, but on an ecclesiastical tradition sufficiently powerful in itself to have nothing to fear from the fluctuations of opinion which scarcely touched the outer fringes of the system. The Bible had its practical value; it was of use for private and common edification; in that respect it lost nothing by being enriched and extended. As to its dogmatic teaching, the elementary truths it consecrated had, from the first and quite independently, become indisputable axioms for every member of the church; and the science of the schools when it did come to discuss questions for which Holy Scripture gave no clear and direct reply, soon ceased to consult it, turning by preference to the authorities which had succeeded in deciding them, and in promulgating their opinions. The discussion of the scriptural canon presented no practical interest whatever, and that explains how a question which to us seems all-important, should have remained without answer for six centuries.

But it also explains why this same question remained undecided even when the attempt was made to resolve it officially. Down to the close of the Middle Ages, the see of Rome had not delivered any categorical opinion on the canon of the Bible. The letter of Innocent I. to the bishop of Toulouse had not been promulgated solemnly as a general law of the church; the decree of Gelasius or of Hormisdas could scarcely have had any greater authority, as may be seen from successive alterations of its text. The papacy was not therefore bound by its antecedents in such a way as to be obliged to regard as heresy all freedom of opinion on the subject of the canon, while at the same time it remained in the narrow circle of the traditional reserves; it had no motive powerful enough to make it break through the neutrality. At the time of the Council of Florence (1439), or at least in consequence of the efforts then made to win back the schismatic Greeks, it chanced that Pope Eugenius IV. published a bull regarding the canon. This bull may be considered to be the first document of the kind emanating from the holy see in a perfectly authentic way, and professing to represent the belief of the whole church of which the Pope was head. It does not indeed form part of the acts of the council,[1] and on that account voices were raised even at Trent in the denial of its authority. But the opposition did not succeed, and, since the decisions formulated on these two occasions are after all textually the same, I have no reason for lessening the importance of the earlier decision. At any rate, from my own point of view, that creates no difficulty; though from the standpoint of ecclesiastical tradition, it may be said that if the Council of Trent had recognised the bull of Eugenius IV. as a synodal decision, it would never have permitted the question of the canon to be debated anew within its pale. Be this as it may, the bull of which I am speaking declares all the books contained in the Latin Bibles then in use to be inspired by the same Holy Spirit,[2] without distinguishing them into two classes or categories; Tobit and Judith are placed between Nehemiah and Esther; Wisdom and Ecclesiasticus between Canticles and Isaiah; Baruch before Ezekiel, and two books of the Maccabees at the end of the Old Testament. In the New there are reckoned fourteen Pauline epistles, that to the

[1] It may be found in the collection of P. Hardouin, *Act concil.*, ix. 1023, and elsewhere.

[2] *Unum atque eundem Deum V. et N. T. h. e. legis et prophetarum atque evangelii profitetur (ss. ecclesia romana) auctorem, quoniam eodem Spiritu s. inspirante utriusque Testamenti sancti loquuti sunt, quorum libros suscipit et veneratur, qui titulis sequentibus continentur.* . . .

Hebrews being last, and the Acts coming immediately before the Apocalypse. This catalogue hardly interests us but for one fact of very slender importance: throughout the list it consecrates no book which had not had its place in the Latin Church for a thousand years; but it did not go so far as to give canonical honours to the Epistle to the Laodiceans, which we have found some of the most illustrious scholastics extolling. To repeat once more, there is therefore ground for saying that the Church of Rome concerned herself very little with the caprices or the theories of its great writers, and continued to walk with a firm step in the path marked out by the ancient usages of its ritual.

All that did not prevent theologians, in the second half of the fifteenth century, from expressing themselves on the subject of the Apocrypha with the frankness of their predecessors. Their frankness was more simple than daring; for, while protesting their profound admiration for these books, they reject them from the canon, and, while apparently desirous of contesting their authority, they extol their qualities, so that for lack of any precise conception of the canon, the mass of Christians and even the majority of clerics must have despaired of grasping the true difference. In a note I quote, as an example, the opinions of Alphonsus Tostatus, bishop of Avila in Spain (†1455) and of the Carthusian Dionysius de Rickel, surnamed the ecstatic doctor (†1471), two of the most fertile exegetes of their day; the one having left twenty-seven, the other twelve folio volumes of commentary on the Bible.[1]

---

[1] Alphonsi Tostat. *Praef. Quaest.* i., *in Scr.* . . . . . *Alii sunt libri qui ad s.s. pertinent qui in canone non sunt sed quartum locum obtinent . . . hos apocryphorum loco censent. Quanquam horum doctrina ad convincendum . . . minus idonea sit et auctoritas non ita ut caeterorum solida, s. tamen ecclesia etsi prioribus minorem eis tamen auctoritatem accommodat.* Dionys., Carthus., *Prolog. in Sirac.; Liber iste non est de canone quanquam de eius veritate non dubitatur.*

But it was quite another matter when, at the opening of the following century, the vivifying breath of a new literary and scientific life was added to that general need of religious reform, which to all time constitutes the glory of that epoch. We shall see by-and-by how, in the bosom of Protestant societies, this movement exercised a powerful and profound influence on the question of the canon. I content myself here with stating that, even beyond this sphere, the arena of learned debate was opening up, and that the first tottering steps of historical criticism were attempted by a science which had to pass through a second childhood, before being to any extent sure of itself. No doubt this criticism had no very remarkable results, but it must not be forgotten that the absolute necessity for conservative stability, felt all the more keenly that the attack from without was energetic and the crisis perilous, tied the hands even of the most enlightened Catholic doctors, who were afraid of compromising graver interests by yielding too much to the impulses of subjective thought, even in ordinary questions. But just because the position of affairs was governed by considerations of this kind, I must set down even the slightest attempts at innovation among those who belonged to the party of resistance.

Among the representatives of the higher Romish clergy who are quoted as witnesses during the first years of the epoch of the Reformation, a eulogistic appeal is made to the Cardinal Thomas de Vio, bishop of Gaeta, and known by the name of that see (Cajetanus.) From him there has come down a series of biblical commentaries in the literal sense, and the research displayed in them was of itself an immense advance for the science of those times. These commentaries are accompanied by introductions to the various books, in which the author does not shrink from dealing with questions of criticism. In regard to the Old Testament, he gets out of any difficulty by means of a definition of canonicity which might be applied to any kind of book;[1] still behind the procedure there was a mental reservation, which becomes more obvious in what he says regarding the antilegomena of the New Testament. Thus he disputes overtly the Pauline origin of the Epistle to the Hebrews; he avails himself of St. Jerome's doubts to cover his criticism; but he discusses very seriously some of the internal arguments which justify him in reproducing these doubts. Only he professes to say at the end that he is not anxious to insist on the result obtained, and that he will conform to usage in choosing the name of the author.[2] His book contains similar opinions regarding the Epistles of James, of Jude, and the second and third of John.[3] Still he defends the canonicity of the second Epistle of Peter. This is intelligible so soon as we recollect that the doubts expressed regarding the other epistles relate only to the apostolic dignity of the authors, who seem to him to have been of an inferior rank, and that they do not affect the authenticity of the names given to them. On the other hand, the case is quite different with Peter. The author of the second epistle pretends positively to be the apostle, and the criticism of the learned cardinal was not strong enough to discuss such a pretention.

Similar reservations, or if you will, criticisms, are found in the exegetical writings of Erasmus of Rotterdam. They are bolder even, more decidedly independent of tradition; on the other hand, the protestations of submission to the

---

[1] *Possunt dici canonici—i.e., regulares, ad aedificationem fidelium.*

[2] *Prooem. in ep. ad Hebr.*, fol. 374, ed. Lugd. 1556: *De auctore huius epistolae certum est communem usum ecclesiae nominare Paulum; Hieronymus tamen non audet affirmare, etc. Et quoniam Hieronymum sortiti sumus regulam ne erremus in discretione ll. canonicorum (nam quos ille canonicos tradidit canonicos habemus), ideo dubio apud Hieronymum epistolae auctore existente dubia quoque redditur epistola, quoniam nisi sit Pauli non perspicuum est esse canonicam. . . Nos tamen loquentes ut plures Paulum auctorem nominabimus.*

[3] *Ibid.*, fol. 410, 454, 455.

judgment of the Church, I might almost have said, the author's palinodes, are more explicit, more ardent. Erasmus, whose historical knowledge, critical instincts, and literary taste were incessantly drawing him farther away from Rome, was easily brought back again by his need of repose and his religious indifference. He in no way felt the vocation of the martyr, and easily endured that he should not be permitted to say what he could not be prevented from thinking. His controversies with the theologians of the Sorbonne, the vigilant guardians of orthodoxy, are very instructive in this respect.[1] "The arguments of criticism, estimated by the rules of logic, lead me," he says, "to disbelieve that the Epistle to the Hebrews is by Paul or Luke, or that the second of Peter is the work of that apostle, or that the Apocalypse was written by the evangelist John. All the same, I have nothing to say against the contents of these books which seem to me to be in perfect conformity with the truth. If, however, the Church were to declare the titles they bear to be as canonical as their contents, then I would condemn my doubts, for the opinion formulated by the Church has more value in my eyes than human reasons, whatever they may be."

Thus, at the very opening of the new era, there arose this cardinal question, which, as we shall see, was clearly put and courageously approached by the Reformers: "Is canonicity exclusively attached to the name of a certain number of privileged persons, so that a purely literary doubt involves the rejection of a book, or does it depend on the book's

---

[1] *Declar. ad censuram facult. theol. paris* (*Opp.*, ix., 864): *Juxta sensum humanum nec credo epistolam ad Hebraeos esse Pauli aut Lucae, nec secundam Petri esse Petri, nec Apocalypsin esse Joannis apostoli. . . Si tamen titulos recipit Ecclesia, damno dubitationem meam ; plus apud me valet expressum Ecclesiae judicium quam ullae rationes humanae.—Supput. errorum Beddae* (*Opp.* ix., 594): *Scripsi semper fuisse dubitatum (de ep. ad Hebraeos), non scripsi ab omnibus dubitatum . . . et ipse, ut ingenue fatear, adhuc dubito, non de auctoritate, sed de auctore.*

intrinsic value so that it may exist even when the tradition is accepted with reservations? We have hardly any right to be astonished that Catholicism in the sixteenth century was startled to see such a question raised. Protestantism followed closely enough in that direction. Neither Erasmus nor Luther foresaw the consequences it entailed; but their adversaries and their successors, without perceiving them more clearly, were guided by unerring instinct when they sought to crush them from the first. I shall return afterwards to what concerns Protestant science. In the Catholic camp, the official declarations of the authorities and the half-arguments of conservative erudition vied with each other in trying to bridle the boldness of those who, from a literary necessity rather than in religious revolt, were emancipating themselves from the yoke of tradition. The Sorbonne proscribed purely and simply all doubts regarding canonicity.[1] A provincial synod, held at Sens in 1528 and transferred later to Paris, denounced as schismatical and heretical every one who should refuse to recognise the canon of Carthage, of Innocent or of Gelasius, or who should have the presumption to interpret the Scriptures otherwise than the Fathers did;[2] while the learned Dominican of Lucca, Pagnini, knows no other means of neutralising the inconvenient effect of Jerome's liberties than to send his readers back to the authority of Augustine, who, without being more certain of his facts, has at least the assurance of prejudice.[3]

[1] D'Argentré, *Collect. judic.*, ii. 52; *Jam non est fas Christiano de illis dubitare.*

[2] Conc. Senonse. *Decr.*, 4, *ap.* Hard., ix., 1939: *In enumerandis canonicæ scripturæ libris qui præscriptum ecclesiæ usum non sequitur, Carthaginense concilium* iii., *Innocentii et Gelasii decreta et denique definitum a ss. patribus librorum catalogum respuit, aut in exponendis scripturis non pascit haedos juxta tabernacula pastorum, sed fodit sibi cisternas dissipatas quae continere non valent aquas, et spretis orthodoxorum patrum vestigiis proprii spiritus judicium sequitur, is veluti schismaticus et haerescon omnium inventor . . . reprimatur.*

[3] Santis Pagnini *Isag. ad ss. litt.*, 1536, c. 15.

CHAPTER XV.

OFFICIAL AND MODERN CATHOLICISM.

According to the pragmatism of history, we should now turn our attention to the influence which the reforming movement of the sixteenth century exercised on the notion of the biblical canon. But this influence was so powerful, and the consequences drawn from the new principles, partly immediate, partly evolved in the growth of ideas, continued so long to dominate over the progressive march of the whole of Christian Theology, that I prefer to discuss this development as a whole, instead of interrupting my narrative with facts foreign to the sphere of Protestant science. I propose therefore to proceed at once with my statement of the facts belonging to the history of the churches that remained faithful to tradition. These are not at all numerous, and they are generally easy to grasp.

The questions connected with Holy Scripture had not been the last to be raised in the great debates which agitated Central Europe during the second quarter of the sixteenth century. In certain aspects they might be considered as the most important of all, because they dealt with the supreme criterion of truth, and led to nothing short of shaking the very foundation on which rested the edifice of the Roman Church. No doubt the mere discussion regarding the catalogue of the sacred books, the canonicity of the Apocrypha and the Antilegomena, a discussion which up to this point we have been following out in all its phases with scrupulous attention, would not of itself have been a very new or very important matter of controversy, had it not been connected with other theological problems which were far more important in their bearing, and were solved by the Reformers in a sense contrary to tradition. Among these problems were the authority of Scripture and its original text, which was vindicated against tradition, the current Latin version and patristic comments. Before questions so entirely novel as these, the confused reminiscences, the timid caprices of a petty literary criticism vanished. Hence, when the theologians of the Council of Trent, after hesitating for a long time, had decided to formulate the orthodox Catholic dogma in all particulars in order that they might have a precise system to oppose to heresy, they began with articles concerning the Holy Scriptures.

The council being constituted in the last days of 1545, the first months of the following year were partly occupied in drawing up, in preparatory meetings or *congregations*, the decree which, its authors thought, would for ever put an end to all quarrel or divergence of opinion regarding the Bible and its canon. These preliminary debates were long and interesting,[1] and prove more than anything else how much reason I had for saying that never before had the canon been officially fixed. If it had been fixed, the prelates and canonists assembled at Trent would not have failed to make appeal purely and simply to the authority of the former decision; whereas we learn, not without some agreeable surprise, that the question was treated as if it were still untouched. For, after decreeing without much difficulty that the tradition of the Church was of irrefragable authority, they proceeded to draw up a catalogue of the canonical books just as had been done formerly at Laodicea and Carthage, as well as by Popes Innocent and Gelasius. But there were four different opinions regarding the manner of drawing

---

[1] For details, I must refer my readers to the historians of the Council, particularly to Sarpi (French edition of Basle, 1738, tom, i., p. 266. f.), and Pallavicini (*Istoria del conc. di Trento*, vi.).

up this catalogue. Some wished the books to be divided into two classes, one containing those that had always been received without contradiction, the other those which had sometimes been rejected or regarding which doubt had existed. This proposal was virtually a return to the division of Eusebius, and was of no value, practical or theoretical. Its supporters, among whom is named the Dominican Louis of Catana, appealed to the example of St. Augustine, St. Jerome, and St. Gregory, alleging that these fathers had followed an identical or analogous procedure. Other orators, amending the preceding proposal, wished the books to be distinguished into three kinds—those that had always been acknowledged as divine; those that after some dispute had finally been included in the canon (the six epistles and the Apocalypse, as well as certain pericopes of the Gospels to which I shall have to return); finally, those which had never been acknowledged—viz., the seven Apocryphal books of the Old Testament,[1] with the additions to Daniel and Esther. This second proposal agreed in principle and very closely in nomenclature with that of the Protestants, especially of Luther. A third proposal was simply to recommend the example of the Council of Carthage—*i.e.*, to neglect all distinctions and place in the catalogue all books usually contained in the Bible, without adding anything which would open up the dogmatic question. This proposal, if it had been carried, would have been an official consecration of the existing state of things. The biblical canon would have included all the books used in the offices of the Church; the thorny question would have been avoided of examining whether they had all an equal right to be there, a question of small importance so long as the authority of tradition was reserved, but one that might become compromising by

[1] Wisdom, Ecclesiasticus, Tobit, Judith, two books of the Maccabees, and Baruch.

bringing into conflict the most illustrious vouchers of tradition. The last proposal was to declare all the books as they are found in the Latin Vulgate to be equally canonical and of divine authority. It is curious to find that there was great perplexity about the book of Baruch, which is not mentioned by name in any of the old catalogues that had been used as precedents; but the consideration that the Church sometimes uses it in her offices, turned the vote in its favour, and in support of this vote it might also be said that the Fathers had regarded this book as an integral part of that of Jeremiah.

When all the theologians present had expressed their opinions, a special sitting was held on the 9th March to take the vote and proceed with the formation of the catalogue. On this occasion, the partisans of the first system joined those of the second and voted for the triple distinction, while the proposal of those desiring to leave the dogmatic question untouched did not receive sufficient support, and was brought up again in the form of an amendment demanding the suppression of all detailed nomenclature. There were therefore three proposals laid before the council, and as no agreement could be come to, the course was taken of drawing up three different minutes of the decree to be given, and of proceeding to the vote at a later sitting when the question should be more thoroughly considered. This sitting took place on the 15th March, and the majority, we are not told in what proportion, voted for the system I mentioned last, and accordingly all distinction between the various books, whatever might be its origin and purpose, was peremptorily suppressed and condemned. Thus the council did not hesitate to place itself in contradiction with most of the orthodox Greek Fathers and a good number of the most illustrious and esteemed Latin Fathers. The dogmatic principle of the authority of Scripture had been put beyond attack by the prominence which the Reformation gave to it, and the council saw no other means of bringing the principle into harmony with the traditional usages of the Church which at first had been founded on a different basis. There was perhaps another motive still for this decision, a motive less exalted but more pressing; this was the desire and need, one might even say the moral necessity, for upholding the Vulgate. As an actual fact, several sittings during the second half of March were devoted to the question, which text was to be canonized. Voices very eloquent and very learned were heard, pleading the cause of the originals, and pointing out the defects of the received translation. The need of a new official translation, or eventually the liberty of revising the work from time to time, was the natural consequence of that opinion. But the same majority that had just voted the entire and absolute canonicity of the Apocrypha, shrank from the prospect of a work so difficult or a liberty so perilous, and preferred to decree the privilege of inspiration to St. Jerome, or to claim it for themselves that they might provide a guarantee for the work of the too modest translator. The power of the secret motives for this second decision will be understood when we estimate the value of the reasons given publicly in support of it. God, it is said among other reasons, had given an authorized Scripture to the Synagogue and the New Testament to the Greeks; it would be doing injustice to Him to think that the Roman Church, His well-beloved, should not have received the like benefit; the Holy Spirit therefore dictated the translation just as He had before dictated the originals.

After discussing the question of the perspicuity of Scripture or the right of interpretation claimed for individuals, as well as the question of the anathema to be pronounced against opponents, a solemn sitting, the fourth of the council, was held on the 8th of April. It was the first sitting at which articles of dogma were formulated, and two decrees were then promulgated. The one was intended to make the authority of tradition and Holy Scripture equal, as well as to consecrate the official catalogue of the books of Scripture, and ended in a formula of anathema. The other declared the Vulgate to be the authentic and approved version, of which a proper and official edition was to be printed, interdicted further the free and uncontrolled interpretation of the Bible, and at the same time established a censorship of the religious press. This second decree was not accompanied by any formula of anathema, because it was thought too much to condemn as heretical everyone who should give a new explanation of some particular passage, perhaps unimportant.[1] I do not give the catalogue itself, for all my readers are acquainted with it from the existing Catholic Bibles, in Latin or other languages. It is the same as that of Eugenius IV., or that of the Council of Florence, with this exception only, that the Acts of the Apostles are placed immediately after the Gospels.

[1] DECRETUM DE CANONICIS SCRIPTURIS: *SS. synodus. . . . perspiciens hanc veritatem et disciplinam contineri in ll. scriptis et sine scripto traditionibus, quæ ab ipsius Christi ore ab apostolis acceptæ aut ab apostolis Sp. s. dictante quasi per manus traditæ ad nos pervenerunt, orthodoxorum patrum exempla secuta omnes libros V. et N. T., quum utriusque unus Deus sit auctor, nec non traditiones ipsas tum ad fidem tum ad mores pertinentes, tanquam vel ore tenus a Christo, vel a Spiritu s. dictatas et continua successione in eccl. cath. conservatas pari pietatis affectu ac reverentia suscipit et veneratur. Sacrorum vero librorum indicem huic decreto adscribendum censuit ne cui dubitatio suboriri possit quinam sint qui ab ipsa synodo suscipiuntur. Sunt vero infra scripti, etc. . . . Si quis autem libros ipsos integros cum omnibus suis partibus, prout in eccl. cath. legi consueverunt et in veteri vulgata latina editione habentur, pro sacris et canonicis non susceperit et traditiones prædictas sciens contempserit, anathema sit. . . .*
DECRETUM DE EDITIONE ET USU SS. LIBRORUM : *Insuper eadem ss. synodus, considerans non parum utilitatis accedere posse ecclesiæ Dei, si ex omnibus latinis editionibus quæ circumferuntur ss. librorum, quænam pro authentica habenda sit innotescat, statuit et declarat ut hæc ipsa vetus et vulgata editio, quæ longo tot sæculorum usu in ipsa ecclesia probata est, in publicis lectionibus, disputationibus, prædicationibus et expositionibus pro authentica habeatur et ut nemo illam rejicere quovis prætextu audeat vel præsumat.* . . .

I shall say nothing further of the other parts of the decree, as they are not connected with the history of the canon.

As to the parts connected with the canon, I cannot but insist on the point I have already brought forward, that in the circumstances the Catholic Church could hardly come to any other conclusion. Had the Protestant Reformation not taken place, the indecision regarding such questions might have continued. Perhaps science would have had some liberty in its development, even if that were to be slow and timid; but, when face to face with a rival and conquering principle, there was no alternative but to give way or to extol the opposite principle no less decidedly. What took place in regard to this special question, reappeared at almost every point along the whole line of attack; and it has long been an obvious fact that, when the Council of Trent succeeded in erecting a barrier against the advance of Protestantism, which was for the time insurmountable, it repressed and crushed out all that remained of expansive vitality in the Catholic theology, thus sacrificing a fair part of its future to the necessities of the moment, which were not well apprehended. The Protestants, who rightly deplore the victory gained on this last great occasion by the spirit of hierarchy over the reform desired by peoples and kings, would do well to meditate on the natural results of a policy which styles itself conservative, but is in reality pregnant with dangers and suicidal. When they break out into bitter reproaches against those who dared to raise to the level of a sacred original a Latin translation, imperfect in sense as well as in language, they should not forget that, till recently, they have practically done the same in regard to current translations which are no less imperfect, and have not even the privilege of great antiquity.

In my opinion, there cannot be the least doubt as to the bearing of the decree of Trent. The council most certainly wished to efface every trace of difference between the books included in the current Latin Bible, so far as such difference affected their authority and inspiration, and to raise the Vulgate to the dignity of the original in this sense, that the science of exegesis or dogma was not to have the right of citing the primitive texts against the interpretation given by the ancient translator. This last thesis has had a considerable number of opponents among Catholic theologians themselves, who think they can mitigate the force of the decree by regarding it merely as a measure of protection against the dangers of an unlimited liberty of translation and interpretation. As this question is foreign to my special subject, I shall not stop to discuss it. As to the other point, it may be said that Catholic orthodoxy has always considered the debate as definitely closed, all the more that the solution of the council gave to the polemic against Protestants a means of attack, which was easy to manage, and, above all, intelligible to the masses.[1] At the same time it is interesting to state that, since the promulgation of the decrees of the council and down to our own day, there have always been theologians of the Roman Church who affected to maintain the distinction between what they called proto-canonical and deutero-canonical books. Only, according to them, this distinction was founded solely on this, that the canonicity of some having come into recognition more lately than that of others, it had no theological value. No doubt from the standpoint of the Church's abiding infallibility, such a method of classification has nothing offensive; still it is difficult not to see in it a last attempt of historical criticism to protest against the silence imposed on it, or, if you will, an argument paltry enough in the mouth of those who were trying to make official theory prevail over the in-

[1] See the special works, such as, Bellarmine, *De Verbo Dei*, i; Jos. Barre, *Vindiciae ll. deuterocan. V. T.*, Paris 1730; Alo. Vincenzi, *Sessio iv. conc. trid. vindicata*, Rome, 1842 tom. iii., etc

defeasible claims of history. At any rate, there is ample testimony to the fact in the Catholic literature of the three last centuries.

The Dominican Sixtus of Sienna[1] makes the distinction indicated with a curious frank simplicity. The canonical books of the second order, he says—viz., Esther, Tobit, Judith, Baruch, the Epistle of Jeremiah, Wisdom, Ecclesiasticus, the stories of Susannah, of Bel and the Dragon, the Song of the Three Children, the two first books of the Maccabees, the last chapter of Mark (v. 9-16), the passage in Luke about the angel assisting the Lord (xxii. 43 f), the story of the woman taken in adultery (John viii.), the Epistle to the Hebrews, five of the Catholic Epistles, the Apocalypse—all these were regarded as apocryphal by the Fathers; but they were read to the catechumens, who were not believed to be capable of understanding the canonical books;[2] later, they were given to all the faithful, but only for edification, and not for the purpose of finding in them confirmation of dogma; finally, it was decreed that they should be received as having irrefragable authority. This manner of understanding or expounding the history of the canon does not require discussion; it is more important to say that it was very popular, and was reproduced more than once by other scholars.[3] The authority of all these books, they say, was not always the same; now their dignity is perfectly equal. Although new revelations are no longer granted to the Church, she may, after some time, be more assured of the truth of a work than she was before. The

---

[1] Sixti Senensis *Bibliotheca sancta*, 1566, p. 1.

[2] *Eosque apud solos catechumenos, nondum canonicæ lectionis capaces* (!) *legi permiserunt; deinde procedente tempore apud omnes fideles recitari concesserunt.... demum inter S. S. irrefragabilis auctoritatis assumi voluerunt.*

[3] Bellarmine, l.c. Anton. a Matre Dei, *Præludia ad ss. ll. intell.*, 1670, p. 85 f. L. E. du Pin, *Dissert. Prélim.*, 1701, I, 1, § 6. Mt. Gerbert, *Princip. theol. exeg.*, 1757, p. 101. J. B. Glaire, *Introd. aux livres de l'A. et du N. T.*, 1843, I, 79 f. Scholz, *Einl.*, 1845, I, 263.

opinion of some theologians,[1] who think that the difference between the two classes was not completely effaced at Trent, that it was not spoken of because it was quite well known—this opinion is declared rash, as all books are equally inspired and canonical, and must have for Catholics the same force and the same authority. Only it is agreed that in controversy with Jews and Protestants, the books rejected by the latter cannot be of so much use as the others.[2]

The history of the canon in the Latin Church terminates, therefore, with the Council of Trent. Then it was closed and fixed, but not before. Since that epoch, the question has no longer been agitated in a sense contrary to the official decision.[3] The vast patristic erudition of that illustrious phalanx of Benedictines by which the age of Louis XIV. was glorified never touched on it. Richard Simon himself, though his bold criticism alarmed all parties and all schools, and his great work explores all the details of the history of the text and of versions of the Bible, seems to have been ignorant that there was also a history of the canon. This silence can certainly not be explained by want of knowledge; quite as little can I attribute it to religious indifference. But the historical fact, which should be discussed by appeal to testimonies and examination of documents, had become an article of faith, sanctioned by an anathema, and was thereby placed beyond all discussion.

The Greek Church, again, built on the same dogmatic basis as its sister-church, and living by the same traditions, was not slow in arriving at a similar conclusion after fluc-

[1] Bern. Lamy, *Appar. bibl.*, 1696, p. 355. J. Jahn, *Einl. ins A. T.*, 1802, I, 140, etc.

[2] Glaire, *l. c.*, p. 118.

[3] In our times, some Catholic scholars have dared to express doubts—*e.g.*, regarding the origin of the Epistle to the Hebrews (Feilmoser, *Einl.*, 1810, p. 241. Lutterbeck, *Neutestl. Lehrbegr.*, II., 245); but they do not speak of exclusion from the canon, and such opinions are too isolated to permit me to say that Catholic science has entered on a new path.

tuations still more serious and no less prolonged. It will be remembered that at the time of the Reformation, the Greek Church was able to extol at one and the same time the contradictory decrees of Carthage and Laodicea. In other words, the old theory of its great theologians, who wished carefully to distinguish between the normative documents of the faith and the simple books of popular edification, was forced to give way insensibly in practice to usage. The usage was all the more imperious that the science which should have counterbalanced it had grown more feeble and more estranged from biblical studies. The two series of books were, in fact, confounded with one another in the East as in the West, and anything that scholars knew and said about their difference scarcely crossed the threshold of their cells.

Only during the course of the seventeenth century did the question of the canon become the subject of a sort of controversy among the Eastern churches, and then, by a strange combination of circumstances, it was settled in harmony with the decree of Trent. That we may better understand the importance of the changes which came at last to be generally adopted, I shall begin by citing several declarations made by prelates in high places who were anxious to maintain as far as possible the theory of the early Greek Fathers. The first of these is a confession of faith by a Macedonian monk, Metrophanes Kritopoulos, afterwards patriarch of Alexandria, composed about 1625[1] when he was travelling in Germany. It declares that the word of God is partly written, partly preserved orally, in the tradition of the church. The written word is contained in the books of the Bible, in number 33, representing the number of years which the Saviour spent on this earth. Of these books, 22 form the Old Testament, 11 the New. This cal-

[1] *Monumenta fidei eccl. or.*, ed. Kimmel, 1850, tom. ii. p. 104.

culation is obviously based on the names only of the authors in each category of the apostolic books, Paul counting as one, the Catholic Epistles as four. In the Old Testament, he excludes the Apocrypha, at the same time saying that they are to be esteemed for their practical utility without claiming for them the honour of canonicity which the church had never granted them.[1] The author is here faithful to the customs of the early church, with this exception, that he includes the Apocalypse in the number of canonical books. We find the same views in a still more famous theologian, the Cretan Cyrillus Lucaris, patriarch of Alexandria, later (after 1621) of Constaninople, and well-known from the tragic end to which he was brought by the theological jealousies of his co-religionists and the under-hand policy of the Porte. He too published in 1629 a confession of faith, in which[2] he treats the Apocrypha in the same way as his colleague and contemporary, and explicitly adds[3] the Apocalypse to the New Testament by a certain turn of phrase which shows that the addition, though not made from his own personal predilection, was at least an innovation, and that he was bound to notice it in passing, since he had promised to give the canon of Laodicea. There exist other documents of this epoch, which prove that the insertion of the Apocalypse in the canon of the East was neither rare nor isolated.[4] In general, the doubt which before had been justified by the recollections of tradition or

---

[1] ἀποβλήτους μὶν οὐχ ἡγούμεθα. πολλὰ γὰρ ἠθικὰ πλείστου ἐπαίνου ἄξια ἐμπεριέχεται ταύταις. Ὡς κανονικὰς δὲ καὶ αὐθεντικὰς οὐδέποτ' ἀπεδέξατο ἡ τοῦ Χριστοῦ ἐκκλησία κ. τ. λ.

[2] *Cyrilli Lucaris confessio*, in *Monumentis* (loc. cit. i. 42).

[3] αἷς συνάπτομεν καὶ τὴν ἀποκάλυψιν τοῦ ἠγαπημένου.

[4] A catalogue in very bad verse, and to all appearance a little earlier in date, is reported by the author mentioned in the note below, and ends with these lines:

θεολογικὴ δ' ἀποκάλυψις πάλιν
σφραγὶς πέφυκε τῆσδε τῆς βίβλου πάσης.

the prejudices of dogma, could no longer be maintained at a time when there was no science to defend or dispute it, and when the whole life of the church was concentrated in a purely exterior worship. Besides, the two theologians I have just named had gone to study in the Protestant universities of Switzerland, Germany, and Holland; they had maintained intimate and continuous relations with different scholars in these countries; all of which no doubt furnished additional reasons to the mass of the Greek clergy for being suspicious of biblical studies, so far as they had any tendency to follow their leaders into such forbidden ground. They preferred to speak of criticism in the way it was spoken of at Rome, as a thing henceforth settled and complete,[1] and Cyril especially, as the most prominent and the most envied, had cruel experience of the result of the suspicions he had awakened regarding his orthodoxy. They cost him his life, and not even his death could satisfy his adversaries. He was condemned for heresy by a synod held at Jassy in 1642, and thirty years later at Jerusalem, a new confession of faith was sanctioned which canonized also the Apocrypha of the Old Testament. The terms used in it for this purpose are somewhat curious. Clearly the bitterness of the orthodox against Lucaris had much to do with the decision, and the frank simplicity with which they pretended to confirm the existing rules, while at the same time they were making light of the Catholic theologians and even of the synods to which they appeal, is worthy of an assembly which very probably was acquainted with the Fathers only

---

[1] *Leo Allatius* (†1669) *de libris ecclesiasticis Graecorum*, p. 36, *ap.* Fabric. *Bibl. gr. T. V.*: *Alio tempore de scripturis hisce disceptatum est in eamque itum sententiam a plerisque, non esse eorum auctorum quos praeferunt* . . . . *attamen hisce temporibus, tanta est vis veritatis, fixum in Graecorum animis mansit.* . . . . *epistolas catholicas et apocalypsin veram et genuinam esse scripturam et uti talem publice in officiis per totam Graeciam, quemadmodum et alias divinas scripturas, legunt.*

by hearsay, and was all the more able to lavish epithets on those with more acquaintance.[1] It roundly declared that to deny the canonicity of the story of Judith, of Susanna, or of the Dragon, is to reject the Gospels themselves, neither more nor less, and it is easy to suppose that such language was used to influence the uncertain and confirm those already convinced.

And in this respect it may be added that these results were fully attained. So far as I am acquainted with the modern theological literature of the Greeks, no voice has since been raised to make appeal from the Fathers of Jerusalem to those of Laodicea. I have before me a splendid quarto edition of the Greek Bible, printed at Moscow in 1821 by the order, and under the auspices of, the Holy Synod of the Russian Empire. It contains all the texts of the Septuagint,[2] and even more; for we find in it the two recensions of Ezra, and four books of the Maccabees, added to the other historical books: the minor and major prophets also come before the seven hagiographa. At the same time I must state certain symptoms which go to show that the Eastern church attaches no great importance to the solution of the question of the canon. No opposition, in fact, is made to the reception of the Apocrypha; their legitimacy is not openly questioned; but neither is it thought necessary to

[1] *Confessio Dosithei*, 1672, Quæst. 3 (*Monumenta, l.c.*, i. 467): στοιχοῦντες τῷ κανόνι τῆς καθολικῆς ἐκκλησίας ἱερὰν γραφὴν καλοῦμεν ἐκεῖνα πάντα ἅπερ ὁ Κύριλλος ὑπὸ τῆς ἐν Λαοδικίᾳ συνόδου ἐρανισάμενος ἀριθμεῖ καὶ πρὸς τούτοις ἅπερ ἀσυνίτως καὶ ἀμαθῶς εἴτ' οὖν ἐθελοκακούργως ἀπόκρυφα κατωνόμασι. . . . (here comes a list of the Apocrypha of the Old Testament). . . . ἡμεῖς γὰρ καὶ ταῦτα γνήσια τῆς γραφῆς μέρη κρίνομεν, ὅτι ἡ παραδόσασα ἀρχαία συνήθεια καὶ ἡ καθ. ἐκκλησία γνήσια εἶναι τὰ ἱερὰ εὐαγγέλια καὶ ταῦτα εἶναι τῆς ἁγίας γραφῆς μέρη ἀναμφιβόλως παρέδωκε, καὶ τούτων ἡ ἄρνησις ἐκείνων ἐστὶν ἀθέτησις κ. τ. λ.

[2] Thus, of course, the book of Baruch is intercalated between the Prophecies and the Lamentations of Jeremiah, and the Apocryphal Epistle of the same author is put before Ezekiel. The book of Esther is completed by additions, and the volume of Daniel contains all that forms chaps. xiii-xvi. in the Latin Bibles.

insist on them. Thus in the confession most approved in the East, the confession of the Patriarch of Kiew, Peter Mogilas, which is usually known as the *Catechism of the Russians* (1640), no catalogue of the books of the Bible is given.¹ Again in an official declaration by the patriarch Dionysius of Constantinople, annexed to the very acts of the Synod of Jerusalem,² it is simply said that the catalogues of the Apostolic Canons of Laodicea and Carthage do not agree with one another, but that the omission of certain books in the Old Testament does not imply that they are to be rejected as profane; on the contrary, they are anything but contemptible.³ While reading such phrases, we might be tempted to say, that between the Latin Church and the

---

¹ Further, this document which is very minute in every part, and enters into many subtleties regarding the practice of religion, does not contain the smallest paragraph concerning Holy Scripture. It is merely said (Quest. 4) that an orthodox Christian must believe that all the articles of faith taught by the Church have been transmitted to it by the Lord through the apostles, and have been interpreted and approved by the œcumenical councils (τρίτει τὰ κρατῇ. ... πῶς ὅλα τὰ ἄρθρα τῆς πίστεως τῆς ὀρθοδόξου ἐκκλησίας εἶναι παραδεδομένα ἀπὸ τὸν κύριον μὶ τὸ μέσον τῶν ἀποστόλων τοῦ εἰς τὴν ἐκκλησίαν καὶ αἱ οἰκουμενικαὶ σύνοδοι τὰ ἑρμηνεύουσαν καὶ τὰ ἐδοκίμασαν); and, by way of explanation, it is added that the authority of these articles rests in part on Holy Scripture, in part on ecclesiastical tradition and the teaching of synods and Fathers (ἔχουσι τὸ κῦρος καὶ τὴν δοκιμασίαν, μέρος ἀπὸ τὴν ἐκκλ. παράδοσιν καὶ ἀπὸ τὴν διδασκαλίαν τῶν συνόδων καὶ τῶν ἁγίων πατέρων.) In Quest. 72, it is said that the Holy Spirit is the author (εὑρετής) of Scripture, and has preached it (ὡμίλησε) by means of many fellow-workers (συνεργῶν). *For this reason* (διὰ τὴν ἀφορμὴν τούτην), we must believe that everything decreed by the orthodox synods came to them from the Holy Spirit. Further, texts are frequently quoted in this catechism, both for dogmas and moral precepts. But the peoples who follow the Greek rite are acquainted with Scripture only by the regular reading of the pericopes, which is everywhere done in a language not understood—*e.g.*, throughout Greece in ancient Greek, throughout Russia in Sclavonian of the tenth century.

² *Monumenta, l. c.* ii. 225.

³ ὅσα μέντοι τῶν τῆς παλαιᾶς διαθήκης βιβλίων τῇ ἀπαριθμήσει τῶν ἁγιογράφων οὐ συμπεριλαμβάνονται, οὐκ ἀποτροπιάζονται ταῦτα ἕνεκεν τούτου ὡς ἐθνικά τινα καὶ βέβηλα. Ἀλλὰ καλὰ καὶ ἱδρυμένα προσαγορεύονται καὶ οὐκ ἀπόβλητα τυγχάνουσι διόλου.

Greek Church, there is still some difference in the conception of the canon, though their official catalogues are the same. The Greek Church, having lost the thread of its dogmatic tradition, no longer possesses, it would seem, the energy necessary to take hold of it again, or to create a new one, and the apathy of indifference marches on side by side with the obstinacy of ignorance and routine. I do not know at this present moment whether any change has taken place in this respect.

CHAPTER XVI.

THE THEOLOGY OF THE REFORMERS.

I USE the term *theology* designedly in the title of this chapter, with which we enter on the most interesting part of this history, and at the same time conclude our investigations. Up to this point we have constantly seen that the collection of the Holy Scriptures, formed at first by practical needs and according to varying local usages, was also preserved and transmitted under the rule of a tradition sometimes uncertain and capricious, and that science made vain efforts to determine its form and contents in a definite manner and according to theoretical principles. For the Catholic Church, as we have seen, the official definition of the canon was not given till the Council of Trent, and even then it was not guided by any theological axiom; it was simply and purely the consecration of a state of things founded on usage.

It may be said, without fear of error, that the leaders of the reforming movement had from the first some perception of the necessity for placing the question of the canon on another basis, and connecting it with some ruling principle which should be based on the theology of the Gospel. At the beginning of their work, they saw themselves forced to break with the tradition of the Church on more than one point; and in order to justify their opposition, and maintain the struggle with confidence and success, they had constantly to appeal to the holy books. These very facts compelled them to place the authority of these books on an independent basis, to free them, so to speak, from the tutelage of the Church, and vindicate for them a position which would shelter them from the caprices of opinion and the weaknesses of exegesis. For just as it became necessary to seek the criterion of the true meaning of the texts elsewhere than in the homilies of the Middle Ages, so it was henceforth impossible to appeal to St. Jerome for a decision regarding the canonicity of each book in the usual canon, all the more that the learned Father had hardly been in the habit of settling these questions.

Still, it would be wrong to suppose that it was easy to decide which part to take, which line to follow, in determining the canon and formulating the theory of it. In our days, it is true, we persuade ourselves that it was quite a simple matter. A great number of our contemporaries imagine that the Reformers, inscribing on their banner the principle of *free investigation*, began by sweeping away all traditional beliefs, in order to reconstruct anew a system of Christianity, and that, if our age still finds some elements to be suppressed, it is solely because the principle was imperfectly applied in former times. It is supposed, without saying it in so many words, that this free investigation must have been made in name and by means of the emancipated reason. In other words, there is a tendency to regard the founders of the Protestant Churches as the first pioneers of the philosophical rationalism which began to prevail in last century. I shall not stop to refute this view, which could only find currency among those ignorant of the history and literature of that memorable period. It will be sufficient to observe that a theology which, wrongly or rightly, but always with imperious energy and powerful unanimity, proclaimed as its fundamental dogma the absolute incapacity of the moral faculties of man, ought not to run the risk of either praise or blame, for having vindicated for the human reason the perilous privilege of the initiative or of supreme jurisdiction in religious matters. It could not then in any shape subordinate the Bible, the immediate work of God, to that same reason, which had fallen so sadly from what it was in the beginning.

I call the Bible the immediate work of God; for it is to be remembered here, that the dogma of the inspiration of the Scriptures was not in the least weakened by the anti-hierarchical tendencies of Protestantism. On the contrary, it acquired all the force that was taken from that of the authority of the Church. Indeed this dogma, while existing theoretically in the theology of the Fathers and Pontiffs, was to some extent neutralised in practice by the fact, that the privilege of being the channel of the Holy Spirit did not belong exclusively to the prophets and apostles, but also to the Catholic Church as a constituted body. It is conceivable enough that the authority of the latter, being more permanently and visibly exercised, should, in the eyes of the masses, throw into the background, and to some extent absorb, the authority of a code with which most of the faithful were hardly acquainted except by hearsay. On this head it is not wrong to say that the Reformation, when it opposed the Bible to tradition and to the authority of popes and bishops, assigned to the written word of God the first place in the order of religious facts.[1] When we see the Protestant theologians of the first half of the sixteenth century, with the exception of some undisciplined spirits who prided themselves on a special, inward illumination, all make appeal to Scripture, and to it alone without reserve, for the confirmation of the truth they taught, and the settlement of all

[1] I very much regret that the necessity of confining myself to my special task prevents me from developing further this fundamental point. The history and influence of the scriptural principle, sometimes opposed to the principle of tradition, sometimes combined with it, and thus giving birth both to Protestant theology itself, and to the divergence of the parties which arose among the churches of the Reformation, would be a fine subject for a writer who was impartial and familiar with the literature of the time. I take the liberty of directing the attention of my readers to the work of M. Holtzmann, *Kanon und Tradition*.

vexed questions, we cannot deny that the conception of the canon had become eminently and essentially theological, such as the Greek Fathers of the golden age of ecclesiastical theology had already conceived it, though they had not been able to gain general acceptance for their point of view. There is no longer any question of liturgical proprieties to be settled, provincial usages to be preserved, means of edification to be multiplied, practical considerations, such points in short as we have so often observed before in the vicissitudes of this history. The canon was henceforth what the term meant—a rule, a norm, a law, or rather the law of creeds.

But this is the very reason why I said just now that the question of the canon, so far from being simplified, seemed of necessity to bristle with new difficulties. When the dignity of the code was increased, and a special place was assigned to it among the providential means which might aid in the religious education of men—when, so to speak, it was made divine—it became all the more vitally important to mark out its limits, withdraw from it all impure alloy, and distinguish carefully its proper contents from the additions made to it at various times by the ignorance or the piety of men. So long as the chief point was to know what public or private readings would edify Christendom, the presence of a doubtful book, provided it served the purpose of edification, caused neither trouble nor danger; the Church was there to watch over the purity of dogma. It was quite otherwise when authority was transferred from the Church to the Scriptures exclusively. How then was a test to be applied without the risk of falling into uncertainty or even into error? That was the problem which had to be solved, and the problem was all the more difficult that it was raised by a more absolute theory, and was complicated by all the prejudices and contradictions arising from ancient usage.

Those who now think otherwise, and who suppose or profess that the question of the canon was definitely settled by the Reformers, make it evident that they have never gone back to the original sources, and that the question has never been presented to their minds in any other aspect than that which it must have had in the Catholic Church—viz., that the canonicity of the books was decided by the testimony of the Synagogue and the Fathers. Now, nothing was further from the thoughts of Luther, Calvin, and their illustrious associates—nothing was more fundamentally opposed to their principles, than to base the authority of the holy books on that of the Church and its tradition, to have the Fathers turned out on guard, and to bring their catalogues on parade, with the reservation of removing their obscurities and contradictions by forced and violent interpretations, as is the custom now. They understood perfectly well that nothing could have been more illogical—nay, more ruinous—to their system than to assign to the Church the right of making the Bible, when they had disputed her right of making dogma, for the one includes the other.

As the theology which in our day calls itself orthodox has forgotten—I might almost say, has denied—this principle, it will be right to place before the eyes of my readers some authentic and explicit texts. Let us first hear what is said by Calvin. He was one of the first to deal with this question, not in any casual way, but in a thoroughgoing fashion. He says:[1]—"*There are several in this pernicious error that the Scripture has no more weight than is given to it by the consent of the Church, as if the eternal and inviolable truth of God were founded on the pleasure of men. For they, showing contempt of the Holy Spirit, make this*

---

[1] *Institutes*, first French edition, 1541, p. 19 (translated from the Latin of 1539, p. 11. The *editio princeps* [Latin] of 1536 does not contain any treatise on the Scriptures). In the last edition of the work, see B. I., ch. 7.

demand: *Who will certify to us that the Scriptures come from God; who will assure us that they have been preserved in their entirety down to the present day; and who will persuade us that one book is to be received and another rejected, if the Church is not our guarantee on all these matters? Hence they conclude that it lies in the power of the Church to determine what reverence we owe to the Scriptures, and what books ought to be included among them.*[1] *Thus these blasphemers, wishing to exalt an unlimited tyranny under cover of the Church, care not in what absurdities they involve themselves and others, provided they can gain this point among the simple that all things are in the power of the Church. Now, if this be so, what would become of the pure consciences that seek certain assurance of eternal life, when they saw all the promises concerning it based solely on the judgment of men?*[2] *On the other hand, to what contempt from the unbelieving would our faith be exposed? Under what suspicion would it be placed in the eyes of all, if it were founded on the mercy and good pleasure of men? . . . As to their question, how are we to know that the Scriptures came from God, if we cannot refer to the decree of the Church, we might as well ask how we are to learn to distinguish light from darkness, white from black, bitter from sweet."*[3]

[1] *The liberty of distinguishing between the apocryphal books* (edition 1562).

[2] *When it is said to them that it is enough that the Church has settled it, will they be content with such an answer?* (Edition of 1562.)

[3] *Il y en a plusieurs en cest erreur pernicieux, que l'Escriture n'a non plus d'importance que ce qui luy en est donné par le consentement de l'Eglise ; comme si la vérité de Dieu eternelle et inviolable estoit fondée sur le plaisir des hommes. Car ilz font ceste demande non sans grand opprobre contre le sainct Esprit: Qui est celuy qui nous certifiera que l'Escriture est procedée de Dieu? et qui nous asseurera qu'elle a esté gardée en son entier iusques à nostre temps? qui nous persuadera que l'un des liures doit estre receu en obéissance et l'autre peut estre reietté? n'estoit que l'Eglise baille reigle de toutes ces choses. Pour tant ilz concluent que cela gist en la determination de l'Eglise, de sauoir quelle reuerence nous deuons à l'Escriture et quelz*

I have quoted from Calvin first, because in France he is the best known of the writers to be cited in this connection, though, unfortunately, he is still too little known. In chronological order, however, he does not come first in the illustrious phalanx of witnesses I am going to bring forward. Long before him, Zwingle summed up the same principles in the first of the theses proposed by him for the conference at Zurich (1523). "Whoever," he says, "pretends that the Gospel is nothing without the patronage and approbation of the Church is in error, and speaks blasphemy."[1] And this thesis he developes by supporting it with a series of Scriptural passages, which give to divine truth and the Scripture containing it a higher guarantee, and at the same time exalt them both above the assault of human weaknesses.

"It is not true," says Petrus Vermilius in his turn, "that the Scriptures take their authority from the Church. Their certitude is derived from God and not from men. The Word came before the Church. It is from the Word that the Church holds its vocation. The Spirit of God wrought in the hearts of the hearers and readers of the Word, so that they recognised the speech to be not of human origin but truly divine. The Spirit, therefore, and not the Church,

liures doiuent estre comprins en icelle. En ceste maniere ces blasphemateurs, voulans eleuer une tyrannie desbordée souz la couuerture de l'Eglise, ne se soucient de quelles absurditez ilz s'enueloppent eux et les autres, moyennant qu'ils puissent gaigner ce poinct entre les simples que toutes choses sont loisibles a l'Eglise. Or si ainsi estoit, que deuiendroyent les poures consciences qui cherchent certaine asseurance de la vie eternelle, quand elles verroyent toutes les promesses d'icelle consister et estre appuyées sur le seul iugement des hommes? D'autre part à quelle moquerie des infideles nostre foy seroit-elle exposée? En quelle suspition viendroit-elle enuers tout le monde? si on avoit celle opinion qu'elle eust son fondement au mercy et bon plaisir des hommes? . . . Touchant ce qu'ilz interroguent comment nous cognoistrons que l'Escriture est sortie de Dieu, si nous n'auons recours au decret de l'Eglise, autant vaut comme si quelqu'un demandoit dont nous apprendrons à discerner la lumiere des tenebres, le blanc du noir, l'aigre du doux.

[1] *Quicunque Euangelion nihil esse dicunt, nisi ecclesiæ calculus et adprobatio accedat, errant et Deum blasphemant* (Zwinglii Opp. ed. Sch., I, 195).

establishes the authority of Scripture."[1] It is true that the canonical writers began by being members of the Church; but it does not follow that the Scriptures derive their dignity from this and not rather from God and his Spirit. The kind of authority which the canon can draw from the testimony of the Church is good, strictly speaking, for common minds; it is not sufficient to assure consciences.[2] This point of view is diametrically opposed to that of the Catholic Church, which no one formulated in more decided fashion than St. Augustine when he said:[3] "I would not believe in the Gospel without the authority of the Church." It is curious to see how much pains were taken by all the Protestant theologians, Calvin especially, to interpret in an inoffensive way this declaration made by an author on whom they were more dependent than they were aware of, and much more than they dared confess.[4]

With such explicit testimonies before us, we shall without difficulty understand the meaning and drift of the declarations regarding the notion of the canonicity of the holy

[1] P. M. Vermilii *Loci communes.* cl. iii., 1. iii, § 3 : *Non est verum quod assumunt, Scripturam habere auctoritatem ab ecclesia. Ejus enim firmitas a Deo pendet non ab hominibus. Et prius est verbum, et quidem firmum ac certum, quam ecclesia. Nam ecclesia per verbum vocata fuit. Et Spiritus Dei agit in cordibus audientium verbum et illud legentium ut agnoscerent non esse humanum sermonem sed prorsus divinum. A Spiritu itaque accessit auctoritas verbo Dei, non ab ecclesia.*

[2] Wolfg. Musculus, *Loci communes,* p. 228 (Bas. 1560): *Agnosco scriptores canonicos esse membra ecclesiae, verum quod inde colligitur scripturam non esse authenticam sine autoritate ecclesiae, plane nego . . . canonicae scripturae autoritas suprema ac perpetua non est aliunde quam ex Deo, et sacri scriptores non ecclesiae, sed Sp. S. instinctu, ideoque non tanquam membra ecclesiae sed tanquam interpretes Dei et ministri Spiritus scripserunt. Scriptura autoritatem ex eo habet apud rudes et inexercitatos quod ecclesia eam habet pro canonica, verum hoc genus autoritatis non est tantae firmitudinis ut conscientias fidelium securas reddere possit.*

[3] Augustine, *Contra epist. fundamenti,* ch. 5 : *Ego evangelio non crederem nisi me moveret ecclesiae auctoritas.*

[4] Calvini *Instit.,* c. i. § 23. Edit. postr. 1, c. 7, § 3. Muscul., *l. c.,* p. 229. Vermigli, *l. c.*

books which were inserted in most of the Reformed Confessions of Faith.[1]

The first Helvetic Confession of Faith, composed at Basle in 1536, contains the above principles by implication, but does not set them forth very clearly. It simply says in few words that the *canonical* Scriptures, the Word of God transmitted by the Holy Spirit and communicated to the world by the prophets and apostles, is the most perfect and most ancient philosophy, and alone contains in a perfect way the whole of religion and the whole of morality. The interpretation of the Scriptures ought to be sought from themselves, and themselves alone, with the help of the rule of faith and charity; the Fathers may be usefully consulted *in so far as* they themselves practised this kind of interpretation.[2] If in this text the criterion of canonicity, such as I have indicated above, is not directly formulated, it is at least contained in it indirectly. For if the organs of the Church, as such, are not qualified to determine the meaning of Scripture, and the privilege of authoritative interpretation is expressly reserved for the Scriptures themselves, it is evident *a fortiori* that the same will be true in regard to the composition of the canon.

The second Helvetic Confession, composed in 1566 by

---

[1] The Lutheran formulas nowhere touch on this question, and for the most part are silent regarding the Scriptures altogether. The Augsburg Confession and the *Apology* only indicate in passing the superiority of the Scriptures over tradition. The *Formula of Concord* (1576) alone expresses in plain terms the principle universally recognised by Protestants that the Bible (*prophetica et apostolica scripta V. et N. T.*) is the only and supreme rule of faith and teaching (*Epit.* p. 570).

[2] *Conf. helv.*, I. art. 1: *Scriptura canonica, verbum Dei Spiritu S. traditum et per prophetas apostolosque mundo propositum, omnium perfectissima et antiquissima philosophia, pietatem omnem, omnem vitae rationem sola perfecte continet.*—Art. 2: *Huius interpretatio ex ipsa sola petenda est, ut ipsa interpres sit sui, caritatis fideique regula moderante.*—Art. 3: *A quo interpretationis genere, quatenus patres non discessere, eos ut interpretes scripturae recipimus et veneramur.*

Beza and Bullinger, enters into more positive detail on these principles, but with the same general meaning. "We believe and confess," it says, "that the canonical Scriptures of the holy prophets and apostles are the true Word of God, and that they hold sufficient authority from themselves and not from men."[1] Then after establishing the nature and bearing of this authority and the manner in which the Christian is made to feel it, the text discusses at length the value of the authority of the Fathers and of the Church, and declares, "We recognise as orthodox and authentic no other interpretation of the Scriptures than that which is drawn from the Scriptures themselves, by means of the preliminary study of the languages, context, parallel passages, those specially that are more clear, and which, being conformable to the rule of faith and charity, turns to the glory of God and the salvation of men."

The Confession of the churches of France proclaims the same principle. "Just as the word contained in the *canonical* books comes from God alone," it says, "so can its authority have no human foundation, and for that reason too, no one, not even the angels, has a right to add anything to it or take away anything from it."[2]

Not to multiply quotations too much, I shall confine myself to mentioning one other, the Scotch Confession of 1560, which has a very forcible statement to the same effect. In its nineteenth article, after vindicating in the previous article for the Scriptures themselves—*i.e.*, for the Holy Spirit that dictated them—the exclusive right of interpreting them, it goes on to say: "As we beleeve and confesse the

---

[1] *Conf. helv.*, II. c. i.: *Credimus et confitemur scripturas canonicas . . . ipsum esse verum verbum Dei et auctoritatem sufficientem ex semet ipsis, non ex hominibus habere.*

[2] *Conf. Gall.*, Art. 5: *Credimus verbum his libris (canonicis Art. 4) comprehensum ab uno Deo esse profectum, quo etiam uno, non autem hominibus, nitatur ipsius autoritas, etc.*

Scriptures of God sufficient to instruct and make the man of God perfite, so do we affirm and avowe the authoritie of the same to be of God and nether to depend on men nor angelis. We affirme therefore that sik as allege the Scripture to have na uther authoritie bot that quhilk it has received from the kirk to be blasphemous against God and injurious to the trew kirk, quhilk alwaies heares and obeyis the voice of her awin spouse and Pastor, bot takes not upon her to be maistres over the samin."[1]

After these quotations there can be no doubt about the Protestant principle, nor about its intimate connection with the special question we are studying with the help of history. It is proper, however, to remark that this principle had not equal prominence in all the countries that took part in the movement of the Reformation. Thus the Anglican Confession (the Thirty-nine Articles) says coldly, "In the name of the Holy Scriptures, we do understand those canonical books of the Old and New Testament, of whose authority there was never any doubt in the *church*," and further—" All the books of the New Testament, as they are *commonly* received, we do receive and account them canonical." Usage therefore, tradition, the Church, in the eyes of the authors of this confession, presented a sufficient guarantee, so sufficient that there was no need to seek one more elevated or more solid. In the same way we read in the Confession of Bohemia, composed in 1535, at a time when the Protestant principle could not yet have been understood in all its clearness and in all its applications: "Our party teach in common agreement that the Holy Scriptures are to be recognised as indisputably true and authoritative, as they are contained in the Bible, received by the Fathers,

---

[1] The only allusion in this confession to the canon is in these words, "*The buiks of the Auld and New Testamentis, those buiks, we mean, quhilk of the ancient have been reputed canonicall.*" [Trans.]

and *endowed* by them with canonical authority."[1] Among the Lutheran formulas, there is also one which might be mentioned here. It is the one composed by Brentz for the Duchy of Wurtemberg in 1552.[2] But we shall see afterwards that the formula employed in it was, on the contrary, intended by its author to consecrate a very important reservation.

But since, according to these formulas expressed in more than decided terms, the Christian does not need and is not bound to consult ecclesiastical tradition, in order that he may learn to discern the authentic and genuinely inspired elements of the Bible from those which error or fraud may have added, what criterion then will he have, what means more infallible can be offered him? If we continue to read the pages of Calvin following the one above quoted, we shall find the answer to this question. The Scriptures themselves, their character, their teaching, their spirit, their very forms, and above all the effects they produce on us when we do not hinder their working—these reveal their origin and truth, and thus impress on us the truths they proclaim with an indisputable authority, but not in spite of ourselves nor by any kind of constraint. For it need hardly be said that the heart, still hardened by sin, is not apt to receive from the word of God such an impression at once demonstrative and salutary. So, too, Protestant theology, when it wished to put in a more scientific form the fact I have just described, did not hesitate to say that it is the Holy Spirit[3] which in our very hearts bears witness to the

---

[1] *Conf. Bohem.* Art. 1. . . . . *docent scripturas sacras quae in bibliis ipsis continentur et a patribus receptae autoritateque canonica donatae sunt pro veris habendas etc.*

[2] *Conf. Wurtemb.* p. 540: *sacram scripturam vocamus eos canonicos libros V. et. N. T. de quorum autoritate in ecclesia nunquam dubitatum est.*

[3] P. Viret, *De vero verbi Dei ministerio* (1553), I. c. 5: . . . . *quotiescunque nobis externus sermo, sive scripto, sive viva voce proponitur, hoc apud nos confestim statuamus oportet, nullam illi quidem voci corporeae vim inesse atque*

Scriptures, whether by convincing us of their canonicity (*i.e.*, of their character as inspired and authoritative books) immediately and directly as by intuition, or by teaching us to distinguish from them all that has not this same character. Far from fearing that this kind of demonstration was insufficient, they expressly proclaimed it as preferable to every other. Those very men who did not hesitate to acknowledge that the canon had been formed under the auspices of the early church insisted, nevertheless, that the church had been able to proceed only in so far as it was guided by the Holy Spirit, and that it by no means derived therefrom an authority superior to that of Scripture.[1] "If we wish," says Calvin, "to make provision for consciences, so as to keep them from being agitated in perpetual doubt, we must take the authority of the Scriptures as higher than human reasonings or proofs or conjectures. In other words, we must found it on the inner witness of the Holy Spirit. For granting that in their own majesty, there is sufficient ground for reverencing them, yet they begin truly to touch us when they are sealed in our hearts by the Holy Spirit. Being then illuminated by His power, we believe, not on our own judgment nor on the judgment of others, that the Scriptures are from God; but above all human judgment, we decide beyond dispute that they were given us from the very mouth of God, just as if with the eye we were contemplating in them the Essence of God. . . . . Such a sentiment can be produced only by celestial revelations. I say nothing but that which every believer experiences in

---

facultatem, nisi Deus sui spiritus magisterio in animos illapsus rivo illo suo et efficaci verbo intus docuerit hominum mentes arcanoque suo afflatu aspiraverit.—II. c. 3: *Deus solus suo Spiritus afflatu corda movet. . . . . Nam ne ipsum quidem externum Christi ministerium quo in hac mortali vita defunctus est, hoc fuit præditum facultate nisi quoties arcano sui spiritus instinctu pater quos filio adducturus erat trahere voluit. . . . .*

[1] Vermigli, *Loci commun.* cl. I. l. vi. § 8.

himself, except that the words are far beneath the dignity of the argument."[1]

I regret that I am not able to transcribe at greater length this entire chapter of our great French theologian, and to add similar extracts from other Protestant authors of that period. They at least still understood the generous words of the apostle in 1 Cor. vii. 40, and did not fear to go wrong in applying it.[2] But I hold it important above all to establish the fact that it was not merely Calvin's own private opinion, for in that case my assertion would not be proved. On the contrary, the thought which he was the first to develop systematically, and with as much eloquence as conviction, appears everywhere beneath the discussions, particularly the polemical discussions of the period, and has even

---

[1] The original French runs thus: "*Si nous voullons bien pourvoir aux consciences, si qu'elles ne soyent point agitées en perpetuelle doubte, il nous faut prendre l'auctorité de l'Escriture de plus hault que des raisons ou indices ou coniectures humaines. C'est à scauoir que nous la fondions sur le tesmoignage interieur du Sainct Esprit. Car iacoit qu'en sa propre maiesté elle ait assez de quoy estre reverée: neantmoins elle commence lors à nous vrayement toucher quand elle est scellée en nos cœurs par le Sainct Esprit. Estans donc illuminez par la vertu d'iceluy, desià nous ne croyons pas ou à nostre iugement, ou à celuy des aultres, que l'Escriture est de Dieu: mais par dessus tout iugement humain nous arrestons indubitablement qu'elle nous a esté donnée de la propre bouche de Dieu, tout ainsi que si nous contemplions à l'œil l'Essence de Dieu en icelle. . . . C'est un tel sentiment qu'il ne se peut engendrer que de reuelations celestes. Ie ne ditz aultre chose que ce qu'un chascun fidele experimente en soy: sinon que les paroles sont beaucoup inférieures à la dignité de l'argument.*"

[2] *Nullius hominis mortalis animus verbi divini et cælestium rerum capax esse poterit nisi a Deo illustretur et doceatur. Mox, ut hoc fit, tam certum et indubitatum fit homini verbum Dei ut veritate divina firmius et certius nitatur quam omnibus literis utcunque obsignatis. . . . Solus spiritus docet omnia quæ de Deo scire hominem convenit* (Zwinglii Opp., i. 196 seq).—*Dixerint aliqui: nos spiritu destituti sumus. Quibus ego regeram: si spiritu vacui estis, quomodo audetis vos appellare christianos? Nemo est vere christianus cui tam parum spiritus huius concedatur quin valeat ex sacris literis haurire et iudicare quæ necessaria sunt ad salutem* (P. M. Vermilii Loci communes, cl. i. l. vi. § 5).—*Donum divinum est vera interpretatio et iudicii rectitudo*, etc. (Melanchthon. Opp., vii. 396.)

been placed by Protestant theology in official formulas. Thus, the second Helvetic Confession distinctly declares, that the effect of the preaching and reading of the Holy Scriptures, which are the only source of true wisdom, theology, and piety of the reformation and government of the Church, depends on the internal illumination of the Holy Spirit.[1] The Confession of the Churches of the Low Countries after enumerating the books of the Bible, adds:[2] "These are the only books we receive as holy and canonical, *i.e.*, as a supreme rule of our faith, and we believe without reserve all that is contained in them, not *so much* because the Church receives them as such, as because the Holy Ghost witnesses in our hearts that they proceed from God and bear in themselves His seal." The French Confession speaks to the same purpose, though using an expression which is a little less exclusive. It says:[3] not *merely* according to the unanimous feeling of the Church, but much more according to the witness of the Holy Spirit and the inward conviction He gives us; for He it is who teaches us to distinguish them from other ecclesiastical writings."[4]

This theory, which bases canonicity on the internal witness of the Holy Spirit, is not an isolated idea, an accidental conception, an expedient devised in some parti-

---

[1] *Conf. Helvet.* II. c. 1: *Neque arbitramur prædicationem externam esse inutilem, quoniam pendeat institutio veræ religionis ab interna Spiritus illuminatione. Quanquam enim nemo veniat ad Christum nisi intus illuminetur per Sp. S., scimus tamen, etc.*

[2] *Conf. Belg.*, Art. 5: *Hosce libros solos pro sacris et canonicis recipimus. . . . idque non tam quod ecclesia eos pro huiusmodi recipiat et approbet, quam imprimis quod Sp. S. in cordibus nostris testetur a Deo profectos esse, comprobationemque eius in se ipsis habeant.*

[3] *Conf. Gall.*, Art. 4: *. . . . idque non tantum ex communi ecclesiæ consensu sed etiam multo magis ex testimonio et intrinseca Sp. S. persuasione, quo suggerente docemur illos ab aliis libris ecclesiasticis discernere.*

[4] The French edition, published at Montpellier in 1825, effaced this little touch of distinction. It does not contain an authentic text of the sixteenth century, but a somewhat free edition of it in modern French.

cular case to meet polemical necessities, to escape from the pressure of the Catholic principle that tradition is authoritative. On the contrary, it is very closely and very naturally connected with the fundamental theses of Protestantism, with the dogmas of regeneration, justification, faith, in short with that precious element of evangelical mysticism which was not foreign even to the spirit of the Middle Ages, but which had been banished from official theology by the ascendency of Scholastic rationalism, and the crushing sway of the constitution of the Roman Church. In so far as it concerned the new theology to demonstrate, not that such a book was by such an author but that it contained the word of life, arguments purely historical, and the testimonies of the Fathers lost all value and had to give place to what the apostle long ago had called "demonstration of spirit and power." Let me add that Calvin did not go too far when he appealed to the experience of the faithful to confirm his views. Indeed, in the domain of evangelical facts, purely rational proofs are always incomplete, or they move in a circle of ideas which gives them no hold over the religious conscience, as may be seen from the despairing impotence of ordinary apologetics; whereas inward experience is the surest control over theory. This truth is as old as Christianity, for it was proclaimed first by Jesus himself (John vii. 16, 17). But it has never been to the taste of scholars, orthodox or neologian; they have always had stout faith in the power of their dialectics. On the other hand, pure and simple piety, especially in the sphere of Protestantism, did not fail to hear the word of God, to feel it, so to speak, in virtue of that mysterious contact of the eternal Spirit there revealed with the soul which opens itself to his beneficent working. It has been remarked that this action is not uniform in all individuals, and that, according to the dispositions of character and temperament, according to the current of ideas at each epoch or in a particular circle, the impression received from reading the Holy Scriptures would vary very considerably, that one might be edified and touched by a writing which might have little or no influence on another, and *vice versa*. The Psalms and Gospels, the Prophets and Epistles, the Song of Solomon and the Apocalypse, have in turn had a greater or less attraction for hearts and minds, and these varying phenomena must not be neglected since they are still visible among ourselves. In the main, they do not constitute a triumphant instance against the Protestant theory above stated, because that theory is not intended to deny the variety of dispositions among men, nor the diversity of God's ways in the work of salvation.

Still the conscientious historian cannot help showing that this theory, in spite of its intrinsic truth, its elevated point of view, and its conformity with the essence of the Gospel, has proved to be insufficient in practice, and that those who had formulated it were the first to diverge from it, and to drift into strange inconsistencies. The reason of this is very simple. The Bible did not fall from heaven as a complete whole: it is composed of numerous elements, which were added one after the other in the course of time; and this work of collection is a fact of history which calls for the expression of a deliberate judgment by the ordinary ways and means of historical science. Now, as soon as an absolute theory comes into direct contact with the concrete facts which are independent of it, it must either seek to fashion them in its own way, which is alway dangerous and creates unceasing difficulties, or, preserving an instinctive perception of the realities it encounters, it relaxes its own rigidity, and thus sacrifices, by concessions or negligence, that which constituted its vitality. Nothing is more interesting, but nothing also is less known and studied in France, than the embarrassments, the hesitations, the inconsistencies of the old

Protestant theology on the question of the canon. The primitive theory was clear, broadly conceived, homogeneous with the entire system, which makes the attempts at application all the more astonishing to us in their diversity and uncertainty. My readers have already perceived this from some of the extracts from the confessions of faith which I have put before them; but these same documents, together with the Protestant editions of the Bible and the writings of the Reformers, furnish us with a mass of instructive details on this point deserving consideration for more than one reason.

Let us consider for a moment the first fact, the fact most generally known and therefore apparently very easy to understand or justify—I mean the separation of the so-called Apocryphal books from the body of the Old Testament. My narrative has sufficiently shown how, at the time of the Reformation, the question of the place to be assigned to these books was still in suspense, between the routine which placed them on a level with the others, and the re-awakening science which remembered, a little confusedly, the secondary rank they had formermly occupied. Now it is well-known that from the first, the Reformers and their adherents, with remarkable unanimity, refused to recognise these books as canonical in the sense indicated above. In the editions of the Bible they were placed apart, with a special collective title, and usually with a notice explaining the purpose of the separation, or guiding the readers how to form their opinion. That I may not dwell too long on a fact which needs no demonstration, I shall content myself with transcribing in a note [1] some of these titles or extracts

[1] The Bibles of Zurich, the oldest that are complete (1529), present this inscription: *Disz sind die bücher Die bey den alten vnder Biblische gschrifft nit gezelt sind, auch bei den Ebreern nit gefunden.* Then follows a preface which begins with these words: *Dise bücher, so hie den Biblischen angehenckt, sind der meinung von vns getruckt, nit das sy in wärd vnd acht der heiligen*

from these notices, taken from the German editions and reproduced with some slight changes in the French Bibles. In the latter the historical element, contained in the notice to readers, shows some superficial appreciation of the usages of the early Church, and the utility of these writings is not so much insisted on. The Genevan Bibles of this first period—and I have a whole series before me—thus express themselves :—" These books, called the Apocrypha, were at all times distinguished from those which were without difficulty held to be the Holy Scriptures; for the ancients, wishing to anticipate the danger of some profane books being mixed up with those that did certainly proceed from the Holy Spirit, made a roll of them which they called the *canon*, signifying by this word that all included therein was a certain rule to which adherence must be given. In regard to these books, the name Apocrypha was given to them, denoting that they were to be considered private writings, and not authentic like public deeds. Wherefore, there is the same difference between the first and the second as between a deed passed before a notary and sealed for reception by all, and the note of hand of a private individual. It is true that they are not to be despised, inasmuch as they contain good and useful doctrine. At the same time, it is very right that what was given us by the Holy Spirit,

gschrifft gleich gehalten werden söllind, sunder das denen so auch liebe zu diesen bücheren habend zeläsen, weder mangel noch klag wäre, vnd das ein yetlicher funde das jm schmackte: dann ob schon dise bücher vnder die Biblischen heyliger schrifft bücher, weder von den alten noch von vns gezelt, sind doch vil ding darinn, die Biblischer gschrifft, dem glauben vnd liebe, keins wägs widerstrübend, ja auch etlich jren grund in Gottes word findend. The Bibles of Luther (1534 et seq.) have only a general and very simple title : *Apocrypha, das sind bücher so nicht der heyligen Schrifft gleich gehalten, vnd doch nutzlich vnd gut zu lesen sind.* There is no general preface, but there are special introductions to each book which, while remarking on their inferiority, take care to direct attention to the qualities for which they may be commended to the notice of Christian readers. [Regarding English Bibles, see note at the end of the chapter.]

should have pre-eminence above what came from men."[1] Then follow a sentence or two which were omitted from the editions after 1559. "Wherefore, according to the saying of St. Jerome, let all Christians read them and take from them doctrine of edification. But let them, however, be warned that they ought not to take thence full assurance of the articles of their faith; because it is not sufficient testimony, etc.[2] There are also Protestant Bibles of this period which, while maintaining the separation, speak of the Apocrypha with a certain favour, on the ground that the fundamental cause of their rejection by the synagogue was nothing else than the difference of language, and the fact that *they treat of things not conforming to the customs of the Jews*. . . . . Wherefore, reader, seeing that from all flowers the fly may draw liquor to make honey, without regarding where it is planted, whether in the field or in the garden, so from all books thou shalt be able to draw matter suitable to thy salvation without being guided by the Jews. . . . . Since, therefore, all have the same source and wholesome root, in spite of any pruning the Jews may have

---

[1] The old French original runs thus: *Ces livres qu'on appelle Apocryphes, ont esté de tout temps discernez d'auec ceux qu'on tenoit sans difficulte estre de l'Escriture saincte. Car les Anciens voulans preuenir le danger qu' aucuns liures profanes ne fussent entremeslez auec ceux, qui pour certain estoyent procedez du sainct Esprit, en ont fait vn rolle qu' ilz ont nommé Canon: signifians par ce mot, que tout ce qui estoit là comprins estoit reigle certaine, à laquelle il se falloit tenir. Quant à ceux cy, ilz leur ont imposé nom d'Apocryphes: denotant qu' on les deuoit tenir pour escritures priuées, et non pas authentiques, comme sont les instrumentz publiques. Parquoy il y a telle difference entre les premiers et les secondz, comme entre un instrument passé deuant un notaire, et seellé pour estre receu de tous, et vne cedule d'vn homme particulier. Il est vray qu'ilz ne sont pas à mespriser d'autant qu'ilz contiennent bonne doctrine et vtile. Toutesfois c'est bien raison, que ce qui nous a esté donné par le sainct Esprit ait preeminence pardessus tout ce qui est venu des hommes.*

[2] The original runs: *Parquoy, suyuant le dire de sainct Jerosme, que tous Chrestiens les lisent et en prennent doctrine d'edification. Mais qu'ilz soyent cependant aduertiz qu'ilz ne doyuent point là prendre pleine asseurance des articles de leur Foy: pource que ce n'est pas tesmoignage suffisant, etc.*

made on them, do not fail to read them and to take from them doctrine and edification"[1] (Lyons, de Tournes, 1551, etc). I willingly admit that Calvin's pen took no part in this composition. The authoritative edition of 1588 presents a new composition of some extent. This reviews the testimonies of the Fathers and sums them up in the following propositions: "These books are not divinely inspired like the rest of the Holy Scriptures, and being of private declaration, they ought not to be received nor produced publicly in the Church so as to serve as a rule for the articles of our faith. At the same time we may use them privately to draw instruction from them, as much because of several fine examples set forth in them, as because of notable sentences they contain."[2]

This arrangement was easily proved to be an innovation, and much advantage was taken of it by Catholic polemics, with the view of prejudicing the people against the Protestant Bibles. The authors, therefore, of most of the Reformed Confessions judged it right to lay down the principle of it in these charters of their respective churches.[3] In this way,

---

[1] In the original French: *Parquoy, lecteur, veu que de toutes fleurs la mouche peult tirer liqueur à faire miel, sans avoir esgard ou elle soit plantée, au champ ou au jardin, ainsi de tous ces liures icy tu pourras retirer chose duisante à ton salut sans te reigler par les Juifs. . . . Puis donq que tous ont vne mesme source et saine racine, pour vne resecation qu'en ont faite les Juifs ne laisse de les lire et en prendre doctrine et edification.*

[2] The original is: *Ce ne sont pas liures diuinement inspirés comme le reste des sainctes Escritures, mais qu' estans de particuliere declaration ils ne doiuent point estre receus ou produits publiquement en l'Eglise comme pour seruir de reigle aux articles de nostre foy. Toutesfois on s'en peut seruir en particulier pour en tirer instruction tant à cause de plusieurs beaux exemples qui nous y sont proposés, que de notables sentences qu'ils contiennent.*

[3] Conf. Helvet., II. art. 1: *Interim nihil dissimulamus quosdam V. T. libros a veteribus nuncupatos esse Apocryphos, ab aliis Ecclesiasticos, utpote quos in ecclesiis legi voluerunt quidem, non tamen proferri ad auctoritatem ex his fidei confirmandam.*—Conf. Gall., art. 4: . . . *(libri ecclesiastici) qui, ut sint utiles, non sunt tamen eiusmodi ut ex iis constitui possit aliquis fidei articulus.*—Thirty-Nine Articles, art. 6: *And the other books, as Hierome*

the distinction assumed an official and dogmatic character, and thus served to consecrate the theological conception of the canon. The Lutheran formulas disdain to elevate this custom to the dignity of an article of faith; and, truth to say, they found no need for it, as I shall show in the course of this narrative.

Having now established the fact, I have still to connect it with the theory. Here I am naturally led to put two questions, diametrically opposed, but equally embarrassing. First of all, if the so-called Apocryphal books have not that essential quality which gives a special value to the others, why have they been preserved in the collection, placed even in the very midst of those which are regarded as emanating from divine inspiration, and therefore authoritative? The orthodox Calvinist theologians, who in our days have applied the principle more rigorously, and have completely eliminated them from the Bible, will readily grant to me that it was illogical to retain them under any reservations whatever. For no amount of usefulness which one or other of these books might present ought to be a sufficient reason for assigning to them that honour, otherwise the Bible might have been further enriched by preference with numerous monuments of Christian piety, from the Apostolic Fathers, who at one time were admitted, down to the books of the Reformers themselves, which were eagerly read by thousands every day. The insertion, let me rather say, the

---

saith, the Church doth read for example of life and instruction of manners; but yet doth it not apply them to establish any doctrine.—Conf. Belg., art. 6 : *Differentiam constituimus inter libros sacros et apocryphos, quos quidem ecclesia legere et ex iis documenta de rebus cum libris canonicis consentientibus desumere potest. At nequaquam ea ipsorum vis et autoritas est ut ex ullo testimonio ipsorum aliquod dogma de fide aut religione Christiana certo constitui possit, etc.* The Waldenses, after consulting Œcolampadius (see the letter he wrote to them in Scultetus, *Annal. evang.*, ii., 313), expressed themselves in the same way in their Confession of Faith. On this point I refer my readers to what was said above at the end of Chap. XIII. (p. 264).

preservation, of these books, by means of a note distributing blame and praise in uncertain proportions, was evidently a compromise between theory and practice, a concession made to usage, to tradition, nay even, as the translators of Zurich frankly confessed, to individual taste. They had not the courage altogether to suppress an element to which the custom of so many centuries had given a kind of consecration.

But I may also raise the opposite question, and ask by what motive they were influenced in making the separation? Was it really in virtue of the sovereign principle of the inward testimony of the Holy Spirit? Would it be quite true to say that the first Protestant theologians, while unmoved by the enthusiastic eloquence of the author of Wisdom, so much extolled by the Alexandrians, felt the breath of God in the genealogies of Chronicles, or the topographical catalogues of the book of Joshua? Did they really find so great a difference between the miracles of the Chaldean Daniel and those of the Greek Daniel, that they felt bound to remove two chapters from the volume which bears Daniel's name? I have some difficulty in believing that they arrived at the *distinction* they drew by any test of that kind. On the other hand, it is very simple to suppose, or, rather, it is very easy to prove, from their own declarations, that their purpose was to re-establish the canon of the Old Testament in its primitive purity, such as it must have existed, according to common opinion, among the ancient Jews—*i.e.*, as we know it in our Hebrew Bibles. As an actual fact, they do not fail to invoke the custom of the *Hebrews* in the notices of which I have given extracts. Speaking frankly, it was the best thing for them to do. They had for this the example of the most learned Fathers, and we must guard against reproaching their still imperfect science that they did not beforehand submit to more careful criticism the tradition in regard to the formation of the Hebrew canon. But I must call attention to this fact that their procedure was exactly that which in principle they had condemned; they implicitly acknowledged the authority of tradition, and thus they returned to the very position which they had loftily declared their intention of quitting as untenable. The theologians were not slow in seeing this. They tried to place the authority of the Hebrew canon on a more solid basis than that of the inspiration of the Jewish doctors, who were absolutely unknown, but to whom the collection in its actual form was attributed. They derived this authority from the testimony of the New Testament, from Jesus and the Apostles. As the value of this testimony was beyond dispute, and the fact of quotations being made from the Old Testament pre-supposed the homogeneity of the Spirit that had inspired them both, it must be acknowledged that this kind of demonstration adapts itself without difficulty to the theological principle above set forth. But if it respects the principle, it also limits its application. Indeed, the canonicity of every book in the Old Testament will depend now on its being quoted by an apostolic writer; for the collection, taken as a whole, is usually quoted with this formula: *the law and the prophets*, which formula, as we know, includes only those parts of the Bible which were used in public readings and recital. Only once *Psalms* is added, in order to be quite complete (Luke xxiv. 44). And even though this circumstance should not form a complete proof, it must be said that the absence of all quotation from a particular book proves of itself that the spirit of that book is not in intimate contact with that of the gospel. In a passage to which I shall afterwards refer, Luther recognises this very clearly, inasmuch as he declares that it is not the title of a work nor the name of its author which assures to it canonical dignity, but the position it takes in regard to the evangelic faith;[1] and we shall see afterwards how freely he pronounces judgment regarding the hagiographa. It was from this point of view, no doubt, that the Fathers set out when they removed the book of Esther from the canon. What I am saying may appear a little rash: I hasten, therefore, to add that the most orthodox Protestant theologians did not shrink from this logical consequence when they perceived it. Thus Flacius, the Lutheran *par excellence*, does not hesitate to say that, in default of any positive declaration by the Apostles regarding the number of the authentic books of the Old Testament, this number may be known without much difficulty from the quotations, direct or indirect, contained in the apostolic writings. And, in this way, he sets himself to draw up a catalogue in which naturally most of the hagiographa are wanting—Ecclesiastes, Canticles, &c.;[2] and he thinks thereby to have proved that the Apostles approved exactly the same books regarding which there had never been any doubt among the Jews. And Flacius had learning enough to know that the books just named had been matter of serious controversies among the doctors of the Synagogue. By this inference, he returned into the circle of ideas dominated by the theory of the Spirit, a circle from which there had been an unconscious departure when an attempt was made to settle the question by rabbinical tradition.

If the definition of the canon of the Old Testament placed the Reformers in a difficulty, the work to be done on that

---

[1] By way of example, I direct the attention of my readers to Canticles, which the apostles could not have passed over in silence, if the mystical interpretation given to it by their successors had the least foundation. It is well known that Luther rejected it also.

[2] *Centuriae Magdeb. s. Hist. Eccl. N.T.*, ed. Semler, i., 29, 451: *Etsi numerus librorum authenticorum V.T. ab apostolis ex professo nominatim non est expressus, tamen hund obscure ex citationibus conjectari potest quod eos pro certis et probatis habuerint de quibus antiquitas iudaica nunquam dubitavit. Citantur* ENIM, etc.

of the New was to produce many more uncertainties; for unless they put themselves at the feet of the scholastic doctors, they had not even a uniform and early enough tradition on which to fall back. Hence on this point there is apparent amongst them a great divergence in methods and results. The theologians in the two churches—at least, the Germans and the Swiss—were perfectly acquainted with the state of the critical questions in so far as it could be learned from reading the Fathers: they knew that several books had been received into the canon only at a very late date and after long fluctuations of opinion. But in regard to this fact, they did not all pronounce the same judgment nor follow the same principles in their judgment. This of itself shows that the question of the canon, more particularly that of the list in its details, was not practically a cardinal question for Protestant theology whose centre of gravity was placed elsewhere. Let us, therefore, pass in review the different solutions given, beginning with the Reformed.

As a general thesis, the theologians of the Swiss churches, while recognising the uncertainty of tradition regarding certain books, and themselves professing doubts about their origin, do not concern themselves much about that fact, and are not alarmed by it. Thus Musculus mentions the seven antilegomena, and under that name assigns them a secondary rank, but nevertheless includes them in the general catalogue of the New Testament.[1] In the same way Œcolampadius, when consulted by the Waldenses on the Scriptural canon, tells them of six antilegomena as holding an inferior rank among the books of the New Testament.[2]

---

[1] Wolfg. Musculi *Loci Communes*, p. 221: *Meæ modestiae non est ut de illis pronunciem, sintne eorum sub quorum nominibus exstant, vel secus. Judicia tamen veterum hoc efficiunt ut minus sim illis quam cæteris scripturis astrictus, licet haud facile quaevis damnanda censeam quae in illis leguntur.*

[2] Œcol. ap. Scultet. l.c.: *In N.T. quatuor evangelia cum actis app. et quatuordecim epistolis Pauli et septem catholicis una cum Apocalypsi reci-*

The Epistle to the Hebrews is not included in this exception. But neither he nor his compatriots show any hesitation in making appeal to the testimony of these same books in theological discussions. It was, therefore, a simple question of historical criticism, which was not brought into opposition with the Protestant principle, or which was decided in favour of these books according to that same principle. Since their contents appeared to Christian sentiment to emanate from the Holy Spirit, the name of the authors, who were perhaps not Apostles, made little difference. Or, perhaps, was it the lack of that inward and immediate demonstration which prompted the distinction? That is certainly the case with Bucer and Zwingle. The former insists on this point that the early Church recognised only the twenty homologoumena[1] as undoubtedly proceeding from the Holy Spirit. The latter rejects the Apocalypse, declaring himself unable to regard it as a Biblical book;[2] whereas he quotes, incessantly and without distinction, the authority of the other books named above, especially the Epistle of James and that of Paul to the Hebrews, having written commentaries on both these books. Calvin is still more instructive on these matters. He is profoundly convinced that the Epistle to the Hebrews is not the work of Saint Paul,[3] and he has a very learned discussion on this head, taking up the historical and internal arguments for and against. But this does not prevent him from pronouncing the most brilliant eulogium on the work, as furnishing

pimus, tametsi apocalypsin cum epp. Jacobi et Judae et ultima Petri et duabus posterioribus Joannis non cum caeteris conferamus.

[1] Buceri *Enarrat. in Ev.*, fol. 20.

[2] Berner Disputation (Zwinglii, *Opera.* ii. 1, p. 169): *Us Apocalypsi nemend wir kein kundschafft an dann es nit ein biblisch buch ist.* [With the Apocalypse we have no concern, for it is not a Biblical book.] Comp. *De clarit. verbi Dei*, p. 310: *Apocalypsis prorsus non sapit os et ingenium Joannis. Possum ergo testimonia si velim reiicere.*

[3] *Ego ut Paulum autorem agnoscam adduci nequeo* (*Praef. in Comment.*)

material for Christian teaching, nor of quoting it at every moment as an authority in his own dogmatics.[1] Here, evidently, the canonicity [2] was decided by the Spirit, and not by the Apostolic origin, still less by the tradition of the Church, which for that matter was quite uncertain. In the same way, Calvin defends the canonicity of the Epistle of James, while at the same time he confesses his ignorance in regard to the author, and willingly admits that the latter may not have been an Apostle. The essential point to him is still the certainty which he gained as an exegete that the text of the book may be placed in perfect harmony with what is preached elsewhere. His opinion regarding the second Epistle of Peter is still more remarkable. The religious impression he receives from it appears to him decisive for its canonicity; critical reasons make him actually lean towards its non-authenticity. And he is prevented from purely and simply rejecting this epistle, not by the testimony of the Fathers, which seems to him insufficient, nor by certain analogies which might be drawn, but solely by the consideration that the excellence of its contents appears to be irreconcilable with the fraud which would result from the name of the Apostle being put to a writing altogether fictitious. He concludes from this that a disciple of Peter may have written it under the auspices of his master, and according to his directions.[3] The same reason

---

[1] Once only, in the edition of 1536, he names Paul as the author, never elsewhere nor afterwards. Nor does he wish to avoid expressing his opinion. Thus, when introducing a passage of this epistle in continuation of one taken from Colossians, he says explicitly that it is from *another* apostle (*teste altero apostolo*). *Instit.* ii., 16, 6. (Tom. ii., p. 374).

[2] *Boni quidam viri hanc supposititiam epistolam crediderunt, quae omni tamen ex parte apostolicum spiritum vere redolet* (*Opp.* i., 678).

[3] . . . . *Quamvis aliqua notari possit affinitas, fateor tamen manifestum esse discrimen quod diversos scriptores arguat. Sunt et aliae probabiles coniecturae ex quibus colligere liceat alterius esse potius quam Petri. Interim omnium consensu adeo nihil habet Petro indignum ut vim spiritus apostolici et gratiam ubique exprimat. Quod si pro canonica recipitur Petrum autorem*

also determined the place he assigns to it; for he alone, among all the Reformers, separates it from the first epistle by inserting those of John and James,[1] a very curious peculiarity which modern editions, modified by orthodoxy, have taken care to efface. Thus everywhere Calvin is guided by that kind of religious intuition which I have characterised above, so that ecclesiastical tradition is consulted only to a very subordinate extent, and never prevails over the other criterion. And certainly, from a theologian and dialectician so skilful, so certain of himself and his axioms, we could not expect an illogical conclusion. Some have believed it possible to affirm that he rejected the Apocalypse, because it was the only book of the New Testament, except the two short Epistles of John,[2] on which he wrote no commentary. But that conclusion is too hasty. In the *Institutes*, the Apocalypse is sometimes quoted like the other Apostolic writings, and even under John's name. If there was no commentary, it was simply that the illustrious exegete, wiser in this respect than several of his contemporaries and many of his successors, had understood that his vocation called him elsewhere.[3]

fateri oportet quando . . . . fictio indigna esset ministro Christi. . . . Sic igitur constituo, si digna fide censetur, a Petro fuisse profectam, non quod eam scripserit ipse sed quod unus aliquis ex discipulis ipsius mandato complexus fuerit quae temporum necessitas exigebat. . . . Certe quum in omnibus epistolae partibus spiritus Christi maiestas se exserat eam prorsus repudiare mihi religio est.

[1] I have before me six editions, Latin as well as French, of the *Commentary on the Catholic Epistles*, all issued under the author's own eyes between 1551 and 1562.

[2] It might be said with more probability that Calvin did not acknowledge the canonicity of these two writings. He never quotes them, and he quotes the first Epistle of John in a way to exclude them: *Joannes in sua canonica. Instit.* iii., 2, 24; 3, 23. (*Opp.*, ii., 415, 453.)

[3] When the second Helvetic Confession, art. ii., declares: *damnamus iudaica somnia quod ante iudicii diem aureum in terris sit futurum saeculum et pii regna mundi occupaturi oppressis suis hostibus impiis*, that proves, not that there was a desire to reject as an apocryphal writing the Apocalypse which literally promises that golden age, but that ordinary exegesis had succeeded in effacing from it *these Jewish dreams*.

The few notes that have just been read already show that the Protestant principle of canonicity may, in application, lead to different opinions. The Swiss theologians felt this; but, in place of modifying it for that reason, or abandoning it, they preferred to yield to it all the liberty of action it could claim. It must be granted that in this they were right; for they thereby showed, in regard to the truth they were called to defend, sounder faith, more praiseworthy confidence, than if they had been anxious to place it under the safeguard of an official and authoritative catalogue. No Helvetic Confession of Faith gives the list of books that are to be recognised as apostolic and canonical. They all confine themselves to the principles of the Gospel, judging that its substance, faithfully formulated and accepted, would guide every member of the Church in the *distinction* to be made between the books.

But the Reformed theologians of some other countries were not of the same opinion. The Confession of La Rochelle, in its third article, contains the complete list not only of the Hebrew canonical books, but also of those of the New Testament, such as it was in every one's hands. Any further examination into the canonicity of any book whatever, whether made by the methods of historical criticism, or made in application of the principle expressly consecrated by the very next article and quoted above, thus became not simply superfluous, but forbidden and dangerous. I merely state that, according to the literal expression of this third article, it is permitted to Frenchmen, and even enjoined on them, not to believe that Paul is the author of the Epistle to the Hebrews, since a clear separation is made between it and Paul's other epistles.[1] This small liberty is refused to the Reformed of the Netherlands, whose Confession (art. 4)

---

[1] *Epistolae Pauli, nempe ad Romanos una, ad Corinthios duae . . . . ad Philemonem una. Epistola ad Hebraeos, Jacobi epistola etc.*

likewise contains a list, and in this list fourteen epistles of Paul. Finally, the Thirty-nine Articles of the Anglican Church do not give themselves the trouble of enumeration. They limit themselves to registering the canonical and apocryphal books of the Old Testament, and in regard to the New simply say that common opinion will be followed.[1]

But even these last facts are such as might in some sort be adduced in favour of the Protestant principle of the demonstration of the Spirit. For, to some extent, if less directly, they show that the fundamental thesis of the Gospel, as it had been conceived by Protestantism, seemed so thoroughly established, so completely raised above all dispute, so positively guaranteed by Biblical teaching, that no necessity was anywhere seen for fortifying it or defending it by a preliminary scrupulous examination of the Scriptural authorities, thereby getting rid of some books which might appear to favour a different conception. From this side no danger was perceived, either for the faith itself or for the system which was its expression. On the contrary, as we have just now seen from the instance of the Apocalypse, the dogmatic theory already had so much predominance that it regulated even the interpretation of the texts. It is not surprising, therefore, that it was considered quite superfluous to sift the canon. We are thus not at all compelled to believe that the French, English, and Dutch theologians came to insert these official lists of sacred books in their Confessions of Faith, only by forgetting and denying the principle which had formed the point of departure for their theology, and by falling back into the beaten paths of the traditional method.

Still, at a much earlier period, and with a boldness of logic which he did not show in everything, Luther had given

[1] "*All the books of the New Testament, as they are commonly received, we do receive and account them canonical.*"

prominence to this same principle in such a way as to lead to quite different applications of it. For him, too, as for Calvin and his school, the Gospel, the whole of Christianity, was summed up in the great thesis of salvation by grace, of the sinner's justification by faith alone in Christ and His expiatory death, to the absolute exclusion of all merit by works. This truth was the cardinal point of all his theology, of all his spiritual and religious life. Criticism, exegesis, historical opinion, all his science, in short, was subordinated to that axiom. Whether he arrived at this conviction from the study of Augustine or the reading of the Bible, it matters little; he had always found it confirmed beyond dispute in all parts of Scripture, by the Old Testament as by the New, so that in his eyes the theological principle of the Gospel and that of a Scriptural revelation were very much identified with one another. But as the former took the lead of the latter, both by its intrinsic importance and the priority of its conception, it thus became the rule and criterion. Later on, Calvin said, in somewhat general terms, that the Holy Spirit, speaking in us, teaches us to recognise the Scriptures as truly inspired by God; whereas Luther, expressing himself more clearly and positively, and at the same time putting his principle more within the grasp of the body of the faithful, said that canonicity was determined by what each Biblical book, real or pretended, taught regarding Christ and the salvation of men. All the other criteria, even the names and dignity of the authors, true or supposed, were of no importance. Thus, in his celebrated preface to the translation of the New Testament, after setting forth the nature, purpose, and conditions of the new economy, he adds that it is also the means of estimating all the books and distinguishing the best. According to this standpoint, the Gospel of John and the Epistles of Paul (especially the Epistle to the Romans) together with the First of Peter, are the very kernel and marrow of all the books, those which ought to be the daily bread of the Christian. They are much to be preferred to the others, particularly to the three first gospels, which speak more of Christ's miracles than of His teaching, though the latter leads us to salvation, while His works profit us nothing. In these books, to which may be added the Epistles to the Galatians and the Ephesians, as well as the First of John, may be found everything necessary to salvation, even if one were never to see any other book.[1] "There, too," he says elsewhere,[2] "is the true touchstone for testing all these books, when it is apparent whether or not they insist on what concerns Christ, since all Scripture ought to show us Christ (Rom. iii.); and Saint Paul (1 Cor. ii.) wishes to know nothing but Christ. That which does not teach Christ is not Apostolic, though Peter or Paul should have said it; on the contrary, that which preaches Christ is Apostolic, even if it should come from Judas, Annas, Herod, and Pilate!"

---

[1] *Preface to the New Testament*, 1522 (*Opera Germ.*, LXIII. ed. Erlangen, p. 114): *Aus diesem allen kannst du nu recht urtheilen unter allen Büchern und Unterschied nehmen welches die besten sind. Denn nämlich ist Johannis Evangelion und S. Pauli Episteln, sonderlich die zu den Romern, und S. Peters erste Epistel, der rechte Kern und Mark unter allen Büchern. . . . denn in diesen findist du nicht viel Werk und Wunderthaten Christi beschrieben, du findist aber gar meisterlich ausgestrichen wie der Glaube an Christum Sünd Tod und Hölle überwindet und das Leben Gerechtigkeit und Seligkeit gibt, welches die rechte Art ist des Evangelii. Denn wo ich je der eins mangeln sollt, der Werke oder der Predigt Christi, so wollt ich lieber der Werk mangeln. Denn die hülfen mir nichts, aber seine Wort die geben das Leben. . . . (darum) ist Johannis Evangelion das einige zarte recht Haupterangelion und den andern dreien weit fürzuziehen und hoher zu haben. Also auch S. Paulus und Petrus Episteln weit über die drei Evangelien Matthæi Marci und Lucæ fürgehn. Summa, S. Johannis Evangel. und seine erste Epistel, S. Paulus Episteln, sonderlich die zu den Romern, Galatern und Ephesern, und S. Petrus erste Epistel, das sind die Bücher die dir Christum zeigen und alles lehren das dir zu wissen noth und selig ist, ob du schon kein ander Buch nummer sehest noch hörest.*

[2] *Preface to the Epistle of James* (*Works*, l. c., p. 157): *Das ist der rechte Prüfestein alle Bücher zu tadeln wenn man siehet ob si Christum treiben oder nicht; sintemal alle Schrift Christum zeiget* (Rom. iii.), *und S. Paulus nichts denn Christum wissen will* (1 Cor. ii.). *Was Christum nicht lehret, das ist noch nicht apostolisch, wenns gleich S. Petrus oder Paulus lehrete; wiederumb was*

We may not be able to follow Luther in all his conclusions, and we may make reservations in regard to his critical estimates; but we are bound to acknowledge that he was consistent in the application of the principle, and that he knew how to place it on a more solid basis than did Calvin. The latter might be reproached with supplying a somewhat subjective criterion, which would leave it possible to each individual to take his tastes and prejudices as a testimony of the Holy Spirit. Luther, on the contrary, when he found the measure of canonicity in a religious axiom which he had not invented, which was actually and textually preached in many passages of Scripture itself, and to which no other could be opposed—Luther, I say, occupied a stronger position, one much less exposed to the chances of a fluctuation in opinion, to a sudden change in the ideas and systems of men. It is true that, from this point of view, the material principle of Protestantism is placed above the formal principle, the Gospel of grace above the written word which bears testimony to it; but an attentive study of the history of the origins of the Reformation shows us that this step was quite natural at the beginning of the movement, and it is in accordance with strict logic to give precedence to the truth itself, over the witness that attests it.[1] And those who affirm their desire to preserve and faithfully continue the theology of the Reformers, ought to be the last to reverse the order of ideas which prevailed at its formation. But when some in our days go so far as to speak of Luther's

Christum prediget das wäre apostolisch, wennsgleich Judas, Hannas, Pilatus und Herodes thät.

[1] This applies specially to Lutheran theology. As to that of the Calvinist Churches, the fact is not quite so perceptible, as I have already shown in part; and the further we go from the beginning of the Reformation movement, the greater the preference shown for the formal principle, *e.g.*, in Holland, in France, and especially in England. That is obvious in all the later development of Protestant theology. I shall note the cause of this divergence when I come to the next period.

foolishness, in connection with the method of which I have just given an account, because in some detail they do not share his opinion, that only proves that, with the modern champions of an orthodoxy, professing to be privileged, ignorance and fatuity go hand in hand.

The words just quoted from Luther may serve at the same time as commentary on a proposition with which we have already met in the confessions of faith, and which was destined ultimately to become the sovereign principle of exegesis in the schools. When it was declared that all interpretation must conform to the rule of faith, the latter was certainly understood to mean the fundamental doctrines of the Gospel as Protestantism conceived them. There was a conviction that these doctrines present so faithful a summary of the essentials of revealed truth, that the Bible could not possibly contain anything opposed to them; and hence, passages more obscure or apparently at variance with the dogma, would naturally enough receive their true meaning, or their most fruitful application, when brought into more direct contact with one another, and with the dogma itself. Whenever, therefore, a conscientious study of the texts led to the conviction that there was a certain incompatibility between what was regarded as the very foundation of the Gospel and what professed to be part of Scripture, there could be no hesitation about the choice to be made. They had to adhere to the Gospel in whose name they had dared to break with Rome, and on which was founded the salvation of individuals and the entire Church: they had to decide, though with regret, on the sacrifice of some pages whose absence would in no way compromise the truth, rather than enfeeble the truth by making too easy a concession to traditional usage. He who is willing to acknowledge this fact, that the Reformation was not a simple reaction against religious tyranny nor the product of a philosophical criticism, but the claim of a positive religious belief, profoundly felt and raised to the dignity of an absolute principle, will also grant that the procedure I have just spoken of hypothetically, would have been natural enough and perfectly legitimate. Indeed, the canon was not to the Reformers a more or less complete collection of all that could have been written at a certain date, or by a certain class of persons, but the body of books believed to have been destined by God to bear testimony to a certain religious truth, which was clearly defined, and could admit of no contradiction or compromise. It followed, therefore, that the contents, the teaching, the spirit itself, must finally decide regarding the canonicity of each book.

What I have suggested by way of hypothesis, became for Luther at the very outset of his career as a Reformer a very serious reality. He thought himself bound, for the very reasons I have been indicating, to dispute the canonical dignity of several books of the New Testament, I mean, of course, the Epistles of James and Jude, the Epistle to the Hebrews and the Apocalypse. He did not indeed suppress them in his editions, but from the first he relegated them to the end of the volume; and in the tables of the contents placed at the top, he separated their titles from those of the books reputed to be canonical by an interval all the more significant that the twenty-three first alone were numbered while the four last were not. But still more interesting to us is his statement of the motives for this separation. It is found in the various prefaces he gave to his translation. Everywhere he mentions the doubts or the opposition these books encountered in antiquity, though that is a very secondary matter with him. But, while passing lightly enough over the facts, he exaggerates their importance.[1]

[1] *Preface to the Epistle to the Hebrews*: *Bisher haben wir die rechten gewissen Hauptbücher des N. T. gehabt. Diese vier nachfolgende aber haben*

Nor is he quite impartial, since he represents the Epistles of James and Jude as generally rejected, while he does not say a word about the nature of the reception formerly given to the Second Epistle of Peter. Still it is easy to see that the decisive reason to him for the rejection is precisely that dogmatic incompatibility of which I have just been speaking, and which, rightly or wrongly, was henceforth for him and his exegesis an incontestable fact. Luther does not hesitate to acknowledge anything fine and excellent he may, with his fastidious views, find in these books—the austerity of James in vindicating the divine law, the practical teaching which he ingeniously extracts from the Apocalypse, and specially the *masterly* statement of the Epistle to the Hebrews regarding Christ's priesthood. He forgets however that if the latter epistle is not canonical, the very idea of that priesthood has no longer any authentic guarantee. But he insists more on the points that are opposed. The Epistle of James[1] derives justification from works; in interpreting the Old Testament, it contradicts Paul; it does not speak of Christ, His death, His resurrection, His Spirit; it speaks of a law of liberty, while we know from Paul that with the law are

vorzeiten ein ander Ansehn gehabt. [Hitherto we have had the right and genuine books of the New Testament. The four that follow have in former times been otherwise regarded]. . . . He quotes in particular the passage ii., 3, as not coming from an apostle, and certainly not from St. Paul.— *Preface to the Epistles of James and Jude: Diese Ep. Jacobi, wiewohl sie von den Alten verworfen ist, etc.* [This Epistle of James, though it is rejected by the Fathers, etc.] . . . That of Jude is a simple extract from the second of Peter, and is, moreover, filled with quotations drawn from apocryphal books, *welches auch die alten Väter beweget hat diese Epistel aus der Hauptschrift zu werfen* [which also moved the early Fathers to reject it from the canon of Scripture.] See also the two prefaces to the Apocalypse.

[1] *Aufs erste dass sie stracks wider S. Paulum und alle andre Schrift den Werken die Gerechtigkeit gibt. . . . Aufs ander dass sie will Christenleut lehren und gedenckt nicht einmal des Leidens, der Auferstehung, des Geistes Christi. Er nennet Christum etlich mal aber er lehret nichts von ihm sondern sagt von gemeinem Glauben an Gott. . . . Dieser Jacobus thut nicht mehr denn treibet zu dem Gesetz und seinen Werken und wirft unördig eins ins ander. . . . Er nennet das Gesetz*

associated bondage, sin, anger, and death. The Epistle to the Hebrews,[1] in three places (ch. vi., x., xii.), refuses repentance to sinners after baptism, contrary to all the gospels and to all Paul's epistles. The Epistle of Jude[2] also, when judged by what is fundamental in the Christian faith, is useless. In the Apocalypse[3] there are only images and visions, such as are found nowhere else in the Bible; and notwithstanding their obscurity, the author has the boldness to add to them threats and promises, while no one knows what he means; and after all Christ is neither taught nor acknowledged. It may be compared to the fourth book of Ezra; the inspiration of the Holy Spirit is not perceptible in it.

I am not called on to discuss here the real value of these opinions. I adhere, however, to my statement, that, though the different standard applied to the literature of the first century prevents the modern historical school from subscribing to Luther's opinions, it does not prevent them from acknowledging that these were natural and legitimate in any one who set out from a purely dogmatic standpoint and subordinated Scripture to his system exclusively Pauline, or, if you will, Augustinian. Nevertheless, it may be said that he did not intend to pronounce peremptory and indisputable verdicts. In spite of his strong convictions, he is aware of the subjective nature of his reasonings, and willingly

ein Gesetz der Freiheit, so es doch S. Paulus ein Gesetz der Knechtschaft, des Zorns, des Tods und der Sünde nennt. . . .

[1] *Ueber das hat sie einen harten Knoten dass sic. . . . stracks verneinet und versaget die Busse den Sündern, nach der Taufe. . . . welches, wie es lautet, scheinet wider alle Evangelien und Episteln S. Pauli zu sein. . . .*

[2] *Darum ists doch eine unnöthige Epistel unter die Hauptbücher zu rechnen die des Glaubens Grund legen sollen.*

[3] *Mir mangelt an diesem Buche nicht einerlei dass ichs weder apostolisch noch prophetisch halte. Aufs erste und allermeist, dass die Apostel nicht mit Gesichten umbgehn. . . . denn es auch dem ap. Ampt gebuhrt klärlich und ohn Bild oder Gesicht von Christ zu reden. . . . Auch ist so kein Prophet im A. T. . . . dass ichs fast gleich mir achte dem 4ten B. Esras u. allerdinge nicht spüren kann dass es von dem H. Geist gestellet sei. Dazu dunkt mich das allzuviel dass er so hart sein eigen Buch befiehlt, und drüuet wer etwas davon thue, run dem werd*

admits that every one is not of his opinion. He writes a second preface to the Apocalypse [1] in order to attempt an interpretation of the book which at first he professed not to understand, and this interpretation is not grounded on a science sure of its methods, but on his own polemical prejudices. He exalts the good intentions of the unknown disciples who composed the epistles in question, and making use of an image borrowed from Paul, and applied to all the doctors in turn, even to those he recommends,[2] he regrets only that the straw and wood are mingled with the precious materials in these works of edification.[3] It has often been charged against him as a crime that he employs this image. But his premises being granted, it is both exact and spiritual, and can only offend those who have ceased to be his faithful disciples, and wish to impose on others a yoke he had broken.

Still it must not be supposed that the opinions of Luther were only casual suggestions, sallies of the moment. It is true that at times he yields to some momentary impulse, that we find in his works many inconsistencies and many contradictions; in other words, that to the last he continued to learn and to advance. But if his criticism of the canon is always limited to these few protestations more or less

---

Gott auch thun; wiederumb sollen selig sein die da halten was drinnen steht, so doch niemand weiss was es ist.... Mein Geist kann sich in das Buch nicht schicken, u. ist mir die Ursach gnug dass ich sein nicht hoch achte dass Christus drinnen weder gelehrt noch erkannt wird....

[1] Preface to the Apocalypse: *In this book I leave it to every man to make out his own meaning; I wish no one to be bound to my views or opinion ... let every man hold what his spirit gives him....* Preface to the Epistle of James: *Therefore I cannot place it among the right canonical works, but I do not wish thereby to prevent any one from so placing it and extolling it as seemeth good to him.*

[2] *Opera Germ.* ed. Erlangen, LXIII., p. 379.

[3] Preface to the Epistle to the Hebrews: *And though he does not lay the foundation of faith, still he builds gold, silver, precious stones* (1 Cor. iii.); *therefore it should not hinder us, if perhaps there are mingled with these*

subjective,[1] and that it nowhere enters on the discussion of any settled and consistently applied scientific theory, it is not the less fitted to show that his theology, while fully extolling the Word of God and its inspiration, always placed the spirit above the letter, the Gospel above its organs, and that it received the truth for its own sake and not because of any external guarantees.

In order to bring out more clearly the high value he attributed to his theological criterion, I ought further to mention here some of his opinions regarding different books of the Old Testament. These latter were positively better defended, as a whole, by that same tradition which did not afford equal protection to all the writings composing the apostolic canon, and it was generally thought that, after eliminating the Apocrypha, the canon of the Synagogue was raised above all criticism. But Luther's exegesis was skilful in discovering the evangelical element in the documents of the Old Covenant, and he did not hesitate to acknowledge his disappointments in this respect when his sagacity was deceived, and at once to draw from this fact conclusions similar to those he had uttered regarding the four deutero-

---

wood, straw, or hay, but we should receive such fine doctrine with all honour. . . . Preface to the New Testament: *These are the books which show thee Christ, and teach all that is necessary for thee to know.* . . . *Wherefore St. James' Epistle is a true epistle of straw compared with them, for it contains nothing of an evangelical nature.*

[1] They are, however, not so rare as might be supposed. An attentive reader finds numerous traces of them in almost all parts of his works. I take the liberty of pointing out a few. In his *Sermons on the Epistle of Peter*, he speaks disdainfully of that of James, as saying not a word of the most essential part of the Gospel, and infers that the author was not an apostle (*Opera Germ.*, LI. p. 337; comp. X. 366). He complains (VIII. 267) that among the pericopes used in the Church, there are some taken from the Epistle of James, *which cannot be compared with the apostolic writings*, as neither conforming to pure doctrine, nor written by an apostle. Nevertheless, he takes them as texts for his sermons, and makes use of them for edification. In the exordium of another sermon on the first chapter of the Epistle to the Hebrews (vii., p. 181), he makes a stately eulogium of tha

canonical books of the New Testament. On this point I shall quote from the interesting collection of *Table Talk*,[1] some examples which so clearly carry the stamp of his genius, and owe so little to the spirit of his ordinary surroundings that their authenticity cannot be doubtful. They will show how far his intelligence, more practical than learned, was able sometimes to grasp the meaning of the facts, or decide beforehand questions which had not yet arisen in his day. Thus, speaking of Ecclesiastes,[2] he says: "This book ought to be more complete: it wants many things; it has neither boots nor spurs, and rides in simple sandals as I used to do when I was still in the convent. Solomon is not its author," etc. Evidently this criticism applies to the theology of the book in which Luther, with justice, did not recognise the spirit of his own—*i.e.*, of the theology of the Gospel. "The Proverbs of Solomon," he continues, "are a book of good works; they are collected by others who wrote them when the king, at table or elsewhere, had just uttered his maxims. There are added the teachings of other wise doctors. Ecclesiastes and Canticles, are, besides, books not of one piece: there is no order in these books; all is confused in them, which fact is explained by their origin. For Canticles too were composed by others from the sayings of Solomon, who therein thanks God for

---

work for its christological doctrine; but he drily declares that it is not by Paul, whose style is not so rhetorical. Some, he adds, attribute it to Apollos. Now the fact is that he himself was the first to venture on this conjecture (*Comm. in Genes.*, c. xlviii. *Opera Latina*, Erlangen, XI., 130), which is now widely adopted. Elsewhere (*Opera Germana*, XVIII, p. 39) when preaching on the allegory just mentioned (1 Cor. iii.), he thinks that with the test there spoken of, we shall find that Paul preached Christ more purely than Peter, etc. Any apostolic origin is distinctly denied to the Epistle of Jude, vol. X. 366; LII. pp. 272, 284 (*Germ.*)

[1] *Opera Germ.*, LXII. pp. 128 ff.

[2] The original German runs: *Dies buch sollt völliger sein, ihm ist zu viel abgebrochen, es hat weder Stiefel noch Sporn, es reitet nur in Socken, gleich wie ich da ich noch im Kloster war.*

the obedience which is a gift of heaven, and the practice of which at home, or in public, brings peace and happiness, like to conjugal harmony."[1] "As to the second book of Maccabees," he say elsewhere, "and that of Esther, I dislike them so much that I wish they did not exist; for they are too Jewish and have many bad Pagan elements."[2] "The preachings of the prophets were not composed in a complete fashion. Their disciples and their hearers from time to time wrote fragments of them, and thus what is now found in the Bible, was formed and preserved." "The books of Kings are a hundred thousand steps in advance of those of Chronicles, and they also deserve more credit. Still they are only the calendar of the Jews, containing the list of their kings and their kind of government." "Job may have thought what is written in his book, but he did not pronounce these discourses. A man does not speak thus when he is tried. The fact at bottom is real; but it is like the subject of a drama with a dialogue in the style of Terence's comedies, and for the purpose of glorifying resignation."[3] "Moses and the prophets preached; but we do not there hear God himself. For Moses received only the law of angels and has only a subordinate mission. People are not urged to good works by preaching the law. When God himself speaks to men, they hear nothing but grace and mercy. The intermediate organs, angels, Moses, emperor, or burgomaster, can only command; we ought certainly to obey them: but only since God spoke by the Son and the Holy Spirit, do we hear the paternal voice, the voice of love and grace."[4]

[1] *Opera, l.c.* p. 128, and Vol. LXIII., pp. 35, 37, 40.
[2] Vol. LXII., p. 131 : *Ich bin dem Buch und Esther so feind dass ich wollte sie wären gar nicht vorhanden; denn sie judenzen zu sehr und haben viel heidnische Unart.*
[3] Vol. LXII., pp. 132 f.
[4] *Interpretation of the Sixth ch. of John*, 1532. *Opera Germ.*, XLVII., p. 357.

After all I have just said, it will be easy to convince my readers that to Luther the authority of Scripture was nothing but an abstract principle, in other terms, that he never studied, reasoned, or taught, so as to begin by fixing the canon, reserving only the right of seeing afterwards what truths this authority would reveal to him, and would ordain him to believe. On the contrary, his supreme rule, his own special canon, was always a very concrete principle, anterior and superior to all Scripture: Christ crucified and a Saviour. According to him, all the Bible from one end to the other should preach Christ; each one of its parts should be judged according to the measure in which it fulfils that end. The faults, the weaknesses that may be discovered and observed on this point in more than one book, do not compromise the essential matter. What matter all the verses that remain above and beyond, provided we have and know him who is the Master and Lord of Scripture? "If, in the debates in which exegesis brings no decisive victories, our adversaries press the letter against Christ, we shall insist on Christ against the letter." As Luther's theory ended consistently in this, it is evident that the opposition between it and the Catholic system was not the same as the difference between Scripture and tradition; it was rather the difference between a living, active faith in the person of the Saviour, and implicit, passive submission to the authority of the Church. If we had no other proof of this man's genius, it would be sufficiently established by this fact, that after three centuries of hesitations, contradictions, and misunderstandings, the question which he solved is again proposed in the same terms in the very bosom of Protestantism.

Let us not forget to say that Luther, armed with the theory I have just expounded, was perfectly justified in pleading the cause of the Bible against those who prided themselves on a pretended internal illumination and rejected the authority of Scripture. On his part this polemic was not inconsistent; for according to him, the Holy Spirit promised and granted to the believer acts in an immediate manner, but connects this action with the external (*i.e.* written) word, which thus serves as a kind of form or body for it. On the other hand, Luther avoided quite as certainly the opposite excess of those who would have liked to *canonize* the letter, since he demanded, first of all, an explicit and positive adhesion to what he had recognised as the fundamental thought of the Gospel, and thus ran no risk of confounding the eternally true and salutary word of God with the collection of books, which only bears testimony to it in very unequal proportions. For a man so profoundly pious as Luther, this distinction was not an error, nor a piece of weakness, as minds of another kind might suppose it to be: it was an absolute necessity.

Objection will of course be taken that such a theory could hardly issue in any rigorous definition of the canon, even less so than with the unscientific methods of the early Church. That is perfectly just; but I see no great harm in it, and, what is more, Luther's fellow-workers and immediate successors were of the same opinion. Indeed, we find among them some little variety on points of detail, as their common theory permitted great freedom in estimating and using various parts of the sacred code. I shall bring this chapter to a close by some notes taken from writings of the first generation of Lutheran theologians, while I reserve for the following chapter the study of the retrogression made by their successors.

Melanchthon, who makes no explicit statement on this point when formulating his principles, frequently quotes the Epistle to the Hebrews, above all in regard to Christ's sacrifice; but he carefully avoids attributing it to Paul, and always introduces it with an anonymous designation. As to the Epistle of James, he has occasion more than once[1] to discuss its texts when he wishes to refute the doctrines opposed to the fundamental thesis of Protestantism; but he does not enter on the critical question. His exegesis enabled him to neutralise the author's propositions, where Luther could refute them only by the absolute rejection of the book.[2] Finally, the Apocalypse leaves no mark anywhere on his theology, and is passed over in silence. Above this detailed criticism there is in Melanchthon, as in his colleague and friend, the supreme principle of the Christian faith dominating the question of the canon. Thus we may explain how, in the preface of the last editions of his *Loci*, and when recapitulating the component parts of the Bible, in order to characterise them from the doctrinal point of view, he could confine himself in the New Testament to naming the Gospels and the Epistles of Paul. It was not that he rejected the rest, but he thought the point to be of little importance.

Brentz, the reformer of the Duchy of Wurtemberg, is equally acquainted with the non-canonical books of the New Testament, and puts them in the same rank as the Apocrypha of the Old. These, as we may well suppose, are what had formerly been the antilegomena. He does not propose to reject them absolutely, but he asks by what right they were put on the same level as the canonical scriptures.[3] He insists specially on this point, that the

---

[1] *Apol. Confess. August.*, pp. 107 f., 182, 254 f., 263, 296, Rechb.

[2] Luther somewhere jests about the trouble Melanchthon had taken to bring the statements of Paul and James into agreement. "Faith justifies; faith does not justify. I shall put my doctor's bonnet on the man who will make that rhyme, and I wish to pass for a madman." (*Opera Germ.*, LXII., p. 127.)

[3] *Scio in his apocryphis libris multa pietatis documenta contineri. Sapientia Sal., etc. . . . Habent et epistolae quae inter catholicas enumerantur et apocalypsis Joannis suam utilitatem. Non igitur iudicamus hos libros prorsus abiiciendos. Sed illud nunc quaeritur . . . . num liceat vel uni creaturae.*

Epistle of James could not be put in harmony with the apostolic doctrine, without the help of a forced interpretation.

Flacius, the ardent champion of pure Lutheranism, the fiery adversary of Melanchthon, in his great work on hermeneutics,[1] divides the books of the Bible into three classes—the canonical writings, the doubtful, and the apocryphal. By these last, which according to him have no great authority, or none at all (for his definition is ambiguous),[2] he means the Apocrypha of the Old Testament. The doubtful books—*i.e.*, those which have been suspected[3]—are the second epistle of Peter, that to the Hebrews, those of James and Jude, the two latter of John, and the Apocalypse. But he does not insist on this distinction, nor base it on any principle of criticism, nor deduce from it any practical consequence. The separation he makes between the doubtful and the apocryphal is always in favour of the former. Elsewhere,[4] in a work in which he was aided by friends devoted like himself to exclusive tendencies, he applies himself to a more thorough discussion of the value of the antilegomena of the New Testament. He tests them in complete accordance with Luther's example—*i.e.*, from the dogmatic point of view. Only he puts in a plea for the Apocalypse, in which he finds nothing contrary to the analogy of faith. But as for James, Jude, and the Epistle to the Hebrews, he simply reproduces his master's arguments.

quamvis apostolicae, quamvis angelicae, vel alicui hominum coetui, quocunque nomine, ad scripturam (ad libros veros canonicos) alios incertae originis addere, eandem iis autoritatem tribuere. . . . (Brentii *Apol. Confess, Wirtemb.*, pp. 824 f.)

[1] Flacii *Clavis S. S.*, part ii., 1, p. 46.

[2] *Apocryphi quibus nulla eximia autoritas tribuitur sunt: Sap. Sal. etc.* . . . *Hi libri licet biblico canoni nunc addantur, tamen nullius autoritatis apud intelligentes scriptores habentur.*

[3] *Dubios dico de quibus dubitatum est.*

[4] *Centur. Magd.*, ed. Semler i., 452 f. Comp. U. Regii *Int. locc. comm.*, p. 42.

I shall mention one author more, to whom I should, perhaps, have given even the first rank, had I followed the chronological order. He was the only one of the Protestant doctors of that age who wrote a special work on the theory of the canon. This was the celebrated colleague of Luther at Wittenberg, Andreas Bodenstein, who is better known by the name of Carlstadt,[1] and died in 1541 as a professor at Basle. As is well known, he stood out among all the prominent theologians of his time as the most logical champion of the exclusive authority of Scripture, and pushed his radical hostility to ecclesiastical tradition to iconoclastic extremes, which Luther was equally energetic in opposing. This very man became the advocate of tradition on this special point, and in such a way as wittingly to contradict the theory which would have pleased him best. The following is shortly the substance of his book. After speaking with enthusiasm about the majesty of Scripture, and establishing its indisputable authority in everything connected with dogma and institutions, he comes to inquire what basis there is for the canonicity of each book, and begins by analysing in succession the texts of Augustine and Jerome in relation to this question. Then expressing a preference for the distinctions drawn by the latter, and adopting the division usual among the Jews, as well as the information furnished by Eusebius and the Fathers of the fourth century, he concludes by combining these two elements, and establishing three *orders* or classes of books, to which he assigns a different dignity—at least, in so far as the New Testament is concerned. The first class contains the Law, or the five books of Moses (though he does

---

[1] *De canonicis scripturis libellus*: Witt. 1520, quarto. He issued a brief summary of it in German: *Welche bücher heilig und biblisch seind* (*ibid. eod.*). The original, become extremely rare, was reprinted in 1847 by Credner with notes (*Zur Geschichte des Canons*, pp. 291 f.)

not hesitate to declare that Moses is not their author in the rigorous meaning of the word), and the four gospels, which are the most brilliant lamps of Divine truth.¹ To the second class belong, on the one hand, the prophets—*i.e.*, the books of Joshua, Judges (with Ruth), Samuel, Kings, Isaiah, Jeremiah (with Lamentations), Ezekiel, and the twelve Minor Prophets; on the other hand, the fifteen epistles universally received and undoubtedly Apostolic — viz., thirteen by Paul, one by Peter, and one by John. To the third, finally, are relegated the hagiographa, as they are brought together in our Hebrew Bibles² (with the exception of Ruth and Lamentations), and the seven antilegomena of the New Testament, which occupy the lowest rank in regard to canonical dignity. The chief, or rather the sole motive, which the author advances for this distinction, is the amount of attestation given by early writers. Thus, in his eyes, the Apocalypse and the Epistle to the Hebrews are put still lower than the Epistles of James, Jude, and John, because the latter were admitted to the canon at an earlier date. Carlstadt expressly adds that the rank he assigns to the Epistle to the Hebrews is not determined by any inferiority in its intrinsic value. In short, Carlstadt's theory is absolutely different from that of Luther. This is evident from his preference for the Gospels over the writings of St. Paul, and especially from his polemic on the question of the Epistle of James,⁴ to which polemic he returns on several occasions with a certain bitterness. He also avails himself of the famous saying of Augustine, to which I have

[1] *Libri primæ notæ summæque dignitatis N. T. totius veritatis divinæ clarissima lumina.*

[2] See note on p. 10.

[3] *Infimum autoritatis divinæ locum.*

[4] *Jacobi epistola nihil usque sententiarum habet quod non possit canonicis literis communiri. Si fas est vel parvum vel magnum facere quod placet, futurum tandem erit dignitates et autoritates librorum e nostra pendere facultate.*

before directed attention; for, he says, it is by the recognition and the testimony of the Church that we know what books are genuinely evangelical, and how many epistles there are by the apostles.

If Luther's personal opinions were not adopted by all the theologians of his school, they at least prevailed in practice, in so far as all the editions of the German New Testament down to our times have preserved the order and arrangement he introduced, separating the Epistle to the Hebrews from the Epistles of Paul, and those of James and Jude from the other Catholic Epistles. There exist even editions of the Greek New Testament, not very old, which were made by Lutheran theologians, and in which the canon is thus modified.[1] Further, Luther's prefaces for a long time were put at the head of each book, and thus gave currency to his critical opinions.[2] These determined also the form of the Bible in several other national versions, made originally from Luther's version, in countries ranged under the banner of the Augsburg Confession, for instance, in Lower Saxony, the Netherlands, and partly in Sweden. There are even editions which give to the four books set apart by Luther a special title, designating them as *Apocrypha*, like those of the Old Testament. I shall have occasion to return to these details.

Whatever impression my readers may have received from the facts stated in this chapter, I have at least proved that the Reformers, while claiming a very important place in the dogmatic system for the notion of the canon, and while successful in connecting it very closely with the general

---

[1] Halle, Orphan House, 1740, etc.

[2] In our days these prefaces, which are no longer found in the current Bibles, have been several times printed by themselves in collections intended for the public, but in such a way as to efface all the characteristic peculiarities I have been pointing out. Marcion, who is called a forger, did not do so much as that.

principles of their theology, did not attain to any uniformity in the application of the theory to facts and questions of detail; that their science was not able to determine the natural and legitimate relation between the testimony of tradition and the intrinsic religious principle; that the symbolic books even contain on this point divergent rules or assertions, and in more than one instance contradict themselves. Still we have also seen that, in spite of these differences, no serious controversy arose among them or their churches about the settlement of the canon, while the fraternal bond that should have united the various fractions of the friends of the Reformation, was enfeebled or broken by lively theological discussions on so many other points which, to us now, have lost much of their importance. That shows most convincingly that the question of the canon was something more to our illustrious fathers than the question of drawing up a literary catalogue, and in this way of viewing it they were all agreed.

[Note on the position of the Apocrypha in early English Bibles.—In the early English Bibles (excepting the Douay version, 1609) the Apocrypha stands detached between the O. and N. T. The first English Bible (Coverdale's, printed at Zurich, 1535) has this title for the collection—" The books and treatises which among the Fathers of old are not reckoned to be of like authority with other books of the Bible, neither are they found in the canon of the Hebrew." The preface is in the same strain :—" These books which are called Apocrypha are not judged amongst the doctors to be of like reputation with the other Scriptures, as thou mayest perceive by St. Jerome *in Epistola ad Paulinum*, and the chief cause is this, there are many places in them that seem to be repugnant unto the open and manifest truth in the other parts of the Bible. Nevertheless, I have not gathered them together to the intent that I would have them despised or that I should think them false, for I cannot prove it." In what is usually called Matthew's Bible, the preface runs thus :—" In consideration that the books before are found in the Hebrew tongue received of all men . . . the others following, which are called Apocrypha (because they were wont to be read, not openly and in common, but as it were in secret and apart), are neither found in the Hebrew nor in the Chaldee, in which tongues they have not long been written . . . and that also they are not received nor taken to be legitimate, as well of the Hebrews as of the whole Church, as St. Jerome showeth, we have separated them and set them aside, that they may the better be known to the intent that men may know of which books witness ought to be received and of which not." This preface goes on to quote the authority of Eusebius for asserting that these books had been corrupted and falsified in many places. The critical knowledge of these early translators may be judged from the fact that in several editions (1539, 1540), the word *Hagiographa* is substituted for Apocrypha in the above preface, and the same explanation made to serve. In later Bibles two lines of treatment may be observed. In all editions of Cranmer's Bible and the Bishop's Bible, the distinction between the other books and the Apocrypha is very much effaced. The title of the still separate collection is, "The volume of the books called the Hagiographa," or "The volume of the books called the Apocrypha, containing the books following," or "The fourth part of the Bible." No note is added to draw attention to any difference in the authority of the books. On the other hand, in the Genevan version (commonly called the Breeches Bible), which was much favoured by the Puritans, the preface draws a strict line of distinction. "The books that follow in order after the prophets unto the N. T. are called Apocrypha—*i.e.*, books which were not received by a common consent to be read and expounded publicly in the church, neither yet served to prove any point of Christian religion, save inasmuch as they had the consent of the other Scriptures called canonical to confirm the same, or rather whereon they were grounded; but as books proceeding from godly men were received to be read for the advancement and furtherance of the knowledge of the history and for the instruction of godly manners, etc." In King James's version (1611), usually called the Authorised Version, the books stand between the O. and N. T., under the title Apocrypha, but without preface or note. The Douay Bible (1609-10), printed for English Roman Catholics, distributes the Apocrypha among the canonical books of the O. T., and maintains a polemic in their favour in the prefaces. One sentence will show the critical standpoint, "Who seeth not that the canon of the Church of Christ is of more authority with all true Christians than the canon of the Jews?" When the house of tradition is thus divided against itself, how can its authority continue?] Trans.

CHAPTER XVII.

THE CONFESSIONAL SCHOOLS.

THE theologians, who followed the generation of the Reformers down to the beginning of the eighteenth century, are much less known outside the narrow circle of professed historians; and even in regard to a still more recent epoch, it may be said that those at least, who simply continued the dogmatic tradition of the early schools, are in our day almost completely forgotten. They are, in particular, seldom consulted for their opinions on the questions which here concern us. We have been so accustomed to represent the scientific work of that period as sterile and stationary, that we have thought it unnecessary to make any detailed study of it; and the unattractive form of the works it produced has in general the stamp of a dull, dry scholasticism, such as to give ample excuse to exacting or timid readers. Nevertheless, the writers of this middle age of Protestantism do not deserve all the disdain of their successors. Not to speak of the great scholars, of the philologists who did honour chiefly to the Calvinistic countries and academies, I take leave to affirm that the interpreters of the theory also, however dependent in regard to the formulas elaborated by their predecessors, frequently rise above the level of routine, and may be studied to good purpose by those who wish to form an exact conception of the movement of modern ideas. The great revolution which took place in this sphere last century, cannot be understood nor justly estimated without some more intimate acquaintance with what preceded it and prepared for it. I propose, therefore, to take a glance through dusty quartos containing the dull and prolix science of the confessional schools, that I may draw from them a new series of materials for my history of the canon.

Note the phrase *confessional schools* which I have put at the head of this chapter. It is intended to characterise a particular phase of the development of Protestant theology, a phase which began about the time of the death of the last great Reformers, and during which the Confessions of Faith were the exclusive and official standard of teaching. From that time, science, but lately regenerated and quickened by the powerful action of a supreme religious principle and deriving increased energy from its recent proclamation, was subordinated to the no less powerful but much less vivifying law of the formulas, in which that principle, with its most important applications, had finally found an expression both rigid and precise. Whereas at first the theology of justification by faith in Christ had drawn its strength directly from the word of God, so much so that it could make claim to limit the latter in accordance with its own fundamental axiom, the nearest source from which it now drew strength was the Symbol, the Gospel turned into a system and composed, not under inspiration from above, but often amid the din of controversies, and sometimes with the afterthoughts of compromise. That which had been an excellent rallying-cry, whether to organize opposition against Rome or to serve as a charter of liberty, became the barrier which divided the churches and arrested progress. The effects of this change in the position of the doctors and the doctrines naturally made themselves felt, though in different degrees, in all branches of ecclesiastical science and government. I have only to concern myself here with what relates to my special subject. As to this latter, the influence of the new methods made itself felt, even when the texts of the symbolic books in no way prejudged the composition of the scriptural canon. But the imperious need of defining everything, systematizing everything, subordinating everything, in short, to a work of dialectic reasoning, soon led the Swiss Calvinists, and a little later the Lutherans of all countries, to the result which the English, Dutch, and French had consecrated from the first—viz., to a definite settlement of the canon, based essentially on usage and tradition.

I shall first note this interesting fact, that the dogmatic works of that period contain chapters more and more lengthy on the Scriptures, their origin, composition, authority, and other qualities, whereas, formerly, and especially in the Lutheran Church, no need had been felt of investigating a point which in its fundamental conception was an axiom for every one. As to this fundamental conception, I must say in the first place that, at first sight, what I have been able to call the Protestant theory of the canon is not changed by the successors of Luther and Calvin. The permanent antagonism of the Romish polemics did not permit the possibility of losing sight of the principle which exalted the authority of Scripture over that of tradition.[1] We, therefore, find everywhere great prominence given to the theses which have been already developed in the preceding chapter, and which I need not again discuss at length, such theses as: Scripture holds its authority from itself, *i.e.*, from God who inspired it; Scripture is the supreme judge in matters of faith and for everything relating to salvation; Scripture is the source of all authority in the Church, and the latter can

---

[1] In practice, frequent appeal was made to the testimony of the orthodox Fathers of the first five centuries, in the interest of the purified dogma, and especially in questions of sacred criticism, it being understood always that this testimony was favourable to the thesis defended. But when some theologians, with the purpose of conciliation, wished to raise this practice to the dignity of a principle, it was very quickly remembered that this was illogical, and an outcry was raised against the syncretism.

as little pretend to exercise any patronage over Scripture as it can pretend to have inspired it.[1]

That is not all. The theory explicitly maintained, in the two churches, the difference already noted between the imperfect, insufficient, pedagogic conviction, in regard to the value of Scripture and its contents, which was produced by historical testimonies and arguments furnished from external facts, and the immediate, absolute, saving conviction, which was produced by the inward action of the Holy Spirit in the believer's heart. Without the active concurrence of this divine power, the true faith which accepts the word of God as such does not exist.[2] The theory (I insist on this term) did not therefore repudiate the mystical element of the theology of the Reformers. On the contrary, the difference between Catholicism and Protestantism was sometimes, and rightly, reduced to this simple expression, that the former regards the Church, the latter the Spirit, as the supreme guarantee of Scripture, and thereby of all revelation. The apostles themselves, it was added, had need of this guarantee to obtain a hearing from the people they addressed, their authority not residing in their own personalities, though they were incontestably the organs of God.[3] Their successes were gained beyond doubt, because the

---

[1] See among a hundred others: Hier. Zanchius *de S. S.* (*Opp.*, Gen. 1619, tom. viii., P. i.) p. 339. J. Cameron, *Prælectt. de verbo Dei* (*Opp.*, Gen. 1642), p. 492. H. Alting, *Loci communes* (*Opp.*, Amst. 1646, tom. i., pp. 271, 296). Mos. Amyraldus, *De testim. Sp. S.*, in Thes. Salmur. i., p. 125. L. Cappellus, *De summo controvers. iudice*, ibid., p. 101. J. H. Heidegger, *Corpus theol. chr.*, 1700, p. 30. M. Chemnitz, *Examen conc. trident.*, loc. i., c. vi., § 7 f. J. Gerhard, *Loci theol.*, ed. Cotta, tom. i., pp. 9 f. Abr. Calovii *Criticus sacer*, 1673, pp. 57 f. J. Musæi *Introd. in theol.*, p. 290. J. W. Baier, *Compend. theol. positivæ*, 1712, p. 81. J. Fc. Buddei *Instit. th. dogm.*, 1724, pp. 147 f.

[2] Zanchi, *l. c.*, pp. 332 f. D. Chamier, *Panstratia cath.*, 1627, P. i. B. vi., c. i., § 7 and c. iv. J. Cloppenburg, *Exercitt. super locos comm.* (*Opp. theol.*, Amst. 1684, tom. i.), pp. 704 f. Calovius, *l. c.*, pp. 43 f. etc.

[3] Cameron, *l. c.*, pp. 458 f.

word they preached was true, sublime, and efficacious; but these qualities were manifested only to those on whom God wrought by the simultaneous action of his Spirit.[1] And since the Roman Church also claimed that Spirit for itself, as its permanent guide, a distinction had to be drawn between what was called the *public* Spirit and the *private* Spirit, and the thesis had to be proclaimed as a Protestant principle, that the action of the Spirit is private—*i.e.*, is addressed directly to the individual without the intervention of the Church.[2] Up to this point we have been on the ground of the principles set forth in the preceding chapter.

Notwithstanding, when we study more profoundly the use which theology made of these principles, we soon see that it hardly ever descended from the abstract, I had almost said glacial, heights of theory into the lower and better explored region of practical questions; and nothing is so curious as the movement of ideas, withdrawing more and more from what had been at first an intuitive conception, a conception belonging to the sphere of the religious sentiment, rather than to that of intelligence and demonstration. Thus, in the controversy against Catholicism, much stress was laid on this action of the Holy Spirit in favour of Scripture; but the need for guarding against the pretensions of the illuminated, who disdained the written word and subordinated it to individual, permanent inspiration, as well as against the subjective criticism of which Luther had set a dangerous example, led theologians on to a series of definitions, analyses and restrictive clauses dictated by prejudices foreign to the primitive conception they were defending. Hence in the end, all was regulated by conventional combinations, and the action of the Holy Spirit, maintained as a theory, became

---

[1] Amyraldus, *De testim. Sp. S.*, in Thes. Salmur., i., pp. 117 f. Buddeus, *l. c.*, p. 103.

[2] Chamier, *l. c.*, iv., § 4. Cameron, *l. c.*, p. 467.

in fact useless and superfluous. I should add that the fundamental contradiction between the old point of view, and the principles now prevailing, makes itself felt chiefly in a certain obscurity, which generally reigns in the exposition of these matters. Let me try, however, to bring out the most salient points of the system as we find it developed in the authors of this period.

Of the two kinds of conviction which might exist regarding the authority of the Word of God, that derived from the action of the Holy Spirit *(fides divina)* and considered the most important, was treated in general with much brevity, I might even say, with decreasing interest. It must also be said that soon there were appended to it discussions altogether scholastic which prove of themselves that the primitive thought of the Reformers had been dropped out of sight. The first point was to determine the part of the Spirit and the part of Scripture in the influence to be exercised; then to indicate precisely the succession of the elementary facts in the action itself;[1] finally, to consider whether the power of the Spirit is a proper force added to that of Scripture, or whether the spiritual effect is produced by the latter, inasmuch as the Spirit acts in it without any need for distinguishing two active principles.[2] All these anatomical processes applied to inward religious experiences, betray dispositions and tendencies very different from those which had formerly guided Protestant theology in its theory of canonicity.[3]

[1] *Form. Conc.*, p. 656 : *Homo verbum Dei prædicatum neque intelligit neque intelligere potest, donec virtute Sp. S. per verbum prædicatum convertatur.*—Man remains a stranger to the Word of God, so long as he is not converted by the Spirit, and the Spirit is to touch him only by means of the Word. Comp. Buddeus, *l. c.*, p. 107. Quenstedt, *Theol. did. pol.*, i., 169 f. etc.

[2] See the article by M. Saigey on *Pajonism* (*Revue de theol.*, first series, vol. xiv., p. 339.)

[3] A similar impression is received from the dialectical attempts made (e. g.

On the other hand the theologians of this period discussed at great length the elements and sources of what was called the human conviction (*fides humana*). They rightly said that this only furnished probabilities in regard to Scripture, and that it needed to be sanctioned by the other to convey to us entire certainty. But the very care bestowed on this part of the dogma proves that, practically, it was considered the most essential, and the arguments supporting it were held to be more efficacious than any others. The proofs which were to produce this purely human and preparatory conviction, were divided into internal and external.[1] The former were derived both from the form and contents of Scripture; the latter from its antiquity, the providential propagation of the Gospel, the faith of the martyrs, the manifestations of the divine justice in history, the credibility of the Biblical narratives, the character of the authors, miracles and predictions, finally and specially the testimony of the Church. All these proofs, according to the theologians, were only to produce a strong presumption in favour of the Bible; still, the power attributed to them was such that the argument kept in reserve to give what was called the divine conviction, could add nothing more conclusive or more palpable. Nevertheless, they adhered to the traditional formula, which consecrated it, and defended it with vigour when Cartesianism,[2] invading the schools of Holland, supposed it possible to rest satisfied with the others. They in-

by Calovius, *Crit. sac.*, pp. 44 f.) to demonstrate that the proof of the authority of Scripture derived from the Word of God is not stained by the logical vice of *petitio principii*.

[1] Comp. Cameron, *l. c.*, pp. 417 f. 475. Zanchi, *l. c.*, p. 337. Heidegger, *l. c.*, pp. 25 f. Baier, *Comp. theol. posit.*, pp. 84 f. Buddeus, *l. c.*, pp. 101 f., 134 etc.

[2] See the literature of this controversy directed especially against Herm. Alex. Roëll, professor at Utrecht, in Buddeus *l. c.*, p. 107. Comp. Gisb. Voëtii *Problem. de S. S.* (*Dispp. sel.*, *Utr.* 1669, P. V.), pp. 3 f. Val. Alberti *Cartesianismus Belgio molestus*, 1678.

stinctively felt that, if they abandoned it even in theory, their dialectics would thenceforth be hardly distinguishable from that of their rationalistic adversaries.

Let us consider for a moment these two sets of proofs, in order to bring out some very characteristic symptoms of the change that was taking place in the science whose history we are studying. In regard to the internal proof which, as we said, consisted in founding the authority of Scripture on its contents, they did not hesitate to acknowledge that absolute certainty about the names of the authors was not indispensable, provided the judgment to be passed on the ground-work, the doctrine, is such as to dispel doubt.[1] Still we should not lose sight of the fact that this kind of demonstration, familiar as it is to most of our theologians, is hardly applied by them except to Scripture considered as one whole and with reservation of the critical questions in detail or the doubts which might arise in regard to one or other of the books. In these special discussions, they preferred to use the historical arguments which thus came to hold a more and more important place in the history of the canon.[2] I am far from blaming this prejudice in every legitimate case since the facts under discussion were historical. I only wish to notice that science was in a period of transition and crisis, consequently in a false position. Scholars began to see that the canon is properly the object of an historical science; but on the one hand the methods and resources of that science were still but little developed and were entirely dominated by a theory independent of them, and on the other hand this theory had already lost the fresh energy of its origin

---

[1] Cameron, *l. c.*, p. 473. Voëtius (*l. c.*) frankly declares that the titles of the books and the inscriptions of the psalms do not form an integral part of the canon.

[2] Amyraut (*De testim. Sp. S.*, § 27, inserted in the first vol. of the Theses of Saumur), very clearly avows that, by means of this distinction, the proofs were more easily managed.

and was finding it necessary to seek in history the supports it had formerly been able to disdain.

Among the historical or external arguments, there was one in particular which deserves the attention of my readers. It is the argument derived from the testimony of the Church. This is a most important point to us, because we are concerned to know in what sense Protestant theology intended to use this argument (which it did use more and more) without falling back into the paths of Catholic traditionalism. On this point they had of course to determine the rights and the duties of the Church in relation to Scripture. In conformity with their theory, they had to limit the Church's part to that of a witness, and in general to insist on the services it might render in watching over the preservation of the collection, rather than on its professed privilege of defining the collection on its own authority.[1] But this reserve was not made by all the dogmatic writers. The necessity for making very complete enumerations imposed on the Church the duty[2] of approving and receiving Scripture, recommending it by attestation, drawing up the official catalogue of the canonical books, preserving the manuscripts, making a faithful translation of them, composing in harmony with it the symbolic books and catechisms, giving the interpretation of difficult and obscure passages, &c. I do not very well see the difference between this list of duties and the list of rights claimed by the Catholic Church. Chamier[3] before this, when recounting

---

[1] Hence the formulas: χειραγωγία, ministeriale iudicium, non magisteriale iudicium; ansa, non causa; medium per quod, non propter quod; non quia ecclesia scripturas authenticas dicit, tales sunt, sed quia sunt, ecclesia tales iudicat etc. Comp. Heidegger, l. c., pp. 28 f. Chemnitz, Examen conc. trid., l. c., §§ 9 f. Gerhard, l. c., p. 10. Quenstedt, Theol. didact. polem., i., 94. Baier, l. c., pp. 113 f. Calov., Crit. Sacr., pp. 66 f. etc.

[2] Officia ecclesiæ, Cloppenburg, l. c., p. 708.

[3] Panstrat. cath., B. vi., ch. i., § 5.

the proofs for the authority of Scripture, had placed in the first rank the testimony of the Church, and had spoken of internal arguments as only secondary. It is quite superfluous to enter into any more detailed criticism of these facts in order to show that the theory, having ceased to express any immediate and personal conviction, was no longer powerful enough to arrest science on the slope which was leading it back, as regards this particular dogma, to the principles so strongly condemned, or, at any rate, despised by the Reformers.

On the whole, the fact is worthy of notice that theology did not succeed in extracting from these numerous and learned discussions any clear and precise definition of the notion of canonicity. The theological element, to which alone the growing science of Protestantism gave heed, was more and more mixed with the historical element, and was specially influenced by the necessity for stability and uniformity, so that the one embarrassed the other, and even corrupted it to some extent. There are still some special facts of a nature to show the embarrassment which this confusion was incessantly creating, and which they attempted to overcome by insufficient or even unfortunate combinations.

The celebrated professor of Saumur, Joshua de la Place,[1] well says that the term *canon* may be taken in two senses—as a body of regulating and authoritative dogmas, and as a list or collection of books regarded as containing the word of God. But, in place of seeking to reduce these two notions to unity, he contents himself with enumerating the signs by which it may be known whether or not a dogma is canonical, and then with discussing a series of quite different arguments to prove that the canonical collection of the Old Testament ought not to

[1] Placæus, *De canone* (in *Syntagm. thes. Salmur.*, tom. i.), pp. 63 f.

include the Apocrypha. These are two facts which thus remain completely isolated from one another.

His no less famous colleague, Moses Amyraut,[1] is not more happy when he tries to combine the principle of the direct intervention of the Holy Spirit with that of the relative authority of the testimony of the Church. He distinguishes three degrees of intensity in the communication of the Spirit which was made with a view to the *discernment* (διάκρισις) of the canonical Scriptures. Those who originally formed the two collections (the author hazards no conjecture on this point) must have possessed the Spirit in an exceptional degree—viz., on a level with the prophets and Apostles. Those who simply had the mission of preserving them in their integrity, by preventing heretics from mutilating them or introducing into them anything heterogeneous, needed the Divine assistance only in a less degree; such was the case with the great councils. Finally, the last degree is that given to the faithful in general, who do not need to make the canon or preserve it, but have to be convinced in themselves of its authenticity. It is difficult here to say which creates most wonder, the idea the author appears to have formed of the working of the Holy Spirit, or the frankness of his historical prejudices, or the distance separating him from the theory of the Reformers. It is evident that science was being fatally dragged in a direction it wished to avoid, and in place of taking the courageous resolution of retracing its steps, was seeking to hide from itself the feebleness of its position.[2]

The explanation I have just been reproducing made

[1] Amyraldus, *De testim. Sp. S.* (ibid.), p. 129.
[2] A third theologian of Saumur, the illustrious Cameron, expresses himself with much greater circumspection. The Church, he says, when making the canon, recognised the books that were to form it by certain characteristics; it did not, therefore, proceed on its own authority, but with the use of means which are still at the disposal of every believer (*Prælectt. de verbo Dei*, *l.c.*, p. 475).

immense concessions to the Catholic system, and on that account it does not appear to have been much favoured by a generation of theologians with whom polemics formed the science or, if you wish, the art *par excellence*. At least I have found it nowhere else. Still I have found something approaching it. While abstaining carefully from pronouncing the name of the Church as the author of the canon or distinguishing various degrees of the spirit, certain Protestant writers were content with admitting that there were, whether among the ancient Israelites or the Christians, pious individuals possessing the gift of discernment, and that to them the honour is due of having composed the two canonical collections.[1] Evidently by placing these individuals in an antiquity sufficiently remote, they could pass over the uncertainties of the Fathers and do without a repetition of the investigation, which threatened to be inopportune, though two centuries before it would have been considered the right and even the duty of all Christians.

There is still another critical reflection to make, and perhaps I have done wrong not to make it sooner. Almost all the strange turns given to a question which at the bottom is simple enough, proceed from a circumstance to which I have not yet directed express attention and to which I shall have to return. It must be remembered that in the eighteenth century the only point of difference to be discussed between Catholics and Protestants (so far as concerned the names of the sacred books), was the canonicity of the Apocrypha of the Old Testament. Sufficient account is not taken of the influence that fact exercised on the exposition of principles. I am prepared to affirm, for instance, that the passages of the various authors I last named, were written by men prejudiced by this special fact. Every means was sought to escape from the dilemma, proposed by their adver-

---

[1] Buddei *Institt. theol. dogm.*, pp. 142 f.

saries, who insisted on the illogical reasoning of opposing now the privilege of individual inspiration to the judgment of the Church, and again the authority of tradition to the caprices of innovators. That will also explain the curious paragraph from Du Moulin,[1] which we would not understand rightly if we consider it as a kind of absolute theory. But, just because I make allowance for the special occasion which inspired its author, I have a right to say that the latter, absorbed by the details of his controversy, lost sight of large principles and got confused to the extent of moving in a circle. For his reasoning, when freed from all extraneous matter, amounts to this: we first accept the Bible because we believe in the Church that gives it to us, then we shall accept the Church because we have believed in the Bible. As an actual fact, things went on and do still go much in this way; but obviously there is neither theological principle nor scientific method in it.

It will not be wrong then to speak of a notable change passing over the current of ideas, and the construction of system in the schools of Protestantism. Let me add that to

---

[1] The Church places Scripture in our hands, but since by this Scripture God has touched our hearts, we do not believe that it is Holy Scripture because the Church says so, but because it has made itself felt and God has touched our hearts by it; without which virtue the testimony of the Church is only a probable aid, producing a confused belief and a slight impression. For no one can have certain knowledge that the testimony his Church renders to Scripture is true, if he does not previously know that this Church is orthodox and well grounded in the faith, and this can be known for certain only after knowing the rule of the true faith, which is the word of God (*Buckler of the Faith*, new ed. 1846, p. 51).

[2] Comp. Gerhard, *Loci theol.*, i., ch. i., § 30 : *Testimonium ecclesiæ nec unicum nec præcipuum est argumentum (librum aliquem esse canonicum) sed accedunt interna κριτήρια et ipsius Spiritus S. testimonium. Initium quidem fieri potest ab ecclesiæ testimonio sed postea scriptura et Spiritus S. per scripturam luculentissime de se testatus.* Theory said (*ib.*, § 33) : *Scriptura est αὐτόπιστος. Credimus scripturis canonicis quia sunt scripturæ canonicæ—i.e., quia a Deo profectæ et immediata Sp. S. inspiratione sunt perscriptæ, non autem ideo illis credimus quia de illis ecclesia testatur.*

my mind this change was only very natural, from the moment that it was recognised, and proved that the masses cannot rise to the height of the few who are gifted minds and accomplished Christians. It may even be said that time and habit were of themselves sufficient to produce this change. According to Luther, the canon was to be determined exclusively by the evangelic principle of justification by faith; according to Calvin, Scripture was guaranteed as a whole and in its parts by its own qualities, regarding which the internal testimony of the Holy Spirit furnished the necessary illumination. Insensibly the conclusion was reached that this guarantee is an admitted fact, and that there is no room for verifying a result universally accepted. The testimony of the Holy Spirit became superfluous; the analogy of faith was recognised; the authority of the previous opinions—i.e., of the tradition of the Church, was substituted for the criteria formerly extolled. The only thing left was to seek out some formula for reconciling two points of view so utterly different, and to give to the early Church the advantages of the conquests made by the new Church.

This transformation of ideas may be regarded in still another aspect, which will perhaps better reveal to us its meaning. At the outset of the Reformation, the two terms *Scripture*, and *Word of God*, were not employed as identical, and Lutheran theology especially maintained the distinction for a very long time. In our symbolic books,[1] the Word of God is the *doctrine* revealed even before Scripture, written in the Bible and preached from it. In that sense, this notion is both wider and narrower than that of Holy Scripture. For though everything, in the holy books, may serve for edification, everything does not directly relate, is not necessary, to salvation—i.e., canonical in the special sense.

[1] See, for instance, *Apol.*, p. 267. *Smalc.*, pp. 331, 333. *Form. Conc.*, pp. 670, 818, etc.

On the other hand, the word of God, known even to the patriarchs, appears still in every sermon that is conformable with evangelic truth, even though Biblical expressions are not literally reproduced in it. Now, it is impossible to avoid observing that gradually the two notions were confused with one another. *Scripture*, and *Word of God* became synonymous terms. That took place with tolerable rapidity in the Calvinistic schools,[1] because they were accustomed from the first to regard the Bible as a homogeneous whole.[2]

That I may not seem intentionally to forget it, I shall only remind my readers in passing that with the increasing ascendency of the traditional principle in the constitution of the canon, the definition of inspiration became more rigorous. In both churches, it was finally extended to the very words of the sacred texts; and, if some theologians still spoke of a certain accommodation of the Holy Spirit to the character or particular style of his *secretaries*, others held that the purity of that style, called in question by some Hellenist philologists, ought to be made an article of faith. But all these details belong rather to a history of dogma than to that of the canon, and I put them aside in order to speak further regarding some special applications of the new theories.

The canon of the Old Testament was not the object of any critical discussion during the period under consideration, with the exception of the great question of the Apocrypha, on which I am about to enter. When any author took the trouble to make a defence of Ecclesiastes, or Canticles, or the

[1] See already the second Helvetic Confession, Art. I.

[2] If we wish to form an idea of the simplicity with which the questions concerning the canon were finally treated, we have only to see how Du Moulin refutes his adversary. His adversary reproaches Protestants with being necessarily illogical, since they cannot deduce the authentic list of the canonical books from a text of Scripture, though they appeal to Scripture as the only source of all truth. "*It is enough*," he says, "*to take the Bible in the original tongues and run over the titles of the books*" (*l. c.* p. 38). In other words, a book is canonical because it appears in my copy.

story of Esther, he had before him none but imaginary foes, and the arguments for the defence were in keeping with the attack.[1] The worthy exegesis of the seventeenth century had its resources, and could, with little difficulty, make light work of the importunate scruples of Athanasius or Luther. But it is interesting to observe that the canonicity of the code of the Old Covenant was demonstrated solely by means of historical proofs, or proofs pretending to be historical. The Jewish Church, it was said, had known the authors and seen the autographs; it was therefore quite in a position to furnish all the guarantees required.[2] The closing of the canon is officially mentioned in the last lines of the last prophet, which declares clearly enough that inspiration would cease till the coming of the new Elijah.[3] The Apostles declared that God had confided his oracles to the Jews, and neither the apostles nor the primitive Christian Church accuse the Jews of having arbitrarily increased or diminished the collection. Christ and his disciples borrow testimonies from it, thereby bearing their own testimony to it. This last argument, however, is hardly used except in a negative form and against the Apocrypha; for it was remembered that all the books of the Old Testament are not quoted in the New, and this fact was used by controversialists to overwhelm Protestant criticism.[5]

But there is one fact which in quite another way shows

---

[1] Canticles and Esther should be translated as types and allegories. The absence of the name of God in these books, so far from betraying a profane spirit, is a warning to the reader admonishing him to seek it under the figure of one of the personages therein represented (Placaei *Opp.*, tom. i. pp. 666, f.).

[2] Placaeus, *De Canone*, l. c., p. 67. Buddei *Institt.*, p. 136, etc.

[3] Heidegger, *Corpus theol. chr.*, loc. ii. § 43.

[4] Gerhard, *Loci*, tom. i. p. 5.

[5] *Si ideo canonici non sunt quia non citantur, ergo Nahum et Sophonias, qui non citantur, canonici non sunt; Aratus contra, Menander et Epimenides profani poetae, canonici quia citantur* (ap. Alting, *Loci comm.*, p. 285).

the tendencies of the Reformed theology, when the reaction had set in towards the authority of the tradition. The learned works of my illustrious countryman, L. Cappellus, on the criticism of the text and the various readings of the Old Testament, had roused the distrustful orthodoxy of the Swiss theologians, and after the launching of many quartos against the rash professor of Saumur, whose colleagues also were suspected to be unsound on predestination, the orthodox succeeded in drawing up the formula called the *Consensus Helveticus* (1675), and procuring its adoption by the government of some cantons. In this formula the vowel-points and the accents were declared to be divinely inspired and to form an integral part of the canon.[1] This Confession of Faith, the last that was officially promulgated in the Protestant Churches, was also the most advanced expression of the despotic traditionalism which had invaded the theology of the Reformed schools; and the violent commotions which it soon provoked, and which led to its revocation, were, in the sphere of dogmatic science, the first symptom of an awakening which had already begun to regenerate the Lutheran Churches in the sphere of practical religion. That did not prevent the points from being canonised, as the result not of any individual caprice but of the general spirit of the studies of the times, nor did it prevent the majority of theologians[2] from accepting that canonisation. Nor did it prevent others from growing impassioned on a

[1] Art. i.: *Deus verbum suum non tantum scripto mandari curavit, sed etiam pro scripto vigilavit, ne Satanœ astu vitiari possit. Proinde. . . . ne apex quidem vel iota unicum peribit.*—2: *In specie hebraicus V. T. codex quem ex traditione ecclesiœ judaicœ accepimus, tum quoad consonas, tum quoad vocalia s. puncta θεόπνευστος.*

[2] See, for example, Gerhard, *Loci*, ii. 267, f. Voëtius (*l. c.*, p. 4) thought that the accents, in so far as they are musical signs, are of human invention; but, in so far as they are signs of punctuation, they share in the canonical dignity of the text. He extended this privilege to the Greek accents of the New Testament.

point no less doubtful, viz., the form of the consonants which was supposed to have remained the same since the deluge.[1]

As to the apocryphal books of the Old Testament, Protestant science never deviated from the principles of the Reformers by which they were excluded from the canon. Still, on this particular point, as on others more important, ideas and procedure varied. Some were content with maintaining the dogmatic distinction as an accepted fact, and did not enter on any criticism of detail. Others, while continuing to speak of these books with much moderation and with some esteem, were led by their polemics to oppose the Catholics who asserted their absolute canonicity. This they did not only with denials based on their general principles, but also with charges so impassioned, attacks so virulent and exaggerated, that they were at the same time aiming a blow at the sounder opinion of Protestant theologians themselves, and preparing the ground for analogous attacks on the Bible in general. Of these two tendencies, the first showed itself somewhat generally in the Lutheran schools; the second gradually prevailed among Calvinists, though I do not mean to say that on the two sides there was perfect agreement on such points. At bottom this divergence is explained very naturally by the different progress which the conception of the canon had made in the two churches. The number of special treatises on this question was considerable, because the anti-Romish controversy was one chief source of the literature of the day.[2] I shall confine myself here to some characteristic extracts.

[1] Critical science began to turn its attention to the comparatively recent origin of what is called square writing. It is assailed by Buddeus (*Instt. dogm.*, p. 98. *Hist. eccl. V. T.*, p. 997).

[2] See, for example, J. Rainoldi *Censura ll. apocr.*, 1611. Æg. Hunnius, *Dica pontificiis scripta ob falsi crimen in S. S.*, 1622. Chr. Kortholdt, *De libris apocr. V. T.*, 1664. Gl. Wernsdorf, *Quod l. Sap. et Eccl. pro canonicis non sint habendi*, 1728. H. Benzel, *De ll. V. T. apocryphis*, 1733, etc.

Those who desired to place themselves at the standpoint of the Reformers were ingenious in finding formulas which might justify, against the two extreme opinions, the secondary place commonly assigned to these books, and should also be intelligible to the people, growing more and more indifferent to scholastic subtleties. Thus Hollaz said: *in codice sunt, non in canone*, they are in the Bible, but not in the canon, a phrase which has meaning only from the standpoint of primitive Lutheranism, for this set up an exclusively theological and non-traditional standard for the notion of canonicity. Others[1] insisted that the term *apocrypha* is intended to recall a fact, the doubtful origin of these writings, and not an opinion, as if it was forbidden to read them. In England, Prideaux, whose orthodoxy on other points is beyond all suspicion, distinguished between a canon of faith and a canon of manners, and thus with one stroke of his pen and without incurring the reproach of syncretism, justified both the separation and the addition of the books, in conformity with the usage introduced into the Bibles of the sixteenth century. From this point of view some theologians, not many it is true, regarded this controversy as of small importance, since salvation did not depend upon it. The Apocrypha added no new truth to those taught by the canonical books, and the Protestant Church lost nothing essential by refusing to place them in the canon.[2] They were rejected therefore to save any recantation.

Still, when we inquire into the motives for depreciating the Apocrypha, we generally find criticism availing itself of arguments which infringed on the principle of Protestantism,

---

[1] *Absconditi* i.e., *originis occultæ*, non *abscondendi* i.e., *quasi non legendi*. They were also called *canonici κατά τι*, i.e., *relatively canonical*. Gerhard, *Loci*, tom. i., p. 3. Chemnitz, *Exam. conc. trid.*, *l. c.*, § 20. Baier, *l. c.*, p. 119. Quenstedt, *l. c.*, pp. 61, 235.

[2] Placæus, *De canone* (*Synt. thes. Salm.*, tom. 1.), p. 64.

or, at least, proved that that principle had no longer its primitive energy. Criticism insisted on the silence of the Synagogue without remembering that the authority of the Church had been cast off; on the absence of prophetic types, though with small effort these would have been found in the Apocrypha quite as much as in hundreds of the passages in the Hebrew code that were arbitrarily interpreted; on the want of originality, the unfavourable opinions of some Fathers, and other like faults.[1] A greater number condemned them because they are not in Hebrew, the proper language of the Old Covenant, the natural language of God,[2] the primitive language of humanity.[3] This point was a favourite theme of criticism, because, while vindicating the use of Greek for the New Testament only and Hebrew for the Old Testament, it attained the double purpose of refuting the canonicity of the Apocrypha and the authority of the Vulgate.

Those, on the other hand, who preserved more positive remembrance of the old criterion, the witness of the Holy Spirit, diligently sought in the Apocrypha for historical errors, heresies, absurdities, all sorts of faults, to establish the point that religious sentiment was not wrong in excluding them from the canon. It is fair to say that on many points of detail, the learned sagacity of the criticism deserves praise; only, it may be asked, on what principle was it so severe on this occasion and so extraordinarily lax at other times? But so very far from this severity being joined with dignity of language, an enlightened appreciation of literary forms, good taste and impartiality, the critics rivalled one another in heaping on the Apocrypha the epithets

---

[1] Zanchi *De Scr. S.*, *l. c.*, pp. 439 f. Placæi *Comp. theol.*, i., ch. 6. (*Opp.*, tom. i., p. 667). Baier, *l. c.*, p. 110. Buddeus, *Institt. dogm.*, p. 144, etc.

[2] Du Moulin, *l. c.*, p. 33.

[3] Buddeus, *Hist. eccl. V. T.*, i., 235, etc.

suggested by contempt and prejudice. The Apocrypha were hated because the Catholics were hated; they were said to be filled with fables, errors, superstitions, lies, impieties;[1] and the violence of such attacks is surpassed only by the silliness of the proofs urged in support of them. One chides the son of Sirach for having said that the witch of Endor called forth the spirit of Samuel, orthodox exegesis pretending that it was only an evil spirit. Another discredits the story of Susanna, by finding it absurd that Joachim should have had a garden, since the Jews were captives. One is scandalised by the costume of Judith as she went to the camp of Holofernes; another laughs over the name of the angel Raphael; a third protests against the method of driving away demons by smoke. I have read one who is genuinely grieved because the demon of the book of Tobit is sent for ever to Upper Egypt, whereas Jesus only banished others into a desert from which they had a chance of returning.[2] Not one of these ardent champions of the purity of the canon foresees that criticisms so puerile, so unworthy of the subject, and so pointless, will end in showing to superficial and scoffing minds the ways and means of sapping the authority of the whole Bible; and that the scoffs thrown at the head of the little fish of Tobit,[3] will sooner or later destroy Jonah's

[1] *Falsa, superstitiosa, mendacia, suspecta, fabulosa, impia.*—Comp. Chamier, *Panstr. cath.*, P. i., B. v. Alting, *Loci, l. c.*, pp. 282 f. Du Moulin, *l. c.*, p. 34. Cloppenburg, *Exercitt., l. c.*, pp. 709 f. Alb. Regis *Exercitt. de ll. can. et apocr.*, i.-iii., 1715, *passim.* Heidegger, *Corpus th.*, p. 37.— Most of these arguments are found among Lutherans, but are discussed by them with less passion. See, for example, Gerhard, *Loci*, ii., pp. 134 f.

[2] It is curious to compare this unmeasured bitterness with the consideration shown towards the most pitiful apostolic lucubrations, not canonised by the Catholics, *e.g.*, the letter of Jesus to king Abgarus (Alb. Regis *Exercitt, l. c.*, iii., 49).

[3] *Quid primum deprehendam? An quod piscis ita exsiliit et dum clamat puellus non potuerit resilire? Et magnum oportuit esse quia resilire non potuit et quia devoraturus erat Tobiam. Idem tamen a puero trahitur in siccum. Hem, quam subito immutatus! Nam quum prius sturionem aut*

whale. All this arose, first from the bad taste of the times, then, too, from the need for overwhelming adversaries whose arguments were not a whit better; but still more it presents an unmistakeable symptom of a fact which emerges during the whole of this period—viz., that the question of the canon assumes a different aspect. The canon, so to speak, is no longer in a permanent state of formation according as the Holy Spirit speaking in its acts immediately on the men deriving instruction from it. It exists now as a fact, with limits determined by tradition and consecrated by usage. All contained in it is *a priori* different from what is outside of it; it is exempt from all imperfection, raised above all inquiry, and cannot but gain from the depreciation of what has remained without. The theory is changed, and we need not be astonished that the demonstration of it is also changed both in nature and means.

It will perhaps be asked how came it that Churches, which were neither scandalised nor disgusted by criticism so poor and desperate, did not go a step further and exclude simply, and purely, the Apocrypha from the Bible they were printing. That would have been rational, and less hurtful to the people. This question of suppressing the Apocrypha was actually raised in the Synod of Dort,[1] by the representatives of all the Reformed Churches. The rigorous dialecticians with Gomar of Leyden and Diodati of Geneva at their head, took the lead in all the fundamental discussions, and urgently demanded that, once for all, an end should be put to the unhappy mixture of heterogeneous elements. They seized the occasion for heaping up against the books to be proscribed, critical arguments of every kind, though

thunnum credebamus, nunc nobis apparet lucius aut gobio (Chamier, *l. c.*, ch. v., § 4).

[1] *Acta Syn. Dordrac.*, 1620, Sess. viii. f. Comp. the supplementary notes taken from the journal of the deputies from Zurich in *Zeitschr. für hist. Theol.*, 1854, p. 645.

one single argument, that of the theological conception of the canon, might have been sufficient, had the preceding generation succeeded in raising it to the dignity of a clearly defined axiom. They remained a minority. Ecclesiastical usage, the habits of the people, the opinion of the early Fathers, the fear of the storm which an innovation might cause, all the reasons which routine and indecision throw into the balance of the debate, finally carried a conservative vote. The vote showed the inability of the Church, and of science, to settle a question which both of them obstinately placed on a false basis. The new official translation of the Bible, which had just been decreed, was bound therefore to include the Apocrypha; only for the consolation of the vanquished, an offer was made to bestow less pains on them than on the canonical books, to print them in small characters, and put them at the very end of the volume after the New Testament. Even still, the foreign deputies reserved to their respective churches the right of taking their own course on this last point.

As to the canon of the New Testament, the Reformed theologians were spared all further labour. Calvin's treatment of the subject was to serve them as a rule; their hands were in part bound even by the Confessions of faith. Hence many dogmatic writers do not touch this question as, indeed, it was not a question to them, and there was no actual controversy about it. Those who consider it in passing, and who vouchsafe to remember that there exist what are called *antilegomena*, merely mention the fact as a curiosity in literary history hardly worthy of notice,[2] all the less that the canon was officially closed by the apostle John himself.[3] Or, if they do enter into details, they reason in such a superficial

---

[1] Chamier, *l. c.*, P. i., B. iv., ch. 2. Cloppenburg, *l. c.* Alting, *l. c.*

[2] Placæi *Opp.*, *l. c.*, p. 666: *Dubitatum est quidem aliquando sed nulla iusta causa fuit dubitandi.*

[3] Heidegger, *l. c.*, §§ 61, 62.

way that one wonders whether they expected to convince any one. The early Church, says one, was on its guard because of the great numbers of apocryphal books that were circulating everywhere; time was needed in order to make sure of the canonicity of certain epistles. And an explanation like this was believed sufficient to maintain the axiom according to which the word of God can be recognised intuitively and without mistake! Doubts, says another may have existed even in the second age, because the testimony of the first had not the same degree of assurance for all the apostolic writings; later on, the Holy Spirit put an end to these doubts by completing the canon. But this would lead us to suppose that the Holy Spirit failed those who were nearer to the beginning of the church, and ought to have had a better chance of being well instructed ! The Epistle to the Hebrews was rejected by the presbyter Caius in the third century, and then by the Socinians; besides, there are certain difficulties, and the readers to whom it was addressed were people quite obscure. That is what the criticism, not the knowledge, of a third amounts to. It is exactly the same as the knowledge, not the criticism, of his successors. In his first ardour, we read elsewhere, Luther

---

[1] J. H. Hottinger, *Quaestt. theol. centuriae*, 1659, p. 178. J. Cameron, *Praelectt., l. c.*, pp. 476 f. Alb. Regis *Exercitt. l. c.*, iii., pp. 41 f. Even at an earlier date, Zanchi (*Opp.*, viii., P. i., pp. 328, 443, 481; P. ii., p. 673; *Miscell.*, ii., p. 1) simply quoted the favourable testimonies of the Fathers and suppressed the others. Theodore Beza, in his annotated editions of the New Testament, pauses only over the Epistle to the Hebrews, and the Apocalypse in his critical considerations. Like Calvin, he declares these two books to be really inspired and therefore canonical; but, regarding the authors, he has no definite conviction. As to the Epistle, *sunt probabiles conjecturæ ex quibus nec Pauli esse nec hebraice unquam fuisse scriptam apparet*, a phrase which he omits in the later editions. As to the Apocalypse, he sees no peremptory reason for not assigning it to the apostle John, though the style rather betrays the pen of the evangelist Mark. Of this conjecture no notice was taken at the time, but it has been adopted in our days by a criticism, whose sagacity is become proverbial.

made light of the Epistle of James; but now it is better appreciated. However Calvinistic a theologian might be, he would rather overlook this peccadillo than enter on a somewhat ticklish discussion; now-a-days, however Lutheran a theologian may be, he makes no scruple of calling Luther a fool. Such comparisons will not be out of place when they show the particular kind of progress which was still to be made.

The history of the canon of the New Testament in the Lutheran schools during this period presents more interest and gives indication of more serious study; the result is the same, but reasons are given for it. At first, during the rest of the sixteenth century, there was no hesitation in following Luther's course in regard to the four books which he had separated from the others; it would be quite superfluous to quote names since, as I said before, the very editions of the Bible attest the fact.[1] But the distinction is further established by official documents, so familiar had it become even to laymen. Thus, to cite only one example, the *Agenda* or *Ecclesiastical Constitution* published in 1598, by the magistrate of Strasburg, very explicitly confirms it.[2]

---

[1] By way of example, I shall quote the polyglot Bible published at Hamburg in 1596, in six vols. folio, by Pastor Dav. Wolder. It is preceded by a table of contents in which the books of the New Testament are divided into canonical and non-canonical. These latter include the Apocalypse (without the author's name) and three epistles, of which one (Hebrews) is of an uncertain authorship, the two others (James and Jude) are by known authors (*certorum auctorum*). It is important to note that the canonicity is not determined here by the certainty of the origin.

[2] P. 6 : *Dieweil aber beydes von alters hero und auch heutigestages it geringer streit ist welches die wahre echte und unzweivelige bücher seien. . . . so erklären wir dass wir desshalb gänzlich der Meynung seien wie D. M. Luther lehret. . . . im N. T. aber die Ep. an die Ebräer wie auch Jacobi und Judæ und die Off. Joh. nit so gewiss für Schriften der App. können gehalten werden ob es sonst wohl gute und nutzliche bücher seynd welche wohl mögen in der Kirche gelesen werden aber allein zur Aufbawung der Gemeinde und nit streitige Artikel damit zu bekrefftigen.* [But since there has been, both in old times and now, no small strife as to which are the true, genuine

Still from the moment that theological science took hold of this question, it was put on another basis. It cannot be concealed, that Luther's separation of the Epistles of James and Jude, the Epistle of the Hebrews and the Apocalypse, had not been made on strictly scientific principles. His successors, without exactly repudiating his criticism, combined its results with the old distinction between the homologoumena and the antilegomena to which they attached great importance. In this way they came to differ from Luther on two points. Instead of four books being omitted from the list of those undoubtedly canonical, there were seven; and, in place of basing this classification on a dogmatic theory, they took their stand on historical facts. They thus abandoned Luther's great principle; but at the same time they were making some distant preparation for the return, whether in the Church or in science, to traditional usages, precisely as had been done a thousand years before.

The Lutheran theory, on the special point before us, is clearly set forth, as it was formulated from the middle of the sixteenth century in the celebrated polemical work of Martin Chemnitz, entitled: *Examination of the Council of Trent*.[1] The author there shows that canonicity ought to

and indisputable books. . . . we declare that we are entirely of Luther's opinion. . . . in the N. T., however, the Ep. to the Hebrews, as also, of James and Jude and the Apoc. of John, cannot so certainly be considered writings of the Apostles, though otherwise they are good and useful books which may be read in church, but only for the edification of the congregation and not for the support of disputed articles.] This passage was suppressed in the edition of 1670, and in 1751 Prof. Lorentz proved in an academical dissertation that the two texts are not contradictory, the first saying the same as the second.

[1] *Examen concil. trid.*, loc. i., sect. 6, §§ 9 f.—§ 15: *Quæstio est, an ea scripta, de quibus in antiquissima ecclesia dubitatum fuit, ideo quod testificationes primitivæ ecclesiæ de his non consentirent, præsens ecclesia possit facere canonica? Pontificii hanc autoritatem usurpant, sed manifestissimum est ecclesiam nullo modo eam habere; eadem enim ratione posset etiam vel canon-*

rest on the fact of inspiration, and the testimony of the primitive Church. Where the latter is wanting, it cannot be replaced by opinion or the usage of a more recent age. For this reason the seven books that in early times were held to be doubtful, should still be considered doubtful. The demand for some testimony from the *primitive* Church, in order to establish the canonicity of the apostolic writings, may seem a very hard condition; but Chemnitz thought otherwise. According to him, John had seen and approved of the three first gospels; he had had his own approved by the Church of Ephesus (xxi. 24, 25). Paul had set a special mark on his epistles, and Peter (2 Ep. iii. 15) had seen and recommended them. It is curious to see that the illustrious controversialist professes to found the canonicity of Paul's Epistles on the testimony of a text which itself seems doubtful to him.

This distinction then was maintained, and there does not appear to have been any opposition on the point. Even the Reformed theologians saw no necessity for entering into controversy with the Lutherans, which clearly proves that the question was not regarded as affecting dogma.[1] The seven books were boldly termed *apocrypha*, and this name was justified by the assertion that they could not be used in the same way as the others for establishing dogmas.[2] I may also cite here the remarkable fact that the faculty of theology at Wittenberg, in its official censure of the catechism of the Socinians, charges them, among other heresies,

icos libros reiicere vel adulterinos canonisare. Tota hæc res pendet e certis testificationibus eius ecclesiæ quæ tempore apostolorum fuit, etc., § 25 : *Nullum igitur dogma ex istis libris exstrui debet quod non habet certa et manifesta fundamenta in canonicis libris.* . . .

[1] W. Whitaker, *Dispp. de SS.* (1590), contr. i., qu. i., ch. 16: *Si Lutherus aut qui Lutherum sequuti sunt aliter senserint aut scripserint de quibusdam libris N. T., ii pro se respondeant. Nihil ista res ad nos pertinet qui hac in re Lutherum nec sequimur nec defendimus.*

[2] L. Osiander, *Instit. theol. chr.* (1582), p. 37: *Qui sequuntur libri non*

with the heresy of effacing the difference between the canonical and apocryphal books of the New Testament.[1]

The first step was made in a contrary direction when to the latter there was accorded a value superior to that of the Apocrypha of the Old Testament.[2] This was done, because the O. T. Apocrypha, which had formerly been spoken of with much esteem, suffered afterwards from the polemic waged against the decisions of the Council of Trent, but also because, from the Christian standpoint, a difference had to be recognised between the two groups of books. Others tried at least to claim a greater authority for some of the contested

prorsus in pari sunt cum prioribus autoritate, propterea quod de autoribus eorum subdubitatur. Itaque in diiudicandis religionis controversiis non eandem vim probationis cum prioribus obtinent. . . . Apocalypsis propter magnam obscuritatem et quia Ioannis theologi, non apostoli, inscriptionem habet, non inter authentica app. scripta numeratur.—N. Selneccer, *Exam. ordin.*, 1584.—M. Hafenreffer, *Loci theol.*, 1603; *Apocryphi libri N. T., sunt: posterior ep. Petri*, etc. *Hi apocryphi libri quanquam in diiudicatione dogmatum autoritatem non habent, quia tamen quæ ad institutionem et ædificationem faciunt plurima continent cum utilitate et fructu privatim legi et publice recitari possunt.*—J. Schrœder, *Aphorismi e comp. th.*, 1599, Disp. I, thes. 16 : *Apocrypha N. T. sunt: Ep. ad Hebræos*, etc.

[1] *Ausführliche Widerlegung des arianischen Catechismi welcher zu Rakau 1608 gedruckt. . . . durch die Theol. Fakultät zu Wittenberg*, 1619, p. 13.

[2] Hafenreffer, l. c. : *Si apocryphos libros inter se conferimus illi qui in Novo quam qui in Vetere Test. comprehenduntur, maiorem habent autoritatem.*—F. Balduin, *idea dispos. bibl.*, p. 68, sq. *Est discrimen inter apocryphos V. et N. T. Ex illis nulla confirmari possunt dogmata fidei sed propter moralia tantum leguntur in ecclesia; horum autem maior est auctoritas ita ut nonnulli etiam ad probanda fidei dogmata sint idonei, præsertim ep. ad Hebræos et Apocalypsis.*—C. Dieterich, *Instit. catech.*, 1613, pp. 19 f. : *Apocryphi N. T. non sunt usque adeo dubii nec quidquam e diametro canonicæ scr. contrarium continent. . . . etsi de iisdem in ecclesia fuit dubitatum a quibusdam, ab aliis tamen fuere recepti. Dubitatum fuit de autore, non de doctrina. Errant autem pontificii qui absolute parem autoritatem cum canonicis apocryphos ll. habere dictitant.*—L. Hutter, *Loci comm.*, 1619, p. 17, claims for the Apocrypha of the N. T. *auctoritatem quandam*, such that they occupy a place immediate between those of the O. T. and the canonical books.—B. Menzer, *De S. S.*, Disp. i., th. 25 f. : *Libri apocryphi primi ordinis s. ecclesiastici N. T. in nostris ecclesiis fere eandem obtinent cum canonicis autoritatem.*

books.¹ In the course of time, people grew more and more familiar with the idea that the difference between the two classes of apostolic writings consisted at bottom only in the degree of certainty regarding their respective origins and not in dogmatic variations of greater or less importance.² Now, provided that, from the nature of the teaching, the characteristics of the direct inspiration of the Holy Spirit could be recognised in it, the canonicity was sufficiently established and it was not necessary to this result that the name of the authors should be known in an equally indisputable way.³ It was preferred therefore to choose for classifying them terms that were quite inoffensive; *e.g., canonical books of the first and second series, or of the first and second canon.*⁴

But this purely formal distinction finally disappeared. The doubts it recalled were no longer shared by the theologians, and no one felt disposed to maintain the negative in questions of criticism. It therefore rested solely on a long-past fact, almost forgotten, with no actuality. The Lutheran authors of the eighteenth century who make any

---

¹ Æg. Hunnii *Disp. de Scr. can.*, 1601 (*Dispp. Witt.*, 1625, tom. i.) pp. 156 f. He sacrifices only the Epistles of James and Jude, while he says of all the seven antilegomena: *extra canonem sunt et apocryphis accensentur.* Comp. too Balduin, *l. c.*

² Abr. Calovii *Syst. locc. theol.*, 1655, tom. i., p. 513: *Nonnulli ex orthodoxis ep. ad Hebræos, etc. . . . deuterocanonicos libros vocant quod in ecclesia iis aliquando contradictum fuerit; qui tamen agnoscunt eosdem pro θεοπνεύστοις habendos esse nec canonicam illis autoritatem in firmandis fidei dogmatibus derogant.*—Andr. Quenstedt, *Theol. did. pol.*, c. iv., qu. 23, p. 235: *Disceptatum fuit de his libris, non ab omnibus sed a paucis, non semper sed aliquando, non de divina eorum autoritate sed de autoribus secundariis. Sunt æqualis autoritatis cum reliquis non autem æqualis cognitionis apud homines.*

³ Schrœder, *De princip. fidei*, c. i., p. 146: *Ut liber pro canonico habeatur, non requiritur necessario ut constet de autore secundario s. scriptore, satis est si constet de primo autore qui est Spiritus sanctus.*

⁴ *Libri canonici primi et secundi ordinis, proto-deuterocanonici.* J. Gerhard, *Loci theol.*, ed. Cotta. i., p. 6; ii., p. 186. Quenstedt, *l. c.* Baier, *Comp. theol.*, p. 120. J. Ens, *De ll. N. T. canone*, c. 6, 12.

mention of it in passing,[1] merely do so to defend Luther from the charges made against him on this point; and they make a very expeditious defence by perverting his meaning.[2]

[1] Buddeus, *l. c.*, p. 146 : *Dubitatum olim fuit ; etiam nostri doctores aliquando hæsitarunt ; postquam autem cuncta adcuratiori studio discussa et explorata sunt, nullum temere, cur recipi non debeant, superesse potest dubium.*—J. G. Pritii *Introd. in N. T.*, 1737, pp. 37 f. : *Inter canonicos libros nullum ordinem nullamque eminentiam agnoscimus: etsi quoque daremus incertum esse auctorem, inde tamen immerito ad negandam libri autoritatem canonicam concluditur.*—J. W. Rumpæi *Comm. crit. ad ll. N. T.*, 1757, p. 188 : *Hodie distinctio illa expiravit.*—J. A. Dietelmaier, *Theol. Beitr.*, 1769, i., 377 : *Heutiges Tages kønnten wir diesen Unterschied zur Noth entbehren ; weil er aber doch noch einigen Gebrauch hat und besorglicher Massen bald noch einen mehrern bekommen möchte* (!), *so ist fleissig zu erinnern dass die Zusätze* proto- deutero- *nicht einen verschiedenen Werth anzeigen sollen, sondern eine frühere oder spätere Aufnahme.*—Ch. F. Schmidt, *Hist. et vind. canonis*, 1775, p. 56 : *Impune et sine ulla impietatis nota licuit priscis ambigere de ll. N. T. quorum divina origo istis temporibus nondum satis nota esset. . . . quod nunc post perspecta clarissima argumenta, traditionem perpetuam ecclesiæ constitutumque publicum eorum usum indulgeri nequit.*

[2] Pfeiffer, *Crit. sac.*, 1688, p. 359. Gerhard, *l. c.*, ii., 223.

CHAPTER XVIII.

CRITICISM AND THE CHURCH.

I HAVE narrated the History of the Canon of the Holy Scriptures in the Protestant Church down to the middle of the eighteenth century. To say truth, it ends there. The canon—*i.e.*, the official collection of the sacred books—has not changed since. In so far as we have to consider it as one of the forms of the religious faith and life of the Christian community, it has undergone no variation. The doubts of scholars, which have since been put forward, sometimes timidly, sometimes with a certain amount of noise, have had the value only of individual opinions; and their influence on usages and institutions has been the less that in most cases they have remained unknown to the general public. The results of a science too bold and rash to inspire universal confidence have in no way encroached on the heritage of tradition. At most, they have increased the number of the elements of dissolution, which for nearly one hundred years have been secretly mining the theological edifice erected in the sixteenth century, and that edifice on some future day will be replaced by a new construction more in harmony with the primitive thought of the Gospel, and therefore more enduring.

With this fact before me, I might have considered my task as ended. The readers who had kindly followed me thus far, in order to gain acquaintance with the various evolutions of a principle seldom well defined and more seldom still applied with any rigour, the readers who are attentive to the teaching of history, would have, at least, carried away the feeling that the ways and methods of former days had ended only in the result we have stated, and that, this result being unsatisfactory, the science of Christianity must build the conception of the Scriptural canon on another basis. Theology is already seeking this basis; it has tried, and is still trying, to prepare it and consolidate it, either by the processes of theory or by the help of history. But the work is only begun. Those who are devoting to it their powers do not deceive themselves about the small success as yet obtained, nor about the greatness of the difficulties to be overcome. Even the need for this vast and uncertain work is still so far from being generally felt, that the historian who would wish to present a summary of what has already been done would run the risk of exaggerating the importance of his facts, or, at any rate, his own power of appreciating them.

In adding, therefore, one more chapter to my history of the canon, I do not desire to continue a narrative which I consider finished; still less do I desire to begin a new narrative which might never be finished. There is no doubt that, if only I succeeded in giving things their true colour, the very actuality of the subject would increase its attractions both for myself and for the public. But the elements and materials on which I should have to work are so different in nature, the interests concerned are so new, the predominating tendencies quite as remote from old prejudices as old methods are recognised to be insufficient, and the whole is so profoundly permeated with the spirit of modern science, that I should certainly be wrong in presenting the actual state of things as the simple continuation of what formerly existed, the movement of to-day as the direct effect of the stagnation in which, as we have seen, the generous efforts of the Reformers ended. My purpose is more modest. I wish simply to bring my work to a suitable close, to round it off, by first casting a retrospective glance over the results acquired. These results, to some definite, to others provisional, deserve both these epithets, according as we regard them from the scientific or practical point of view. This will lead me in the second place to indicate summarily the new elements introduced by our fathers into this particular sphere of the vast field of theology, elements cultivated with more or less success by our contemporaries, and in any case destined to play a great part in the future development of Christian studies. Finally, I shall try to state precisely the divergence existing between the traditional path and the innovations extolled by independent science, and to mark out the route by which one day perhaps the school and the Church will come to a reconciliation of their equally legitimate interests.

It is impossible to deny that Protestant theology had made, in regard to Scripture, an important and salutary progress over the theology of the Middle Ages. When it claimed for the sacred code, as a right and as a fact, the first place, the supreme authority, it had at the same time experienced the need of formulating the conception of the canon clearly and precisely, and of not being content with vague eulogiums. These vague eulogiums had accommodated themselves in early times to the caprices of custom, and more recently had not prevented the holy books from falling into oblivion among the faithful, and into the bondage of tradition among the learned. Unfortunately this progress did not succeed in ripening all the fruits it might have borne. The fundamental principle regarding the definition of the canon and common to the two fractions of the growing Protestantism had consisted, as we have seen, in building the authority of the written word on the internal testimony of the Holy Spirit—*i.e.*, on the assent of the Christian conscience, an assent spontaneous, instinctive, free from all reserve and hesitation, independent of tradition and delivering itself with confidence to the mysterious and salutary action of the principle of life placed by Providence in that particular *means* of grace. We have seen with what astonishing rapidity this point of view was abandoned in the schools to give place to another diametrically opposed to it; or rather how, by transitions which explain the fall but do not excuse it, theologians came to neglect, to weaken, at last to bury a theory which from the vital element of the system had become a dead letter, and then to substitute for it a scaffolding of conventional arguments, for the most part without solid basis, and at all events quite unknown to the body of the faithful. The same stiffness of the formulas, the same dialectical routine which had changed the living and victorious faith of the Reformers into a catalogue of abstract and powerless theses and their inspired eloquence into a dry, arid scholasticism, finally banished from the study of the Bible, and consequently from the conception of the canon among orthodox Lutherans and Calvinists, everything of the nature of immediateness in the religious sentiment, though that is the indispensable correlative of the fact of inspiration.

It is very remarkable and very significant that at the close of the development which I have just characterised in two words, and which we have been studying thoroughly, the scriptural canon was the same among Protestant as among Catholics, with one single exception hardly worth mentioning. This result would certainly be deeply important if the two sides had reached it by different routes, if Protestant theology with its new principle had furnished a verification of Catholic tradition. But I have shown that, where that principle was freely used—*i.e.*, with Luther and his friends or immediate disciples, and to some extent with Calvin—it brought out some manifest differences of details, and that these differences finally disappeared not by applying the theory of the Reformers more firmly, perhaps more legitimately, but by abandoning it by returning to the old methods, the time-honoured customs. In spite of the energy of the religious movement of that epoch, neither the Church nor the school felt itself equal to following their new leaders in a path apparently so hazardous; and what might be permitted to these illustrious men seemed much too perilous and compromising to men of the second and third rank. On this point, therefore, we must make allowance for the reserve of such men even while we regret it. The shock had been sudden and deep; the reaction was equally intense. The desire for stability, though unfortunately pushed to excess, was a natural manifestation of the spirit of the time, I might call it the result of circumstances. That desire hastened the fixing of the canon and settled the list of the sacred books. The dogma of inspiration could tolerate no hesitation about the details and still less the preservation of an intermediate class of deutero-canonical writings, by establishing which science had at first avoided the embarrassing necessity of coming to any conclusion regarding questions not yet clearly seen. An illusion was kept up regarding the little progress made by the new theology in the department of history. There was no hesitation in pronouncing judgment on points regarding which inquiry had hardly been commenced. In places where the Reformers had sought above all to make themselves acquainted with the spirit, examining their own inward experience, their successors confined themselves to ascertaining the proper name, and for this purpose were very often content with reading the current ticket and accepting the current mark. The proofs of these facts have been given at length in the preceding chapters. Besides, there is no one, even in France, but knows how theological tradition, after Luther was established in the Lutheran Churches regarding the

Apocalypse, and historical tradition, after Calvin, in the Reformed Churches regarding the Epistle to the Hebrews. These examples may be sufficient.

I have just said that with one single exception the Scriptural canon was the same among Protestants as among Catholics, but that this difference was hardly worth mentioning. This assertion may appear strange and hazardous, when it is remembered how desperately the canonicity of the Apocrypha of the Old Testament was discussed between the two parties. No doubt the canon proper, in the doctrinal sense, contained in the one church some books more than in the other; but this difference had no great weight, neither from the grounds on which it was based, nor from the use which science could make of it, nor in ecclesiastical practice. In this last respect it amounted for the faithful to a different order of the books in the different copies. The dogmatic theory was nowhere trammelled by disputes regarding the validity of a quotation, or rather these quotations, handed down from one generation to another, were no more than one of the conventional forms of debate, and did not exercise the smallest influence on the march of ideas. Finally, as to the grounds for the difference maintained in principle, there is no harm in saying that if there was anything more feeble than the arguments of the defenders of the Latin tradition, it was the arguments of their adversaries. For the latter, without knowing it or desiring it, went far beyond the mark, and, by neglecting the only solid basis on which Protestantism could rest a theological notion of the canon, persisted in placing it on the very same ground on which Catholicism had done nothing but go astray.

But I shall go further, and say that this deviation from the principles of the Reformers entailed other consequences of a deplorable kind, not only for science, but also for the Church. Luther and Calvin, in vindicating the exclusive authority of the Bible as opposed to the Catholic principle of tradition, had intended to remain in close and permanent communion with the Word of God, so as to submit to its control their conceptions, their teaching, and their institutions. The very freedom with which they criticised the composition of the traditional collection was both a symptom of the direct interest taken in it by their religious sentiment and a guarantee for the sincerity of their affirmations. Now, though the principle of which I am speaking subsisted in theory and was constantly invoked in the controversy with Rome, the fact is that secretly its authority was soon divided with a totally different principle, the very principle which was publicly disputed. This principle had been only imperfectly recognised and conquered at the origin of the Reformation, but its empire would have disappeared of pure necessity if advance had been made in the path so gloriously opened, if the fertile germ of the Gospel had been developed and freed from all extraneous elements. Protestant theology, in place of becoming more and more biblical, which it could not be altogether at first, became traditional, as the Catholic theology had always been. On both sides, orthodoxy included many things of which neither prophets nor apostles had ever dreamed. The confessions of faith, though they had been generous manifestos of evangelic emancipation, became stiff and cold as codes, all the more imperious that they were more scholastic, more void of Christian life, and more unintelligible to the general body of the faithful. It was not the spirit of the Bible, but rather the spirit of Aristotle, which inspired that conventicle of Bergen, whence issued the Formula of Concord, as it was called, and the condemnation of Melanchthon; and the unfortunate debates which long before had been agitating French Switzerland on the question of predestination, and which ended in the trial of Bolsec, might have foretold the rapid fall of a science too fond of its own logic and too careless of acquiring fresh vigour by constant contact with the simple and legitimate aspirations of sentiment and conscience. And if that happened in the middle of the sixteenth century, what was to take place later when the current of ideas, at first so powerful and limpid, had slackened and grown troubled? Protestant theology, founded, as it said, on the Bible, came at last not to open it; in more than one university there was not a single course on exegesis; the students no longer needed it; everything was defined, settled, fixed. Thousands of passages had received their official explanation, which was maintained all the more doggedly that it was arbitrary, and the generous efforts of a more thoughtful piety, endeavouring to restore to the people the book whose treasures scholars believed themselves to have exhausted, were reviled quite as furiously as were the feeble attempts of science itself to correct the methods and sweeten the language of the discussion.

Such was the state of things brought about by the spirit of traditionalism which had carried Protestant theology away, such was the price given for an advantage which the early Church (I mean the Church of the martyrs and not the Church of popes and councils) had foregone and run no risk. That advantage was the absolute certainty of the canon, a catalogue of the holy books officially fixed, a legal inventory of the archives of inspiration. It was still the theology of the old Judaism so well characterised by St. Paul, when he calls it the ministry of the letter and of death, διακονία γράμματος καὶ θανάτου. Fortunately, the power of life inherent in the gospel, though neutralised for a time by the persistence of the work of systematizing, at length regained its liberty of expansion and freed itself from the restraints of the school. This salutary revolution, which had been long prepared or at least desired, manifested itself in the last quarter of the seventeenth century. It appeared simultaneously in the three great fractions of the Christian Church, but its chances for the future varied according to the respective nature of these fractions. In all three, the Bible was replaced, not theoretically but in actual usage, on the pedestal of honour. From it, and not from tradition, instruction and edification were sought, and theological studies, placed henceforth in more direct contact with the needs of the community, entered on a new course of development. Not that the discussion of the canon itself was revived; but the use made of what had been handed down, proved that there was something better to bed one in this sphere than to write dissertations on the forms without penetrating into the spirit. At any rate, as I have already said, the fate of these attempts at regeneration was not the same everywhere, and the effects they produced had scarcely any resemblance to one another.

Within the pale of the Catholic Church, Jansenism, vainly recommended by the best and most serious men of the time, men who united the eloquence of good taste to that of a good example, appeared only to prove a truth, often confirmed since and now generally recognised. That truth is the immutability of the Romish institution, the impossibility of its retrograding a single step, of changing ever so little in direction, of playing a wider part in individual development, of suffering the least encroachment to be made on its visible and permanent authority, by making any concession whatever to a principle which would threaten to cast off its control. It was vain for the Jansenists to start a controversy with the Protestants, their nearest neighbours, that they might obtain forgiveness for their own assertions of independence. That piece of feebleness did not save them, and they had not even the consolation or honour of buying with their own pains and mortifications the liberty of a more fortunate generation.

In the churches of the Reformed rite, the movement was more varied and more powerful. It succeeded in breaking down the artificial barriers which hindered it at first, but not without falling into various errors. While in Switzerland the exaggerations of orthodox literalism went so far as to give birth to theories more compromising than conservative, the arid scholasticism of the school was strongly shaken in the Low Countries by the increasing ascendency of the Biblical system of Cocceius. This celebrated professor of Leyden attempted a complete restoration of theology, by basing it on Holy Scripture without subjecting himself to the traditional scheme of its elements, or to the rule of its prescribed methods. He frankly recognised the gradual evolution of the divine revelations as they appear in their authentic monuments; and, when transferring this principle into the teaching of dogma, he introduced for the first time the historical point of view in a science which for more than a century had lived on hardly anything else than abstraction. Unfortunately, an immoderate taste for types and allegories, and hence a preponderating influence of imagination in exegesis, deprived this principle of much of its proper fruits; and, as his disciples, according to the general rule, imitated the master's faults most of all, history has not inscribed his name among the genuine reformers of the science. At the same period, France, Holland, England showed rival zeal in the arena of philological labours. Louis Capellus at Saumur, and the editors of the polyglot Bible of London, were collating texts, and creating critical science in spite of the obstacles put in their way by routine. The Arminians of Amsterdam were already beginning to employ criticism in discussing graver questions. But everywhere the first energy of the work evaporated; nor should this relaxation of zeal, which was felt all along the line, be attributed to external causes, such as the revocation of the Edict of Nantes. The true cause seems to me rather to lie in this fact, that towards the end of the seventeenth century, theology, chiefly by its own fault, ceased to be the first of the sciences, the science which had almost exclusively engaged the attention of the studious for a hundred and fifty years. It was now the turn of philosophy, the mathematical and physical sciences, history, law. All disposable powers, those above all that were conscious of themselves, turned their backs on a study in which, according to its accredited representatives, there was nothing more to be done, and nothing more to be gained but anathemas or worse. This almost universal desertion was fatal to theology, and might have been fatal to Christianity, had Christianity been dependent on the tendencies of the age. This movement also, joined to the moral effects of the political fermentation, and to the influences of a superficial philosophy, led in England to the arbitrary and superficial lucubrations of the freethinkers, or to that luke-warm and colourless latitudinarianism, whose knowledge consisted in masking indifference, and whose tactics were only the making of concessions. The very natural reaction produced Methodism and its fervour, at times eccentric, revived tottering convictions and created new ones. Its road, rough as it was, was far removed from the thorny paths of science, and, as it addressed itself specially to the masses, it needed missionaries and not theologians. In the national Church, theology, neglecting too readily the knowledge acquired by study, and believing no longer in progress, was soon reduced to a mere polemical parade, made with rusty weapons against exploded or misunderstood theories, and to drawing-room apologetics in which conventional arguments drawn up by people unacquainted with history or philosophy, are well suited for tranquillizing souls more afraid of doubt than of error. Thus, by quite different means, the development of ideas was arrested in all the camps. The increasing division into sects, was neither the result nor the forerunner of intellectual work. All ecclesiastical activity tended in a different direction; it continues to produce numerous fruits of Christian charity, which, at the same time, have often a very pronounced flavour, and resemble manufactured products bearing a trade mark.

The Lutheran Church, specially in Germany, got entangled in other ways and arrived at different results. There appeared first in it the great religious movement known in history under the name of *Pietism*. This powerful and happy reaction against orthodox scholasticism did not tend in the least degree to bring into question any dogma of Protestantism, to raise irreverent doubts regarding any one book of the sacred collection, to break up the canon and, consequently, the system. What it wished was to restore the Bible to the people, to the gospel its popularity, to nourish those who had been famishing for the word of God, with other food than incomprehensible definitions, hollow formulas, and savage denunciations. It sought to awaken the inner life, to bring the sinner face to face with his Saviour without hiding Him by parchments, to raise the voice of peace and consolation, too long choked by the confused noise of theological quarrels as desperate as they were superfluous. Pietism, like every reaction, had its weak side, its defects and its troublesome consequences; it concerns us here merely to show the change it produced, more by instinct than of set purpose, in the conceptions regarding Scripture and its place in the Church—in other words, in the notion of the canon. To begin with, the symbolic books and the formal theology derived from it were put aside, not because of any sceptical or aggressive criticism, but simply because each believer was brought directly to Christ and the apostles. That which did not proceed from their mouth lost the value hitherto attributed to it. Not so much the essence as the form of traditional teaching was put in question. Unfortunately this form had finally pervaded everything, so that the defenders of orthodoxy soon foresaw, and rightly foresaw, that encroachment would be made also on the essence. From this time forward, the distinct formulas of Lutherans and Calvinists were no longer absolute in importance. At the feet of Christ there was room for all who experienced the need of hearing him, and he who had welcomed publicans and harlots, he in whose name the apostles had called men of every nation, the children of God, on the sole condition that they repented and believed, he could not possibly be thought to demand a preliminary guarantee provided by the theological police. This was not said: there was no clear consciousness of it; but principles were loudly proclaimed which were bound to lead to it; and principles never fail to produce their natural consequences. Some preparation was made for the union of the two churches; the necessity for that union was felt more and more; but it was accomplished only by sacrificing that which had formerly rendered it impossible. In another direction, as religious life was brought back to a personal communion with the Saviour, the Bible, destined to nourish that life, was of more use in maintaining it than when it was only a repertory of arguments, an arsenal of weapons; but it was of use just according to the dispositions of individuals and the ease with which its truths were assimilated. Each one found in it what he needed and no more, and each one was sure of not failing in his search; but all did not seek in the same manner. Convinced beforehand that the entire volume encloses an inexhaustible treasure of the wisdom and grace of God, each one made confident use of the part most accessible to him, or of the part which furnished the richest product for his particular needs. There might be in this illusions and eccentricities. Thus, the

Apocalypse, so miserably maltreated by orthodox exegesis, became, in a certain sphere of Pietism, the centre of spiritual studies and aspirations. Still there was assigned to the religious conscience a large part in the appreciation of the elements of Scripture, so far at least as their practical importance was concerned; and the theory of the internal witness of the Holy Spirit, without being spoken of in so many words, again became the essential principle, much more even than it had been in the time of Luther himself.

Pietism had made a breach in scholastic orthodoxy, not so much by learned and solid arguments as because it had met a need long felt vaguely, and because the liberty of expansion, claimed by it for the religious sentiment, conciliated the suffrages of all those who detested the tyrannical monopoly of the official theology. But it had not power to maintain itself at the head of the movement it had called forth. Every emancipation, even the most legitimate, gives rise to tendencies which go beyond the original mark, or, profiting by the greater latitude granted for the time to new ideas, push out in a direction quite opposed to it. Pietism made the mistake or had the inherent defect of despising, of suspecting science, which at this very period was preparing to usher in a glorious era. No doubt it did not advance at first with well-assured step. Adventurous and rash, it believed itself often to be at the end of its labours when they were not seriously begun; it boldly marked out routes across regions still unexplored; it pretended to reap before it had even cleared the ground; it created systems before it had gained experience; and traditional prejudices which were the result of long toil and which habit had made dear to less fickle or less exacting minds, were continually replaced by other prejudices, which had sprung from a passing caprice to be overturned on the morrow. Science of such a kind had to contend with theology regenerated by piety quite as much as with the theology that condemned all reform on principle. Unfortunately neither the one nor the other had arms powerful enough to contend with success against the spirit of the age which was plunging with enthusiasm into the path of progress and light, in no way careful to measure its steps by its strength, spurred on by the resistance it met with, and carried forward by the impetuous current of opinion. What I am now saying applies much less to Germany where the influence of Pietism neutralised a good part of the force which might have become hostile to positive theology or even to religion, than to other countries where the new ideas came into direct opposition with the rough and inflexible theories of a past age. But there is no need that I should paint this conflict in detail. The insipid pleasantries of the author of *La Bible enfin expliquée* did no injury to the essence of Christianity, any more than the ill-humoured attacks of the *Wolfenbüttel Fragments;* and the sacred trust of the Church resisted with equal success and with no great efforts the atrabilious sallies of Chubb and Toland, the romantic frivolities of Doctor Bahrdt, and the ignorant prating of a De La Serre or a Maréchal.

Let us, however, consider for an instant a phase of modern development, or rather a party name which in our days and specially in France is made responsible for all the opinions, which, in regard to the canon, depart from the fixed conclusions of ancient theology. I mean the Rationalism which prevailed almost universally at the beginning of this century, and whose traces have not yet wholly disappeared. This rationalism was not simply a method as it had been to the scholastics in the Middle Ages, or more recently to Descartes and Wolf. It had formed itself into a system and pretended to construct Christianity and theology with the sole help of the human reason, aided no doubt by the teaching of the Gospel; but the Gospel, continually controlled by reason, was to be considered only as a more antique summary of truths, quite analogous in origin and meaning to those which might now be discovered and demonstrated, and which belonged essentially to the domain of morality. This rationalism, an essentially theoretical system of theology, or, if you will, of philosophy, ignorant of all history or rather incapable of turning attention to it in consequence of its complete subjectivism, may deserve the reproach of having impoverished the conception of Christian facts, exalted the power of the human faculties at the expense of the action of God, and despised the most precious element of teaching; but it is quite wrong to accuse it of having assailed the Biblical canon and used criticism to get rid of an inconvenient and indisputable testimony. Rationalism never made any attempt in this direction. Inspired by the moral philosophy of Kant, it sought with pleasure in the Bible itself the foreshadowings of its own axioms, and did not hesitate to use for this purpose the arbitrary processes of an exegesis recommended by the illustrious philosopher of Kœnigsberg himself. But this art of knowing how to find in the texts precisely what is sought—*i.e.*, what had been previously declared to be necessarily true, this art now justly decried but once in fashion among others than rationalists and still a little in fashion among those who are not rationalists at all, this art, I say, practised frankly by the exegetes of this school and with the avowed purpose of defending Scripture against those who rejected it altogether, freed them completely from the trouble of getting rid of any particular part of the Bible by violent operations. The meaning of texts was twisted; but whole members were not amputated from the body of revelation; the canon was not changed. The rationalists, like the orthodox and the Pietists, might have a certain predilection for one book of the Bible over another; but, as they attached no great value to any book, they accommodated

themselves to all, or rather accommodated all to their system.
We have seen Dr. Paulus of Heidelberg assert vigorously that
the Epistle to the Hebrews was Pauline, in the very year in
which Dr. Tholuck abandoned the defence of the Pauline
authorship as hopeless. When Schleiermacher, the first theologian to deal Rationalism a mortal blow, was the first also to
deny the authenticity of the Epistle to Timothy, Wegscheider,
the chief of the rationalist party, took on himself the reply.
The Mosaic origin of the Pentateuch was valiantly maintained by the rationalist Eichhorn, long after the supernaturalist Vater had proved it to be inadmissible.

But these examples, which might easily be multiplied, remind me that I am not writing a history of theology; I
have promised only to finish the history of the canon of the
Holy Scriptures. Let me then recapitulate what I have just
said, in order to prove that, if modern theology has entered
on other ways and formulated other views than those of our
fathers in regard to the composition of the canon, this was
not the result of a mere change of theory. There may be—
I willingly believe there are—among contemporary writers
who till now have not yielded to the arguments of a doubt-creating criticism, some who find themselves compelled by
their dogmatic convictions to refuse consent; but this
criticism, though it was sometimes turned into a party
question, sprung, nevertheless, from a different soil than that
of theory. It is the legitimate daughter of a principle, or, if
you like, an instinct which was almost unknown to the
ancients, Pagans, Jews or Christians, Catholics and Protestants, and which modern critics even, both orthodox and
rationalist, have hardly recognised, or, at any rate, have
hardly placed at the service of the science—the historical
sense. I say the historical sense, just as we say the sense
of seeing or hearing; for, just as the man deprived of
certain organs cannot receive the impressions that come

through these organs, so a particular kind of mind is needed in order to estimate rightly and without any subjectivity facts outside of us or long past. By one of these mysterious evolutions of the human mind to which we have no key, it was the eighteenth century, the century of theories, the century which gave birth to a subjectivism so boundless as to end in denying the reality of the world, it was this same century which first awakened the historical sense. From that time it gradually became a power of the first rank in the vast domain of intelligence, an instrument which, in the hands of the workers of scientific progress, has enriched the labourers by increasing their field of activity.

It was a little after the middle of the last century that the historical and objective method began to free itself from the bonds of history, and was applied for the first time to the questions now before us. This change in the direction of theological work is connected with the name of a man whom nature had not fashioned for a prophet or the leader of a party. John Solomon Semler had none of those qualities which make reformers, neither the consciousness of a great purpose, nor the enthusiasm of a noble cause, nor the sentiment of personal superiority. He had been reared in the atmosphere of a somewhat narrow Pietism, but the taste for study, the passion for books, had won the day over the contemplative and sentimental tendencies fostered in him by his education. He was dominated by the need for reading, learning, acquiring, not only in his youth, but all his life long, so much so, that he had never any leisure for examining into the riches of his immense knowledge, nor the patience for bringing it into any kind of order. He did not know how to bring clearness into his conceptions, precision into his opinions, lucidity into his expositions. When reading the innumerable volumes he has written, prefaces, notes, and appendices rivalling the text itself in length, we have difficulty in gathering from them his system, in grasping his fundamental ideas. It was therefore not his talent, still less his genius (he had less genius than most celebrated men), that placed him at the head, not of a school, for he did not form one, but of a movement for which men's minds were ripe, and which was all the more vigorous that it was not dependent on the personal ascendency of one man over others. I would even say that he rather followed it by instinct, than called it forth with full consciousness. Too feeble to direct it, too dim-sighted to settle beforehand its future march, he bequeathed to it his name, only because he was the first to enter on that path, and because he long remained the most erudite, the most indefatigable, the most fortunate in making real or illusory discoveries, and the most frank in communicating them to the public, in an age when the powers directed to this kind of work were in general deficient, and when the courage of novelty was hardly shared by any but the forlorn hope of investigation. Profoundly pious, eminently conservative by conviction, he delivered the rudest blows against traditional conceptions. He wrote against the Deists, and unintentionally furnished them with materials and arguments. Wholly occupied with the polemics of the day, he never came to construct an edifice on the ruins he heaped together. Such were the beginnings of modern historical studies, as applied to the question of the Biblical canon. If the ideas of this pioneer of the science came down to succeeding generations to serve them as principles, it was not due to his superior mind, but to their intrinsic worth, and this same worth has preserved to posterity the remembrance of Semler.[1]

[1] Semler, *Abhandlung von freier Untersuchung des Kanon*, 1771 f. 4 vols. In directing attention to Semler's influence, I have no desire to pass over those who prepared for his coming (J. Alph. Turretin, *De S.S. interpretandae methodo*, 1728,) or who along with him vindicated the rights of criticism (Lessing. *Theol. Nachlass*, 1784.)

Semler's innovations had a bearing on various parts of the question of the canon. I shall note three of the leading points, which will, at the same time, serve as terms of division for a brief summary of the later development of the science.

His attention at the very outset was directed to this fact, that the canon had not always been the same in the early Church, or at least, that the witnesses to be consulted differ from one another, and that, in regard to certain books, tradition is not merely wavering but is actually unfavourable to their canonicity, or even to any presumption of their apostolic origin. He thus came to the conviction that it was impossible to harmonise witnesses equally early, and from our point of view, equally authoritative. He also felt an instinctive and justifiable antipathy to the means employed by conventional orthodoxy for getting rid of these inconvenient testimonies, means which consisted sometimes in ignoring them entirely, sometimes in altering their meaning by forced interpretations. All this led him by preference to search in the texts themselves for information regarding their origin, since the statements of tradition were not enough to place the history of the apostolic literature on a solid basis. In other words, what we now call internal criticism was added to the study of external testimonies. And, as these external testimonies did not go back to so early a date as the writings under discussion, writings, too, which might be heard in their own case, it followed that, in all cases of doubt and even where doubt had never existed, the science rested on solid ground only when the arguments drawn from the sacred writers themselves had confirmed or corrected tradition. I shall not enter on the details of Semler's investigation, or on the immediate results of his criticism. I shall rather repeat with some emphasis that these results do not concern us so much as his method. That method has never since been abandoned; its legitimacy was at last generally acknowledged; it is only its application to details that has continued to foment controversy. Not only did the partisans of the new ideas make use of them, as weapons of war; the defenders of the old opinions had to follow their adversaries on their own domain, more than once finding occasion to reduce too hasty conclusions to their just value, or to be the first to say the truth regarding literary facts before understood imperfectly. These researches and debates have been going on for more than a hundred years, without losing any of their importance or their interest. Advancing by roundabout ways, getting entangled in wrong paths, exaggerating sometimes the value of a clue, sometimes the solidity of a conjecture, borne along by the need of the intelligence to arrive at something definite, criticism has committed many mistakes, seen many hypotheses come into the world stillborn, had often to retrace its steps after apparently wasting its strength. I grant all that. I shall even say frankly that the results universally adopted by all scholars worthy of being heard without distinction of school, are not very numerous; that it is very improbable that the controversy will ever end in a general and complete agreement; in fine, that the science ought never to take rank as having nothing more to learn. Still immense progress has been made; ground has been conquered, which will not be disputed by any one who has learnt to distinguish between these radically different things—facts and theories. Criticism (I mean that which seeks truth sincerely and unreservedly), is no longer the weapon or the privilege of a party; it is not now a weapon at all, unless against historical error. It is a method for finding the truth of facts, a method for the use of all, indispensable to all, suspected only by ignorance, neglected and decried solely by those who tremble instinctively for what they had previously learned, and who for that reason wish facts to bend to their theories instead of basing their theories on facts. On this very point we can show the immense advantage of this method over that which makes facts dependent on axioms, and judges them according to preconceived theories. The philosopher, the theoriser will many times be tempted to sacrifice the facts to his principles; when these are laid down, he will pass over everything inconvenient, deny or pervert everything contradictory. Besides, theories do not correct nor transform one another; they replace and succeed one another; they are overturned by facts. The historian, on the other hand, though liable to be deceived like any other man, does not fear this experience because his work, as he pursues it, is of necessity a verification, and the discovery of error, far from being to him matter of discouragement, or an obstacle to be persistently got rid of, is, in his eyes, an advance, a conquest.

But I am forgetting that I have not to write an apology. Let me resume, then, by saying that, touching this first point, the generation which preceded us entered frankly into the new arena opened to it, and that our generation followed it all the more successfully, that long use has given to the science an exact knowledge of its methods, and the first gropings have given place more and more to intelligent and rational work. Now-a-days, all the details regarding the composition of every Biblical writing are carefully studied before the theological explanation is undertaken; the possibility of writing the history of Hebrew literature is more visible; the history of the literature of Christianity in its dawn is already marked in firm outlines; in short, the history of the formation of the collection, the sources of which, on the whole, run with all desirable abundance, has positively reached a degree of certainty which will be further increased, and which theorists are making vain efforts to depreciate.

A second point, to which Semler called the attention of his contemporaries, is the special character of the Biblical writings or their inspiration. As the question here is not one simply of method, but one of positive views directly affecting dogma, the adoption of Semler's view has naturally been much less general, the opposition more vigorous, and the systems to this day have remained more at variance. This, however, has not prevented the professor of Halle from exercising great influence on the question; on the contrary, there are very few comtemporary schools whose doctrines do not in some way bear traces of his ideas. Semler was one of the first among Protestant theologians to think seriously of modifying the received notion of inspiration. That notion had already in his day been strongly shaken, but it still preserved officially all the rigidity bequeathed to it by a scholasticism, deficient in sentiment, and without the slightest tinge of psychology. Unfortunately, Semler on his part, or rather his whole century, was equally deficient; only he was more disposed to deny what he did not experience, while orthodoxy, without being less dry and prosaic, at least admitted the fact of inspiration as an inexplicable privilege of certain mortals holding a special place among men. To Semler, inspiration meant the moral illumination of men in general. He has, therefore, been often called the coryphaeus or chief of rationalism, and indeed there was much greater affinity between him and the rationalistic school, though the latter, as I have already remarked, remained indifferent to what had most occupied the learned critic. Still it is more accurate to say that rationalism was in the air, and that the philosopher could not free himself from it any more than the historian, since the illustrious thinker of Kœnigsberg made it one of the corner-stones of his system. This may be some excuse for Semler. Besides, neither the one nor the other deserves to be confounded with the crowd which professed to march under their glorious flags, while taking as little as possible of the work. In any case, it ought to be sufficient to have noted, in passing, this particular element in the revolution which passed over theological ideas. Every one understands that the theory of inspiration is very closely related to the conception of the canon; we have been meeting with it all through our history; but, just because it is a matter purely of theory, I may dispense with entering on details. I shall confine myself to the statement that dogmatic science continued to develop, to be changed, to advance in a notable way on this point as on so many others. The present generation, without being able to flatter itself on having for ever fixed the scientific conception of a fact, which, as essentially mystical and individual, eludes all purely dialectical processes, is very far in advance of the formula that prevailed a hundred years ago. But an immense advantage has been gained by recognising the necessity of conceiving the fact of inspiration, otherwise than as a mechanical pressure exercised by a motive force on a passive instrument, of connecting it with another faculty of the soul than the pure intelligence, of bringing it into closer relation with what constitutes the essence of the spiritual life of all Christians, of radically reforming the traditional theory of the Spirit of God and bringing it back to the Biblical conception which on no other point has been so sadly disfigured or rather abandoned by the rationalism of the orthodox schools. I may dispense here with any profound treatment of this subject, the French public having frequently had to consider it in recent years. For among us, too, the scholastic conception, put forward in all its crudity, has provoked very general protestations. French theology, born but yesterday, is trying in its turn to find a formula more adequate for defining a religious fact which science formerly disfigured by its sophisms, but which our science, fortunately for itself, cannot do without. If only it succeeds in understanding the fact, its regeneration will be effected.

Nevertheless, modern theology, a daughter of that reaction whose primitive character we are at this moment trying to grasp, has not confined itself to correcting the theoretical conception of inspiration. By its very refusal to attribute the origin of the apostolic books to a cause absolutely external to the will and conscience of their authors, it naturally undertook to point out some other cause more in harmony with the laws of psychology and history, and at the same time more fitted for resolving the innumerable exegetical problems which from the old point of view had been insoluble, and had sapped the basis of the theory itself. Here, again, Semler marked out the new route. Taking up the ideas already followed instinctively by Grotius and Le Clerc and more openly professed by Turretin, profiting, too, by the tendencies of Pietism which had restored to the sacred writers a good part of their individuality, he entered resolutely on the path of historical interpretation and applied himself to the study of the social and religious conditions amid which the convictions of the disciples of Jesus were formed. On this study he based his explanation of their books. I do not hesitate to say that he was not altogether fortunate in this work of exploration and reconstruction. He, too, brought to it his share of prejudices; and, what is still worse, though he showed much sagacity in eliminating the errors with which traditional history swarmed, he was not equally skilled in recognising and defending the real facts. Thus, for instance, he had dwelt on a fact, which no one before him had noted with so much clearness, the presence and influence of certain Jewish ideas in the primitive Church. He taught science, which has since improved on his conception but has not abandoned it. to distinguish Jewish Christianity from Paulinism; but he was quite wrong in marking off their limits, assigning to Jewish Christianity more than one element which was an integral part of the Gospel itself, and neglecting too much the objective study of the Gospel, or rather betraying generally a certain awkwardness, it might even be said, a radical incompetence, in seizing its true essence. Thus, again, he was able to recognise everywhere in history (he was himself the creator of the history of dogmas) the variety, the divergence of the systems; he destroyed for ever the old prejudice of orthodoxy that the dogma of the Church has always been the same; but the intimate relations of the phenomena he was observing, the supreme law of these evolutions of religious thought, in a word, the pragmatism of that history, escaped him. In spite of these faults which I have no desire to conceal, I am bound to say that his fundamental ideas, especially where they tended to change methods, have been justified by experience. I shall cite as one more proof only this fact very easy to verify—viz., that the exegesis of our century, even the most conservative, bears the stamp of the historical point of view while rationalistic exegesis has disappeared without hope of return. The natural origins are studied on the soil where the Bible was formed, which by no means excludes the belief in the providential action of the Spirit of God; and consequently the question of the canon, in so far as it depends on the study of the texts, has entered irrevocably, not into the sphere of a *doubt* which would be the enemy of *faith*, but into the sphere of facts which can only give to faith a more solid basis.

But the question of the canon is also closely allied with the theory, and this is the third and last point I have to treat. On the subject of the canon, modern science has been least sure of its beginnings: its progress has been least visible and most disputed. All this just because it is not a question of the facts in themselves, but of their subjective appreciation, let me say rather, their relation to systems which, without exception, have been partly formed in independence of facts. In very truth, the whole history of contemporary theology lies in this. It cannot of course enter into my views to exhaust such a subject by introducing it incidentally. But I wish to point out some salient and characteristic points in what is universally recognised to be the most profound religious crisis since the Reformation, a crisis suspected and cursed by some, extolled by others, and confronting all.

From the very first, when in consequence of the historical discoveries true or false which had been made, the apostolic writings were deprived of that absolute authority they had hitherto enjoyed, and of that character of intrinsic homogeneity which justified their distinct separation from all other literature, it became necessary to seek a definition of the canon which would take into account the results of historical criticism and still explain what makes the Biblical writings a really distinct and special literature. On this point, the first attempts of science were not happy. By one of these caprices to which the human mind so readily yields, Semler, the champion of rights of history, began by substituting for it what was simply his own personal conviction. He pretended that the canon, even in the early church, had only been the catalogue more or less official of the books read to the people for their edification, thus neglecting the dogmatic element which was the main point, and adhering only to one of the forms of its application. Not but that in certain respects this opinion may be defended, and some support to it is given by the customs and usages of the Latin Church; but, after all, the theology of the Fathers, chiefly that of the golden age of the Eastern Church and the very history of the institutions, are anything but favourable to it. In any case, its author combined it with another thesis, proclaimed as the principle henceforth to be followed, which thesis made the canonicity of every book depend on what he called its practical or moral utility. The historian here was completely effaced by the moralist, the preacher, the man charged with the instruction of the people; and as such, when the point is closely examined, he received the mission of making and unmaking his own canon according to the moral needs he was able to advance, and the corresponding qualities he was able to recognise in each Biblical writing. I shall not waste time in proving that Christianity is not merely a system of morality, above all in the sense which Semler and his age meant; that point of view has long been left behind. Still less is it necessary to prove that the sacred authors did not wish to be simple echoes of the natural law. Let me rather point out here some details. First of all, I should say in defence of Semler that his test of canonicity, though it could not be accepted by Christian theology, and the theology of Protestantism in particular, had a distant analogy with that of Luther, inasmuch as the great Reformer also set up a theoretical axiom as the supreme rule determining the value of each element in the traditional canon. Only Luther's axiom was an evangelic truth, the very truth which brought about the rupture with Rome; while Semler's contained nothing specially Christian or Protestant. This being recognised, it may be asked what interest he had in speaking of a Biblical canon at all. This question will seem less superfluous when it is found to help us to a better acquaintance with the somewhat arbitrary methods which Semler used for reconciling theory and practice. As an actual fact, he did not go very far in his negations, and the parts of the canon which he eliminated purely and simply were by no means numerous. On this point he was not so bold as Luther. Esther,

Canticles, the Apocalypse, were the chief victims on the altar of his principle, and the two latter were immolated with equal stubbornness and bad taste. But what he did not reject, he *accommodated* by interpretation to the general tendencies of his theology, and in this, the chief defect of his method, he had the most numerous and faithful disciples. It is difficult to understand how a criticism undertaken in the name and for the benefit of history—*i.e.*, of objective knowledge—could have been involved in the least justifiable errors of a narrow and poor subjectivism. Still this defect is exceeded by another eccentricity which did not form a school. That was the distinction established by Semler between private religion and public or official religion, for which he not only professed a respectful deference, and which he would not deliver to the mercies of an independent discussion. Was not this antithesis of an esoteric and an exoteric teaching, a confession of feebleness, an anachronism, which nothing seemed to justify for there was nothing to make it necessary.

All these gropings, all these errors and inconsistencies, are explained when we remember what studies must be that have been freed suddenly from rigid tradition and a jealous authority, but have before them an obstacle more difficult to surmount, a danger more likely to disturb their vision. These were the very novelty of the situation which came face to face with the empire of habit, the old prejudices unwittingly retained and added to new prejudices which hastened to take the vacant place of the old. On the one hand, there was the pleasure of criticising, discovering, advancing, a pleasure all the more irresistible that it had been long denied; on the other hand, there was that conservative instinct so profoundly rooted in the German mind. They might be called two poles exercising their attraction alternately, and increasing thereby the uncertainties of the present moment, while guaranteeing progress for the future. These inconveniencies may be regretted; suffering even may arise from their immediate effects; they are inherent in human nature. Providence, in promising to man so richly endowed that he would find satisfaction for his aspirations after truth, desired also that he should seek it; success is the reward of the work. The truth is that science has advanced, and by advancing it has grown fond of movement. It has traversed distances which render a return to its former position, not only difficult, but impossible; it has entered on paths from which before all else it must seek the issue; and it will certainly not discover the issue by returning on its steps or stopping half-way: it must finish its work.

But its route is strewn with ruins! But the doubt which professes to illumine it, begins invariably by extinguishing the only lamp that gave security! But the sacred books are descending more and more into the rank of simple historical documents! But the authority of Scripture is sapped, and with it how many other authorities! These complaints are the order of the day; they are almost general in France. They do not proceed only from the ignorant mass whom the spirit of party can terrify by phantasmagoria; they reach us also from those who, strong in their convictions and satisfied with what they possess, desire nothing more. These latter, on their own authority marking out in the garden of science trees with forbidden fruit, believe that reason, now more prudent than in the beginning, will prefer the nakedness of an eternal infancy to the knowledge of good and evil, lest it should be driven out of a paradise without labour, and be compelled unceasingly to pull up the thistles and thorns which have been permitted to grow abundantly in the field of the human mind. But such complaints are largely exaggerations, arising from a false estimate of the facts, or from personal impressions which cannot give the true measure of things. Where they are well-founded, they are far from authorising any absolute condemnation of historical criticism in itself; they rather mark the elements of a real progress, I might say, the young fruits which are already visible in spring, and with the aid of heaven, will one day form the harvest expected in autumn. There may indeed have been sometimes too great haste in destroying; wrong roads may have been pursued and false lights followed; but, in almost all cases, the science itself was the first to discover the true cause of error, while traditional and conventional opinion was simply putting forward denials that refuted nothing and proved nothing. If doubt still seems to occupy too large a place in modern science, that is because science has recognised the great value of doubt as a means of research. Science has no fears for itself nor for the truth; science knows that reason is forced by its own nature to overcome doubt before attaining any positive result, and that there is no worse method of overcoming doubt than that of stifling or proscribing it. If now the books of the Bible are consulted chiefly as the documents of religious thought, such as was long ago formed in circumstances favoured by Providence, at decisive epochs of history, the part thus assigned to them is certainly nobler than that they played, when, under pretext of regulating by them the religious thought of the times, men made them the passive instruments of the current philosophy or of partisan interests, the humble servants of dogmatic argument, the weapons of controversy unceasingly re-shaped on the anvil. If the Old Testament is now no longer used as in the days of our fathers, for constructing Christian dogma by means of exegetical manipulations as repugnant to good taste as to common sense and fairness, its own nature, its religion and poetry, its morality and legislation, the holy enthusiasm of its prophets, and the epic simplicity of its traditions, these, considered in their true light, have gained by the change; and the radiance which Hebrew literature thus casts across the centuries, stands out against the profound night of pagan antiquity, and becomes more brilliant when the air is freed from the mists of theology. If, in establishing the authority of the New Testament, we no longer pause over proper names open to doubt, but go straight to the truth which it proclaims and enforces on the conscience, are we acting contrary to the counsel which Jesus was the first to give regarding his own claims? Will his claims vanish away if we give heed to do what he commands us, to draw inspirations from his example, to enter into communion with his living holiness, in place of losing precious time in dissecting his personality? When his claims are verified by the process which he gave to his disciples and all are bound to follow, will they not continue to assure to him that absolute authority from which we derive the right of bearing his name? And inasmuch as his regenerating personality was reflected with greater brilliancy on his immediate surroundings, men, ideas, or books, will not that privileged circle for ever continue to possess a legitimate influence on the Church and on theology, an influence better assured than if it were founded on claims purely literary and therefore open to dispute? In short, the part of the Holy Spirit will not be less, far from it, if, according to modern theology, its action extends to remote spheres, if it is recognised in the most varied forms, if its power is revered in effects whose greatness is perhaps revealed only to exercised intelligences. It will not be less if, instead of enclosing it in narrow formulas with no trace of its quickening contact, theology permits it to blow where it listeth, and studies it first in the inner experiences of the soul, before seeking to define it in the phenomena of history.

I have thus given in rapid outline the direction taken by theology since it began to seek a solid basis for itself in historical criticism. The conviction has grown that the question of the canon of Scripture is more or less closely related to all the problems that have been most discussed in these latter days, even when that particular question has not been raised. The question has assumed larger proportions than formerly, and I was right in saying that the scheme of narration, sufficient for the narrow circle of early times, would have to be greatly enlarged for recounting the various phases that have appeared in contemporary literature. The time is not yet come for science to draw its final conclusions; still some facts are now placed above discussion and will no longer lose their weight. Among such facts, there is first, in regard to theory, this fact, that inspiration has appeared and still appears in different degrees, and that no formula will succeed in drawing an absolute distinction between the inspiration of all Christians and that of the sacred writers; and secondly, in regard to practice, this, that theology has no longer any interest in altering the traditional composition of the canon, since it returns with full conviction to the Protestant principle of appealing to the testimony of the Spirit of God, and therefore claims no longer to stand between that Spirit and the believer, controlling their mutual relations. For theology, to believe in the Bible means before all else to believe that it is revealed directly to heart and conscience; but it is also to believe that the power of this revelation is not diminished by the inequality of its forms, or the inferiority of one or other of its organs. Theology, in short, does not believe Christianity and the Church to be in danger, though the same credit be not given to the story of the massacres caused by a Persian queen, a story containing all the persistent hatred of the Synagogue, as is given to the holy eloquence of an apostle of Jesus

Christ: or though the Wisdom of the Son of Sirach, extolled by the Fathers, be placed, as Luther wished, side by side with the sentences of Solomon. In other words, the question of the canon no longer consists in the problem of drawing up a list of books: that conception has had its day. Theology aims henceforth at a higher mark, and the very fact that it has learned to place before itself a more elevated task, is some assurance that the task will in the end be accomplished.

THE END.

S. Cowan & Co., Strathmore Printing Works, Perth.

www.ingramcontent.com/pod-product-compliance
Lightning Source LLC
Chambersburg PA
CBHW050844300426
44111CB00010B/1124